OXFORD CLASSICAL MONOGRAPHS

Published under the supervision of a Committee of the
Faculty of Literae Humaniores in the University of Oxford

The aim of the Oxford Classical Monographs series (which replaces the Oxford Classical and Philosophical Monographs) is to publish books based on the best theses on Greek and Latin literature, ancient history, and ancient philosophy examined by the Faculty Board of Literae Humaniores.

Rome and Baetica

Urbanization in Southern Spain
*c.*50 BC–AD 150

A. T. Fear

CLARENDON PRESS · OXFORD
1996

Oxford University Press, Walton Street, Oxford OX2 6DP
Oxford New York
Athens Auckland Bangkok Bombay
Calcutta Cape Town Dar es Salaam Delhi
Florence Hong Kong Istanbul Karachi
Kuala Lumpur Madras Madrid Melbourne
Mexico City Nairobi Paris Singapore
Taipei Tokyo Toronto
and associated companies in
Berlin Ibadan

Oxford is a trade mark of Oxford University Press

Published in the United States
by Oxford University Press Inc., New York

© A. T. Fear 1996

British Library Cataloguing in Publication Data
Data available

Library of Congress Cataloging in Publication Data
Rome and Baetica: urbanization in southern Spain
c. 50 BC–AD 150/A. T. Fear.
(Oxford classical monographs)
Includes bibliographical references and index.
1. Andalusia (Spain)—History. 2. Romans—Spain—Andalusia.
3. Urbanization—Spain—Andalusia—History. 4. Municipal corporations
(Roman law). 5. Acculturation—Spain—Andalusia—History.
6. Andalusia (Spain)—Antiquities, Roman. 7. Excavations (Archaeology)—Spain—
Andalusia. I. Title. II. Series.
DP302.A49F43 1996   946'.8—dc20   95-41324
ISBN 0-19-815027-X

1 3 5 7 9 10 8 6 4 2

Typeset by Best-set Typesetter Ltd., Hong Kong
Printed in Great Britain on acid-free paper by
Bookcraft (Bath) Ltd., Midsomer Norton

ACKNOWLEDGEMENTS

I should like to thank Professor Fergus Millar and Dr Barbara Levick for their help and advice. The errors here are of course mine.

CONTENTS

ABBREVIATIONS

A.e.A.	*Archivo español de arqueología*
AE	*L'Année epigraphique*
AJA	*American Journal of Archaeology*
Antiquaries' J.	*Antiquaries' Journal*
Arch. J.	*Archaeological Journal*
BAR	British Archaeological Reports
BMCGC	*British Museum Catalogue of Greek Coins*
BMCRE	*British Museum Catalogue of Coins of the Roman Empire*
BRAH	*Boletin de la Real Academia de la Historia*
BSAA	*Boletin del Seminario de Estudios de Arte y Arqueología*
CHM	*Cahiers de l'histoire mondiale*
CMH	F. Alvarez Burgos, *Catalogo general de la moneda hispánica* (1979)
CIL	*Corpus Inscriptionum Latinarum*
CNA	*Congreso Nacional de Arqueología*
CRAI	*Comptes rendus de l'Academie des Inscriptions de Belle-Lettres*
EAE	*Excaviones arquelogicas en España*
EE	*Ephemeris Epigraphica*
FHA	*Fontes Hispaniae Antiquae*
FIRA	*Fontes Iuris Romani ante Iustiniani*
HSCP	*Harvard Studies in Classical Philology*
IA	*Itinerana Antonini Angusti*
IAM	*Inscriptions antiques du Maroc*
ICERV	*Inscripciones cristianes de la España romana y visigoda*
IG	*Inscriptiones Graecae*
ILER	*Inscripciones latinas de la España romana*
ILS	*Inscriptiones Latinae Selectae*
IRPC	*Inscripciones romanas de la provincia de Cádiz*
IRT	*The Inscriptions of Roman Tripolitania*
JCS	*Journal of Classical Studies*
JRS	*Journal of Roman Studies*
KAI	*Kanaanäische und aramäische Inschriften*
MCV	*Mélanges de la Casa de Velazquez*

MEFRA	*Mélanges d'archéologie et d'histoire de l'École Française de Rome*
MI	A. M. Guadan, *La moneda ibérica* (Madrid, 1980)
MM	*Madrider Mitteilungen*
NAH	*Noticario arquelogico hispanico*
NAMSC	*Nouvelles Archives des Missions Scientifiques*
PBSR	*Papers of the British School at Rome*
PG	*Patrologia Graeca*
PIR	*Prosopographia Imperii Romani*
PL	*Patrologia Latina*
RA	*Reserches angustiniennes*
REA	*Revue des études anciennes*
RHDFE	*Revue historique de droit français et étranger*
RIB	*Roman Inscriptions of Britain*
RIC	*Roman Imperial Coinage*
RIDA	*Revue internationale des droits de l'antiquité*
RSF	*Rivista di studi fenici*
SHA	*Scriptores Historiae Angustae*
TAPA	*Transactions of the American Philological Assocation*
ZPE	*Zeitschrift für Papyrologie und Epigraphik*

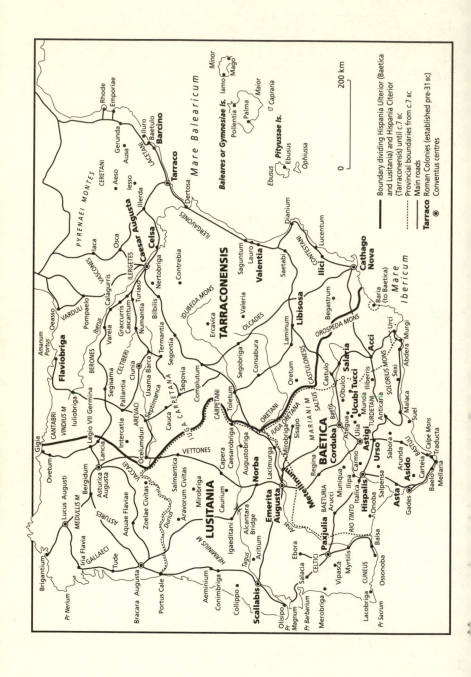

Minor
Iamo
Mago

Baleares or Gymnesiae Is.
Pollentia
Palma
Maior

Capraria

Mare Balearicum

Pityussae Is.
Ebusus
Ebusus
Ophiussa

Mare
Ibericum

Boundary dividing Hispania Ulterior (Baetica and Lusitania) and Hispania Citerior (Tarraconensis) until c.7 BC
Provincial boundaries from c.7 BC
Main roads
Tarraco Roman Colonies (established pre-31 BC)
● Conventus centres

0   200 km

Rhode
Emporiae
Gerunda
Ausa
Iluro
Baetulo
Barcino
Tarraco
Dertosa
LACETANI
CERETANI
Iesso
Aeso
Illerda
Iaca
Osca
PYRENAEI MONTES
VASCONES
Pompaelo
Oeasso
Amanum Portus
Calagurris
Iluro
ILERGETES
Caesar Augusta
Celsa
Nertobriga
Contrebia
ILERCAVONES
Dianium
Saguntum
Lauro
Valentia
Saetabi
CONTESTANI
Lucentum
Ilici
Cathago Nova

TARRACONENSIS
IDUBEDA MONS
Ercavica
Valeria
OLCADES
Laminum
Begastrum
OROSPEDA MONS
Libisosa
Baria (to Baetica)
Urci
Abdera Murgi
Acci
SOLORIUS MONS
Sexi
Malaca
Suel

VINDIUS M
CANTABRI
BERONES
Iuliobriga
Varia
Graccurris
Cascantum
Turiaso
Numantia
CELTIBERI
Bilbilis
Segobriga
Consabura
Segontia
Uxama Barca
Clunia
Pallantia
Segisama
AREVACI
Intercatia
Ocelumduri
Cauca
IUGA CARPETANA
Segovia
Complutum
CARPETANI
Toletum
Mirobriga
ORETANI
Oretum
Sisapo
MARIANI M
IUGA ORETANA
SALTUS
CASTULONENSIS
Castulo
Salaria
Obulco
Ucubi Tucci
Munda Iliberris
Iliberis
TURDETANI
ANTICARIA
Anticaria
Sabora

Amanum Portus
MEDULLIS M
Lucus Augusti
Ovetum
Gigia
Brigantium
ASTURES
Iria Flavia
GALLAECI
Flavia
Tude
Bracara Augusta
Portus Cale
Aquae Flaviae
Asturica Augusta
Bergidum
Lancia
Zoelae Civitas
Aravorum Civitas
Salmantica
Mirobriga
VETTONES
Caurium
Norba
Lacimurga
Capera
Caesarobriga
Augustobriga
Alcantara Bridge
Igaeditani
Aritium
Emerita Augusta
Regina
Metellinum
BAETURIA
Arucci
Paxiulia
CELTICI
Ebora
Salacia
Vipasca
Myrtilis
CUNEUS
Merobriga
Lacobriga
Ossonoba
Balsa
Onoba
Italica
Ilipa
Munigua
Carmo
Ulia
Ategua
Corduba
BAETICA
Astigi
Urso
Hispalis
Salpensa
Arunda
Iliturgi
BASTULI
Carteia
Asta
Asido
Baelo
Mellaria
Traducta
Calpe Mons
Gades

LUSITANIA
HERMINIUS M
Tagus
Anas
RIO TINTO
Conimbriga
Aeminium
Collippo
Olisipo
Pr Magnum
Pr Barbarium
Pr Sacrum

Scallabis

Pr Nerium

Flaviobriga
VARDULI
VACCAEI
Durius
Iberus
Termantia
Nertobriga
Legio VII Germina

Mare
Ibericum

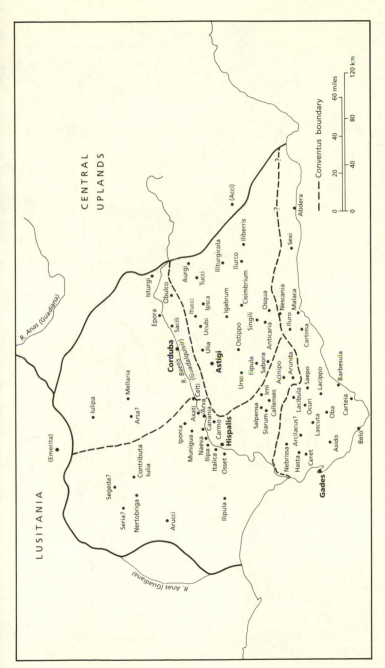

MAP 2. Baetica (L. A. Curchin, 'The Creation of a Romanised Elite in Spain', thesis (Ottawa, n.d.))

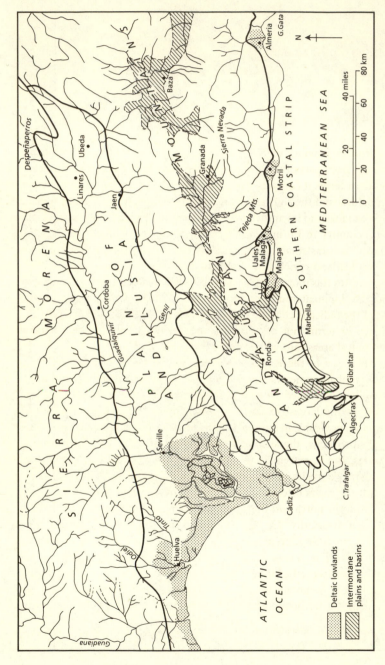

MAP 3. The Physical Divisions of Southern Spain (HMSO, *Geographical Handbook: Spain and Portugal,* i. *The Peninsula* (London, 1941))

I

Introduction

THE Roman province of Baetica was created in *c*.16 BC by the emperor
Augustus from part of the old republican province of Hispania Ulterior.
In modern terms it comprised most of the present-day Spanish province
of Andalusia and the southern part of that of Extremadura. It comes as a
surprise to many to learn that, after Switzerland, Spain is the most mountainous country in Europe. The Iberian peninsula is one of strong geographical contrasts, and perhaps Baetica, though often portrayed as
simply a lowland region given over to arable farming and arboriculture,
demonstrates this more than any other region of the country.[1] An analysis
of the development and the nature of life in the province must take into
account the radically contrasting landscapes found there, and examine the
evidence in terms not of a unitary whole, but of the various natural
geographical areas into which the region is divided.

At the heart of the Roman province lay the valley of the river from
which it took its name, the Guadalquivir, known as the Baetis in antiquity.
This valley, combined with that of its tributary, the Xenil, the ancient
Singilis, is the largest expanse of low-lying land in Spain. Both these
rivers were navigable in antiquity, the Guadalquivir as far as Cordoba and
the Xenil to Ecija, the ancient *colonia* of Astigi.[2] The land surrounding
them was, and is, extremely fertile, and provided the agricultural basis of
the province's wealth: the production of corn, wine, and, above all, olive
oil, with the rivers offering a ready means of transportation.

To both the north and the south of the Guadalquivir valley the terrain
changes dramatically. On the northern side the Sierra Morena rises
steeply from the valley in a complex chain of several ridges of sharply
folded hills. The Sierra is some 40 miles deep, and its height is, on
average, 3,500 feet (the highest point, La Bañuela, is over 4,000 feet high).
Beyond these mountain ranges the country once again flattens out, but
into much less fertile moorland. Farming here, which is hindered by the

---

[1] For a detailed account of the physical geography of the region, and Spain in general, see
A. Cabo, *Historia de España Alfagura*, i. *Condicionamientos geograficos* (1973).
[2] Baetis: Strabo 3. 2. 3; Singilis: Pliny *NH* 3. 1. 12.

large numbers of boulders found on the land, is mainly restricted to the rearing of livestock, especially the pig, and cultivation of the cork oak, which may well also have been the case in antiquity.[3] The area also contains a substantial number of mines worked in our period: the most notable examples can be found around the Rio Tinto area, but smaller workings are scattered throughout the region.

To the south similar changes are found. The group of mountain chains known collectively as the Andalusian Cordillera, including most famously the Sierra Nevada, rises sharply from the valley floor, making a stark boundary between the lowlands of the valley and themselves. This range, though more broken than Sierra Morena, is on average higher; its highest point, also the highest point in the peninsula, El Mulhacén, measures 11,420 feet high, with a further nineteen peaks exceeding 6,000 feet. Within the Cordillera, as in the Sierra Morena, small plains are found, divided from one another by intervening parts of the mountain range. The general wildness of these areas can be seen from the fact that they were plagued with bandits until the nineteenth century.[4]

The two ranges meet in the north-east of the province (both are readily visible from the capital of the Roman province, Cordoba), isolating Andalusia from the rest of Spain to such a degree that in the Arabic period a common name for the region was 'Yesira Andalús', or 'the island of Andalusia'. Passage to the central Meseta of Spain is only to be had with difficulty. The pass of Despeñaperros provides the only major geological break in the Sierra Morena, at the head of the Guadalquivir valley. To the west of this other roads running north from the valley are few in number; only three are mentioned in the *Antonine Itinerary*.[5]

The final geographical region of the province is the narrow coastal strip extending along the Mediterranean and Atlantic coasts of the province to the Bay of Cádiz, a genuine bay in antiquity rather than the tidal marshland found today. This again is a low-lying fertile region, presenting a contrast in this respect to the Costa Brava of Catalonia for example, and was heavily colonized by the Phoenicians in the pre-Roman period. However, it must be emphasized that the strip of land concerned is extremely

---

[3] These two naturally coexist, as the pigs eat the acorns from the trees. Aracena has a high reputation for 'pata negra', as does this area of the province of Huelva in general. A friend of Varro's records the death of a giant sow in Lusitania (*RR* 2. 4. 11), probably near to this region, and Pliny (*NH* 22. 8) talks of the quality of the *coccus*, a grub which lives on oak trees, found near Mérida, again possibly a reference to this region.

[4] See C. Bernaldo de Quirós and L. Ardila, *El bandolerismo andaluz* (1988), *passim*, esp. pp. 61 ff. For ancient times, Cicero, *Ad Fam.* 10. 31.

[5] See J. M. Roldán Hervás, *Itineraria hispanica* (1965). lam. VI.

narrow, and in parts almost non-existent. As with the Guadalquivir valley, the Andalusian Cordillera rises steeply from it to the north, forming a clear topographic break. From Cádiz the coast continues to Huelva at the mouth of the Rio Tinto via a complex system of riverine estuaries which were probably far more marshy in antiquity than today, and possibly drained by canals.[6] This marshland continues to the mouth of the Guadiana, the boundary between the *provinciae* of Baetica and Lusitania. However, the passage west to Lusitania through the present-day province of Huelva, like the passage north, is difficult and would have been even more so in antiquity.

Baetica therefore was not a geographical unity, and in addition it was also in antiquity racially diverse. The Guadalquivir valley was inhabited by Iberians, inheritors of a distinct, urban-based, culture, while the uplands to both the north and south were the province of Celtic tribes. As well as these two 'indigenous' groups, the Mediterranean coastal strip contained a large Punic population who had settled here during the period of Barcid rule in Spain. Reaction to the Roman presence and its effects on the region must therefore take account of the possible differences in outcome among these diverse racial and topographical features.

It is also important to ascertain the attitude taken by ruler and ruled towards one another. One starting-point here is the schema for colonial models designed by Horvath.[7] Horvath divides the colonial experience into two categories, 'colonialism' where a large number of settlers from the ruling power are present, and 'imperialism' where there is no settlement involved. These two are then divided, in turn, into three sub-models, 'extermination', 'assimilation', and 'relative equilibrium'. This produces six possible outcomes. The rarest sub-model, total extermination of the ruled, involves the land being entirely occupied by settlers in the case of colonialism, or simply being left empty in that of imperialism. The second sub-model, assimilation, involves the adoption of the rulers' culture by the 'host' society in the case of 'colonialism', the adoption of its economic, or other salient administrative structures in the case of 'imperialism'. Finally 'relative equilibrium' involves the two cultures living side by side, with some cultural exchange, but no cultural dominance by the rulers in the case of 'colonialism' and the simple retention of indige-

---

[6] This area is mainly taken up with the present-day Parque Nacional de Doñana. For the canals, see Strabo 3. 2. 5.

[7] R. J. Horvath, 'A Definition of Colonialism', *Current Anthropology*, 13/1 (1972), 45–56. See also B. Bartel, 'Colonialism and Cultural Responses: Problems Related to Roman Provincial Analysis', *World Archaeology*, 12/1 (1980), 11 ff.

TABLE. Horvath's model

	Colonialism (settlers)	Imperialism (no settlers)
Extermination	Replacement of population	Land left empty
Assimilation	Acculturation of 'host' society	Adoption of ruling power's key structures
Equilibrium	Two cultures side by side	Maintenance of indigenous culture

nous culture in the case of 'imperialism'. The model is presented here in tabular form.

Although Horvath's model gives us a starting-point for the analysis of provincial development, it is too simplistic to apply directly. Further factors need to be taken into account: for instance, the potential diversity of the reactions of the different racial groups within the province to Roman rule, the possible differing reactions of different status groups within these groups, and changes in perception of the ruling power as its structures changed or privileges were granted to the ruled. The fact that if 'assimilation' did occur, it may have happened only in certain spheres of life, must also be taken into account, along with the reasons for such selectivity. It is also, on the other hand, necessary to examine the motives of the ruling power, where there will be differences in policy according to whether inculcating their own cultural values among the subject population was regarded in a positive light, or with indifference. Horvath draws our attention to the need to determine whether a large number of settlers were present in the province or not; however, his divide between large-scale settlement and the total absence of settlers seems too sharp. A further possibility is small-scale settlement, in selected areas—areas which may consequently have been affected differently from those without settlers. Again the social class of the settlers may be of importance in determining their effects on the host community. A further factor to consider is the nature of settlement itself: whether it is 'informal' or 'organized'.

Such a model could be applied to the 'countryside' of the province, but as classical civilization was urban-based, as were two of the 'host' communities concerned (the Iberian and the Punic), the towns of the province and their development provide an ideal focus for an examination of these phenomena.

In the context of Baetica the 'extermination' sub-model can be ruled out. More interesting is the question of which of the two sub-models of 'assimilation' and 'equilibrium' appears more applicable to the province, and whether variations are found as between its different ethnic and geographical divisions. Also of interest is the question of whether the 'colonialism' or 'imperialism' model seems more appropriate, and again whether regional variations appear in this analysis.

The time-limits for the study allow an examination of the significance of two major developments in the province: first, the change at Rome from the republic to the empire, normally regarded, both in ancient and modern times,[8] as the beginning of directed policy towards the provinces rather than the simple exploitation which had gone on before; and Vespasian's grant of *Latinitas* to the peninsula, which has frequently been seen as an indicator of urban development. The limits proposed allow us to look to both sides of these two events and to analyse the factors leading up to any changes which occurred at these points and their consequent impact on the province.

[8] For ancient opinion, see Tacitus, *Ann.* I. I. 2; Justin, *Epit.* 44. 5. 8. For modern views, see C. H. V. Sutherland, *The Romans in Spain* (1939), ch. 6, significantly entitled 'Julius Caesar and the Urban Experiment', and his remarks on p. 152, and E. S. Bouchier, *Spain under the Roman Empire* (1914), ch. 2, pp. 21 ff.

2
Urbanization and Rome: An Overview

'L E T wild beasts live in fields and woods, men ought to draw together into cities.'[1] This opinion of Cassiodorus, writing at the end of antiquity, can be seen as a summary of the constant belief of the classical world that civilization consisted in urban life.[2] Aristotle, writing a millennium earlier than Cassiodorus, regarded the city-state as the natural end of man's evolution; hence his now hackneyed statement that man is a political (i.e. a city-state dwelling) animal.[3] For Aristotle the *polis* made not merely life, but the good life, possible. Plato held similar opinions. In the *Laws*, although some citizens of his theoretical Cretan state are to live in country villages rather than its main town, these villages too are to have the typical features of a classical city.[4] Roman authors hold out a parallel ideal. Lucretius speaks of man's evolution to the city-state, depicting the steps on the way in terms of Roman history.[5] Tacitus too regards the touchstone of civilization as the fostering of cities, the 'urbium cultus'.[6] The same analysis of the good life was found even amongst the early Christians. Tertullian, arguing that all God's works are acceptable, says the Christians live in a world of *fora, macella, balnea, tabernae* (town-squares, market-places, baths, and inns), and various other typical constituents of a city-state.[7]

When considering the spread of classical city-state urbanization to areas where it was not native, for example all of the provinces of the western empire, including southern Spain, two questions need to be asked. First, what were regarded as the defining characteristics of a town in the classical world? And second, what were the mechanisms by which this form of settlement was diffused into new areas?

---

[1] Cassiodorus, *Ep.* 8. 31.
[2] C.f. Philostratus, *Epistles of Apollonius* 11: Πρῶτον εἰς πάντα θεῶν ἄνθρωποτ δέονται καὶ περὶ παντός, ἔπειτα πόλεων . . . ('Above all and for all men have need of the Gods, their next need is for cities . . .').
[3] Aristotle, *Pol.* 1252ª20–1253ª3.   [4] Plato, *Laws* 848d.
[5] Lucretius, 5. 925–1240.   [6] Tacitus, *Ann.* 2. 52.
[7] Tertullian, *Apol.* 42. 2.

The classical city was not simply an agglomeration of people,[8] but was characterized in three distinct, though interrelated, ways. The first of these, as the quotation from Tertullian above suggests, was a community's possession of substantial buildings, in particular public buildings. The second was an independent political life. The third was a communal life extending beyond the political field, though in important respects related to it, including common religious cults and leisure.

Many of the buildings regarded as typical of a classical town were, as will be seen below, connected to political/communal activity, so these two features were normally regarded as linked together: the buildings forming the stage for the political and other communal life of the town, and by their very presence fostering it.[9] The best method of discovering which buildings were regarded as essential for town life is to turn to ancient discussions on the subject. At an abstract level the texts of the *Digest*[10] which deal with the question of who is and is not a resident of a town, make the relevant criterion the use of the town's amenities. These are defined as the *forum, balneum, spectacula* (the town-square, a bath-house, and games), and the fact that 'festi dies' ('holidays') can be celebrated. These passages give us some starting-points for what were regarded as the necessities of town life, implying that a civic centre (the *forum*, although the authors cited by the *Digest* probably had its trading, rather than its strictly legal, functions in mind here), and a bath-house should exist, and suggesting that buildings for *spectacula* and religious rites should also be present.

It is important to note, however, that the passage only mentions the existence of *spectacula* and religious rites. Both of these could be held in the open air or makeshift surroundings, and so, while the presence of buildings for these functions is implied, it cannot be said to be attested securely. However, firm evidence for such buildings comes from the colonial charter of Urso.[11] This document, probably substantially drafted

---

[8] See Isidore of Seville's comments: 'Vici et castella et pagi hi sunt qui nulla dignitate civitatis ornantur, sed vulgari hominum conventu incoluntur' ('Villages, strongholds, and country settlements are places which are adorned with nothing which gives them the dignity of a town, they are lived in by a common herd of people') (*Etym.* 15. 2. 11)

[9] The Spanish philosopher Ortega y Gasset sensed this fusion of the material and political aspects of ancient life when he remarked, 'La urbe [antigua] es, ante todo, esto: plazuela, foro, ágora. Lugar para la conversación, la disputa, la elocuencia, la política' ('The ancient city is above all this: a little square, a *forum*, an *agora*. It is a place for conversation, discussion, eloquence, politics') ('Sobre la muerte de Roma', reprinted in *Las atlantidas y del imperio romano* (1985)).

[10] *Digest*, 50. 1. 27. 1 (Ulpian); 50. 1. 35 (Modestinus).

[11] For a discussion of the implications of this document, see Ch. 4.

at the time of Urso's foundation,[12] is a blueprint for the organization of life in a particular town as opposed to the theoretical speculations found in the *Digest*, and it is of interest therefore to see if the two cohere. The *Lex Ursonensis* contains provisions that the *duoviri* of the *colonia* will take care of the *fana*, *delubra*, and *templa* (shrines, chapels, and temples) of the colony by appointing *magistri* (supervisors) to oversee them;[13] in other words the town is assumed to have religious buildings, of several forms and sizes.

The *magistri* have the further duty of arranging whatever *ludi circenses* (circus games) have been voted by the decurions in connection with these shrines. This is only one of several references to games in the charter, tying in with Ulpian's provision of *spectacula* found in the *Digest*. Both the *duoviri* and the aediles are required to hold games in honour of the Capitoline gods, and in the aediles' case to Venus as well.[14] These are described as 'munus ludive scaenici' ('games or theatrical performances'). Added to the reference to *ludi circenses*, it appears that three different types of entertainment are envisaged. Similar arrangements were no doubt to be found in all the Baetican *coloniae*. Do such provisions for games entail the existence of buildings specifically designed for them? A theatre does seem to be implied, as the law forbids anyone other than certain individuals to sit in the *orchestra* at the *ludi scaenici*.[15] An *orchestra* is specific to the theatre, and this regulation would not make sense if the performance were held in the *forum*. On the other hand, a temporary theatre could have been built for the duration of the spectacle and then dismantled, so the provision could still make perfect sense if Urso did not possess a permanent theatre. Nevertheless the town would no doubt have aspired to a permanent building in time. Less can be inferred from the *locus datus adsignatus* (assigned place) given to the decurions at *ludi* and *ludi scaenici*. Any arena, permanent or temporary, can have a reserved area. More important is the implication that these two events are distinct from one another.[16]

The clearest mention of public buildings in the *Lex Ursonensis* is found in the chapter requiring the town aediles to hold one day's *munus ludive scaenici* for Venus 'in circo aut in foro' ('at the race-track or in the town-square').[17] There is a clear reference to a *circus* (race-track) here, but it is

---

[12] E. Gabba, 'Rifflessioni sulla Lex Coloniae Genetivae Iuliae', in J. Gonzalez and J. Arce (eds.), *Estudios sobre la Tabula Siarensis* (1988), 157 ff. The document in its present form dates from the time of the emperor Domitian.

[13] *Lex Urs.*, ch. 128.   [14] Ibid., ch. 70 (*IIviri*), ch. 71 (aediles).
[15] Ibid., ch. 127.   [16] Ibid., ch. 125 (*ludi*), ch. 126 (*ludi scaenici*).
[17] Ibid., ch. 71.

difficult to determine what sort of structure was envisaged by the drafters of the law. The requirements for a *circus* were the easiest of all classical public buildings to satisfy, a stretch of levelled ground being all that was needed. The provisions at Urso could refer to such a minimal structure, perhaps with temporary stands, put up when games were held. But this again may have created a desire to have a more permanent structure when possible. No evidence of a *circus* has been found at Urso; however, given the very limited excavation which has taken place, and the fact that the *circus* would have to have been sited some distance from the town, which is on a hill, little can be inferred from this. The alternative site proposed by the law, the *forum*, is of more interest. If the phraseology of the duties and sites is parallel, it implies that were the aedile to choose to put on *ludi scaenici*, he would do so in the *forum*, suggesting the absence of a theatre and at most, given the provision of the law discussed above, the erection of a temporary structure in the *forum*. Despite this, the remains of a theatre have been found at Urso, which may show the law here has failed to take into account Urso's specific amenities or, and perhaps more likely, that the permanent theatre was built later to fulfil an aspiration for such a building.

There is no mention of an amphitheatre in the law. It is doubtful if this was because animal-baiting or gladiatorial contests were never held as a *duovir*'s or aedile's *munus*,[18] but rather suggests that such performances would have taken place in the *forum*. This practice persisted into the imperial period, as can be seen from Vitruvius. While discussing the building of *fora*, he notes that their intercolumniation must not be as narrow as found in Greece, otherwise it will hinder the viewing of gladiatorial contests, whose celebration in the *forum* is described as 'a maioribus consuetudo tradita' ('a practice handed down to us from our ancestors').[19] Theatres too appear to have been used for this purpose, as can be seen from the prologue of Terence's *Hecyra* and a gloss on it by Donatus, who states: 'hoc abhorret a nostra consuetudine, verum tamen apud antiquos gladiatores in theatro spectabantur' ('although it appals our tastes, the ancients watched gladiators in the theatre') and Dio Chrysostom notes that the theatre of Dionysus in Athens was used for such purposes in the imperial period.[20] Temporary arenas are another possibility: Plutarch records how a temporary *cavea* (arena) was erected in the *forum* at Rome for a gladiatorial display.[21] It may be that such a temporary edifice, built in

---

[18] Columella's remarks (*RR* 7. 2. 4) that animals were imported to Gades for *munerarii* strongly suggests that this was the case on occasions.
[19] Vitruvius, 5. 1. 1.   [20] Dio Chrysostom, 31. 121.
[21] Plutarch, *Vit. C. Gracchi* 12.

the *forum* as Plutarch describes, is what Urso's charter envisages. This would have the advantage that a mixture of games and theatrical performances could be put on in the three- and four-day show using only one structure.

The *Lex Ursonensis* therefore satisfies the criteria found in the *Digest* for religious buildings and *spectacula*. The provisions dealing with the aediles' games require that these be held in either the *circus* or *forum*. As in the texts in the *Digest*, there is an assumption that Urso will have a *forum*. Chapter 81 of the law requires the *scribae* (clerks) of the *colonia* to swear an oath on taking up their office in the *forum* on market-days. This shows that as well as having civic functions the *forum* is envisaged, as it is in the *Digest*, as having a trading function.

The only criterion found in the *Digest* that the *Lex* fails to meet is a provision for a bath-house. This is at first sight curious as the bath-house was regarded as an important part of Roman urban life. An inscription found on the bath-house belonging to the country estate of C. Legianus Verus near Bononia proudly declares: '[b]alineum *more urbico* lavat [et] omnia commoda praestantur' ('here is a bath-house of the city style with all its facilities').[22] However, the relevant provisions were probably found in one of the lost chapters of the law, as can be seen from an examination of a second document setting out a city charter, the Flavian Municipal Law.[23] Its status, in that it was to be applied to a wide variety of highly different communities, is ambivalent.[24] It is less theoretical in nature than the *Digest*, but not as specific as the *Lex Ursonensis* since it deals with many communities rather than a single one. Therefore it is of interest that its provisions appear to agree with both these other documents. Section 19 of the law charges the town aediles with the upkeep of *aedes sacrae, balnea, macellum, cloacae,* and *viae* (sacred shrines, bath-houses, market-hall, sewers, and roads).[25] A now lost section of the *Lex Ursonensis* probably dealt with *balnea* in the same way. Unlike the *Lex Ursonensis*, the Flavian law does not require the aediles to put on games but does envisage the production of *spectacula*. Provisions for regulating expenditure on them are found in chapter 77 of the law and others, dealing with seating arrangements, an important consideration in status-conscious Roman society, in chapter 81. The obligation of holding games would have fallen on the *duoviri*. Columella refers to animals being

---

[22] *ILS* 5721.
[23] J. González, 'The *Lex Irnitana*: A New Copy of the Flavian Municipal Law', *JRS* 76 (1986), 147 ff.
[24] See the discussion in Ch. 6.   [25] *Lex Irn.*, ch. 19.

brought to Gades, a town with municipal status, for *munerarii* (games-producers).²⁶

Like the Flavian Municipal Law, the *Lex Ursonensis* also concerns itself with the town's *viae publicae* (public roads) and rights of access to them.²⁷ Similarly, provisions for sewer maintenance are also found here.²⁸ The provision for the upkeep of sewers and baths implies the presence of aqueducts.²⁹ That aqueducts, and hence the provision of running water, were regarded as necessities of town life is underlined by a text of the *Digest*,³⁰ which regards the presence of aqueducts in a town as normal. Further evidence is provided by the *Lex Ursonensis*,³¹ which contains details about what is to be done if a public aqueduct cuts through private land. While the relevant section is couched to look to the future, it implies that such aqueducts already existed.

The assumed presence of a *macellum* (market-hall) in the *Lex Irnitana* is not found in our other documents. But, as has been seen, Ulpian regards the use of the *forum* as one of the essential rights of a citizen. He is thinking here of its trading, rather than its legal, functions, so the require-ment of a special building for trade as found in the Flavian law can be seen as an amplification of this demand.

Our written legal sources, therefore, give a generally coherent picture of the minimum requirements for town life. These are a *forum*, religious buildings, baths, the supply of water, areas where games and shows could be held, and facilities for commercial life, either in the *forum*, or, as in the case of Irni, a separate market-place. These provisions cover the basic areas of a classical town's public life: politics, religion, communal leisure, and local trade.

Tacitus' *Agricola* provides a non-legal check on these sources. We are told that Agricola encouraged the native population to build *templa, fora*, and *domus* (temples, town-squares, and houses).³² The Britons are also said to have acquired a taste for *balnea*. Again there is the same strong emphasis on public centres as found above. The inclusion of *domus*, or private houses, is a new feature. This is not normally given a high priority by ancient authors, although private housing which was thought abnor-mally poor, such as that of Athens, would draw comment.³³ However,

---

²⁶ Columella, *RR* 7. 2. 4; other references to municipal status: 8. 16. 9, 11. 3. 26.
²⁷ *Lex Urs.*, ch. 78.　²⁸ Ibid., ch. 77.
²⁹ Given the climate of the region it seems highly unlikely that sewers here would have been flushed by rain-water.
³⁰ *Digest* (Arcadius Charisius), 50. 4. 18. 6.
³¹ *Lex Urs.*, ch. 99.　³² Tacitus, *Agricola*, 21.　³³ Ps. Dicaearchus, 2–4.

what Tacitus is drawing attention to is not any particular style of housing, but merely the fact that the custom of living in towns, something previously alien to the Celtic aristocracy, was encouraged.

A final physical sign of a Roman town was, on occasions, the presence of a planned street-grid. Although not present in many of the older towns of Italy, it was a regular feature of newly created settlements, and its adoption by native settlements should probably be regarded as a conscious attempt to give a more Roman appearance to the town concerned.[34]

The second element in the urban scene was the possession of some form of independent political life. The classical town was the political centre-place for a surrounding, and delineated, territory, and would possess magistrates and a council to oversee its own affairs. This autonomy was the touchstone of the classical concept of a city, as can be seen from Plutarch's comments: παρὰ πάντα ταῦτα λέγεται πολιτεία τάξις καὶ κατάστασις πόλεως διοικοῦσα τὰς πράξεις ('above all things a constitution is the ordering and arranging of a city with a view to managing its affairs').[35] The Pisidian town of Tymandus was granted city status in the late third or early fourth century AD. The imperial rescript making the award states that what it is to be a city is to enjoy an autonomous council and magistrates making their own laws.[36] Similarly the appeal from the Phrygian town of Orcistus to the emperor Constantine to be restored to city status included, as an argument in its favour, that it had once possessed annual magistrates and a council.[37] Finally both the *Lex Ursonensis* and the Flavian Municipal Law contain detailed provisions for the operation of local government, defining both the number and rights of the council and its presiding magistrates.

Beyond political life were the shared religious practices and leisure

[34] See E. J. Owens, 'Roman Town Planning', in I. M. Barton (ed.), *Roman Public Buildings* (1989), 7 ff.

[35] Plutarch, *Moralia* (*De unius in Republica dominatione, populari statu, et paucorum imperio*) 826e.

[36] *CIL* 3. 6866 = *ILS* 6090: 'uti ceteris civitatibus ius est coeundi in curiam, faciendi etiam decreti et gerendi cetera que iure permissa sunt, ipsa quoque permissu nostro agere possit, et magistratus ei itemque aediles, quaestores quoque et si qua alia necessaria facienda sunt, creare debebunt. Quem ordinem agendarum rerum perpetuo pro civitatis merito custodiri conveniet' ('As in all the other towns there is a right to hold a local assembly, make decrees and carry out everything else which is permitted by law, so this town too can do these things as it has been given our permission. They ought to create magistrates, and aediles and quaestors and if anything else is necessary it must be done. It shall be proper for this method of conducting affairs should hold for ever for the benefit of the town').

[37] *CIL* 3. 7000 = *ILS* 6091: '[Orcistus] annuis magistratuum fascibus ornaretur essetque curialibus celebre et populo civium plenum' ('Orcistus was once adorned with symbols of magistrates' office each year, famed for her councillors, full of citizens').

pursuits. Neither of these could be divorced from municipal political life, and they should be regarded as another thread in the complex web of ancient social life. As has been seen, both the *Lex Ursonensis* and the Flavian Municipal Law contain regulations concerning the religious buildings of the community, and games too are assumed to be present in both *coloniae* and *municipia*. Bath-houses were the centre of much Roman social activity, and, as has been seen, were regarded as an integral part of urban life.[38] The physical and non-physical aspects of this as described above were normally assumed to go together; the petition from Orcistus, for example, as well as talking about a council, also mentions the town's baths, aqueducts, and roads. On occasions this was not the case, as is shown by Pausanias' remarks about the town of Panopeus in Phocis. Pausanias was unsure if he ought to call it a town at all. His confusion arose because it possessed none of the physical attributes of a town listed above, yet still enjoyed political autonomy.[39]

If we have outlined what a classical town ought to have looked like, it still remains to see how and to what degree this pattern of urbanization could have spread into the area of Baetica in the late republican and early imperial Roman periods. A crucial question here is: what evidence is there for implementation of positive measures by Roman authorities to promote such a process? Because of the emphasis placed on town life in ancient sources many historians have concluded that Rome, after conquering a new area, did actively encourage urbanization as a means of integrating the conquered area into her empire. Harmand's view that 'le "fait urbain" est par excellence le facteur de cette [i.e. provincial] romanisation . . . C'est cet idéal que le conquérant romain aspire à faire partager aux masses . . . qui composent cet occident', is a typical statement of this viewpoint.[40] Rome is portrayed as concerned with 'civilizing'

[38] J. Carcopino, *Daily Life in Ancient Rome* (1941), 277 ff.

[39] Pausanias, 10. 4. 1–4: . . . πόλιν Φωκέων, εἴγε ὀνομάσαι τις πόλιν καὶ τούτους οἷς γε οὐκ ἀρχεῖα οὐ γυμνάσιόν ἐστιν, οὐ θέατρον οὐκ ἀγορὰν ἔχουσιν, οὐχ ὕδωρ κατερχόμενον ἐς κρήνην, ἀλλὰ ἐν στέγαις κοίλαις κατὰ τὰς καλύβας μάλιστα τὰς ἐν τοῖς ὄρεσιν, ἐνταῦθα οἰκοῦσιν ἐπὶ χαράδα. ὅμως δὲ ὅροι γε τῆς χώρας εἰσὶν αὐτοῖς ἐς τοὺς ὁμόρους, καὶ ἐς τὸν σύλλογον συνέδρους καὶ οὗτοι πέμπουσι τὸν Φωκικόν ('. . . a city of the Phocians, if one can call a city a place which has no official buildings or no *gymnasium*. They have no theatre, nor a town-square, nor water running to a fountain. They live in hovels by a torrent on the edge of the mountains. Nevertheless there are boundary stones marking out their lands from their neighbours and even they send delegates to the assembly of Phocia'). The list of typical amenities to be expected in a town closely parallels those from our Latin sources. The ruins of Panopeus show that Pausanias was heavily overstating his case. However, this does not affect the value of his words for assessing the characteristics which it was thought an ancient city ought to possess.

[40] L. Harmand, *L'Occident romain* (1960), 291. See also E. J. Owens, 'Roman Town Planning', in I. M. Barton (ed.), *Roman Public Buildings* (1989), 7.

its subjects in much the same way as the empires of the nineteenth century.

Do we find traces of such a positive attitude in our ancient sources? One form of attested urbanization which was the result of positive initiative did occur: namely the creation of cities for personal reasons by emperors. Good examples of this process are the creation of Nicopolis by Augustus to celebrate his triumph at Actium, of Antinopolis by Hadrian, and of a *colonia* by Marcus Aurelius at the village where his wife died.[41] A notable Spanish example of this phenomenon is the creation of a new luxury district, the *nova urbs* (new city), by Hadrian at Italica, the town of his birth. Italica, however, demonstrates the fragility of such urbanization. The plan was highly grandiose and bore no relation to local conditions. In fact the *nova urbs* had rapidly to be abandoned because of subsidence.[42] The foundations mentioned above show that the creation of a city was regarded as an act worthy of an emperor and consequently of propaganda value. However, their *ad hoc* nature must not be forgotten. All were provoked by specific incidents in individuals' lives and as such cannot be taken to show the practice of a consistent imperial policy of positive urbanization.

More promising support for the existence of such a policy is found in two late imperial rescripts referred to above. The letter to Tymandus expresses a wish that 'per universum orbem nostrum civitatum honor ac numerus augeatur' ('may the glory and number of cities increase throughout our realm') while the other, concerning Orcistus, speaks of an imperial 'studium' ('eagerness') to 'urbes vel novas condere, vel longaevas erudire vel intermortuas reparare' ('establish new cities, aid long-established ones, and restore those that have fallen into decay'). However, it must be remembered that these documents both come from the Greek East of the empire and date from a period when urban growth was in decline. Consequently what appear at first sight to be wishes to extend the area of urbanization may in reality be simply a desire to shore up a declining system which is already in place. Their value in revealing imperial attitudes to the creation of an new urban system in the western empire in the early imperial period is therefore limited. It is also of interest that despite the fine sentiments expressed in these letters, in neither case was the resulting rise in status due to a conscious imperial initiative, but stemmed from an appeal to the centre from the town concerned. This perhaps

---

[41] *SHA, Aurelius* 26.

[42] J. M. Luzón Nogué, 'Consideraciones sobre la urbanistica de la ciudad nueva de Italica', *Italica* (*EAE* 121 (1982)), 75–132.

suggests that what is being expressed is a rhetorical *topos* reflecting the wish of the emperors concerned to be seen as promoters of culture *post eventum* rather than any positive commitment to bring this about. There seems therefore to be no conclusive evidence that there was an active imperial policy of urbanization.[43] In the republican period too prestige could be acquired by being the founder of a town. Several Spanish examples are known, such as the foundation of Corduba in 152 BC by M. Claudius Marcellus,[44] and of Valentia in 138 BC by Decimus Iunius Brutus.[45] However, here there is an even larger problem than in the imperial period with the nature of such foundations. It is unclear whether these settlements involved the creation of any Roman features at all.[46] As the act of foundation was one carried out for propaganda purposes at Rome, what was actually laid out on the ground was of little importance, especially as few, if any, of the target audience would go to verify the claims made. In Spain, Ti. Sempronius Gracchus certainly made inflated claims about the numbers of 'cities' he captured,[47] and this sort of exaggeration must cast doubts on the nature of his own foundation, Gracurris, and other similar acts by individual governors.[48] It is hard therefore to see such foundations as producing a major diffusion of urban ideas into the local environment. We have no secure way of knowing what form they took, and the *ad hoc* nature of their foundation led to them being random in location and small in number. This, and the fact that they were, above all, propaganda gestures, which were unlikely to have attracted continued interest from their founders, means that they ought not to be seen as an extensive stimulus for change among the local population.

A more widespread form of deliberate urbanization is found in programmes of colonization. Yet it must be borne in mind that the great

[43] See the remarks of S. Mitchell, 'Imperial Building in the Eastern Roman Provinces', *HSCP* 91 (1987), 333 ff. concerning the much better documented eastern empire: 'The evidence for direct financial commitment on the part of emperors in the foundation or refoundation of cities which bore their name is disappointingly thin' (p. 361); 'The absence of evidence makes it hard to argue that the emperors, through cash contributions for city foundation or civic building, were enacting a conscious and deliberate policy to regenerate and transform regions economically, although that may have been a frequent and predictable result of their actions' (p. 364).

[44] Strabo, 3. 2. 1.   [45] Livy, *Epit.* 55.

[46] Italica, for example, founded in 206 BC by Scipio, seems to have remained firmly native in outlook for much of its early history.

[47] For which he is criticized by Strabo. 3. 4. 13.

[48] Was this Aemilius Paullus' intention in freeing the 'Turris Lascutana' from the rule of Hasta (*CIL* 2. 5041)? The resulting 'city' would have born little relationship to a classical city. It is precisely the conflation of *turres* (πύργοι), i.e. towers, with cities that Strabo complains of in the case of Gracchus.

period of planting colonies under Julius Caesar and Augustus was provoked by a wish to solve internal Roman political problems. These settlements were indubitably Roman in form; however they were created, of course, not for the benefit of the local population, but for the colonists. Some colonies did incorporate a native element, but this was to ensure the viability of the town rather than promote a change of lifestyle among the local population so incorporated. Indeed, the imposition of a colony may have been regarded as a punishment, not a benefit, for the natives concerned.[49] It is still reasonable to accept, however, that an epiphenomenon of colonial foundations would have been an alteration in native attitudes towards urban life as relations with the new settlers may well have led to the adoption of certain Roman patterns of behaviour. How far such a process occurred remains to be seen; however, whatever the strength of such a phenomenon, it is not evidence of a general policy to change the local way of life but merely an incidental by-product of the colonization programme.

The examples of active urbanization found so far have been limited in scope. Was there a general intellectual climate in Rome in favour of a policy of promoting urban growth in order to civilize Roman subjects? The existence of such a belief, at least as a majority viewpoint, is not borne out by our sources. Almost all the statements we have on imperial aims from the Roman period are silent on the subject of encouraging the growth of urban civilization. Their emphasis is firmly on the glories of conquest rather than on a civilizing mission.[50] Cicero declared that it behoved a man with *humanitas* to rule his province well, even if it was a barbarian (i.e. western) one, and that the integrity of the governor's rule was more important than obtaining fame.[51] Nevertheless he preferred to dwell on the glory that empire brought to Rome, saying that wise statesmen would do their best 'ut rempublicam augeant imperio, agris, vectigalibus' ('to extend the power, land, and revenues of the state').[52] There is no hint of a beneficent ideology here, even as a justification for conquest. Cicero's injunction to rule well is couched purely in terms of not mistreating the native population rather than actively bettering their lot and it is this negative form of beneficence which finds a continuing emphasis in Roman thought. Livy notes that Hannibal failed to win over

---

[49] See Ch. 4 and P. MacKendrick, 'Cicero, Livy, and Roman Colonisation', *Athenaeum*, 32 (1954), 201 ff.
[50] Cicero, *De Rep.* 3. 24; *Pro Murena* 21 ff.
[51] Cicero, *Ad. Quint. f.* 1. 1. 27; *Ad Att.* 5. 20. 6.   [52] Cicero, *De Offic.* 2. 85.

Rome's allies because they were governed fairly,[53] and sees the advantage for Rome in just rule: 'certe id firmissimum longe imperium est quo oboedientes gaudent' ('certainly the securest rule by far is that which the ruled are happy with').[54] Again any beneficial results for the ruled are merely a side-effect of a policy designed to be of advantage to the rulers. Seneca too uses this theme. While believing that full control in the empire ought to remain with the rulers,[55] he states that after a conquest it should be benefits rather than armed force which secure the obedience of the ruled.[56]

This pragmatic beneficence also underlies the passage which is regarded as the *locus classicus* of the active encouragement of urbanization and 'Romanization': namely Tacitus' account of Agricola's activities as governor of Britain. Here we read of Agricola:

hortari privatim, adiuvare publice ut templa fora domos extruerent... iam vero principium filios liberalibus artibus erudire... et ingenia Britannorum studiis Gallorum anteferre, ut qui modo linguam Romanam abnuebant, eloquentiam concupiscerent. Inde etiam habitus nostri honor et frequens toga. Paulatimque discessum ad delenimenta vitiorum, porticus et balineas et conviviorum elegentiam idque apud imperitos humanitas vocabatur cum pars servitutis esset.

He urged on individuals and helped communities to build temples, town-squares, and houses... he educated the sons of the leading Britons in the liberal arts... and favoured British aptitude over the book-learnt abilities of the Gauls so that those who had previously spurned the language of the Romans now desired to be eloquent in it. Then prestige came to our form of dress and the toga was often to be seen. Slowly they passed on to those charming vices: porticoes, bath-houses, and smart dinner parties—that which is called 'civilization' by those who don't know the ways of the world, but which in fact are a part of slavery.[57]

This cannot be dismissed as the policy of a solitary governor, as Tacitus alludes to the same process taking place in the governorship of Trebellius Maximus approximately ten years previously.[58] Nevertheless the prologue to the passage shows that the policy was designed primarily for Roman

---

[53] Livy, 22. 13.   [54] Livy, 8. 13. 17.   [55] Seneca, *Hanse frag.* 42.

[56] Seneca, *Cons. ad Polyb.* 12. 3: 'melius beneficiis imperium custodiatur quam armis' ('one's rule is better guarded by benefits than arms').

[57] Tacitus, *Agricola* 21. See however the comments of J. C. Mann and R. G. Penman, *Literary Sources for Roman Britain* (2nd edn., 1985), 69 n. 47 and M. Millett, *The Romanization of Britain* (1990), 69 ff.

[58] Tacitus, *Agricola* 16: 'didicere iam barbari quoque ignoscere vitiis blandientibus' ('now the barbarians learnt to turn a blind eye to seductive vices').

security reasons: 'Ut homines dispersi et rudes, eoque in bella faciles quieti et otio per voluptates assuescerent' ('In order that men who had previously lived scattered from one another and in a primitive way and so were ready to make war should become accustomed to peace and quiet through their pleasures'). In other words the plan was to enervate the natives for the benefit of Rome, not to educate them for their own good.

The extent of the programme can also be questioned. Agricola is said to have helped communities (*publice*) to build Roman-style buildings, but it is clear that the initial impulse to build came from the Britons themselves. Roman aid presumably took the form of hiring out army builders to help with this task, as there would have been no suitable artisans in Britain. The similarity in design of British *fora* to military *principia* (headquarters buildings) has often been used to support this belief. However, the most recent work in this field has cast doubt on whether even this sort of assistance was provided.[59] There is no hint that the Britons did not pay for the buildings themselves, and the massive debts which accrued to the imperial exchequer and Seneca before Boudica's rebellion suggest that they did.[60] Aid therefore was an encouragement to a native tendency found to be of advantage to Rome: in this case centralization and the adoption of Roman habits which were believed to help secure the Roman occupation. In addition the concentration of the local élite in one fixed location would have made them easier to police and punish if the need for such action arose.

The education programme was restricted to the nobility, as Tacitus himself says. This was inevitable as Rome, being a pre-industrial state, did not have the resources to set up a national scheme of education, a notion anyway alien to the Roman mind.[61] The education of the chieftains would allow easier communication between the rulers and the highest echelons of native society. It would also bind them closer to the Roman system and detach them from their own people, both making them fit to perform the tasks of local government, as understood by Rome, and removing potential tribal leaders who could be figureheads in a revolt. Again this programme was probably a response to aristocratic native pressure rather than active encouragement by Agricola. The popularity of such schemes can be seen from the enthusiasm with which that of Sertorius was received

    [59] T. F. C. Blagg, 'Roman Civil and Military Architecture in Britain', *World Archaeology* 12/1 (1980/1), 27–42. Millett, *The Romanization of Britain*, 69 ff.
    [60] Dio, 62. 2. 1, with Naber's amendment of ἄκουσιν to αἰτοῦσιν. See also Sheppard Frere, *Britannia* (3rd edn., 1987), 71.
    [61] See Cicero, *De Rep.* 4. 3.

in Spain,[62] and the number of young Gallic aristocrats found at Augusto-
dunum learning Roman manners in AD 21 during the revolt of Florus and
Sacrovir.[63]

While Tacitus underlines Agricola's activities in this field, his emphasis
lies less on the value of civilizing the Britons than on praise of Agricola for
bringing about the pacification of Britain without the loss of Roman life
(compare his account of the use of auxiliaries at Mons Graupius). He also
seizes on it as an opportunity to expand on the ideal of the noble savage
and Roman decadence, one of his favourite themes.

Most statements dealing with Roman rule, however, are concerned
with Rome's achievement in 'pacifying' the world, the most famous being
that of Anchises in the *Aeneid* which is all the more important given the
poem's semi-official status as a 'national' epic and the fact that it was
specifically aimed at a ruling-class audience: 'Tu regere imperio populos,
Romane, memento. | Hae tibi erunt artes, pacisque imponere morem, |
parcere subiectis et debellare superbos' ('You, Roman, remember to rule
over the other nations. These are your skills; to impose the custom of
peace, to spare the subjugated and cast down the proud').[64] Significantly,
just prior to this statement Anchises has disclaimed any of the higher arts
for Rome. The same theme is used by Augustus in his *Res Gestae*. In the
introduction he records how he brought the world under Roman sway,
and when speaking of his achievements abroad the main theme is that of
pacification.[65] This is a constant *topos* running through the praise of
emperors, whereas the civilizing of the provinces never occurs as such a
theme. This is true even in contexts where it might be most expected.
According to Suetonius, Domitian was particularly strict with provincial
officials and eager to prosecute corrupt practices.[66] Nevertheless the notion of acting justly towards the provinces or helping to civilize them is
not used in any of the poems produced in his honour by Martial or
Statius. Instead they dwell on his German conquests. Statius again sees
Rome as the universal law-giver pacifying the world.[67] Fronto, when
writing to Marcus Aurelius, lists the duties of an emperor. Those not
concerned with Italian affairs are: 'reges exterrarum gentium compellare,
sociorum culpas edictis coercere, benefacta laudare, seditiosos com-
pescere, feroces territare' ('to coerce the kings of peoples outside the

---

[62] Plutarch, *Vit. Sert.* 14.   [63] Tacitus, *Ann.* 3. 43.
[64] Virgil, *Aen.* 6. 851–3.   [65] Augustus, *RG* 5. 26: 'pacare'.
[66] Suetonius, *Vit. Dom.* 8, and H. W. Pleket, 'Domitian, the Senate and the Provinces',
Mnemosyne, 14 (1961), 296–315.
[67] Statius, *Silv.* 5. 3. 188 ff.

empire, punish by your edicts the wrong-doings of our allies, praise their good deeds, put down the rebellious, and cow the barbarous by terror') .[68] In a letter to Verus, Fronto praises his military conquests and speaks of the 'respublica imperiumque populi Romani' (the state and rule of the Roman people), implying a view of the provinces which in no way considers them as equal to Italy.[69]

This image of inequality is both common and persists through time. Strabo speaks of Rome's ἐπικράτεια (power), and of the Gauls being δεδουλωμένοι (enslaved) by the Romans.[70] Tacitus also refers on several occasions to the Roman empire being a form of slavery.[71] Aelius Aristides is careful to address Rome as 'you' throughout his panegyric to the city, despite the tenor of universal citizenship which runs through the work. It is also noteworthy that there are few hints of a civilizing mission imputed to Rome in the *Ad Romam*, a fact which will be further discussed below. Justin uses more violent language, speaking of Spain accepting the yoke of Roman rule, 'iugum accipere'.[72] Finally Orosius talks of Augustus not as civilizing but as imposing 'the habit of obedience', 'disciplinae morem', on the world.[73]

No reflection of shame is meant by these references to slavery. For Strabo it is the ἐπικράτεια of Rome which has improved the lot of the conquered peoples concerned (it has stopped them fighting and forced them to take up agriculture).[74] The Elder Pliny, after noting the miserable conditions in which the Chauci live, remarks contemptuously: 'et hae gentes si vincantur hodie a populo Romano servire se dicunt' ('and these tribes if they were conquered today by the Roman people would say that they were enslaved').[75] The advantages of Roman rule, however, tended to be extolled in terms of bringing 'peace' rather than of bringing civilization. This is shown from Cerialis' speech to the Treveri at the time of Civilis' revolt. His appeal for loyalty rests on arguing that Gaul suffered constantly from arbitrary rule and war before Roman intervention, and that the Romans came solely to bring about peace. The tribute levied on Gaul is to pay for the army that keeps that peace. No appeal is made to any civilizing of the country carried out by Rome. Cerialis instead merely threatens the Gauls with a worse set of rulers who will levy higher tribute if Civilis' revolt succeeds. Cerialis does mention that Gauls can and do rise

    [68] Fronto, *De Eloquentia* (Ambr. 404).
    [69] Fronto, *Ad Verum Imp.* 2. 1 (Ambr. 446, col. 2).   [70] Strabo, 4. 1. 5, 4. 4. 2.
    [71] Tacitus, *Ann.* 2. 73, 14. 31; *Agricola* 14. 2.   [72] Justin, 44. 5. 8.
    [73] Orosius, 6. 22. 3.   [74] Strabo, 4. 1. 5, 4. 4. 2.   [75] Pliny, *NH* 16. 1. 4.

to the highest ranks in the empire, but this is a personal rather than a general point. There is no implication that Roman rule has materially changed the Gauls' life for the better.[76] The *Pax Romana*, by removing the threat of tribal wars, produced an environment which would have made the creation of towns easier than it had been in the past; nevertheless this positive aspect of fostering civilization is left very much to the 'pacified' themselves.[77]

There is moreover some evidence of active discouragement of urbanization by Rome. In the republican period we have two examples of this outside the direct Roman sphere of influence, or in a recently incorporated area. These are Appian's recording of Ti. Sempronius Gracchus' prohibition on the Celtiberian tribes against building further *poleis* or fortifying their existing ones,[78] and Strabo's remark that the Romans reduced the majority of the *poleis* of the northern Lusitanians to mere villages, while improving a few and settling there themselves. (The verb used for the reduction of the Lusitanians, ταπεινοῦν (to humble), is one which emphasizes Rome's military triumph and is pregnant with the theme of 'debellare superbos'.)[79] These two statements show that Rome was willing and able to deal with power-structures other than those constructed around a *polis* and on occasions would prefer to do so if it was thought that this would hold some advantage (here that of avoiding sieges of hilltop sites). In turn this may suggest that when Roman-style urbanization did occur, it was for the benefit of Roman settlers, who would expect urban amenities, rather than that of the local population. This is not to say that some urbanizing tendencies would not be adopted by the natives, but to note that we have yet to find evidence that this process was intended by Rome.

Vespasian's letter to the Saborenses of Baetica also shows that at a later period urbanization *per se* was not the primary goal of Roman policy. Vespasian approves of the move of their town down to the lowlands requested by the Saborenses, but does not grant them the extra revenue-raising powers for which they also asked.[80] The money generated from these powers would probably have been used to help adorn the proposed new city. However, Vespasian was obviously more concerned with Sabora's ability to pay its imperial taxes than with its wish to be completely

---

[76] Tacitus, *Hist.* 4. 74.

[77] However, the Roman 'peace' is sometimes portrayed as something entirely negative for the conquered. See, most famously, Calgacus' comments before the battle of Mons Graupius in Tacitus, *Agricola* 30–2, esp. 30: 'atque ubi solitudinem faciunt, pacem appellant' ('and where they make a wasteland they call that peace'). C.f. Tacitus, *Ann.* 12. 33: '[Britanni] qui pacem nostram metuebant' ('the Britons who feared our rule').

[78] Appian, *Ib.* 44.   [79] Strabo, 3. 3. 5.   [80] *ILS* 6092.

urbanized. It is also significant that the desire to move the town originated from the local population, not the central Roman authorities. Similarly Pliny in Bithynia refers all new building projects to Trajan for approval.[81] The criterion for such approval is whether the project concerned will drain the revenues of the town. The emperor's concern here is probably the same as that of his predecessor, Vespasian, namely that the towns of Bithynia should be solvent enough to pay their imperial taxes. Bithynia was a fully urbanized area, so the question of urbanization as such does not arise, but a comparison with Sabora shows that the ability to pay tax, not the form of the tax-paying unit, is foremost in the imperial mind.

Aelius Aristides speaks of Rome training the barbarians of the western empire, but his analogy with horse-training suggests that he is emphasizing Rome's pacification of the provinces rather than a civilizing mission.[82] Aristides was not adverse to using a civilizing theme, but reserves this for his panegyric on Athens, omitting it entirely in the *Ad Romam*, where he chooses to use the *topos* of pacification instead. Dio may imply that Roman troops had created towns in Germany by AD 9, but we need to be wary, given the distance in time between the author and his subject and the fact that the syntax of his statement is unclear and could equally be taken as part of the description of the voluntary adoption of Roman customs by the German tribes which immediately follows this passage.[83]

There is only one unambiguous statement of an intention to civilize the world in Latin literature. This is found in the Elder Pliny. On arriving at Italy in his geographical description of the world he breaks out into the following paean: 'numine deum electa . . . sparsa congregaret imperia ritusque molliret et tot populorum discordes ferasque linguas sermonis commercio contraheret ad colloquia et humanitatem homini daret, breviterque una cunctorum gentium in toto orbe patria fieret' ('land chosen by the wisdom of the gods . . . to gather together scattered empires, to make men's customs more civilized, to gather together through one common tongue into a single forum so many people with dissonant and barbarous languages, to give civilization to mankind, in short to become the homeland of all the people in all the world').[84] This is a manifesto claiming that

---

[81] He was possibly under orders to do so: A. N. Sherwin-White, *The Letters of Pliny* (1966), 593.

[82] Aelius Aristides, *Ad Romam* 96.

[83] Dio, 56. 18. 2–3: καὶ στρατιῶταί τε αὐτῶν ἐκεῖ ἐχείμαζον καὶ πόλεις συνῳκίζοντο, ἔς τε τὸν κόσμον σφῶν οἱ βάρβαροι μετερρυθμίζοντο καὶ ἀγορὰς ἐνόμιζον συνόδους τε εἰρηνικὰς ἐποιοῦντο ('their [the Romans'] soldiers wintered there and founded cities, and the barbarians were gradually changing to the Roman way of doing things, holding markets and peaceful assemblies'). [84] Pliny, *NH* 3. 5. 39.

Rome had pursued an active policy to change her subjects, a policy which Pliny, as his remarks on the Chauci above show, thought would be of major benefit to much of the empire. He appears, however, to be a lone voice, and this is not for want of alternative sources. Perhaps this passage is the opinion of one learned man at variance with his own contemporaries, or represents the views of a substantial minority, isolated from the decision-making élite. Alternatively Pliny, and possibly others, may have needed to justify Rome's rule as a civilizing one, something which most did not feel the necessity of doing.

Whatever the reason, Pliny remains outside the mainstream of Roman thought on the empire, and his view is more reminiscent of that of much later European imperialists. These, however, were given their convictions both through the radical differences between their own lifestyles and those of their subjects, and in possessing a religion, Christianity, which claims sole and universal validity and which lays an injunction on its adherents to proselytize. This attitude to imperialism is summed up by the declaration of the Aborigines' Protection Society that: 'The complete civilisation and the real happiness of man can never be secured by anything less than the diffusion of Christian principles.'[85] Roman religion made no such claims, and the material differences between Rome and her subjects were much smaller than those which existed between ruler and ruled in the later European colonial empires; consequently the two main reasons responsible for developing a civilizing ideology among later European imperialists were not present in the Roman mind.[86] Indeed, far from urging Domitian to 'take up the Romans' burden', the philosopher Apollonius of Tyana could be portrayed instead as encouraging the emperor not to wish to rule over and thus be of benefit to βαρβάροι.[87] Even had the imperial administration wanted to carry out Pliny's wishes, this would have been impossible in practical terms. The Roman empire was run with a very small administrative apparatus,[88] increases in which would have caused extreme political and economic tension. Nor were there the resources to fund schemes of education or provide the large numbers of artisans needed to build cities, even if the will to do this had been present.

There are nevertheless more specific examples of the deliberate crea-

[85] Perhaps its most famous expression is found in Kipling's poem, 'The White Man's Burden'.

[86] For the 19th c., see C. A. Bayly, *Imperial Meridian* (1989), ch. 5.

[87] Philostratus, *Epistles of Apollonius* 21.

[88] See K. Hopkins, 'Taxes and Trade in the Roman Empire', *JRS* 70 (1980), 101 ff., at p. 121, where it is estimated that there was one administrator per 350,000–400,000 head of population.

tion of new towns other than *coloniae* in the empire. Most of these occurred for the prosaic reasons of military or administrative convenience.
Florus notes that Augustus after the Cantabrian wars resettled these tribes
in the lowlands in new towns.[89] His reason was a wish not to civilize them,
but to deprive them of their potential mountain strongholds and make
them more vulnerable to Roman policing.[90] Florus' assertion is supported
by Orosius, who records the use of the mountains for warfare by the
Cantabrians and Astures.[91] Augustus in fact created three centres
in north-west Spain: Asturica Augusta, Lucus Augusti, and Bracara
Augusti, which all appear to have been pre-existing native sites. Unfortunately the archaeological record is poor, and it is impossible to ascertain
the degree of Romanization involved. Asturica however did have sewers,
a street-grid, and some wall-paintings.[92]

Nevertheless this need not be a conclusive sign of a deliberate intention
to Romanize the local population. Asturica may have been the headquarters of a legionary legate, and these developments could have been for
the benefit of, or created by, him and his entourage, rather than by, or for,
the local population. In this case adoption of Roman customs by the local
population would have been a by-product of Roman action rather than its
deliberate goal. Pliny calls Asturica an *urbs magnifica* (a magnificent city).[93]
It is hard, given the archaeological evidence, to see what he meant. Perhaps the description is in comparison to the surrounding towns, or perhaps, as Pliny himself served there, it is a reflection of sentimentality, or
merely an attempt to disguise the town's unimportance and the implicit
comment this has on Pliny's own standing.

Another instance of this policy of Rome establishing new administrative arrangements for purely military/political reasons is Corbulo's imposition, after his defeat of the Frisii, of Roman-style magistrates, a council,
and a binding constitution on the tribe.[94] This can be seen as an attempt
to break the power of the Germanic war council, and thus provide greater
security for the German nobles which in turn would increase their dependence on Rome, the provider of this new security.[95] It is interesting

---

[89] Florus, 2. 33. 59.
[90] 'Fiduciam montium timens in quos se recipiebant' ('fearing their trust in the mountains into which they were accustomed to retreat').   [91] Orosius, 6. 21. 5. 7.
[92] See A. Tranoy, *La Galice romaine* (1981), 191–3, for a general description and further
bibliography.   [93] Pliny, *NH* 3. 3. 28.
[94] Tacitus, *Ann.* 11. 19: 'senatum, magistratus, leges inposuit' ('he imposed on them a
senate, magistrates, and laws').
[95] See E. A. Thompson, *The Early Germans* (1965), 93 ff., for a full analysis of this
process.

that although Roman governing structures are imposed, there is no hint in
Tacitus' account of an urban structure also being created. Corbulo's
actions provide us not with an example of an ideology of 'Romanization'
applied across the empire, but the use of specific Roman institutions as a
tool to solve concrete problems.

This approach can also be seen in terms of administrative convenience.
When Pompey created eleven new cities in Asia Minor he was not aiming
to encourage a Roman model of civilization, but rather to solve the administrative problems specific to this region. The kingdom of Mithridates had
been run on centralized lines,[96] and there were not enough experienced
Roman officials available to take over its running in this form. Entrusting
its administration to the local aristocracy, who had supported Mithridates, would have been to court disaster, by giving potential rebels a
power-base. Therefore a town-based system, not requiring Roman supervision, nor giving a base for rebellion, was created. Few of the new centres
of administration were new creations; rather they were pre-existent towns
given new administrative functions.[97]

If, in contrast, no threat was perceived, non-urban systems of government were allowed to remain in place much longer. The best example of
this is Egypt, which was never fully urbanized and where town councils
only came into existence in the reign of Septimius Severus.[98] Similarly in
Thrace the *strategia* system survived the annexation of the kingdom by
Claudius and lasted until the foundation of cities in the area by Trajan and
Hadrian. These foundations were only made then because the old centralized system was breaking down. According to A. H. M. Jones: 'in all
probability none of the cities was an entirely new creation', and he further
concludes that they 'did little to develop either the political or economic
life of the province'.[99] Clearly there was no sense of urgency on the part of
Rome to change the Thracian style of administration to a city-based one,
and when the change did come it appears to have been made for administrative reasons only, with no intention of urbanizing the population or
encouraging them to change their way of life.

The town of Panopeus mentioned above illustrates this overriding
concern with administration. Panopeus lacked all the features regarded as

[96] A. H. M. Jones, *The Cities of the Eastern Roman Provinces* (2nd edn., 1971), 154: 'The
administrative system of Pontus was a centralised bureaucracy of the usual Hellenistic
type . . . This fact emerges clearly from Strabo's description of the country.'
[97] Ibid., 157.
[98] A. K. Bowman, *Town Councils of Roman Egypt* (1971).
[99] Jones, *Cities of the Eastern Roman Provinces*, 19, 23.

necessary by the classical world to be a town. Nevertheless it was still a fully fledged town in terms of its administrative powers, and was apparently regarded as a useful centre of administration by Rome; no attempt was made to build up the urban centre as befitted its status, despite its being located in one of the most urbanized areas of the empire.[100] Large areas of the empire were administered by such 'skeleton' towns. In Britain urbanization never took a firm hold. There is growing evidence, for example, that the *forum* complex at Silchester was never completed.[101] The size of the town itself was not large enough to have allowed all the local decurions to have maintained houses there, and some houses appear to have been farms rather than town houses. Taken as a whole, this evidence suggests that there was no consistent attempt to inculcate an urban lifestyle among the Britons. Instead it seems that provided some form of centralized centre was present, through which taxes and administrative matters could be dealt with, the form of that centre was of little concern.[102] Recent work on the small towns of Roman Britain has begun to show that far more of these sites have Iron Age origins than was previously thought, again suggesting that the active promotion of urbanization by Rome is not a necessary factor in explaining the development of these sites.[103]

In Transalpine Gaul a similar picture emerges. A recent survey of the territory of the Bituriges in central Gaul shows that the tribe lacked a firmly fixed 'capital' for a considerable period of time, and that the structure of the area was essentially rural with *villae* and villages playing major roles.[104] Nor was this situation confined to the 'barbarian' West. In the East large areas, such as Galilee[105] and the Hauran,[106] were administered by a village system, the towns only providing a convenient point for the collection of taxes. Jones draws the same conclusion for the whole of Syria:

On paper the change in the political aspect of the country is considerable . . . practically the whole of Syria was partitioned into city states . . . In reality

---

[100] Pausanias, 10. 4. 1–4.

[101] M. G. Fulford, 'Excavations on the Sites of the Amphitheatre and Forum-Basilica at Silchester, Hampshire: An Interim Report', *Antiquaries' J.* 65/1 (1985), 39–81.

[102] For a general overview of this *laissez-faire* approach of Rome in Britain, see Millett, *The Romanization of Britain*.

[103] B. C. Burnham, 'The Development of Romano-British Small Towns', *Oxford Journal of Archaeology*, 5/2 (1986), 185–203.

[104] A. Leday, *Rural Settlement in Central Gaul in the Roman Period*, BAR, IS 73 (1980).

[105] M. Goodman, *State and Society in Roman Galilee AD 132–212* (1983); A. N. Sherwin-White, *Roman Society and Roman Law in the New Testament* (1963), ch. 6.

[106] J. M. Dentzer (ed.), *Hauran*, 1. 1 (1985) and 1. 2 (1986).

however the change was superficial . . . the only function the cities had was administrative; they policed and collected the taxes of their territories.[107]

Even this policing function did not exist in Galilee, where it was performed by village watchmen.

A good example of the type of deliberate urbanization found in this area is the creation of Tiberias by the Hellenizing client king, Herod Antipas. Josephus' account of its creation shows its artificial nature and the force that was required to give it a population.[108] The comment of Rabbi Hanina ben Hana (*fl. c.*AD 220–50, i.e. at the height of the urbanized empire), that the Romans created cities merely to inflict forced labour on the local inhabitants, shows both the failure to create an urban mentality in the native population and an overriding concern for administration on the part of Rome.[109]

Finally we learn from Strabo that parts of Italy were not urbanized. Liguria is dismissed with a curt note saying that the people live in villages and plough a harsh country.[110] The Sabine country is described as having only small towns, with villages as the predominant form of settlement.[111] The Marsi and the surrounding tribes are said to live in the main in villages: Τὰ μὲν οὖν ἄλλα κωμηδὸν ζῶσιν.[112] Clearly the programme of positive urbanization had not reached the Roman heartland, and this absence strongly suggests that such a programme never existed.

There seems therefore little firm evidence that Rome pursued an active urbanizing policy. The approach towards the provinces seems rather to have been one of *laissez-faire*. Exceptions to this rule appear to have been pragmatic responses to specific situations rather than reflections of a general policy of Romanization. This question of intentionality bears strongly on the depth of urbanization which occurred and the form it took. Like later imperialists the Romans certainly regarded their form of life as superior to that of their subjects. Nevertheless, unlike them, they were not subject to moral pressure to export it. This suggests that the chances that the classical model was simply transferred to the provinces in its pristine form will have been much lower. Instead we are likely to see a synthesis of native and classical forms. Roman forms would be assimilated more by contact with Rome, with a consequent adoption of her values, than by Roman proselytizing and direct enforcement. The end result would have been an amalgam which reflected to some degree not only what classical civilization thought was necessary for urban life, but what

---

[107] Jones, *Cities of the Eastern Roman Provinces*, 293–4.
[108] Josephus, *Ant. J.* 18. 36–8.
[109] D. Sperber, 'Angaria in Rabbinic Literature', *Antiquité Classique*, 38 (1969), 164 ff.
[110] Strabo, 5. 2. 1.   [111] Ibid. 5. 3. 1.   [112] Ibid. 5. 4. 2.

the local population thought the classical world thought was necessary for urban life. The process would also on occasions have a reverse side, where it was the classical model which was accommodated to the native cultural pattern, not vice versa.

Contact with Roman individuals and institutions was Rome's greatest, if unconscious, contribution to promoting the classical urban lifestyle. One obvious, though limited, source of such contact came through the establishment of *coloniae* as noted above. More widespread than these, however, were the informal *conventus* settlements of merchants and other immigrants involved in farming and the exploitation of the area's mineral wealth.

While such a spread of Roman habits is normally regarded as 'passive', this is true only from a Roman point of view. It would have required a positive desire by the native population to emulate the Roman lifestyle. In the absence of a policy actively to promote urbanization, and the probable technical impossibilities of carrying out such a policy, this factor was of overwhelming importance. Why should this wish to emulate the conqueror have come about? A variety of reasons suggest themselves.

On one level such an accommodation would have been necessary to meet the demands of the Roman state. A large factor here would have been the tribute imposed by Rome both generally and for the upkeep of her army. Such demands were probably couched in Roman terms and so some degree of assimilation would have been necessary in order to meet these obligations. On the other hand the simple power of Rome must have impressed and led to a desire to copy what seemed a winning formula. Moreover the potential benefits of adopting a Roman lifestyle, especially for the local aristocracy, would have encouraged the process. The prime benefit would be potential access to the hierarchy of the Roman world, with the possibilities this offered for prestige, wealth, and power.[113] It is not clear whether these benefits were held out as such by Rome, or were just seen, or merely perceived, to exist by potential urbanizers.

Native aristocrats would have seen a need to adopt some Roman customs therefore, both to impress Rome in the hope of obtaining benefits for doing this, and, on the other hand, to emphasize to their own people that they were still part of the ruling élite. One way of going about this would be to demonstrate their adoption of the urban lifestyle which was so much a part of classical civilization. The creation of the classical-style towns of Caesarea by Herod the Great and Tiberias by his son, Herod Antipas, fits

---

[113] The best Spanish example of this is the success of the Balbi.

into this pattern. Strabo notes that although the majority of the Allobroges lived in villages, their nobles, οἱ ἐπιφανέστατοι, turned Vienne from a mere κώμη (village) into a πόλις (city).[114] A similar magnetic effect occurred at Marseilles, where the presence of the Greek colony led to the adoption of classical habits and the hiring of doctors and philosophers by native communities.[115] Other examples of native aristocracies' desires for Roman education have already been noted above. Nevertheless caution is in order. A desire to create an urban centre did not always feature among those aspects of Roman life which non-Roman communities wished to espouse. This can be seen from Strabo's discussion of the Cavari on the Rhône. While the majority of this tribe are said to have adopted Roman customs, only some, that is, a minority, have adopted a Roman πολιτεία, meaning civic structures analogous to those of the classical world.[116]

If it is true that there was no active Roman policy of urbanization, there are several important implications for a study of a substantially urbanized area such as Baetica. Here Rome was not confronted with the need to create administrative units *ex nihilo*, as she was for example in Britain. The area already had a native urban tradition. The south of the province was heavily influenced by its Punic occupation, and from the remains of Iberian sites in other regions of Spain (there being a dearth of excavation in the south) Iberian culture too appears to have been urban-based.[117] The density of towns in the province thus reflects a history of urban life preceding Roman rule, and not the creation of such a zone by Rome. The impact of Rome on the area therefore must be judged not by the number of towns, but by examining the growth and adoption of those features, discussed above, which can be regarded as particularly 'classical' within the region's towns, and the degree to which they came to predominate over the native features of the region and became its norms. Although this is more difficult, such an examination should also attempt to look beyond the simple recording of the growth of the physical and legal facts of Roman urbanization. As has been seen, many of the structures taken as typical of the classical town presuppose a certain set of cultural attitudes towards urban life. Did the outward manifestation of classical civilization foster the growth of a congruous intellectual environment?

---

[114] Strabo, 4. 1. 11.   [115] Ibid. 4. 1. 5.

[116] Ibid. 4. 1. 12: οὐδὲ βαρβάρους ἔτι ὄντας, ἀλλὰ μετακειμένους τὸ πλέον εἰς τὸν ῾Ρωμαίων τύπον καὶ γλώττῃ καὶ τοῖς βίοις, τινὰς δὲ καὶ πολιτείᾳ ('Nor are they still barbarians, but for the most part have adopted Roman way of life, using both Latin and Roman customs; some have even become Roman in the way they conduct public life').

[117] R. J. Harrison, *Spain at the Dawn of History* (1988), ch. 7; A. Blanco Freijeiro and L. Abad Casal (eds.), *Los Ibéros* (1988); A. Arribas, *The Iberians* (1964), ch. 5.

Cultural differences and geography are also an important considerations, given the diversity exhibited by the region. How far did urbanization extend beyond the riverine and maritime coasts of the province, which are emphasized by Strabo? And was it as extensive here as he suggests? Strabo, it must be remembered, never visited Spain, but relied heavily on the account of Posidonius, who may have had philosophical reasons for emphasizing the civilization of the lowland areas of the province.[118] In social terms, did urbanization create a Roman mentality amongst the inhabitants of the province, and if so, to what groups did this penetrate, and to what degree?

The highlands of the province appear to have had a smaller concentration of towns. Their isolation from the lowlands, leading to less contact with Roman settlers, may explain this to some degree. The poor soil of the area may be another relevant factor. The region also had much stronger Celtic influences bearing on it than the rest of the province. Celtic civilization, unlike the Iberian, was not urban-based, and so the natives of the area may have been more resistant to the notion of town life than their lowland, Iberian, neighbours. A comparison between the towns of the two areas to see if the northern area retained Celtic features or mechanically copied a Roman model would yield useful evidence to check the theory that urbanization was mainly a native-inspired process.

In all events it appears that a study of urbanization should not be simply the study of an imperial power attempting to impose its own structures on its subjects, but rather a study of the cultural interaction and synthesis between the groups concerned. We must also study the reaction of those subjects to the structures of the ruling power and the extent to which they perceived it to be advantageous to imitate them, both by modifying their pre-existing urban structures and by creating new ones.

---

[118] For the influence of Posidonius on Strabo's thought, see P. Thollard, *Barbarie et civilisation chez Strabon* (1987).

3

The State of Southern Spain in *c*.50 BC

THE evolution of the south of Spain in the late republican period is a highly controversial topic. Nevertheless, if we are to understand the development of Baetica in the imperial period it is necessary to look closely at the area of Hispania Ulterior (Further Spain) out of which the province was formed in order to assess whether the region's evolution, marked most notably by the grant of the *ius Latii* (Latin rights) to the peninsula by Vespasian, differed in scale or form in the imperial period from that which had taken place previously, or was simply a continuation of a process whose foundations had been firmly laid down in the earlier period.

The normal view is that Rome had had an extensive impact on the future Baetica by the end of the republican period; this view is not only held by the vast majority of Spanish scholars,[1] but is also supported by, among others, Wilson and Gabba.[2] The hypothesis envisages that large numbers of soldiers, on receiving their discharge, remained in Spain because of its fertility and the increasingly deteriorating political situation in Italy, especially in the first century BC,[3] and that they were the main agents of propagating this proposed Roman influence in the peninsula.

Spain, unlike any other area ruled by Rome, experienced a continual occupation by Roman troops, who would have provided a constant source from which these envisaged settlers could have been drawn, a fact which is seen as strengthening the above position. Such a view might also be seen to gain support from the comments of one of our major primary sources, Strabo, who, while writing in the Augustan period, relies heavily on the work of the late republican philosopher, Posidonius, and states that the

---

[1] e.g. A. Blanco Freijeiro, *Historia de Sevilla*, i. *La ciudad antigua* (3rd edn., 1989), 110.

[2] A. J. N. Wilson, *Emigration from Italy in the Republican Age of Rome* (1966), esp. pp. 29–40; E. Gabba, 'Le origini della Guerra Sociale e la vita politica romana dopo l'89 a.C.', *Athenaeum*, 32 (1954), 41–114, and esp. pp. 293–345.

[3] Wilson, *Emigration from Italy*, 40; M. Roldán Hervás speaks of 'la masiva presencia de cives Romani' in his 'La crisis republicana en la Hispania Ulterior', *Actas de I Congreso de la Historia de Andalucia*, 'Fuentes y metologia, Andalucia en la antigüedad' (1978), 109–30.

Turdetani of southern Spain have forgotten their own language and have become all but Roman, τελέως εἰς τὸν Ῥωμαίων μεταβέβληνται τρόπον.[4]

The first step in examining this position, before going on to look at the actual instances and types of Roman settlement in the region in the late republican period, is to assess the overall state of affairs there at this time: would it have been an attractive area to settle in? Although southern Spain is often portrayed as a peaceful area, unlike the rest of the peninsula, this was far from the case. Raids from the north and west, the region later to become the province of Lusitania, were a persistent feature of its history. Such incursions are attested in 194 BC;[5] 190 BC;[6] throughout the mid-second century when the Lusitanians were led by Viriatus and his successor Tantalus, during which period some of the towns of the region, such as Tucci (present-day Martos in the north-east of Andalusia), sided with the Lusitanians;[7] and in 114 BC, when Marius is said to have put down banditry in this area (Plutarch adds at this point: 'this province was still uncivilized and savage in its ways').[8] Campaigns against the Lusitanians, which may have involved further incursions, are recorded in 112 BC;[9] in 109 BC;[10] in 102 BC;[11] in 101 BC;[12] and possibly in 99 BC.[13] In 98 BC Crassus triumphed from Spain, probably in Ulterior, as we know he was not the governor of Citerior.[14] Caesar campaigned against the Lusitanians in 60 BC, while governor of Ulterior, possibly because of the depredations of bandits,[15] and in the Civil Wars we find Lusitanians coming into the province, and campaigns against them being held in the midst of campaigns connected to the Civil Wars themselves.[16] In this period Pollio complains to Cicero of the banditry found in the *Saltus Castulonensis*.[17]

In addition to these examples of native aggression the province also suffered in the campaigns waged by Sertorius. In 79/8 BC Sertorius de-feated Cotta in a naval battle by the Straits of Gibraltar (a fact which perhaps draws attention to the possible threat of piratical raiding against the province) and then defeated Fufidius, the governor of Ulterior, some-

---

[4] Strabo, 3. 2. 15.   [5] Livy, 35. 1.   [6] Livy, 37. 46. 7.
[7] For the scope of these raids, see J. de Alarcão, *Roman Portugal* (1988), 6 ff.
[8] Plutarch, *Vit. Mar.* 6.   [9] Appian, *Ib.* 99.   [10] Eutropius, 4. 27.
[11] Appian, *Ib.* 100.   [12] Julius Obsequens, 101.   [13] *Ibid.* 99.
[14] Asconius (ed. Clark), pp. 14–15, with Plutarch, *Quaes. Rom.* 13.
[15] Plutarch, *Vit. Div. Iul.* 12.   [16] Ps. Caesar, *B. Alex.* 51.
[17] Cicero, *Ad Fam.* 10. 31. In fact banditry has been a perennial feature of Andalusian life; for a general overview, see C. Bernaldo de Quirós and L. Ardila, *El bandolerismo andaluz* (1988).

where on the banks of the River Baetis.[18] In 76 BC his legate, Hirtuleius, suffered a major defeat at the hands of Metellus outside Italica, losing 20,000 men.[19] The size of these losses suggests that major campaigns took place in the province, with obvious detrimental effects for the regional economy.

The lawless nature of the area at the end of the republican period is also attested by our only eyewitness reporter of Hispania Ulterior, the anonymous author of the *Bellum Hispaniense*, who comments: 'Hic enim propter barbarorum [presumably the Lusitani] crebras excursiones omnia loca quae sunt ab oppidis remota turribus et munitionibus retinentur' ('Here because of frequent barbarian raids all the places far from towns are guarded by towers and fortifications'). He goes on: 'item oppidorum magna pars eius provinciae montibus fere munita et natura excellentibus locis est constituta, ut simul additus ascensusque habeat difficilis' ('indeed a large number of this province's towns are more or less fortified by their mountain locations and built in naturally high places so that they are difficult to approach as they must be climbed up to').[20] There is evidence for these 'turres' existing in the early years of the province, as L. Aemilius' freeing of the *turris Lascutana* from the political control of the town of Lascuta shows.[21] Archaeological evidence shows that a large number of these towers, measuring on average 20 × 20m., and at times perhaps having a penumbra of unfortified buildings round them, continued to be occupied well into the first century AD and beyond in the north-western areas of the province and along the Singilis valley.[22] Taken as a whole, this evidence suggests that there had been only a marginal improvement in the security of the province at the end of the republican period from the state of affairs which obtained at its creation. The picture conjured up is one of a frontier rather than a pacified region, constantly under the threat of incursions. This view receives some support from the fact that many towns remained on hilltop sites throughout the republican and well into the imperial period, the most well known being Sabora, which remained a hilltop site until the Flavian period.[23] Other towns such as Basilippo, although situated in the Baetis valley itself, remained hilltop sites throughout the Roman period.

Defensive towers are also mentioned by the Elder Pliny, who remarks that they are also found in Africa, implying that they were used as refuges

---

[18] Plutarch, *Vit. Sert.* 12; Livy, *Epit.* 90.   [19] Orosius, 5. 23. 10.
[20] Ps. Caesar, *B. Hisp.* 8.   [21] *CIL* 2. 5041.
[22] J. Fortea Pérez and J. Bernier Luque, *Recintos y fortificaciones de la Bética* (1970).
[23] *CIL* 2. 1423.

from pirates.[24] The tower now known as la Torre del Cartagena, near Carteia, and described as a lighthouse by Thouvenot,[25] may well have been a defensive tower of this type. Similar towers exist near Gibraltar, Algeciras, and Velez. This suggests that the south of Spain was subject to raids not only from the north, but also from Mauretania. The Neronian poet, Calpurnius Siculus, writes of the 'trucibusque obnoxia Mauris pascua Geryonis' ('the meadows of Geryon facing the surly Moors').[26] The use of this theme as a poetic *topos* suggests that Moorish raids were not an unfamiliar feature in the life of the province. More concrete examples of this phenomenon are attested by the razzia of the Mauretanian king, Bogud, on the province in the period of the Civil Wars, and the major Moorish incursions in the late second century AD.[27] It is likely that small-scale raiding would have been frequent before the establishment of Roman control over Mauretania. That such a problem still remained even after this is hinted at by an inscription from Corduba, dating from the mid-second century AD at the earliest, recording a *tribunus militum* of a *cohors maritima*, a unit which was presumably used to patrol the province's coastline.[28]

Such a view of the region clashes with the 'civilized' picture given by Strabo. However, there are reasons for thinking that Strabo's account of the province may contain some inaccuracies. In it Turdetania, the area of the province which he regards as its most civilized part, is defined as the region lying between the Anas River and Bastetania.[29] Strabo goes on to say that the *colonia* of Emerita is in Turdulian, (i.e. Turdetanian) country.[30] There is a complete lack of any account here of the region of Baeturia in the Sierra Morena, where Emerita is normally placed and which was, according to Pliny, primarily inhabited by Celtic peoples.[31] Strabo does mention Baeturia once, and both correctly locates it and

[24] Pliny, *NH* 2. 181, 35. 169. Similar structures were used as refuges from pirates in the eastern Mediterranean; see H. A. Ormerod, *Piracy in the Ancient World* (1924), 41–9.

[25] R. Thouvenot, *Essai sur la province romaine de Bétique* (2nd edn., 1973), 526.

[26] *Ecl.* 4. 40–1.

[27] N. Santos Yanguas, 'Las invasiones de Moros en la Bética del siglo II D.N.E.', *Gades*, 5 (1980), 51 ff.

[28] *CIL* 2. 2224.

[29] Strabo, 3. 2. 1: ἀφορίζει δὲ αὐτὴν πρὸς μὲν τὴν ἑσπέραν καὶ ἄρκτον ὁ Ἄνας ποταμός ... πρὸς νότον δὲ Βαστητανῶν οἱ μεταξὺ τῆς Κάλπης καὶ τῶν Γαδείρων στενὴν νεμόμενοι παραλίαν ('Its boundary to the west and north is the river Anas . . . and to the south those Bastetanians who live on the narrow coastland between Calpe and Gades').

[30] Ibid. 3. 2. 15: ἡ ἐν τοῖς Τουρδούλοις Αὐγούστα Ἡμερίτα ('Augusta Emerita in the country of the Turduli'); for the assimilation of these groups, see ibid. 3. 1. 6.

[31] Pliny, *NH* 3. 1. 13.

describes its aridity, but this relatively brief treatment suggests that the region did not feature in the geographer's major sources, and that he was not clear as to its location.[32]

Pliny's division of Baeturia into Celtic and Turdulian zones places Emerita in the Celtic, not the Turdulian, area. His account gives an impression of Baeturia as an uncivilized region; for he comments that it is possible to tell that its Celtic inhabitants came from Lusitania from their religion, language, and the names of their towns. This implies that this area of Baetica was little different from the neighbouring province of Lusitania. Moreover Pliny's language suggests that this was the situation either at the time of his writing, or at that of his Augustan sources.

This impression is confirmed by Varro, who had been a governor of Hispania Ulterior. Varro notes that 'multos enim agros egregios colere non expedit propter latrociniam vicinorum . . . et in Hispania *prope* Lusitaniam' ('it is not expedient to cultivate much good land because of banditry from neighbouring people . . . in Spain this is the case with land adjacent to Lusitania').[33] Varro here refers not to land in Lusitania, but neighbouring land. This is most likely to have been, given Varro's personal history, land in what was to become northern Baetica, that is, in Baeturia. It seems that Strabo, who never visited the area himself, has given an exaggerated impression of the area of Turdetanian civilization. Such exaggeration occurs in another part of his account of Spain, namely where he claims that the developments in the reign of Tiberius in north-western Spain not only pacified, but also urbanized the peoples here, something contradicted by all our archaeological evidence.[34] Furthermore he is forced to admit that the Celts living next to the Turdetani (presumably meaning those living in Baeturia, Bastetania, and Oretania, which lies at the head of the Baetis valley), although civilized by them to some extent, still in the main, τὰ πολλά, lived in villages, κωμηδὸν ζῶσιν.[35] On the southern and eastern sides of the Baetis valley lay Bastetania, the present-day Andalusian Cordillera. Strabo describes this area in terms of primitive Celtic occupation, speaking of ritual dances, Celtic dress, and the habit of sleeping on the ground.[36] It appears therefore that the only part of Hispania Ulterior which could have been described as 'civilized' and would have been attractive to settlers was the Baetis valley and that this too was subject to frequent raiding, which would have been a strong disincentive to settlement.

[32] Strabo, 3. 2. 3.   [33] Varro, *RR* 1. 16. 2.   [34] Strabo, 3. 3. 8.
[35] Ibid. 3. 2. 15.   [36] Ibid. 3. 3. 7.

Bearing these factors in mind, what evidence is there for specifically Roman foundations in the area during this period? Our knowledge of such sites is unfortunately limited. The earliest settlement of this kind was Italica, established by Scipio for his wounded after the battle of Ilipa in 206 BC.[37] The nature of the town, however, is unclear. Although it would have contained some Roman citizens, its name perhaps suggests that it contained as many, if not more, Italians as Romans proper.[38] The type of local government used by the town in this period is also unclear and we have no indications as to whether this was Román in form or not. Nor do we know if the town had the collection of public buildings normally found in a Roman town and earlier interpretations of some structures which were thought to indicate this are now being revised. For example, a structure dating from the republican period previously interpreted as a temple with three *cellae*, and possibly therefore as a primitive *capitolium*, is now seen as a commercial structure; moreover its materials and style of construction are native. Similarly, while the houses excavated in the republican town are ordered and rectilinear in form, they are built in native materials to native designs.[39] The town was walled by the time of the Civil Wars, but this was a feature of many native settlements and cannot be attributed to specifically Roman factors. Iberian pottery predominates, and an *acroterion* found here, and dating from this period, depicts a πότνια θηρῶν (mistress of beasts), a Punic religious symbol.

The site therefore does not suggest that the settlement of Roman troops had an overwhelming impact on local life. The presence of a large amount of Iberian pottery implies that Italica was a mixed settlement, involving the local population, as does Appian's reference to a native of the town, C. Marcius, temporarily put in charge of the war against Viriatus, as an ἀνήρ Ἴβηρ (Iberian). Although Marcius' name shows that some acculturation to Roman norms was taking place amongst the local population, at least at an upper-class level, the finds from the town suggest that this phenomenon was a two-way process, with many Iberian traits being adopted by the settler community.

A much stronger Roman influence is found at the only town which we can be certain was granted a Roman legal status in the republican period. This is the *colonia Latina* founded at the town of Carteia, on the Medi-

[37] Appian, *Ib.* 38.
[38] Ibid.: πόλιν, ἣν ἀπο τῆς Ἰταλίας Ἰταλικὴν ἐκάλεσε ('he called the city Italica after Italy').
[39] M. Bendála Galán, 'Un templo en Italica de época republica', in *13 CNA* (1975), 861–8.

terranean coast, in 171 BC.[40] The town was founded in response to a petition to the senate by some 4,000 *hybridae*, or sons of Roman fathers by native Iberian women. The senate's grant of Latin status in return allowed not only the *hybridae*, but also possibly their freed slaves,[41] and certainly any inhabitants of the pre-existing native town, to enrol as *coloni* of the new foundation.

Carteia was formally founded as a *colonia*, and did have a firmly Roman system of government. The town possessed first a *senatus* and then probably an *ordo*, or town council, members of which were known by the standard title of *decuriones*. The governing magistrates of the town were known as *quattuorviri* throughout its history; aediles and perhaps *censores* are also found. These details are known solely from the town's coinage, which uses standard Roman motifs and carries exclusively Latin legends.[42]

Yet despite these Roman features, Carteia too, like republican Italica, has yielded a large amount of Iberian pottery. A large public building dating to the Augustan period has been partially excavated in the town. Its remnants consist of some column fragments, part of an architrave, and two protomes. The last are in the form of kneeling bulls, and Iberian in style. The form of these remains shows that once more there was a mixing of Roman and Iberian culture rather than a direct supercession of one by the other.[43] The two towns serve to warn us that even if we accept the hypothesis of Roman settlement we cannot simply advance to a position that this entails an adoption of a Roman way of life.

M. Claudius Marcellus was involved in creating a settlement at Corduba in 152 BC. Strabo comments that it was inhabited from the beginning by 'selected' Romans and Iberians.[44] Who performed the selection is not clear. Presumably it was Marcellus. The criteria for inclusion are also left undefined. The problems surrounding the town are further compounded by Strabo's reference to it as the first ἀποικία sent to this region.[45] Is Strabo here using ἀποικία in its technical sense of *colonia*? There is no

[40] Livy, 43. 3. 1–4.
[41] If the reading of the *codex Vindobonensis* 'manumisissent' is accepted rather than Gryaeus' correction 'manumississet', the slaves would have been included.
[42] For a general survey, see F. Chaves Tristan, *Las monedas hispano-romanas de Carteia* (1979).
[43] For a general survey of Carteia's archaeological remains, see F. J. Presado Velo *et al.*, *Carteia*, i = *EAE. 120* (1982) and D. E. Woods, 'Carteia and Tartessos', *5 Symposio internacional de prehistoria peninsular* (1968), 251 ff.
[44] Strabo, 3. 2. 1: ᾤκησάν τε ἐξ ἀρχῆς Ῥωμαίων τε καὶ τῶν ἐπιχωρίων ἄνδρες ἐπίλεκτοι ('there settled here from the beginning picked Romans and natives').
[45] Ibid.: καὶ δὴ καὶ πρώτην ἀποικίαν ταύτην εἰς τοὺς τόπους ἔστειλαν Ῥωμαῖοι ('indeed this was the first colony the Romans sent to those parts').

further evidence that Corduba was a formal *colonia civium Romanorum* from its foundation. Similarly, although Strabo's use of στέλλειν (to send) implies that settlers were despatched to Corduba, there is no additional evidence of this. On the other hand we find that at the time of the Civil Wars a *conventus Cordubensis* of Roman citizens is attested in the town.[46] The presence of such a body suggests that the town of Corduba itself did not enjoy any specific Roman legal status in the republican period. Marcellus' settlement was probably therefore an informal settlement, like Italica. Again there is no indication of the form of local government enjoyed by the town.

The physical appearance of republican Corduba is also difficult to determine. It was the seat of the provincial governor, and regarded as the most important place in the province.[47] We might safely assume that the governor had an impressive personal residence as did, probably, members of his retinue. What evidence is there, however, of public buildings in the town? Our literary sources provide some clues. L. Calpurnius Piso Frugi is said to have summoned a goldsmith 'into the *forum* to the judgement seat of Corduba', when he was *praetor* of the province in 112 BC.[48] The *Bellum Alexandrinum* refers to a *basilica* in the town at the time of the Civil Wars.[49] This evidence when combined suggests that there was at least the nucleus of a *forum* complex in the town. There is, however, no way of determining the size or the form of the buildings involved. Nor can we be sure that these buildings were used for municipal purposes rather than being exclusively devoted to provincial matters dealt with by the governor. Santos Gener has claimed that a bath complex found in Corduba is republican in date and was destroyed during the civil wars. However, no firm reason is given for this date and the styles of mosaic found here imply a date of the second century AD.[50]

Other towns in whose creation Rome may have been actively involved are even more mysterious. A Brutobriga, possibly founded by D. Brutus in the wake of the Viriatic Wars, is mentioned by Stephanus Byzantinus, and coins from the town have been found.[51] However, nothing further is known of Brutobriga: its name implies that it lay in a Celtic area. We do

---

[46] Ps. Caesar, *B. Alex.* 57.   [47] Ps. Caesar, *B. Hisp.* 3.

[48] 'in forum ad sellam Cordubae', Cicero, *2 Verr.* 4. 25.   [49] Ps. Caesar, *B. Alex.* 52.

[50] S. Santos Gener, 'Memoria de las excavaciones del plan nacional realizadas en Córdoba 1948–1950', *Informes y memorias* 31 (1955), 140–1. See the comments of R. Knapp, *Roman Córdoba* (1983), 57. Santos Gener appears to have fallen into the common trap of wishing to attribute archaeological remains to buildings referred to in the literary sources.

[51] *CMH* 964.

not know if the town was intended for Roman troops or native Spaniards, or even whether we are dealing with the foundation of a new settlement rather than a native town simply taking the name of a Roman commander to honour him. As the location of the town too remains uncertain, these questions are unlikely to be resolved. If Brutobriga's name is its only connection with Rome, Iliturgi's connection is even more enigmatic. A inscription from the town refers to Tiberius Sempronius Gracchus as its 'deductor' ('founder'). The inscription itself dates to the imperial period, and so can tell us nothing of the state of the town in the republic. Gracchus' role is mysterious. We know that he exaggerated his conquests in the peninsula,[52] and his title of *deductor* here may simply be honorific and so need not imply that he changed the town in any substantial manner.[53] Sites with a discernible Roman content therefore seem both few in number, and limited in the effect they had on the province. Their own internal structure is in most cases unclear, and in all it seems that many Iberian features remained in the physical appearance of the towns.

Apart from settlements founded by Rome, did native towns themselves take on new Roman features? Our best example of this phenomenon is found at Gades. Caesar, during his praetorship in Ulterior in 60 BC, is said to have set up laws, 'iura statuere', for the town with its consent, 'ipsorum permissu', and to have removed a certain engrained barbarity from the town, 'inveteratam quondam barbariam ex Gaditanorum moribus disciplinaque delerit'.[54] The phrase 'iura statuere' sounds as if it ought to mean that Caesar gave the town a Roman-style law code. Seventeen years later such a structure was certainly in place in the town. From a letter of Pollio[55] we learn that the town possessed *quattuorviri*, elected by *comitia*, who presided over a *senatus*; that *ludi*, including gladiatorial displays, were held in the town; and that the first fourteen rows of seats were reserved for *equites*, as at Rome, on such occasions. However, within those seventeen years Gades had become a *municipium civium Romanorum*,[56] and it is possible that the adoption of the structures described above was a necessary consequence of this and that Caesar's previous alterations were less far-reaching in their effects.

Does Pollio's letter allow us to infer anything about the physical appearance of Gades at this time? The holding of *comitia* would require a

[52] Strabo, 3. 4. 13.
[53] C.f. Agrippa's title of *municip(ii) Parens* (father of the town) on some coins of Gades (*CMH* 1625–9).
[54] Cicero, *Pro Balbo* 43   [55] Cicero, *Ad Fam.* 10. 32.
[56] In 49 BC, Dio 41. 24. 1.

large open public space, a sort of *forum*, but the presence of such a space
need not have been specifically a Roman feature. The theatrical and
gladiatorial games held by Balbus seem more promising in this respect.[57]
Moreover Balbus is said to have burned a Pompeian soldier, Fadius, alive
in a *ludus*, or gladiatorial barracks. We know that Balbus did build an
entire new part of Gades and a new harbour complex on the mainland
opposite the town.[58] Traces of a theatre have been found on the Calle de
Silencio in Cádiz which should have fallen within the area of Balbus' new
city, the Νέα Πόλις.[59] The combination of the archaeological remains and
Pollio's account does suggest that Gades had a theatre by this time, and
that perhaps Balbus had already built his new suburb. Nevertheless no
firm dates have been provided by the excavations carried out. This leaves
open the possibility that the building programme was a product of the
Augustan period; an ideal context would be provided by either Balbus'
consulate which he held in 32 BC, or the triumph which he celebrated in
19 BC. If this is the case, the games of 43 BC may have taken place in a
temporary building or the *forum*. The *ludus* is more interesting, as it
clearly did exist in 43 BC. Unfortunately there is no way of determining
what form this building took. Nevertheless its presence suggests that
Gades already possessed its own troup of gladiators by the mid-first
century BC.

   Whatever the physical shape of the town, the presence of the gladiators
shows that Gades had certainly absorbed a number of Roman cultural
traits. This absorption, however, was tempered with a determination to
continue with some former practices. The Gaditani certainly seem to have
been jealous of aspects of their own judicial customs. The 'inveterata
barbaries' removed by Caesar in 60 BC is normally assumed to be the Punic
custom of burning criminals alive.[60] However as was seen above, Pollio, to
his horror, discovered this practice was still in use in 43 BC, even after the
grant of Roman-citizen status to the town.[61]

---

   [57] The letter is only absolutely clear on the fact that gladiatorial games took place, but
presumably Herennius Gallus, the actor honoured by Balbus on the last day of his *ludi*, was
so honoured because of his performances on the previous days.
   [58] Strabo, 3. 5. 3.
   [59] *Arqueologia*, 81 (1982), no. 74; *Arqueologia*, 83 (1985), no. 1. 12.
   [60] T. Rice Holmes, *The Roman Republic* (1923), i. 303; see Aulus Gellius, *NA* 3. 14. 19.
Another possibility is the banning of the sacrifice of first-born children.
   [61] Cicero, *Ad Fam.* 10. 32, on the execution of Fadius in the town. Although burning alive
was a Roman practice with a history extending from the Twelve Tables well into the imperial
period (see P. Garnsey, *Social Status and Legal Privilege in the Roman Empire* (1970), 122 ff.),
the Punic background of Gades makes it likely that a Punic, not a Roman, punishment was
being carried out in this instance.

Can Gades be regarded as typical of the development of towns in the area? Such an assumption would be unwise. Gades was a large cosmopolitan town with extensive trading links which probably led to the adoption of some foreign customs. In addition it was the home town of the ambitious Cornelii Balbi, confidants and bankers of Julius Caesar. Their behaviour in Gades can be seen as reflecting that of typical Roman politicians in whose milieu they moved; and perhaps their encouragement of certain Roman practices was an attempt to impress a Roman audience rather than a response to demands for such a development in their home town. The Balbi and Caesar are a special factor in the development of Gades which does not occur elsewhere in the province.

However, another factor increasing the likelihood of acculturation at Gades would have been present in other towns: namely an informal settlement of Roman citizens, or *conventus*. The Gaditanian *conventus* should have been extensive. Strabo remarks that the town's *census* returns recorded 500 *equites*, more than any town other than Patavium.[62] Unfortunately we do not know how many of these were native Gaditani and how many Italian immigrants. It is probably to such *conventus* that Strabo is referring to when he remarks that the majority of Turdetanian towns have received Roman ἔποικοι (settlers).[63] The nature of these ἔποικοι is unclear. As can been seen from the evidence from Gades, some were clearly wealthy individuals. Metellus' fêting in Corduba after his defeat of Sertorius, an event which gained considerable notoriety because of its expense,[64] may provide us with an example of a wealthy *conventus*, although the main participants could have been Metellus' *amici* who had come from Rome with him; certainly one of the chief participants was Metellus' *quaestor*, C. Urbinus.[65] Better evidence for the presence of wealthy settlers in Corduba at this time comes from Cicero's remark that Metellus was praised by poets there: 'Cordubae natis poetis, pingue quiddam sonantibus atque peregrinum tamen aures suas dederet' ('he listened to poets born at Corduba in spite of their somewhat thick and foreign accent'). Cicero specifically states that these poets were born in Corduba and that they sounded like *peregrini* (i.e. implying that they were not).[66] The Roman aristocracy always had a taste for poetastry and we have an example of this here.

Caesar's governor, Cassius, clearly upset the local wealthy Romans,

[62] Strabo, 3. 5. 3.   [63] Ibid. 3. 2. 15.
[64] Extensive descriptions of Metellus' lifestyle in Spain are found in Valerius Maximus, 9 (*De Luxuria et Libidine*). 1. 5, and Plutarch, *Vit. Sert.* 22.
[65] Sallust, *Hist.* 2. 70.   [66] Cicero, *Pro Archia* 26.

some of whom attempted to murder him. His would-be assassins all bore Roman names and their wealth is shown by the fact that Cassius was prepared to spare them execution if they paid sufficiently. We are told that he settled openly with Calpurnius Salvianus for 60,000 HS, with Quintus Sestius for 50,000, and presumably with the other conspirators less openly or for lesser amounts.[67] Cassius then held a levy of *equites*.[68] This need not imply that there were a large number in the province although, as will be seen below, there were a substantial number, since it is clear that the levy was not being held to raise troops, but to extort money—the *equites* being unwilling to travel overseas and Cassius inviting them to buy their discharge.

Equites are attested at Italica,[69] Asta,[70] Urso,[71] and Gades, where we learn that the front fourteen rows of seats in the theatre were reserved for them.[72] According to the author of the *Bellum Hispaniense* 3,000 *equites*, some of whom hailed from Rome, others from the province, 'partim ex urbe, partim ex provincia', fell in the battle of Munda. Unfortunately there is no indication of the relative proportions of these two groups. As Munda was the last stand of the 'Pompeian' cause many of the *equites* who died in the battle may have had no strong connection with the area.

Perhaps below these merchants were less wealthy traders, such as freedmen from Italy. However, evidence for such settlers is inevitably poor. Edmondson detects a high proportion of freedmen involved in the garum works at Troía in Portugal, but his conclusions are conjectural.[73] One poor trader may be attested at Gades. Pollio, while complaining to Cicero about the enormities of Balbus at Gades,[74] notes that several Roman citizens have been put to death, including a 'circulator quiddam auctionum notissimus homo Hispali quia deformis erat' ('a certain visitor of auctions, a man well-known at Hispalis because he was a cripple'). The unfortunate victim's description as a 'circulator' may show he was a pedlar or petty trader. His fame at Hispalis would in this case be due to his deformity. But we cannot rule out the alternative possibility that we are dealing with a wealthy merchant being snobbishly derided by Pollio for his banausic activities.[75] In this case the man may well have been 'notissimus' at Hispalis as much for his political influence as his physical

---

[67] Ps. Caesar, *B. Alex*. 52–5.   [68] Ibid. 56   [69] Ps. Caesar, *B. Hisp*. 25.
[70] Ibid. 26.   [71] Ibid. 22. Possibly senators are attested here, but the text is unclear.
[72] Cicero. *Ad Fam*. 10. 32.
[73] J. C. Edmondson. *Two Industries in Roman Lusitania: Mining and Garum Production*, BAR, IS 362 (1987) 132, table 5.7.
[74] Cicero, *Ad Fam*. 10. 32.
[75] 'Circulator' is used in this pejorative sense.

appearance. Whether or not a lower stratum of traders existed, they are likely to have had less influence on the urban development of the province than their richer brethren. It is the latter who would have had the financial ability and political influence to change their surroundings, and would probably have felt less inclined to adopt native customs.

In one sense these *conventus* would have done less to promote urban life than in other provinces simply because a native urban structure already existed in the south of Spain. We cannot therefore attribute the growth of nucleated settlements to external trading stimuli, as has been plausibly suggested in the case of Gaul.[76] However, would such groups have stimulated specifically Roman urban structures by their presence?

It might be expected that wealthy Romans would wish to live in comfort and possibly in a familiar style of housing. Martial mentions a famous plane tree planted by Caesar 'aedibus in mediis' ('in the middle of the house') in Corduba.[77] This sounds like a description of a Roman peristyle house. However, as we have seen, private housing was not normally regarded as important in the context of classical urbanization, and such private houses could easily exist in a town which retained its overall native structures and appearance. Did the *conventus* stimulate the erection of public, as opposed to strictly private, buildings?

At Hispalis we have literary evidence for the existence of a *forum* and porticoes by the period of the Civil Wars.[78] González and Campos have in addition proposed that a republican temple underlies a later structure dating to the second century AD, fragments of which remain along the Calle de Marmoles; but this can only be conjectural.[79] Other structures dating to the republican period have been found nearby, but their nature is unclear.[80]

A *forum* would be a natural structure for a *conventus* to erect, concerned as it was with trading. Nevertheless we must bear in mind difficulties with our terminology here. Any open space in the centre of a town would be called a *forum* by classical authors. For example in 206 BC the

[76] B. Cunliffe, *Greeks, Romans, and Barbarians* (1988), ch. 1.

[77] Martial, 9. 61. 5–6: 'aedibus in mediis totos amplexa penates, stat platanus densis Caesariana comis' ('In the middle of the house overshadowing it all stands Caesar's plane tree with its thick foliage'). The tree's fame was only local; it is not found in Pliny's list of famous plane trees, Pliny *NH* 12. 5. 9.

[78] Caesar, *BC* 2. 20: 'in foro et porticibus'; does this mean a porticoed *forum*?

[79] J. Campos and J. González, 'Los foros de Hispalis, colonia romula', *A.e.A.* 60 (1987), 123 ff. Sadly, in 1989 most of the site was buried under concrete.

[80] These are centred principally on the Calle Argote de Molina.

forum of Oringis in Ulterior is said to have been captured.[81] It seems most unlikely that a classical *forum* is meant in this context, but rather a space which would be naturally called a *forum* by a Roman. Unfortunately apart from Hispalis there is little evidence of Roman-style public buildings, but it must be emphasized that this may solely be due to the lack of excavations in the area.

A late republican date has recently been proposed for both the *forum* complex at Belo and the major monumental temple of Munigua which is modelled on the temple of Fortuna Primigenia at Praeneste.[82] Belo, a trading town on the Mediterranean coast, and Munigua, lying close to valuable silver deposits on the fringes of the Sierra Morena, would both be candidates for *conventus* settlements, although no concrete evidence of such groups has been found. This view is based on the architectural style of the buildings. However, in both cases the evidence from stratigraphical surveys of these sites contradicts this hypothesis, and it seems likely that stylistic developments would have taken place more slowly in the provinces than at Rome.[83] It would seem wise therefore to accept the archaeologically determined dates of the sites concerned, which would place them in the Julio-Claudian period.

A series of reliefs from Urso, where a *conventus* is firmly attested, is normally dated to the late republican period. While some of these, such as the horn-player, who appears to be playing a Roman military *cornu* (horn), have Romanizing tendencies, strong Iberian traits also remain, such as the stylized treatment of hair and drapery.[84] Recently it has been suggested that the walls of Urso were Roman, and were built by the Younger Pompey in 45 BC.[85] The area enclosed by the walls is interpreted as a cemetery, levelled in an emergency, and the few buildings found inside as emptied tombs and barrack buildings. However, it is unlikely that the 'tombs' found would have been emptied so carefully in an emergency, particularly given Pompey's attitude to the native population. Moreover the *Bellum Hispaniense* implies that the commander at Urso was a native, and that the whole population, not just the Roman garrison, was within

---

[81] Livy, 28. 3. 13.

[82] M. Pfanner, 'Muster republikanischer Städte in Spanien' and 'Struktur und Erscheinungsbild augusteischer Städte', in W. Trillmich and P. Zanker (eds.), *Stadtbild und Ideologie: Die Monumentalisierung hispanischer Städte zwischen Republik und Kaiserzeit* (1990).

[83] This was certainly the case in the provincial capital, Corduba and that of Tarraconensis, Tarraco. J. L. Jiménez Salvador, 'El templo romano en la calle Claudio Marcelo en Córdoba', *Cuadernos de arquitectura romana*, 1 (1991) esp. 126–7 and n. 28.

[84] See comments on the individual pieces in A. Garcia y Bellido, *Las esculturas romanas de España y Portugal* (1949). The *cornicen* is no. 429, found on pp. 424–5.

[85] R. Corzo Sánchez, *Osuna de Pompeyo a César* (1977).

the walls. The account is best seen as describing Urso as another fortified Iberian hilltop site.[86] The small amount of the wall excavated suggests that its circuit covered much of the site of the later *colonia*, where some Iberian houses have been excavated, again indicating that Urso was a typical Iberian town.[87] Finally several other major Iberian sites, such as Torreparedones, El Fresno, Cerro de Santa María, and Pajares exhibit the same style of building as that found at Urso, and were probably similar Iberian sites.[88] Even if Urso's walls were constructed under a Roman aegis therefore, like Tarraco's walls built some 150 years previously, they show an adoption of native building techniques by Rome, not their supersession.

Another problem with our extant Roman buildings is the motive for their erection. We are told that Caesar presented the cities of Spain with 'magnificent public works'.[89] These could have included the Corduba *basilica*, the *forum*, and porticoes of Hispalis attested in the Caesarian corpus, and perhaps the theatre at Gades. Caesar may have been responding to local pressure for Roman buildings; however, an alternative is that they were intended as a form of bribe to a key part of the population, the Roman *conventus*, for political reasons.

The impact of the *conventus* on the political life of the towns where they were settled, as opposed to their physical appearance, is also problematic. Although highly influential in local politics, as can be seen, for example, from the leading role taken by the *conventus* of Corduba in the Civil War period, a *conventus* was not the governing body in its host town, but merely an internal component of the town, which regulated its own affairs. In most cases there is no evidence one way or the other for a dissemination of Roman administrative structures into the governing body of the town proper.

Possible evidence for such diffusion is provided by coins from three native communities, Acinippo,[90] Obulco,[91] and Belo,[92] which list local magistrates who have the Roman title of *aediles*. The presence of aediles in such circumstances could show an adoption of Roman structures, but sadly we have no further evidence on this point, and the weaker possibility that it was merely the title that was adopted within an overall native context cannot be ruled out. Knapp unfortunately seems correct in his

[86] Ps. Caesar, *B. Hisp.* 22, 28.
[87] See A. Engel and P. Paris, *Une fortresse ibérique à Osuna* (1906), 377.
[88] J. Fortea Pérez and J. Bernier Luque, *Recintos y fortificaciones ibéricas de la Bética* (1970).
[89] Suetonius, *Vit. Div. Iul.* 28.   [90] *CMH* 946.   [91] *CMH* 837–45.
[92] *CMH* 1259.

conclusion that the coins of the region tell us 'disappointingly little about juridical and political arrangements'.[93]

An example of this partial adoption of Roman administrative forms is provided by an inscription, dating to 49 BC, from La Rambla (ancient name unknown).[94] This records the building of the town wall by two magistrates of the town. One of these is an *aedilis* with the Roman name M. Coranus Alpis. However the other, who appears to be his superior, a *decemvir maxsumus* (*sic*), has a completely native name, Binsnes Vercellionis f. The decemvirate seems to be a native, Iberian magistracy.[95] Here therefore we see a partial adoption of Roman forms, but the dominant strand in the administrative system of the town appears to have remained Iberian.

Some even more nebulous literary evidence for this sort of political transformation is found in Caesar's speech delivered, we must assume, in Latin after the battle of Munda to a *contio* (public meeting) at Hispalis.[96] Caesar reproaches the assembly for the fact that while they were familiar with the law of all civilized men and that of Rome in particular, 'iure gentium civiumque Romanorum institutis cogniti', they have none the less acted like barbarians, 'more barbarorum'. This may suggest that the town of Hispalis used Roman-style laws. But equally it could simply be a comment to the effect that while the Hispalenses knew how to behave in a civilized manner, they chose, perversely, not to do so; the contrast being not simply between the *instituta Romanorum* and 'mos barbarorum', but between also the *ius gentium*, a norm assumed to exist in all civilized societies, and this latter.

The major impact of the settlement of *conventus* was probably an increase in the adoption of general, but individual, aspects of Roman culture, such as Latin literacy, or at least Latin speaking, in the province. This is suggested by Strabo's remarks about the Turdetani, which single out individual traits of acculturation such as this, rather than communal ones.[97] It is of, course, difficult to quantify Strabo's remarks, which are probably taken from the philosopher Posidonius. We cannot be sure how wide a sample of the native population Posidonius drew on for this generalization. Did he mingle with the lower classes of the area, or simply meet local aristocrats who are likely to have been more receptive to foreign cultures? Or, worse still, did he speak only with those interested in

---

[93] A. M. Burnett and M. H. Crawford (eds.), *The Coinage of the Roman World in the Late Republic* (1987), ch. 2, Spain, pp. 19 ff., 30.

[94] *AE* (1986), 369.   [95] See the detailed discussion in Ch. 8.

[96] Ps. Caesar, *B. Hisp.* 42.

[97] Strabo, 3. 2. 15; cf. his remarks on the Cavarii (4. 1. 12) discussed above in Ch. 2.

meeting a Greek philosopher, who are unlikely to have been typical of their fellow Iberians? Moreover, Posidonius may have had philosophical reasons for overemphasizing the 'civilized' nature of the lowland Turdetani as opposed to the highland tribes.[98] These reservations mean that while Strabo's remarks are important evidence for the adoption of Roman customs in the area, they cannot be accepted uncritically.

Beyond these urban-based groups of Romans, the possible contribution of two other groups to the province's development needs to be considered. These are those immigrants involved in mining and those concerned with farming.

Mining is a problematic area to assess. Diodorus Siculus states that there was a 'rush' of Italians into the area after the Second Punic War to exploit its mineral wealth.[99] It is true that Spain had a great deal of such wealth and that *societates* were busily engaged in its exploitation in the republican period.[100] Nevertheless this need not imply a vast influx of immigrants. Although Romans or Italians would have been needed to fill positions of responsibility in these operations, the bulk of the labour force would have been composed of native Iberians. Mining was always a highly dangerous occupation in antiquity, and frequently used as a form of criminal punishment. It is most unlikely that large numbers of Italians would have emigrated to perform such a task, and, as the Carthaginians had exploited the mines with native labour before the Roman occupation, there would have been a sufficiently skilled, and considerably cheaper, labour force to hand. Diodorus' use of πλῆθος (mass) to describe the number of Italians coming to work the mines at this time is somewhat problematic in this context. However, as there had been virtually no Romans in the area prior to this period, it is conceivable that even two or three hundred managers may have been sufficient to constitute a πλῆθος. It is quite possible, of course, that such managers resided in Spain only for a few years and then returned to Italy.

The location of most mining sites, in highland areas and those devoid of good arable land, which was normally a necessity for the survival of a classical town, such as the Sierra Morena and the Sierras of the present-day province of Huelva, would have militated against such activity being a stimulus for urbanization.[101] Moreover, excavations of mining sites from both the republican and imperial periods show little evidence of

[98] P. Thollard, *Barbarie et civilization chez Strabon* (1987). Such theorizing was not uncommon in antiquity; see Polybius 4. 20–1 on the Arcadians.

[99] Diodorus Siculus, 5. 36.

[100] See C. Domergue, 'Lingots de plomb romains de Carthagène', *A.e.A.* 39 (1966), 41 ff.

[101] It appears that in the republican period the only mines in the area which were worked

widespread adoption of Roman practices at such sites.[102] This is not surprising given the low esteem in which mining was held.[103] Recent surveys of mining activity in Hispania Ulterior suggest that the Roman occupation had little impact on the scale and development of mining in this period.[104]

Farmers would seem to offer a greater potential stimulus for changes in lifestyle than those engaged in mining. Wealthy farmers would have had the wherewithal to impose themselves in the province. We have, moreover, positive attestation of their existence at this time. Varro reports a story of an Atilius Hispaniensis, 'minime mendax et multorum rerum peritus in doctrina' ('utterly reliable and well educated in many things'), about a large sow which was slaughtered in Lusitania and sent to the senator, L. Volumnius.[105] Although there can be no doubt that Volumnius was in Spain at the time of this story, we need not believe that he was a settler; he could easily have been an official on a tour of duty in the province. Atilius, on the other hand, sounds like a gentleman farmer with interests in amateur scholarship; just the kind of man that Varro would have associated with when he was governor of Ulterior.

On Sulla's seizure of power in 88 BC M. Junius Brutus and others fled to Spain.[106] It is likely that they fled to rich friends whom they knew there. This was certainly the case with Crassus, who was sheltered by a certain Vibius Paciaecus.[107] Paciaecus was a large landholder; Plutarch mentions the bailiff of his farm and the two slave girls whom he put at Crassus' disposal. His name is of some interest as its suffix '-aecus' is not good Latin, although its stem is. Schulten believed that the suffix was Iberian, which raises interesting questions about Paciaecus' status . It is just possible that he was a wealthy Romanizing native, but the two components of his name would probably have been reversed (i.e. Iberian stem and Latin suffix) if this were the case. It is more likely that he was a wealthy Roman settler who had adopted native customs to some extent, even if it was only

extensively were the silver mines of the Sierra Morena: C. Domergue, *Les Mines de la péninsule ibérique dans l'antiquité romaine* (1990), 189: 'Elles [les mines] sont concentrées presque exclusivement dans la Sierra Morena et dans le Sud-Est [de la péninsule]'. The workings are listed on pp. 190–1.

[102] See e.g. P. Sillières, 'Sisapo: Prospections et découvertes', *A.e.A.* 53 (1980), 49 ff., and the comments below on Castulo, whose wealth rested on mineral exploitation.

[103] M. Finley, *The Ancient Economy* (1973), 72–3.

[104] Edmondson, *Two Industries in Roman Lusitania*, 45; B. Rothenberg and A. Blanco Freijeiro, *Ancient Mining and Metallurgy in South West Spain* (1981), 173.

[105] Varro, *RR* 2. 4. 11.

[106] A. Schulten (ed.), *FHA* 4 (1937), 157–8.

[107] Plutarch, *Vit. Cras.* 4–6; for Paciaecus, see Schulten, *FHA* 4 (1937), 158.

changing his name slightly in order to make it easier for the natives to pronounce. Another alternative which suggests itself is that Paciaecus' unusual *cognomen* was a native formulation which then stuck to his family. When Crassus came out of hiding he raised a force of 2,500 men from a 'multitude' who volunteered to serve him.[108] These need not be assumed to be Roman citizens, but are more likely to have been Iberians eager for plunder, which, if Crassus sacked Malaca, as is alleged, they would have obtained. The allegation is a strong indication that Paciaecus was a land-owner in Hispania Ulterior rather than the north of Spain. This is con-firmed by a L. Vibius Paciaecus, described as a 'hominem eius provinciae notum' ('a man well known in the province'), who is found serving with Caesar's troops in 46 BC in Ulterior, and should be the son of Crassus' benefactor.[109]

Did the presence of such farmers encourage the spread of urbanization in southern Spain? There is little evidence that this was the case. They would have operated beyond the urban environment, and Paciaecus' name suggests that cultural interaction was not entirely one-way in this period. The volume of trade in agricultural produce from the province to Rome appears to have been considerably lower in the republican period than it was to become in the following centuries. The trade in olive oil, Baetica's major export to Rome, was not to reach its peak until the late second century AD, as is graphically demonstrated by the remains of the Monte Testaccio. Surveys of the development of *villae*, around which the trade was based, and whose growth might be seen as a good indicator of the transformation of life in rural Baetica, show that their period of rapid expansion began in the Augustan period, before which there were few such farms in the area.[110]

The other main export of the area, a form of fish sauce known as garum, is more difficult to quantify. However Edmondson sees its rise, in Lusita-nia at least, as not taking place until the first century AD.[111] In the area of Hispania Ulterior which became Baetica, the trade could have had earlier beginnings.[112] The trade probably remained in the hands of local mer-chants, and appears to have been well integrated into the indigenous pattern of town life here; so increased contact with Rome would have caused little disruption or change to traditional life. Garum manufacture

---

[108] Plutarch, *Vit. Cras.* 6.   [109] Ps. Caesar, *B. Hisp.* 3.

[110] J. G. Gorges, *La villa hispano-romaine* (1979), 26–33 and figs. 4–6.

[111] Edmondson, *Two Industries in Roman Lusitania*, 108.

[112] The garum of Gades is mentioned by the 5th-c. BC poet, Eupolis. *Stephanus Byzanti-nus*, s.v. Γάδειρα. See also Edmondson, *Two Industries in Roman Lusitania*, 107.

was concentrated on the Mediterranean coast, and many towns here displayed fish emblems on their coins, which may be an allusion to the trade. These towns are precisely those which Agrippa regarded as Punic when he surveyed the region.[113]

If large-scale farmers cannot be proved to have made a major impression on the province, what then was the role of smaller-scale settlers, who had established themselves individually in Ulterior? This category of settlers is often taken as having been extremely numerous and as having contributed substantially to the province's development. However, what evidence is there for this point of view?

Apart from the general difficulties discussed above, which would have been worse for the small settler than his wealthier counterpart, a variety of other problems present themselves. First, there is the question of where land could be found on which to settle. The Baetis valley would have been entirely occupied by native Iberian farmers, and an ordinary veteran would not have had sufficient resources to buy land from its occupiers. Some land might have been seized by force, something expressly forbidden in the imperial period.[114] However, there would have been considerably less security available to veterans attempting to do this in the republican period, and if the settlements were small, unofficial ventures, as is normally assumed, they would probably have been unable to impose themselves in the face of determined resistance. The best-documented case of abuse in the imperial period comes from Colchester in Britain.[115] Here, however, there was a large official *colonia* and a nearby army to provide protection, while turning a blind eye to abuses. Neither of these factors would have been present in republican Spain to a sufficient degree to allow a similar situation to arise.

Although it is often assumed that many veterans would have wished to stay in the province after their discharge, there is some evidence that on the contrary this desire need not have been strong even towards the end of the republican period. Varro writes of the Veianii brothers from Falerii, who served in his army in Spain, and who, despite having only a *iugerum* of land back home, were making a healthy profit from it by using it for bee-keeping, and envisaged returning to it after their service.[116]

The hypothesis that large numbers of veterans did stay in the province is based on assumptions deduced from references to legionary recruitment

---

[113] Pliny, *NH* 3. 1. 8.   [114] *Digest*, 18. 1. 62 (Modestinus), 49. 16. 9 (Marcianus).
[115] Tacitus, *Ann.* 14. 31.
[116] Varro, *RR* 3. 16. 10 ff. For reluctance to stay in earlier periods, see Livy, 28. 24. 7 (209 BC), 39. 31. 5 (187 BC), and 40. 35. 7 (180 BC).

taking place in the province in the late republican period between 60 and 45 BC, to which we must now turn.

The first mention of recruitment in the province is in relation to Caesar's governorship of Ulterior in 60 BC and his campaign against the Lusitanians. Caesar raised ten cohorts in the province to supplement the twenty already under his command.[117] The twenty previously existing cohorts were probably the army of two legions frequently stationed in the province. As ten cohorts was the number which formed a legion, Caesar's raising of precisely this figure of additional cohorts could imply that he levied an extra legion. As the legions were recruited from Roman citizens, this in turn would imply the presence of a large Roman-citizen body in the province on which he could draw. However, none of these speculations is secure. It is as likely that the force involved was a number of auxiliary cohorts designed to complement the legions in the difficult terrain of Lusitania; auxiliaries, unlike legionaries, were recruited from among the *peregrini*, so it is impossible to draw any firm conclusions about settlement from this incident.

A more substantial argument based around legionary recruitment concerns the *Legio Vernacula* (the Native Legion) found in the province in the Civil War period. This was one of the two legions under Varro's command at the beginning of the Civil Wars. Caesar's reference to it as the legion 'quae vernacula appellabatur' ('which was called the Native Legion')[118] shows that this was its official title, not merely a descriptive adjective applied to it. Such a title suggests that the legion was not composed of Roman citizens. Lewis and Short define 'vernaculus' as meaning either 'of, or belonging to the household slaves' or 'native, indigenous'.[119] On the other hand this contrasts with the unit's undoubted legionary status; legions were normally recruited exclusively from *cives Romani*.

If the legion was raised at the beginning of the Civil Wars, or in the immediately preceding period, there could be little dispute that it was composed of natives, as it would have been raised as an emergency measure when few questions would have been asked about the legal status of its recruits. However, the legion is described as 'veterana' and 'multisque proeliis experta' ('tried in many battles'), implying that it had existed for some time previously.[120]

Yoshimura,[121] using Caesar's comment that the Caesarian governor,

[117] Plutarch, *Vit. Div. Iul.* 12. [118] Caesar, *BC* 2. 20.
[119] C. T. Lewis and C. S. Short, *A Latin Dictionary* (1894), s.v. 'vernaculus'.
[120] Ps. Caesar, *B. Alex.* 64.
[121] T. Yoshimura, 'The Legio Vernacula of Pompey', *JCS* 8 (1960), 74 ff.

Cassius, was particularly hated by the *Vernacula* and Second (which had been in the province so long that it had strong native sympathies) legions,[122] suggested that the legion was levied in Cassius' quaestorship in the province under Pompey in *c*.56–52 BC. This need not be the case. The troops of the *Legio Vernacula*, even had it not been formed at that time, would have been in the province and so have remembered Cassius' former actions. This is also true of the Second Legion. Although it may have been in the province at this date, it is possible that its troops gained their antipathy towards Cassius from the stories of their native camp-followers who certainly would have been. The description of this latter unit as 'diurnitate iam factus provincialis' ('already made provincial through its long stay there') suggests that a considerable amount of acculturation had taken place.

Cassius had undertaken a campaign against Lusitania in his governorship.[123] Nevertheless this cannot be the reason for the *Vernacula*'s description as a veteran legion, as its opponents in the passage concerned, who are contrasted because of their rawness with the Second and *Vernacula* legions, also took part in this campaign. Consequently the reference to the *Vernacula*'s veteran status should refer to campaigns undertaken prior to Cassius' actions in Lusitania by Varro, which are not recorded in our sources. Such campaigns would have been policing measures against the Lusitani, the frequency of which is attested by the fact that one was undertaken in the midst of the Civil Wars themselves.

We must remember that the mid-50s BC was a period of major instability, when irregular practices were frequently followed. It was at this time that Caesar recruited the non-citizen *Legio Alaudae*, and the *Legio Vernacula* is best seen as a Pompeian device, or perhaps response, of a similar kind. After his victory at Ilerda, Caesar remarked that Pompey had sent six legions to Spain and raised a seventh there for no other purpose than to outnumber him.[124] Given that there were five legions at Ilerda, and, that Varro had two in Ulterior, the most likely interpretation of these comments is that they concerned the *Legio Vernacula*.

Finally there is a linguistic argument for the *Legio Vernacula* having been composed of natives. In its final appearance, when it is fighting for the Younger Pompey, it is contrasted with a legion 'facta ex colonis qui fuerunt in his regionibus' ('composed out of the colonists who were to be found in those parts'),[125] implying that it itself was not so composed.[126]

[122] Ps. Caesar, *B. Alex.* 53.   [123] Ibid. 51.   [124] Caesar, *BC* 1. 85.
[125] Ps. Caesar, *B. Hisp.* 7.
[126] L. Keppie, *The Making of the Roman Army* (1984), 141.

The description of some troops from the *Legio Vernacula* as 'loricati' is also of interest.[127] Normally all legionaries could be described in this way, but the context here suggests that other members of the legion were not so equipped. This again suggests that the *Vernacula* was an irregular formation.

The brief mention of this legion 'facta ex colonis' ('composed of colonists') shows that there were some settlers in the area, but it is unlikely that many questions were asked about the legal status of potential recruits at such a low ebb in the Pompeians' fortunes. A maximum of around 4,000 male settlers is implied by the legion's existence. This should approximate to the number of male settlers available in the area. Although some settlers would have taken the Caesarian side, and others would not have been of military age, the *Bellum Hispaniense* records constant desertion to Caesar's forces, suggesting that at least some of Pompey's troops had been conscripted against their will. Moreover, given the desperation of Pompey's position, it is unlikely that those too young or old for normal military service will have been passed over.

This legion may be related to one previously raised in the province by the Caesarian governor, Cassius, the 'Legio Quinta'.[128] We are told that the levying of this legion and the cost involved caused great hatred. As an attempt to assassinate Cassius was made soon after by wealthy Roman citizens, some at least being *equites*, it seems that the legion was raised from Roman citizens, although this is nowhere explicitly stated. The hatred may have arisen simply from a dislike of Cassius and military service, but it is possible that it was also generated partially because the settler community could hardly bear the strain of recruitment. If so, this again implies a smaller settler body than is commonly assumed to have existed. The legion was quietly disbanded after Trebonius assumed the governorship of the province.

Two Titii brothers described as 'Hispani adulescentes' are found serving in a 'Quinta' legion in Africa at a later date, but they were military tribunes and so their origin need not have any connection with that of the legion's rank and file.[129] Moreover the Fifth in Africa is described as a veteran legion in comparison to the Thirtieth, and the Thirtieth is said to be older than the Spanish Fifth.[130] The 'Fifth' of the Titii brothers therefore is likely to have been the *V Alaudae*, not the Spanish unit, and

---

[127] Ps. Caesar, *B. Hisp.* 20: 'loricatus unus ex legione vernacula' ('a man with a breastplate from the Native Legion').

[128] Ps. Caesar, *B. Alex.* 50.   [129] Ps. Caesar, *B. Afr.* 28.

[130] Ps. Caesar, *B. Alex.* 50, 53.

the two tribunes were probably serving with it because they enjoyed
Caesar's favour. We are told that their father was raised to senatorial
rank by Caesar. Whether he was the L. Titius who was a tribune in the
Legio Vernacula is unknown.[131] If he was, this need not imply that the
Vernacula was composed of citizens, as officers could easily come from
a background very different from that of their men, nor that he was a
settler, as Caesar was notorious for introducing enfranchised provincials
into the senate.

Both the above units may have had their genesis from the *colonicae
cohortes* we hear of at Corduba in 49 BC.[132] These two units were used
by the *conventus* of Corduba to help in their rebellion against Varro. The
title of these units might at first lead to the assumption that they were
a purely civic force. If this was the case, it suggests that in Corduba alone
there were at least 800 *cives Romani* of military age. However, the *cohortes*
are said to have come by chance to Corduba, 'cum eo casu venissent'
and to have been kept there to guard the city, 'tuendi oppidum causa apud
se retinuit' by the *conventus*. This implies that the units were province-
wide bodies as otherwise they would have been permanently based at
Corduba and hence would not have come there 'by chance'; nor would
there have been any need to retain the units to guard Corduba as this
would have been their normal function. 'Colonus' here is probably being
used in the sense of 'settler' rather than in the strict sense of 'member
of a *colonia*'.[133]

The recruitment of legions in Spain therefore shows the presence of
some Roman settlement in the area. However, it also appears that the
extent of this has often been overestimated. Given the troubles of the
time, much of the recruitment was probably from the native Iberian
population. A maximum of two legions seem to have been recruited from
settlers. These do not seem to have been in existence simultaneously; and
it is likely that the two formations had a considerable overlap in manpower, as recruitment was certainly involuntary in the first case and may
well have been so in the second.

In conclusion it appears that the number of small-scale settlers in the
area has been frequently overestimated in the past. Again, even if this is
not the case, there must be a question as to how greatly they would have
contributed towards cultural change in the province. If these settlers are
envisaged as being scattered across the country, rather than forming large
blocks, there is little reason to assume that they would retain a great deal

[131] Ps. Caesar, *B. Alex.* 57.   [132] Caesar, *BC* 2. 19.
[133] Cf. the use of *colonus* in the *legio facta ex colonis* discussed above.

of their Roman identity. More recent experience has shown that the common man placed in a new cultural environment will tend to assimilate into his surroundings unless there are positive incentives not to do so. If these settlements were those of individuals, one such incentive, that of group solidarity, would certainly not apply.[134]

Finally, what was the impact on the province not of Roman immigrants, but of local inhabitants who had obtained the Roman citizenship? It is unfortunately impossible to quantify the numbers involved. Our most striking example is clearly the two Balbi of Cádiz who went on to pursue impressive political careers at Rome. Nevertheless we cannot be certain that a grant of citizenship would always have led to such a commitment to the Roman way of life.[135] Roman citizenship could have been regarded simply as a symbol of prestige, or perhaps as an insurance policy which would prevent exceptional maltreatment by the ruling power. Very few enfranchised individuals are positively attested. One is a Gaditanus, whose name exists only in the garbled term †Herosnovem†.[136] It would not be surprising if the Balbi had obtained the citizenship for some of their friends; but equally it is interesting that Cicero in the *Pro Balbo* does not quote a large number of parallels to the younger Balbus, though it would have been to his advantage to do so. On the other hand we know that Pompeius Strabo granted the citizenship to an entire *turma* of Spanish *equites* from Hispania Citerior during the Social War, although this grant may have been provoked by exceptional circumstances.[137] In summary all we can say is that there were some enfranchised natives in the province and that, as in the case of the Balbi, enfranchisement led to the pursuit of a Roman lifestyle; however, this cannot be regarded as universally true.

Since most Roman activity in the area in the republican period was connected with trade, it is legitimate to ask whether the instruments of that trade themselves, as well as the presence of the merchants and settlers, helped to promote the adoption of Roman habits. The areas which spring to mind immediately are those of coinage and systems of weights and measurement.

---

[134] Such acculturation can be seen in British India before the evangelical fervour of the high Victorian period, amongst US troops serving in the Plains Wars of the 19th c. (see E. Donnell, *Son of the Morning Star* (1984), 25), and away from main-force formations in the Vietnam War (see D. Donovan, *Once a Warrior King* (1985), *passim*).

[135] After all, St Paul, the most famous of all Roman citizens, does not appear to have been 'Romanized'.

[136] Cicero, *Pro Balbo* 22. 50. Cicero's text is corrupt here; only one name appears to be mentioned, yet in apposition we have the plural 'Gaditanos'.

[137] *ILS* 8888.

There does appear to have been an adoption of some Roman weights and measures, which would clearly have facilitated trade between Rome and the province. The best potential example of this phenomenon is a silver bowl found at La Granjuela with an Iberian inscription which may refer to its weight expressed in Roman pounds.[138] However, Iberian weights found at the *colonia* Ilici graphically illustrate that such adoption was not universal even at sites which had the strongest reasons to emphasize their Roman standing.

The dating of the province's coinage is highly problematic. Crawford dates the beginning of the native minting in the peninsula to *c*.154 BC,[139] while most commentators place the major period of coining at the end of the republican period. These include Grant,[140] Guadan,[141] Vives,[142] Alvarez Burgos,[143] and Hübner.[144] Some coins may date from slightly later still, for example those of Irippo, Osset, and Laelia which appear to have a bust of Augustus on the obverse. In the case of Irippo the reverse, depicting a seated woman with a cornucopia, closely parallels a commemorative issue of Augustus struck at Italica in the reign of Tiberius, and has some parallels with similar coins struck at Turiaso and Tarraco in northern Spain.[145]

The coins issued by the *propraetor* of Cn. Pompeius in 46–45 BC, M. Poblicius, may also provide some information for dating local issues. Poblicius' coins displayed an obverse with the head of Rome wearing a distinctive style of helmet with two plumes.[146] Parallels to this design can be found on the coinage of Caura and Lastigi, and some coins of Sexi, Urso, Onuba, Osset, and Searo also show some parallels. If these were influenced by this coinage, they should date slightly later than Poblicius' official issues. Hübner believed that the issue of Numit(?ius?) and Terentius Bodo from Lascuta was to commemorate the defeat of Bogud's incursion into the province, which would date the coin to the 30s BC.

---

[138] F. J. Oroz Arizcuren, 'El sistema metrológico de la inscripción ibérica del cuenco de la Granjuela', in A. Tovar *et al.* (eds.), *Actos de II Colloquia sobre lenguas y cultura prerromanas de la peninsula ibérica* (1979), 283 ff.; see however some doubts expressed on p. 363. Other possible examples are listed by K. Raddatz, *Die Schatzfunde der iberischen Halbinsel* (1967), i. 14, 86, 225.

[139] M. Crawford, *Coinage and Money under the Roman Republic* (1985), ch. 6, pp. 84 ff.

[140] M. Grant, *From Imperium to Auctoritas* (1946), 379 ff.

[141] *MI passim.*   [142] *La moneda hispánica* (1926), *passim.*

[143] *CMH passim.*

[144] *Monumenta linguae ibericae* (1893), 6.

[145] Irippo, *CMH* 1109–10; Italica, *CMH* 1680–1; Turiaso, *CMH* 1781; Tarraco, *CMH* 1737–8.

[146] *CMH* 1826.

Given the semi-native names of the magistrates and the Libyo-Phoenician legend carried, if Hübner is correct, the coin provides strong evidence of the persistence of native culture into the late republican period.[147] The name Terentius also appears at Onuba—P. Terent.,[148] and possibly at Iluip Halos—Val. Ter(?entius?).[149] One possibility is that the name may be connected with the governorship of Terentius Varro, which would give the coins concerned a *terminus post quem* of the end of the republican period. In general it appears that the coinage of the province dates, in the main, from the end of the republican period and possibly continued into the principate.

The local coinage of the area differed sharply from the so-called 'Iberian denarii' found to the north. While these latter coins were of silver and closely followed Roman metrological values, the coins in the south of Spain are bronze and seem to have no fixed metrology. This suggests a difference of purpose. The Iberian denarii were produced initially to pay Roman troops and therefore had to conform to a form acceptable to the payees;[150] although obviously the adoption of such standards would also have been encouraged by traders as it would have enabled their own transactions to be carried out more easily. The bronze coins of southern Spain appear to be designed for more local purposes, although some mints have a very wide distribution.[151] The coins, however, suggest the beginnings of a monetized economy in the region; moreover as well as the use of Roman magisterial titles on these coins which has already been mentioned, Latin, in sharp contrast to the issues of northern Spain where Iberian is normally found, is the preferred language of the majority of the issues.[152]

At first sight, therefore, our numismatic evidence appears to show a strong tendency towards Romanization, especially at the expense of the local Iberian culture; however, it is important to look at all aspects of this numismatic evidence and not merely legends. Although Latin is the most frequent language used on the coins, their iconography remains overwhelmingly Iberian. The cavalryman motif, 'el jinete ibérico', found on the coins of many towns in northern Spain, appears on the coinage of Carisa, Iliturgi, Olont(igi?), Laelia, Lastigi, Ilipla, and Ituci. Other Iberian

---

[147] E. Hübner, *Memoirs numismatiques*, i. 18.   [148] *CMH* 1186.
[149] *CMH* 1078.   [150] Crawford, *Coinage and Money*, 94.
[151] Some in fact drifted as far afield as Britain; see J. G. Milne, *Finds of Greek Coins in the British Isles* (1948).
[152] Four alphabets are found in use in the south of Spain: Iberian, Latin, Punic, and Libyo-Phoenician. Out of a total of 58 towns known to have minted in this period, 7 (12%) use Punic, 8 (13%) Libyo-Phoenician, 3 (5%) Iberian, and 40 (70%) Latin legends.

motifs such as the bull and the boar are also common. Motifs copying those of Carthaginian coinage are also found, such as the horse at Sacili, Cilpe, Oba, and Nabrissa, the horse and tree at Sisapo, the horse's head at Obulco, and the bull and tree at Vesci.

The majority of coins with Latin script display only the name of the town. Nevertheless a substantial minority also carry magistrates' names. Some of these are of a standard Latin form, for example C. Aeli and Q. Publili of Onuba,[153] L. Aimil. and M. Iuni, aediles of Obulco,[154] P. Corn. and Q. Manl. of Belo,[155] and Val. Ter. of Iluip Halos.[156] Again, these coins, despite their Latin legends, still retain Iberian iconography. Of those listed above only that from Onuba is influenced by Roman design. Those from Belo display a bust of the Punic god Melqart, influenced by the coinage of Gades, and that of Iluip Halos uses a typical Iberian design, the boar.

The coins of Obulco, mentioning a Roman title, *aedilis*, retain the Iberian bust and reverse found on those which possess Iberian legends. One issue of the aediles Aimilius and Iunius carries a Latin legend running from right to left, showing that its minters had an imperfect understanding of the language.[157] A *terminus post quem* for the coins of these two aediles may be provided by an example found sealed in the rampart of Urso along with a denarius probably of L. Julius Bursicus, dating to 83 BC.

Other coins, while carrying Latin legends, show anomalies of nomenclature and civic forms as compared with Roman norms. At Lascuta, a coin was issued with the names of L. Numit. Bodo and P. Terent. Bodo.[158] Bodo is an Iberian name, and a related form of it, Bodilcos, is found on a coin from Obulco. This coin, in addition to its Latin legend, also carries a Libyo-Phoenician legend, showing that the local language had not been entirely superseded.

At Onuba, a coin refers to 'P. Terent. et Colp.'[159] 'Colp.' may refer to a local, non-Roman form of magistracy, or perhaps a non-Roman name. At (Ba?)Esuri, a coin refers to 'M. An. Ant. et Con(legae?)' which poses similar problems.[160] This is also true of a coin from Obulco with the legend 'Connipp.'[161] At Abra, the Iberian name, A. Titin., is found.[162] At Carteia, although the form of administration, the quattuorvirate, is clearly Roman, some individual *quattuorviri*, such as L. Atini. and P. Mion., have

[153] *CMH* 1187.   [154] *CMH* 840–4.   [155] *CMH* 1257.   [156] *CMH* 1078.
[157] *CMH* 845.   [158] *CMH* 1140.   [159] *CMH* 1186.   [160] *CMH* 958.
[161] Vives, *La moneda hispánica*, iii. 57.
[162] A. Guadan, *Numismática ibérica e ibero-romana* (1969), no. 335, p. 68.

semi-Iberian names.[163] The area's coinage therefore shows a mixture of Roman and native features.

In addition some of the issues from the province were not struck by the local authorities themselves. It is noticeable that the legend 'L. Ap. Dec. Q.' appears on the coins of three towns, Urso, Belo, and Myrtilis in Lusitania. This is a strange coincidence, and Grant plausibly connects these issues with the Pompeian *quaestor*, L. Appuleius Decianus.[164] Similarly the C. Livius who appears on the coinage of Vesci could have been the legate of L. Antonius, the proconsul of Spain.[165] In the same way, perhaps the T. Manlius T.f. Sergia(?nus?) found on the coinage of Brutobriga may not be a local official, but a Pompeian officer from Rome.[166] Beltrán identifies the A. Hirtius on the coinage of Lascuta with the Caesarian commander, Aulus Hirtius.[167] This coin raises interesting questions, as Hirtius' name appears on a coin whose obverse depicts a bust of Melquart, and with a reverse showing a three-stage altar with palm fronds growing from it. There is an identical coin which, instead of Hirtius' name, has a Libyo-Phoenician legend on the reverse. The similarity of these Punic-influenced coins suggests that coining in Latin need not have superseded coining in local languages, but merely ran parallel to it.

Similar questions are raised by the iconography of other coins. A coin from Urso with the legend 'L. Ap. Dec. Q.' displays a sphinx on its reverse closely paralleling sphinxes found on coins from Castulo and Bastele. Many of the coins from Castulo have Iberian legends. Two, however, have Latin legends reading 'Sacal. Iscer. and Cael. M. Isc.' on their obverses, and 'Soced. Cast. and M. Ful[?]' on their reverses.[168] Here we see that although Latin was adopted for legends, native iconography was retained. Isc/Iscer. may refer to a local magistracy. The coin from Bastele is influenced by those of Castulo and has an Iberian legend. If the Urso coin was minted by Apuleius, those from Castulo and Bastele may, given their similarity to it, date from this period, suggesting a strand of Iberian culture continuing down to the end of the republican period. In the same way a coin from Iliberris, with a triskele reverse and bearing the Latin legend 'Florentia', is paralleled exactly by two coins which bear

---

[163] *CMH* 1421, 1426.   [164] M. Grant, *From Imperium to Auctoritas* (1946), 24–5.

[165] Ibid. 379 f. with Appian, *BC* 5. 54.   [166] Ibid. 381.

[167] A. Beltrán, 'Sobre las acuñaciones de Lascuta', *Numisma*, 4 (1954), 9–20.

[168] *CMH* 887–8.

the Iberian legend 'ILBeRIR',[169] again suggesting a continuity of Iberian culture, with a move to Latin as preferred language for legends.

Taken in general, the province's coinage seems to show that an embryonic growth of Roman customs was occurring by the end of the republican period, rather than that there had already been a widespread adoption of them. Some Roman-style names and magistracies occur, but they are paralleled by Iberian forms. As the region would have been populated by a generally illiterate society, the main impact of coins would have been visual for the majority of the population. The general native iconography of the coinage might indicate that the mass of the population and more significantly the moneyers themselves, who would have been from the higher echelons of society, were still happier with coins displaying traditional, rather than Roman, motifs. This, in turn, may suggest that the adoption of things Roman was a phenomenon mainly limited to the upper stratum of native society.

The coins of the Mediterranean coast of the province show even fewer signs of Roman influence. Apart from some coins of Sexi, which possibly copied issues of Poblicius, the iconography of these coins remained firmly Punic, as did the language of their legends, bearing out Agrippa's remarks on the Punic nature of this part of the province.

The distribution of sites minting coins is also significant. Apart from Turricina, Arsa, and other towns whose location is uncertain, the vast majority of minting sites appear to lie along the coast, the Baetis valley, or the foothills of Bastetania. Coining therefore seems to have been mainly limited to the lowland 'core' area of the province, where Roman influences were at their strongest. Large areas in the north and the Sierra Nevada appear to have possessed very few coining communities. Minting coins may well have been a response to Roman pressure in trading, a counter of the local élite to Rome intended to demonstrate to the local population its continuing independence, or possibly to pay soldiers. The latter suggestion gains strength if the coinage is dated to the end of the republican period, when large bodies of troops were present in the province, and obviously would have to have been paid in some way. If this is the case, the production of coins may have been forced on the local population rather than being adopted willingly by them.

In contrast to these signs of the adoption of Roman practices, evidence of the survival of Iberian culture and language can also easily be found. Cicero draws a picture of the Hispani being unintelligible on embassies to

---

[169] *CMH* 918–20.

Rome without interpreters,[170] and Iberian may have been the dominant language spoken among the lower classes even in towns with *conventus*; and this was almost certainly the case in the smaller towns which lacked such settlements.

Castulo in the north-west of the province provides good evidence of the continuing strength of Iberian culture. The town's Iberian wall was repaired in the early imperial period,[171] and a funerary statue of a lion, dating to the first century BC, carved in a pure Iberian style which can be traced back almost 1,000 years before this period, has been found here.[172] An inscription, thought to date from the late republic, records a 'M. Folui Garus . . . Uninaunin . . . Sierovciut'.[173] Although the name here has a slight Roman veneer, for example in its apparent use of the *tria nomina*, it remains basically Iberian.[174] The meaning of what follows the name is obscure, as Iberian remains undeciphered. However, it is normally assumed that some sort of civic function is involved; if this is the case there is no sign of a wish to adopt Roman forms. Castulo may be a better guide to the nature of the average town in Ulterior in this period than either Corduba or Hispalis with their *conventus* of Romans. We find adoption of some Roman forms, but essentially a retention of Iberian customs and traditions.

Another possible sign of the retention of native political structures may be found in the *Bellum Hispaniense*, where the death of a king Indo, who has voluntarily joined the Caesarian forces, is recorded. Indo is a purely native name and kingship obviously a non-Roman office. Unfortunately we cannot be sure that Indo was from this area, although kingship seems to have been a traditional form of government here; he could have come from neighbouring Lusitania. A Lusitanian who provides a contrast to Indo is the Pompeian sympathizer, Caecilius Niger, described as a 'homo barbarus' and leader of a 'bene magna manus Lusitanorum' ('a large band of Lusitanians').[175] The difference in self-image between these two native rulers graphically shows the varied penetration of Roman values into native society.

In general there appears to have been little wholesale adoption of Roman urban values in the south of Spain in the republic. Most towns, including those where there was a formal settlement of Romans, retained,

[170] Cicero, *De Div.* 2. 131. The dialogue was written in 44 BC and its dramatic date is contemporaneous with that of its composition.
[171] *CIL* 2. 3270.
[172] J. M. Blazquez *et al.*, *Castulo 4* = *EAE 131* (1984), 271, lam. 14. 1.
[173] *CIL* 2. 3302.   [174] Cf. the aedile of Acinippo, L. Folce, discussed above.
[175] Ps. Caesar, *B. Hisp.* 35.

as far as can be ascertained, many Iberian features in their physical make-up. Few Roman buildings are found, and there is as yet no evidence of a general adoption of gridded street-planning or of an overall Roman environment. The same is true of the political arrangements of the area. Only Carteia and Gades can be securely said to have used Roman administrative structures, and in both cases the grant of an official status, that of *colonia Latina*, in the case of Carteia, and that of *municipium civium Romanorum* in that of Gades, makes this adoption exceptional.

The impact of Rome in this period was of a general cultural form, such as the spread of Latin speaking and literacy, the adoption of Roman-style nomenclature, and familiarity with Roman metrological systems. All these could, of course, exist and gain ground within a predominantly native cultural environment. The absence of coining from much of the highlands of the province, and the strongly native remains of Castulo, situated in this part of the province, suggest that these areas were more resistant to Roman influence than the lowlands of the Baetis valley. The Punic Mediterranean coast too seems to have been more resilient in the face of Roman pressure.

Some of the reluctance to change can probably be attributed to the more exploitative management of the provinces and the greater instability of Roman politics in the late republic which would have made integration more difficult than it was to be under the principate. Strabo appears to be correct when he singles out Turdetania as the area of the province which had moved most towards Roman norms, but seems to have overstated his case. Even here the move to a predominantly Roman way of life appears to have been in an embryonic stage rather than firmly established, and there is more a synthesis of Roman and Iberian cultures, as shown by the Urso reliefs, than the simple suppression of one by the other.

In sum the Roman practices which we find in the region in the republican period are not primarily those concerned with the development of urban life as understood by Rome, but are of a wider and more diffuse kind. The spread of these more general aspects of Roman culture can be seen as preparing a field in which the urban mentality could later be cultivated, but hardly as sowing the seeds of the process itself.

4

The *Coloniae* of Baetica

THE *coloniae* founded in the future *provincia* of Baetica at, and just after, the end of the Roman republic were the first large-scale settlements of Roman citizens in this area organized directly by the Roman state. As such they were of a markedly different character from previous Roman communities established in Hispania Ulterior, which had taken the form either of informal *conventus*, or possibly of individual settlement. In contrast to these *ad hoc* developments of the past, the new *coloniae* were established according to a firmly Roman model of what constituted a town. This model, to be used for *coloniae* of all provinces, was, not unnaturally, the city of Rome itself: Aulus Gellius calls *coloniae* 'effigies parvae et simulacra' ('little copies and replicas') of Rome.[1]

However, not only does reality often differ markedly from idealistic intentions, but the very nature of such intentions also needs to be examined with great care. Do the *coloniae* of Baetica provide confirmation of Gellius' statement? Did they help to communicate the ideals of a Roman way of life to the native population? If so, which aspects were so transmitted and was such communication, if it did occur, intentional, or coincidental, a mere epiphenomenon of the colonies' true purpose? In attempting to answer the above questions we are hampered, as ever, by the ambiguous nature of our sources and while what is said below will rely mainly on evidence drawn from the *coloniae* in Baetica, on occasions parallels have been drawn from other colonial settlements outside the province.

The question of precisely when, and by whom (i.e. whether by Caesar or Augustus), the majority of the Baetican *coloniae* were founded is controversial, but, as it does not affect their role in the province, it will not be examined here.[2] Similarly the question of whether Latin, as opposed to citizen, *coloniae* were established in the province at this period is a separate question, and is dealt with elsewhere.[3]

---

[1] Aulus Gellius, *NA* 16. 13.
[2] For a summary of foundation dates, see P. Brunt, *Italian Manpower* (1971), app. 15.
[3] See the discussion in Ch. 5.

Baetica, in proportion to its size, had a considerably larger number of *coloniae* than the other Iberian provinces: nine compared with Tarraconensis' twelve and Lusitania's five. These nine *coloniae* were Corduba, Hispalis, Astigi, Tucci, Itucci, Ucubi, Urso, Hasta Regia, and Asido. The number was increased further by at least one, when Hadrian granted his home town, Italica, colonial status and possibly by two if we accept that the town of Iliturgi was also promoted to this rank.[4]

The grant of colonial status to Italica and the subsequent creation of the 'nova urbs' in the town, can be seen as a simple act of imperial munificence to the emperor's home town. As such it tells us little of the aspirations of the inhabitants of Italica or their state of 'Romanization' at the time of the grant. Iliturgi presents a greater problem. The inscription we possess dates, if accepted as genuine, to the reign of Hadrian. As the town is not listed by Pliny as a *colonia*, Iliturgi's putative colonial rank ought to have been acquired at some point after the compilation of Agrippa's map, from which Pliny probably took his information, and the reign of Hadrian. The grant has been linked to a period of rebuilding in the town starting in the reign of Tiberius and ending in the Flavian period.[5] If this is the case, we are still unable to ascertain whether the grant would have been made as a reward for progress in urbanization (an unlikely possibility) or whether conversely Iliturgi's promotion consequently provoked urban development in the town. If the latter is the case, we can have no idea why the promotion originally occurred. A third possibility remains that the two events are entirely unconnected. It would be perilous therefore to see Iliturgi as evidence that a grant of colonial status was used as either an incentive to promote urbanization or a reward for prior urbanization.

Apart from the two cases discussed above, Pliny's list of *coloniae* also raises problems which must be discussed before returning to examine the wider impact of colonial settlement in Baetica. The first of these difficulties concerns the town of Asido. Hübner held that this town could not have been a *colonia*, as its officials are listed as *quattuorviri*, not *duoviri*, using as evidence an inscription (which he dates to the Caesarian period) recording a dedication to a *quattuorvir*, Q. Fabius Senica. In addition to this title, which Hübner believed was not used in *coloniae*, the dedicants of

---

[4] The colonial status of Iliturgi is attested by an inscription (*CIL* 2. 190*) rejected as false by Hübner, but accepted by H. Galsterer, *Untersuchungen zum römischen Städtewesen auf der iberischen Halbinsel*, p. 13, and R. Wiegels, *Die Tribusinschriften des römischen Hispanien* (1985).

[5] C. González Román, 'Las colonias romanas de la Hispania meridional en sus aspectos socio-juridicos', in C. González Román (ed.), *La Bética en su problemática historia* (1991), 87–110, at p. 91 and n. 14.

the stone are described as *municipes*, not *coloni*, *Caesarini* (*sic*).[6] Hübner concluded that this evidence demonstrated that Asido was a *municipium* and not a *colonia*.

To support his case Hübner quoted another inscription, found at Jerez de la Frontera, which records a dedication of thanks to the *quattuorvir* L. Fabius Cordus by the *populus* M.C. for putting on a gladiatorial show. Hübner believed that this stone refers to Asido, and that the abbreviation 'M.C.' should be expanded to read *M(unicipii) C(aesarinorum)*.[7] On the strength of this epigraphic evidence, Hübner proposed that the passage of Pliny mentioning Hasta Regia and Asido as *coloniae* should be amended to make the colonial reference apply only to Hasta Regia.[8] Such an amendment would of course mean that the text of the *Natural History* would no longer contain nine *coloniae* as initially listed at the beginning of Pliny's description. However, this is not a serious objection to Hübner's theory. Pliny frequently fails to name all the towns of a certain status that he has initially listed. This is true, for example, of both *oppida libera* (lists six, but only names two) and *oppida foederata* (lists three, but only mentions two) in the case of Baetica.

Nevertheless more difficult problems remain. Jerez de la Frontera can plausibly be identified with the ancient town of Ceret, allowing an alternative expansion of 'M.C.' to *M(unicipii) C(eretensis)*, which would make it irrelevant to the question of Asido's status. Even if this is not the case, there is still no guarantee that the inscription refers to Asido. Other ancient towns whose names began with 'C' (for example, Colobana and Carisa) lay as near to Jerez as Asido, and Hübner's inscription could equally well refer to one of these. Hübner's strongest evidence is the inscription found at Asido itself, which refers to *municipes* and *quattuorviri*, but neither of these factors need make us question Asido's colonial status. Aulus Gellius complains that virtually everyone, including the inhabitants of *coloniae*, habitually refer to themselves as *municipes*.[9] It might at first be thought that this habit would not manifest itself outside everyday speech; however, we do have evidence from a Trajanic inscription from Auximum in Italy, showing that this loose usage also appeared in more formal contexts. Here Auximum is referred to as a *municipium*, although it had been a *colonia* since *c.*128 BC.[10] A similar phenomenon is attested at Lepcis Magna in Tripolitania, where two inscriptions dating to long after the period when the town had obtained colonial status refer to

---

[6] Hübner, *CIL* 2 s.v. 'Asido'; *CIL* 2. 1315.

[7] *CIL* 2. 1305.   [8] Pliny, *NH* 3. 1. 11.   [9] Aulus Gellius, *NA* 16. 13.

[10] *CIL* 9. 5825.

the town as a *municipium*, not a *colonia*.[11] If the biography of Marcus Aurelius in *SHA* is amended to read that his father was born 'in municipio ⟨s⟩Ucubitano', which seems highly plausible, we have an example of a town of undisputed colonial status in Baetica itself being referred to as a *municipium*.[12] It is therefore possible that this loose usage of 'municipium' is being followed in the inscription from Asido.

Similarly, the long insisted-on differentiation between *quattuorviri* and *duoviri* does not seem to have been as exclusive as has often been thought. Indeed we can find evidence that the terms overlapped in the epigraphic record of Baetica itself. In his reply to the citizens of Sabora, Vespasian addresses the *quattuorviri* and *decuriones* of the town, but it is the *duoviri* who see to the public display of his letter.[13] Similarly at Ilipula Minor, a local dignitary appears to have been both a *quattuorvir* and a *duovir*.[14] It is possible that *quattuorviri* might have been a collective term for all four municipal magistrates. If a man reached the rank of *duovir*, or had acted specifically in that capacity, this fact would obviously be recorded. On the other hand, when all the town's magistrates were involved, *quattuorviri* may have been thought the most appropriate term. If this is the case, we can see how *quattuorvir* might have been thought a more dignified title than aedile, and so used in its place, by an individual who had only reached aedilician rank. Support for this proposed parallel usage of the two terms can be found in the fact that a *duovir*, M. Acilius Silo, is also attested at Asido, which ought not to be the case if Hübner is correct.[15] It seems, therefore, that there is no strong reason to challenge Asido's colonial status.

Our second problem concerns the status of Gades. It has been suggested that this town too was a *colonia*. The hypothesis stems from a coin published by Gómez Moreno, which bore a bilingual legend on its reverse, the Latin legend reading 'COL(onia) A(ugusta) GAD(itana)'.[16] However, Gómez now believes that the coin has been tampered with;[17] and this, along with an absence of other evidence for colonial status, combined with a reference to the town as the *Municipium Augustum Gaditanum* on a tombstone of a *duovir* of the town, M. Antonius Syriacus, found at Asido

[11] *IRT* 286 (Commodus), 544 (late 3rd–early 4th c. AD). The town became a *colonia* in the reign of Trajan.

[12] *SHA, Marcus* 1. 6.   [13] *CIL* 2. 1423.

[14] *CIL* 2. 1470 and p. 702, 'L. Flavius Gallus IVvir, IIvir bis . . .'

[15] *CIL* 2. 1314.

[16] M. Gómez Moreno, 'Divagaciones numismáticas', *Miscelaneas Historia—Arte—Arqueologia* (1949), 165. See also A. Beltrán, 'Sobre los Balbi y Cádiz', *A.e.A.* 25 (1952), 142–5.

[17] See also Galsterer, *Untersuchungen zum römischen Städtewesen*, 17 n. 6.

and dating from the Antonine period, which does seem to refer to its formal rank,[18] appears to rule out Gades' claim to colonial status.[19]

A third problem is found in a passage of Strabo. The geographer, after describing the *colonia* of Hispalis, says that despite remaining the trading centre of the district, τὸ ἐμπόριον, it had been outshone τῇ τιμῇ δὲ καὶ τῷ ἐποικῆσαι νεωστὶ τοὺς Καὶσαρος στρατιώτας ('in prestige, as imperial troops have recently made their home there') by a settlement named Βαῖτις, although this latter town was not heavily populated, οὐ συνοικουμένη λαμπρῶς.[20] This site, clearly settled by veterans, and so perhaps a *colonia* judging by Strabo's language, is never attested again. Strabo's use of νεωστί implies that the settlement took place in his own day, or shortly before, that is, in the reign of Augustus, or possibly that of Tiberius.

The lack of further attestations of Βαῖτις leads to an immediate suspicion that Strabo's text is corrupt here. Schulten[21] suggested that Βαῖτις ought to be corrected to read *Κόρδυβα. However, it is difficult to see how the provincial capital could be described as οὐ συνοικουμένη λαμπρῶς, so this solution appears untenable.

It has been postulated, as a further solution, that there were two *coloniae* on the site of present-day Seville, using two inscriptions which refer to the 'Scapharii Romulae consistentes' and 'Scapharii qui Romulae negotiantur' ('the lightermen based at/trading from Romula'), and contrasting them with a further inscription which refers to the 'Scapharii Hispalenses' ('the lightermen of Hispalis'). The use of both 'Hispalis' and 'Romula' implies, it is suggested, that *Romula* was a separate settlement from Hispalis.[22] This seems unlikely. Pliny refers to the *colonia* of Hispalis as 'Hispal colonia, cognomine Romulensis' ('the colony of Hispal, given the title of Romulensis'),[23] and probably both the old native name and the new colonial title remained in use. This was the case at Corduba, where there is no question of a second settlement, and where inscriptions refer to its

---

[18] *CIL* 2. 1313.

[19] The case for the authenticity of the coin has recently been raised again by Ma. Paz García-Bellido, who believes that Augustus raised Gades to the status of *colonia civium Romanorum* after the death of Agrippa. However, given the lack of further evidence, and that Columella (*RR* 7. 2. 4) and our epigraphic reference to the town is as a *municipium*, the hypothesis seems highly tenuous. See Ma. Paz García-Bellido, '¿Colonía Augusta Gaditana?', *A.e.A.* 61 (1988), 324 ff. On the other hand A. Burnett, M. Amandry, and P. Pau Ripollès reject the coin in their *Roman Provincial Coinage* (1992), i. 80.

[20] Strabo, 3. 2. 1.   [21] *FHA* (1952), vi. 154.

[22] *CIL* 2. 1168, 1169, 1180, with A. Blanco Freijeiro, *Historia de Sevilla*, i. *La ciudad antigua* (3rd edn., 1989), 119.

[23] Pliny, *NH* 3. 1. 11.

inhabitants equally as Cordubenses (the old native name of the town) and Patricienses (its new colonial title). Henderson's solution that Strabo is referring to a small additional deduction of troops by Augustus to the original Julian *colonia* of Hispalis seems a more plausible solution.[24] Such a settlement could have taken the form of a separate suburb with a distinctive name. This would explain the name given by Strabo, and his note that it was not a well-populated settlement. *Baῖτις* implies that the suburb would have been by the river, possibly on the opposite side to that of the main town, Henderson's preferred site, like the present-day suburb of Seville, Triana. Our evidence here is scanty; Triana has been tradition-ally regarded as the home of the late Roman martyrs Stas Justa and Rufina, but no Roman traces have been found in the admittedly limited excavations carried out in here, and no bridge appears to have been built across the river until AD 1171 in the reign of Yusuf Abu Ya'kb, which suggests that the city was confined to one bank of the river until this period.[25]

A final alternative solution is offered by two interesting series of *semisses* struck at Italica in the reign of Tiberius.[26] The obverse of these coins bears a bust of either Germanicus or Drusus, who were widely honoured on coins in Spain,[27] but it is the reverse design which draws attention. This displays two military *signa* and, in the centre of the field, a legionary eagle standard surmounted by a *vexillum*. Several dies were used for both of these series, and the slight variations in iconography are well recorded by Chaves Tristan, who dates the commencement of their issue to AD 19.[28]

The reverse design is not unusual in itself; similar ones are found at several Spanish towns.[29] But what is striking is that all these other sites are *coloniae*, and the coin-type appears to be related to the settlement of troops; on some issues the names of the legions appear beside the stand-ards. At Acci (the modern Guadix), *Colonia Iulia Gemella*, where, as its name suggests, veterans of two legions were settled, coins are found

[24] M. I. Henderson, 'Julius Caesar and Latium in Spain', *JRS* 32 (1942), 1–13.

[25] P. Gayangos, *A History of the Muhommaden Dynasties in Spain* (1840), i. 362–3 = n. 4 in bk. 1, ch. 3.

[26] See Vives, *La moneda hispánica*, iv. 125 ff., and F. Chaves Tristan, *Las monedas de Italica* (2nd edn., 1979), 68–71.

[27] Ibid. 29–30.

[28] Ibid.; discussion of die types, pp. 68 ff.; discussion of date, pp. 106, 108.

[29] Listed by Chaves Tristan, ibid. 31; see also L. Villaronga Garriga, *La numismática de la Hispánia antigua* (2nd edn., 1987), for Corduba, no. 1002; Carthago Nova, no. 1135; Ilici, no. 997; Caesaraugusta, nos. 1062, 1089, 1129; Acci, nos. 1000, 1114; Emerita, no. 1030.

bearing two eagle standards within the same general design to allude to the settlement of two legions.[30] Italica is the only known non-colonial town to issue coins of this type: its municipal, as opposed to colonial, status is made clear by the legend found on the reverse of these coins, 'Per Aug. Munic. Italic.' The most obvious solution to this anomaly is that Italica is recalling its own military foundation. The town was created in 206 BC by Scipio for troops wounded in the battle of Ilipa.[31] Nevertheless the Italian troops after whom the town was named would not, at this time, have been Roman citizens, the eagle had not yet become a symbol of the legions,[32] and there is no hint that the town enjoyed any special legal status after its foundation.[33] All in all it seems that coins struck by the town in the reign of Augustus displaying a standing soldier with the legend 'Roma' were a far more appropriate way of recording the town's martial history than the *semisses*.[34]

The combination of the *semisses* from Italica and the passage of Strabo appears to resolve the dilemma of Βαῖτις completely. A small settlement of veterans at Italica would not make the town a *colonia*, yet would allow it to use the reverse found on the *semisses* without this appearing out of place. Such a small settlement could easily lead to the town being described as οὐ συνοικουμένη λαπρῶς, and the town is sufficiently close to Hispalis to allow Strabo's comment that it outshone this town to make sense. It seems therefore that Strabo's manuscript can be best amended to read *Ἰτάλικα. The confusion in the manuscript probably arose because Strabo, after this sentence, immediately goes on to discuss Italica again, [35] leading a copyist to think that a mistake had been made in the transmission of the text here. However, Strabo's account probably relies on a list of towns from an earlier source, in which, quite rationally, Italica followed immediately after Hispalis. Strabo added a personal gloss concerning the recent settlement at Italica to his source's comments on Hispalis to make his own account more up to date, and consequently reverted to the order of towns found in his original source. The result is that Strabo appears to be repeating himself, but in fact is guilty only of poor editing.

Our final problem concerns the town of Munda. Pliny mentions Munda as a *colonia*, but is careful to use the past tense, 'fuit', of it. Strabo states

---

[30] Ibid., nos. 1000, 1114.   [31] Appian, *Ib.* 38.

[32] See Pliny, *NH* 10. 5. 16, for its institution by Marius.

[33] See the discussion in R. Knapp, Aspects *of the Roman Experience in Iberia* (1977), 111 ff.

[34] Vives, *La moneda hispánica*, type 1, p. 125; Villaronga Garriga, *La numismática de la Hispánia antigua*, no. 1007.

[35] Strabo, 3. 2. 2: Μετὰ δὲ ταύτας Ἰτάλικα καὶ Ἴλιπα ἐπὶ τῷ Βαῖτι . . . ('after these come Italica and Ilipa on the Baetis . . .').

that it was once the μητρόπολις of its area, but again is careful to use the past tense, κατέστη.[36] Colonial status was presumably lost after the battle of Munda, which ended the Civil Wars in Spain. The town does not seem to been totally destroyed, however, as Strabo, Pliny, and Orosius suggest its continuing existence.[37] The loss of colonial status was probably a punishment for backing the Pompeian side so vigorously (as Caesar settled not only his own, but also surrendered Pompeian, veterans in *coloniae*, this could explain the initially surprising disloyalty of the *colonia*). Alternatively it is possible that so many of the settlers had died in the fighting (Munda became a byword in the ancient world for a bloody battle), that it was no longer credible for the town to retain this status.

Pliny's list does therefore seem an accurate account of the *coloniae* to be found in Baetica in the Augustan period. Given that a colonial foundation was an act of state, it is not surprising to find that setting up such a settlement required a large amount of preparatory legislation. A law was required to establish the site and territory of the colony and the number of colonists, and to provide an official founder or 'deductor'. The *deductor* then led the colonists out to the site of their future home, oversaw the physical foundation of the town, and drafted the legal charter for the new *colonia*.[38]

This foundation process appears to have been accompanied with elaborate religious ritual. An augur drew a ceremonial diagram of the town on the earth with an unknotted wand, known as a *lituus*, naming the regions of the town and nearby landmarks as he did so. This process was known as *conregio*. He then ritually watched the skies to ensure that no evil omens had occurred, 'conspicio', while a *haruspex* also took omens by observing the liver of a sacrificed sheep.[39] Following this the boundary of the site was ploughed with a bronze plough, guided by a priest who would have his head veiled by his toga. The plough was drawn by a white heifer and bull, the latter yoked to the right, the former to the left. The ploughing took place in an anticlockwise direction, the bull on the outside symbolizing the strength of the community against external aggressors, and the heifer on the inside the hoped-for fertility of the community within. The plough was raised at the points on the boundary circuit where the gates of the city wall were to be built, and the earth turned by the plough was cast inside

[36] Pliny, *NH* 3. 1. 12; Strabo, 3. 2. 2.
[37] Ibid. (the use of διεχει); Pliny, *NH* 36. 134; Orosius, 6. 16. 9.
[38] See the discussion in E. Hardy, *Three Spanish Charters and Other Documents* (1912), 8–10.
[39] Varro, *LL* 7. 9.

the circuit to form the ritual beginnings of the city wall. This rite of ploughing was acknowledged by the Romans to be Etruscan in origin.[40] Some other ritual acts are also recorded, such as the digging of a ritual pit at the centre of the city known as the *mundus*.[41] This was dug into the virgin earth, and fruit,[42] other 'good things',[43] and soil from the settlers' native land were placed in it.[44] It was then covered by a stone, and had a ritual fire lit over it, so becoming the 'focus' of the city.[45] It may have been at this last ceremony that the town was officially named. According to John Lydus the *lituus* was used for this purpose (presumably the trumpet of this name, not the augur's staff).[46] The naming would have involved the giving of three names: the public, the secret, and the priestly. Rome itself was said to possess three such names, and the Elder Pliny records the execution of a certain Valerius Soranus for revealing one of the forbidden names.[47]

How many of these ancient rituals were still performed in the late first century BC? Vitruvius hints that some may have been dispensed with, as he states: 'Itaque etiam atque veterem revocandam censeo' ('and so I advise that the old custom be revived') when talking about the sacrifices of the *haruspices*,[48] suggesting that such sacrifices were no longer carried out in his day. Moreover, Vitruvius is not so much concerned with the religious aspects of the sacrifice as that it be performed for a rationalized purpose: namely to see if the climate of the proposed site is healthy. Similarly the *agrimensor* (surveyor) Siculus Flaccus talks of 'maiores nostri' ('our ancestors') sacrificing at boundary markers as if this practice no longer went on in his day.[49] Again, as the majority of *coloniae* in Baetica were on previously occupied sites, it could be asked if many of the rituals listed above were relevant.

Nevertheless there is evidence that some ritual did continue. The weakest evidence for this is the depiction of the ploughing ceremony on coins. This is found on the coins of *coloniae* in Lusitania and Tarraconenesis, such as Emerita and Caesaraugusta.[50] However, the use of this motif does not seem to be connected directly with the act of foundation itself; at Caesaraugusta it was used up to the end of local minting in the reign of Caligula. It also appears on the coins of purely titular colonies,

[40] Ibid. 5. 143; Servius, *Ad Aen.* 5. 755.   [41] Plutarch, *Vit. Rom.* 11.
[42] Ovid, *Fasti* 4. 821.   [43] Festus, s.v. 'Quadrata Roma'.
[44] Plutarch, *Vit. Rom.* 11.   [45] Ovid, *Fasti*, 4. 823–4.
[46] John Lydus, *De Mensibus* (ed. Bekker), 4. 50, pp. 85–6.   [47] Pliny, *NH* 3. 5. 65.
[48] Vitruvius, 1. 4. 9–10.   [49] Siculus Flaccus, *De Cond. Agr.* (ed. Thulin), p. 105.
[50] *MI* Emerita, no. 994, Caesaraugusta, no. 325.

such as that of Rome itself when it was renamed Colonia Aeliana by Commodus, and so seems merely to have been a useful way of depicting a town's status as a *colonia*, rather than denoting that a ritual had actually been performed. None of the *coloniae* in Baetica has this image on its surviving coins; some, however, do depict priestly items such as the *lituus* used in the rituals of founding a *colonia*, which again are best seen merely as indicators of the town's status.[51]

Better evidence for the continuation of ritual comes from Tacitus' account of Vespasian's rededication of the Capitol after it had been burnt down in the battle for Rome. Here many of the *mundus* rituals appear to have continued.[52] Our best evidence, however, comes from the colonial law of Urso. Chapter 73, dealing with burial regulations, begins with the prohibition: 'Ne quis intra fines oppidi colon(iae)ve, qua aratro circum-ductum erit, hominem mortuom inferto' ('no one is to bring a dead body within the boundaries of the town or colony which have been marked out by the plough'); an actual ploughing ritual is thus implied. The grammar of this phrase is strange. The disjunctive '-ve' suffix should indicate that two separate classes of towns, 'oppida' and 'coloniae', are being con-sidered, rather than just the *oppidum*, that is, the urban centre, of the *colonia*.

Nevertheless nothing indicates that towns other than *coloniae* had the ploughing ceremony performed at their foundation.[53] Only the coins of *coloniae* use this symbol, including titular ones. The latter would have used an unambiguously colonial motif to advertise their status, strongly suggesting that the ploughing ritual itself was exclusive to *coloniae*. It is best to assume an error in the engraving of the *Lex Ursonensis* here, the most likely mistake being the addition of the '-ve' suffix to the phrase 'oppidum colon(iae)', which refers to the urban centre of the *colonia*, and occurs in other chapters of the law, for example chapter 75. An emenda-tion removing the '-ve' would leave the ploughing ceremony as the sole preserve of *coloniae*, and is highly attractive.

As Urso was a *colonia* founded on a site already occupied, its charter shows that foundation rituals did take place at such locations. From the excavated remains of Iberian houses here it seems that the *colonia* was built directly over the old Iberian settlement. Similarly Corduba and Hispalis were built over previous sites of those names. These two towns already had Roman *conventus* prior to colonization, and this was probably

---

[51] *MI* Emerita, no. 956 (Corduba), no. 1030 (Acci).   [52] Tacitus, *Hist.* 4. 53.

[53] Other towns were not founded *ex novo* like *coloniae*, even if this was only in a technical sense, and hence the ceremony would have been meaningless for them.

the case at Urso too, as some members of a Caesarian delegation, said to have been composed of 'equites Romani et senatores', to the town, are referred to as 'eius civitatis' ('of that town'), suggesting the presence of a *conventus.*[54]

There was no one particular physical type of *colonia*: some, as mentioned above, were founded directly on the site of a previous settlement, the effects of which will be examined below, while others were built alongside pre-existing settlements. At Astigi[55] and Tucci[56] Pliny records the existence of 'vetus' settlements of the same name, suggesting that these *coloniae* were built near an older native settlement, but not directly on top of it. All the *coloniae* of Baetica are of one or other of these two types.

Whatever the extent of religious ritual involved in the foundation of the colonies, the land allocated to them was strictly delineated, a specialized task carried out by the *agrimensores*, or professional land-surveyors.[57] The first step of this process was to determine the two cardinal axes on which the allocated land was to be divided. Ideally their intersection would be fixed to lie at the centre of the new settlement, the land then being allotted in regular blocks. The distribution of land was not performed on a basis of equality, but according to rank. Hyginus notes that *coloniae* were founded 'cum signis et aquila et primis ordinibus ac tribunis' ('with the standards, eagle, senior NCOs and tribunes') and that 'modus agri pro portione officii dabatur' ('the amount of land was allocated in accordance with rank').[58] The quality of the land was also taken into account when determining the size of the allotments.[59]

Coloniae founded on pre-existing sites could present problems for the *agrimensores*. Although Hyginus states that the centre of the city is the 'ratio pulcherrima' ('best place') from which to perform cadastration, he concedes that when 'vetusta municipia in ius coloniae transferuntur, stantibus iam muris et ceteribus moenibus, limites primos nisi a foris accipere non possunt' ('when old towns are given the rank of *coloniae* and there are already town walls and other structures present, the starting-points for cadastration have to be outside the town').[60] Such advice might be thought only to refer to towns which were to receive an honorific grant of the title *colonia*; however, the *colonia* of Ilici in Tarraconensis shows that this

[54] Ps. Caes., *B. Hisp.* 22.   [55] Pliny, *NH* 3. 1. 12.   [56] Ibid. 3. 1. 10.
[57] For a general survey, see O. A. W. Dilke, *The Roman Land Surveyors* (1971).
[58] Hyginus Gromaticus, *Constitutio* (ed. Thulin), p. 141.
[59] Siculus Flaccus, *De Cond. Agr.* (ed. Thulin), p. 120.
[60] Hyginus Gromaticus, pp. 143–4.

practice was also followed when dealing with non-Roman communities. At Ilici the clearly marked centuriation system is not centred on the town itself, which retained its old Iberian street-plan, but, as Hyginus suggests in these circumstances, is centred on a point just outside the city. While the cadastration of Ilici is traceable today, this, unfortunately, is not true at the vast majority of Spanish colonial sites, where the Roman field-pattern has been obliterated by later Arab and Renaissance land-allotment systems.[61]

The centuriation of the *territorium* of Ilici is most marked in the fertile lowland areas near the *colonia* itself, for example the plain of Vinalopo. This has led to the hypothesis that the native inhabitants of Ilici were displaced onto the less fertile areas of its territory. No doubt there is some truth in this, but the loss of traces of centuriation in the outlying areas may simply be because of the nature of the ground there. Equally, parts of Ilici's *territorium* may not have been centuriated. Agennius Urbicus states that there are two forms of *subseciva*, or land left over after centuriation; one is found in the centuriated area itself, the other comprises land which although it was within the *territorium* of a colony lay outside the area that had been centuriated.[62] According to his colleague, Julius Frontinus, this latter form of *subseciva* was not uncommon, 'Multis enim locis adsignationi agrorum inmanitas superfuit' ('in many places the size of the fields surpasses the area of centuriated land').[63]

But there can be no doubt that expulsions did occur. The legal process of *deditio*, or unconditional surrender to Rome, regarded the surrendering party as having forfeited all rights to their land.[64] The land could then be restored to its previous owners, but this was at the discretion of Rome. Siculus Flaccus talks of cases 'cum pulsi essent populi, et deducerentur coloniae' ('when the inhabitants are driven out and colonies founded'),[65] and Tacitus remarks that the *colonia* built at Camulodunum (Colchester) in Britain was constructed on 'agros captivos' ('conquered land').[66] As well as expulsions at the initial foundation of a *colonia*, further encroachments on native land may have occurred. The best evidence for this is Tacitus' account of the *colonia* at Camulodunum. Here we are told that the colo-

---

[61] V. González Pérez, 'La centuriatio de Ilici', in A. López Gómez (ed.), *Estudios sobre centuriaciones romanas en España* (1974), 101 ff.

    [62] Agennius Urbicus, *De Controv. Agr.* (ed. Thulin), p. 41.

    [63] Frontinus, *De Controv. Agr.* (ed. Thulin), p. 9.

    [64] See R. López Melero *et al.*, 'El bronce de Alcántara: Una *deditio* del 104 a.C.', *Gerión*, 2 (1984), 265 ff.

    [65] Siculus Flaccus, *De Cond. Agr.* (ed. Thulin), p. 128.

    [66] Tacitus, *Ann.* 12. 32. 4.

nists 'pellebant domibus, exturbabant agris, captivos, servos appellando' the former inhabitants ('drove them from their homes and banished them from their fields calling them prisoners and slaves').[67] The use of the imperfect tense hints that these dispossessions persisted over a period of time rather than that they were a single act of depredation. Moreover the colonists' acts were condoned by local units of the army 'spe eiusdem licentiae' ('hoping that the same licence would be exercised in the future'), suggesting the practice need not have been uncommon, albeit the level at Colchester may have been exceptional.

Cadastration would have had a major effect on the native population around the *coloniae*, radically transforming the adjacent environment. In the most severe cases it would have deprived some of the indigenous population of their ancestral lands and homes. Others may have retained their land within the new system. Hyginus, for example, defines 'divisi et adsignati agri' ('allotted land') as that which 'veteranis *aliisve* personis per centurias certo modo adscripto, aut dati sunt aut redditi qui[?ve?] *veteribus possessoribus* redditi commutati pro suis sunt' ('land given or assigned to veterans or other individuals in fixed allotments or that which has been assigned to the former owners having been exchanged for their own').[68] This process can be seen at Ilici, where the settlements within the *colonia*'s *territorium* tend to be aligned on the boundaries of the centuriation blocks. As importantly, centuriation will have caused a major change in the way land was registered and regarded in the province. Communities adjacent to the *coloniae* would have had to define their land in terms acceptable to Rome.[69] This could have been a result of a mass centuriation of the province, such as occurred in Tunisia,[70] undertaken when the Spanish *coloniae* were deducted. However, it is equally possible that the process in Spain was a slower, *ad hoc* phenomenon, with towns with *territoria* adjacent to *coloniae* rather than the whole province initially being affected.

The town of Ostippo may provide an example of this process. At El Moralito traces of centuriation on two different alignments have been found. These probably mark the boundary of the *territoria* of Ostippo and the neighbouring *colonia* of Urso. A Claudian inscription marking the *terminus agrorum decumanorum* of Ostippo has been found here.[71] Ostippo,

---

[67] Ibid. 14. 31. 5.   [68] Hyginus Gromaticus, *De Cond. Agr.* (ed. Thulin), p. 80.

[69] A further incentive would have been that this would have helped prevent the creeping encroachment of *coloniae* as described above.

[70] R. Chevallier, 'Essai de chronologie des centuriations romaines de Tunisie', *MEFRA* 70 (1958), 61 ff. See also A. Piganiol, *Atlas des centuriations romaines de Tunisie* (1954) and Dilke, *The Roman Land Surveyors*, 151 ff., esp. fig. 42.

[71] *CIL* 2. 1438.

an *oppidum liberum* at this time,[72] probably centuriated its land in response to the cadastration carried out at Urso, and is unlikely to have been the only native town to respond in this way. The *coloniae* therefore would be responsible for the gradual introduction of Roman-style land-use. Although Frontinus strictly states that 'ager ergo divisus adsignatus est coloniarum' ('centuriated land therefore belongs to *coloniae*'),[73] traces of centuriation have been found in the *territoria* of unprivileged sites in Spain such as Basti,[74] and seem to be examples of the voluntary adoption of Roman practice. In Italy, too, cadastration identical in type to colonial cadastration is found around non-colonial sites,[75] despite instructions by the *agrimensores* that local tradition should be followed here.[76] A commentary on Frontinus, attributed to Agennius, glosses Frontinus' comments on centuriated land, quoted above, with 'sive municipiis' ('or to *municipia*').[77] This implies, like the archaeological remains, that centuriation was not exclusive to *coloniae*. The best conclusion here, to avoid a clash with Frontinus, is that whereas *coloniae* had *adsignatus* land from their inception, *municipia* could have their land centuriated if they so wished. This would make *adsignatus* land found in the provinces at non-colonial sites a sign of adoption of Roman methods of land division, produced either by the pressure of a colonial site nearby, as suggested above, or as a voluntary act to seek enhanced status.

One feature of colonial land allotments in Spain which would probably have been unique to them was the granting of *praefecturae*, or tracts of land which were not contiguous to the main body of colonial *territorium*.[78] At Valdecaballeros, in the province of Badajoz, a boundary marker has been found marking off the territories of Emerita and Ucubi.[79] The marker is 120 km. to the east of Emerita and 182 km. to the north of Ucubi. It seems impossible that it could be in the continuous *territorium* of either

---

[72] Pliny, *NH* 3. 1. 12.   [73] Frontinus, *De Agr. Qual.* (ed. Thulin), p. 1.

[74] G. M. Cano García, 'Sobre una posible centuriatio en el regado de la acequia de Monteada', in López Gómez, *Estudios sobre centuriaciones romanas*, 115–27.

[75] J. Bradford, *Ancient Landscapes* (1957), ch. 4.

[76] Siculus Flaccus, *De Cond. Agr.* (ed. Thulin), p. 103. See the comments of Dilke, *The Roman Land Surveyors*, pp. 141, 178.

[77] Ps. Agennius, *Commentatum* (ed. Thulin), p. 53.

[78] Various non-colonial towns in Italy were assigned lands in other *provinciae*; Atella, for example, possessed land in Gaul (Cicero, *Ad Fam.* 13. 7. 1), and Augustus granted land at Knossos on Crete to Capua (Dio, 49. 14. 5). However, this was probably due to the higher status of Italian towns in Roman eyes and is unlikely to have been repeated in the case of provincial towns. The only parallel we have from Spain is the assignment of the Mauretanian tribe, the Icositani, to the *colonia* Ilici; see N. Mackie, 'Augustan Colonies in Mauretania', *Historia*, 32 (1983), 332 ff.

[79] *CIL* 2. 656.

colonia, as there are too many intervening settlements. Rather it seems to have been an enclave given to these two *coloniae*. Presumably there were valuable mines here which would generate extra income for them. Suetonius remarks on Caesar's habit of not settling veterans *en bloc* to avoid mass dispossessions, but this is in an Italian context, and it is hard to believe that the Roman authorities would care about provincial feelings in the same way.[80] More significant is the fact that this area lay in Lusitania, so the *territorium* of Ucubi straddles two provinces. If the normal functions of revenue-raising and exercising jurisdiction were supposed to be carried out by the magistrates of the *colonia*, this must have caused considerable inconvenience and perhaps required some special arrangements.

Festus notes that a *praefectura* is a place where 'ius dicebatur et nundinae agebantur et erat quaedam respublica neque tamen magistratus suos habebant' ('courts and markets are held and there is a form of settlement, but one which doesn't have its own magistrates'). This would fit the situation of Valdecaballeros very well. However, Festus seems to envisage *praefecturae* as existing only in Italy. In contrast to this though, the *agrimensor* Agennius Urbicus makes it clear that such *praefecturae* could exist outside Italy, and suggests they are exclusive to colonies, stating: 'Coloniae quoque loca quaedam habent adsignata in alienis finibus, quae loca solemus praefecturas appellare. Harum praefecturarum proprietas manifeste ad colonos pertinet non ad eos quorum fines sunt diminuti' ('Colonies have some allotted land in the territory of other communities. Such places we call *praefecturae*. The ownership of these *praefecturae* clearly falls to the inhabitants of the colony and not to those whose territory is lessened by their creation').[81] Siculus Flaccus goes on to add that the *coloniae* had legal jurisdiction over these enclaves in the manner described by Festus: 'magistratus coloniarum iuris dictionis mittere soliti sunt' ('Normally magistrates of the colony are sent there to give justice').[82] A combination of Festus and the *agrimensores* therefore appears to explain the nature of these *praefecturae*. The dispatch of magistrates to them, however, must have been awkward for the *colonia* concerned. The distance and difficult terrain must have made the journey from Ucubi to Valdecaballeros a thankless, and possibly even dangerous task, for the *magistri* chosen at Ucubi.

Ucubi's enclave in Lusitania is paralleled by one of Emerita in Baetica. At the Hito de Montemolin a stone has been recovered recording the

---

[80] Suetonius, *Vit. Div. Iul.* 38.
[81] Agennius Urbicus, *De Controv. Agr.* (ed. Thulin), p. 40.
[82] Siculus Flaccus, *De Cond. Agr.* (ed. Thulin), p. 124.

terminus [Augus]talis [Em]erite[nsium].[83] This is 100 km. south of Emerita and in Baetica. Again some form of revenue must have accrued from this land for it to have been allotted to a distant *colonia*.[84] Three more such *praefecturae* are attested as belonging to Emerita, a *praefectura Turgaliensis* (the present-day Trujillo, 200 km. from Emerita), the *praefectura Mulli-censis* (site unknown), and a third unnamed *praefectura*.[85] Other such *praefecturae* may have been assigned to *coloniae* in Baetica. These would have spread the adoption of Roman land-use, as the land around the *praefectura* would have to be defined in order to delineate the *praefectura* itself. Presumably Roman legal forms in general too would have come into use among the native population, as they would have fallen under the jurisdiction of the *coloniae* which possessed Roman law codes and would have been visited by the colonial magistrates, or their deputies.

The settlement of the *coloniae* in the province therefore would have had significant effects on the life of the local inhabitants: these would have included the loss of land in some cases and its redefinition in others, and the adoption of some Roman customs and legal forms, especially in those regions which feel directly under colonial control. Given this impact, can we see the *coloniae* as having an active Romanizing purpose? It could be argued that Tacitus hints at this when he speaks of the *colonia* at Colchester as 'subsidium adversus rebellis et imbuendis sociis ad officia legum' ('a defence against rebels and a way of impressing upon our allies their obligations to the law'). This can be taken as having a positive aspect.[86] However, a more pessimistic interpretation is also possible. 'Officium' has the sense of obligation, whether legal or otherwise.[87] Caesar certainly uses the word with overtones of subjection: 'huic [i.e. Labienus] mandat, Remos reliquosque Belgas adeat atque in *officio* (Romanorum) contineat' ('he commanded him to advance into the territory of the Remi and other Belgae and hold them to their obligations to Rome').[88] The context of these two passages is the same, namely that a holding operation is being carried out while the main military emphasis is switched elsewhere. Tacitus may have used the phrase seeing its ambiguity, but the tenor of his

---

[83] P. Sillières, 'Centuriation et voie romaine au sud de Merida', *MCV* 18 1 (1982), 437–48.

[84] The site lies near both silver mines and marble quarries.

[85] Hyginus Gromaticus, *Constitutio* (ed. Thulin), p. 136.

[86] Tacitus, *Ann.* 12. 32. 5. For an optimistic approach, see M. Grant's translation (Penguin, 1978): '[to] familiarize the provincials with law-abiding government'.

[87] H. Furneaux (*The Annals of Tacitus* (1891), ii. 256 n. 4) is nearer the sense than Grant with his translation: 'to familiarise the subjects with the due performance of legal duties'.

[88] Caesar, *BG* 3. 11.

work in general suggests that the implication of a civilizing mission by Rome on the historian's part is, at best, ironical. Similarly 'imbuere', although it can mean 'train' in a positive sense, is often used in a pejorative sense meaning to 'taint' or 'stain'.

Other literary references to *coloniae* carry no implications that the *coloniae* had the positive purpose of changing the lifestyle of the local inhabitants. The early *coloniae* established in Italy are called 'propugnacula imperii' ('outposts of the empire') by Cicero,[89] a phrase echoed by Appian when he calls those established by Sulla φϱούϱια ('garrisons') in a context which shows they were a punitive measure.[90] This attitude did not change in the imperial period. Hyginus regards *coloniae* as one of the spoils of the victors in war,[91] while Siculus Flaccus regards their purpose as 'ad ipsos priores municipiorum populos coercendos, vel ad hostium incursos repellendos' ('to keep the previous inhabitants of the towns in order or to repel incursions by enemies').[92]

The *coloniae* in Spain were founded at a time of extreme social tension in the political history of Rome, and it is best to attribute their creation not to a desire to 'Romanize' the provinces as part of an empire-wide master plan, as has sometimes been done in the case of Caesar, but rather to a wish to defuse a highly dangerous political situation by satisfying the aspirations of the two most powerful and volatile groups in the Roman body politic, the urban mob and the army. This makes praise of Caesar and the early years of Augustus' rule for setting up colonies misplaced. *Coloniae* were created by necessity, not choice, and there is no reason to believe that Caesar would have embarked on a programme of colonization had he not been confronted with the particular circumstances of his time. One of the arguments Dio attributes to Caesar in support of his colonization programme in Italy, is that it would alleviate the danger of rioting at Rome.[93] The confiscations of land necessary to set up *coloniae* were highly unpopular. It has already been noted how Caesar tried to avoid mass confiscations in Italy.[94] Augustus' sequestration of land for this purpose

---

[89] Cicero, *De Leg. Agr.* 2. 27; cf. his attitude to the *colonia* of Narbo in Gaul, *Pro Fonteio* 13.

[90] Appian, *BC* 1. 96: ταῖς πλείοσι [i.e. the Italian cities] τοὺς ἑαυτῷ στρατευσαμένους ἐπῴκιζεν ὡς ἕξων φϱούϱια κατὰ τῆς Ἰταλίας τήν τε γῆν αὐτῶν καὶ τὰ οἰκήματα ἐς τούσδε μεταφέϱων διεμέϱιζεν ('He settled soldiers who had served with him in most of the (Italian) towns in order to establish garrisons throughout Italy. He took their land and houses from the original inhabitants and divided them up among his men').

[91] Hyginus Gromaticus, *Constitutio* (ed. Thulin), p. 140.

[92] Siculus Flaccus, *De Cond. Agr.* (ed. Thulin), p. 99.   [93] Dio, 38. 1. 1.

[94] Suetonius, *Vit. Div. Iul.* 38.

when he was a *triumvir* took a long time to live down.[95] Not surprisingly, colonists were extremely unpopular with the previous inhabitants of an area. Cicero records a dispute between the two groups at Pompeii,[96] and makes great play with the injustice of colonization in his speeches against Rullus' land bill.[97] Perhaps the strongest statement of hostility to colonization comes in a speech attributed to Caesar by Appian. Here Caesar says that he will not behave as Sulla, ἀφαιρούμενος ἑτέρων ἣν ἔχουσι καὶ τοῖς ἀφαιρεθεῖσι τοὺς λαβόντας συνοικίζων καὶποιῶν ἀλλήλοις ἐς ἀεὶ πολεμίους ('taking away from those who were the owners and settling alongside those who had been deprived of their land those who had taken it making the two groups enemies for ever'). The phrase ἐς ἀεὶ ('for ever') underlines the strength of feeling generated by colonization.[98] Hatred of colonization can also be seen in the rejoicing which followed Augustus' introduction of cash gratuities for veterans rather than giving them grants of land.[99]

It made sense, therefore, to settle colonists abroad whenever possible. This would have mollified Italian opinion, and, given the number of communities who had supported the wrong side in the Civil Wars, have allowed confiscation without any need for compensation, saving considerable sums of money as well as reputations. Baetica must have been a prime site for colonization, as all of it, save the town of Ulia, had defected to the Pompeian cause in the Civil Wars.[100] In addition to this, although the province was not entirely safe from attack (for example, a Moorish incursion from Mauretania led by Bogud occurred in 38 BC, after many of the colonies had been founded[101]), much of the land was extremely fertile and hence ideal for settlement.

Tsirkin sees the colonization programme in Spain as a punitive measure, contrasting the colonies with the towns listed with honorary titles by the Elder Pliny (the latter, he suggests, obtained their titles as a reward for their loyalty).[102] Ulia's title of *Julia Fidentia* supports Tsirkin's views, but many other towns which defected from Caesar also obtained honorary titles. One solution is to see these as being granted to towns which quickly reverted to the Caesarian cause without armed resistance. However, the theory is faced with a more serious problem in the fact that

[95] Virgil, *Ecl.* 1. 9; Suetonius, *Vit. Div. Aug.* 13.   [96] Cicero, *Pro Sulla* 21.
[97] Cicero, *De Leg. Agr.* 2. 17. 45–6.   [98] Appian, *BC* 2. 13. 94.
[99] Dio, 54. 25. 5–6.   [100] Dio, 43. 31. 4.   [101] Dio, 48. 45. 1.
[102] J. Tsirkin, 'The South of Spain in the Civil War of 40–45 [*sic*] BC', *A.e.A.* 54 (1981), 81–100. See also Hardy's comments on the foundation of a *colonia* at Urso, *Three Spanish Charters*, 7.

although Carthago Nova in Tarraconensis remained loyal to Caesar, holding out against a siege by Pompeian forces,[103] a colony was still founded there. One possible reason for this could be the availability of *ager publicus*, which had existed near the town before the Civil Wars, as attested by Cicero.[104] However, this land may not have been agricultural, but connected with the nearby silver mines.[105] Despite these problems, Tsirkin's account of these titles is more satisfactory than that of Henderson, which has been adopted by scholars such as Nicolet and González, and sees the titles as evidence of a grant of Latin colonial status.[106]

Another advantage of the foundations was that the new loyal settlers could be used to keep watch over the old inhabitants of the former *conventus* who had been behind much of the pro-Pompeian activity in the area. Four *coloniae*, Corduba, Hispalis, Hasta Regia, and Urso, definitely had Roman citizens of this sort already living in them, and this may have been also true of Ucubi. Therefore the colonists would act as a safeguard, as well as a punishment. The relations between members of the existing *conventus* and the new colonists, many of whom may well have been below them in social status,[107] is not recorded; but it would be surprising had there been no hostility.

The geographical position of the *coloniae* also suggests that changing the pattern of native life was not a prime consideration when they were established. The majority command important strategic sites in the province. Corduba stands at the head of the navigable portion of the Baetis river, near extensive silver mines; and since it was already regarded as the most important settlement in the province,[108] the placing of a *colonia* here was inevitable. Hispalis was similarly located near mines, and stood at the head of the stretch of the Baetis navigable to sea-going ships. Astigi too stood at the head of a navigable river, commanded a pass through the Andalusian Corderilla to Malaca and the Mediterranean, and was situated in one of the richest agricultural areas in the province. Tucci overlooked the route to Iliberris, and looked up across to the Despeñaperros Depression, the major route from Baetica into the central uplands of Spain. Hübner, in his introduction to the inscriptions of the town, describes it as

---

[103] Dio, 43. 30. 1.   [104] Cicero, *De Leg. Agr.* 1. 2. 5., 2. 19. 51.
[105] Nevertheless Strabo (3. 2. 10) notes that the mines of Carthago Nova had passed into private hands (εἰς ἰδιωτικὰς μετέστασαν κτήσεις). Depending on the date of this reference the *ager publicus* at Carthago Nova could therefore have been agricultural land.
[106] This issue is discussed at length in Ch. 5.
[107] Men of equestrian and perhaps senatorial rank are attested as members of the *conventus* at Urso, Ps. Caes., *B. Hisp.* 22, and Hasta Regia, ibid. 26.
[108] Ps. Caes., *B. Hisp.* 3. 1.

possessing a dominant and naturally fortified location and makes similar remarks of Ucubi. The strategic position of Itucci had been appreciated since the times of the Viriatic Wars in the second century BC.[109] Acci (in Baetica when founded) commanded another pass through the Andalusian Cordillera running down to the Mediterranean at Almeria. The other colonies overlooked stretches of immensely fertile land. This availability of land, combined with the fact that its previous owners had backed the wrong side in the Civil Wars, has probably more to do with the disproportionate number of *coloniae* in Baetica compared to the other provinces of Spain, than factors concerned with the level of civilization of the natives of the region. The land, because of its fertility, was more valuable to Rome than the rest of Spain, especially as there were rich mineral resources in this area as well; and such advantages meant that it would be easier to persuade veterans to settle here, and hence that there was a greater chance of the *coloniae* being successful. Moreover it must be remembered that large areas of Spain were still unsubdued and therefore too dangerous for settlement. Pliny states that all the *coloniae* in the judicial *conventus* of Astigi had the tax-exemption of *immunitas*.[110] He makes no mention of this right when talking about the *coloniae* of the other judicial *conventus* of the province, but given the partial nature of his survey nothing can be inferred from this. In Lusitania both Emerita and Pax Iulia received the even more desirable exemption of the *ius Italicum*.[111] These concessions were probably to encourage long-term settlement in the *coloniae*, and prevent the sort of drift described by Tacitus, suggesting that their primary function was regarded as military.

Finally, the nature of the colonists themselves makes it unlikely that they were seen as cultural ambassadors for Rome.[112] The majority of the *coloniae* were settled by legionary veterans, as has been seen above. Tacitus, while describing the collapse of Neronian colonies at Tarentum and Antium, notes that this had been the case in the good old days when 'universae legiones deducebantur cum tribunis et centurionibus et sui cuiusque ordinis militibus' ('whole legions had been settled together along with their tribunes and centurions all grouped into their proper centuries').[113] He believed that the new settlements failed because those settled there were from different units and so lacked group loyalty, many settlers simply drifting away. It would be surprising if this phenomenon of

---

[109] Appian, *Ib*. 66.   [110] Pliny, *NH* 3. 1. 12.   [111] *Digest* (Paulus) 50. 15. 8.
[112] For problems with this assumption at a slightly later period, see Millett's comments on colonization in Britain, *The Romanization of Britain*, 87.
[113] Hyginus Gromaticus, *Constitutio* (ed. Thulin), p. 141; Tacitus, *Ann*. 14. 27.

drift did not also occur to some extent in earlier colonial foundations. The more ambitious and wealthy colonists may have decided that life in Rome was better than that in Spain and sold up. This would leave behind the poorer ordinary troops who, although they would not be absorbed into their new surroundings as rapidly as they would have done had they been settled separately, would not be the best propagators of Roman culture.

In addition, some of the veterans settled in Spain were not ethnic Romans themselves. Emerita was colonized by veterans of the Fifth *Alaudae* and Tenth *Gemina* legions. The former was certainly, and the latter possibly, recruited from Gauls, and so the colonists' Roman credentials themselves would not have been perfect. This may have been true of a substantial number of veterans, given the irregular recruitment practices of the Civil War period. In addition to this, Caesar settled large numbers of the Roman poor abroad. In Spain this can be seen in chapter 105 of the *Lex Ursonensis*, which allows freedmen to become *decuriones*. Again it is legitimate to doubt whether such colonists would be effective exporters of Roman culture: the inhabitants of a similar colony established by Caesar at Corinth became notorious for grave robbing, and plundering the ruins of old Corinth for antiques to sell.[114]

Our evidence therefore leads to the conclusion that *coloniae* were not founded with a 'Romanizing' purpose in mind. Nevertheless this is not to say that they did not fulfil such a role unintentionally. One way of seeing if this did happen is to observe to what extent they lived up to being the *effigies* and *simulacra* of Rome that Aulus Gellius claimed they were.

We are fortunate in having the partial remains of the legal charter of Urso. Although our copy of this document dates from the time of Domitian, it appears to be substantially unchanged from the time of the law's original promulgation at the foundation of the *colonia*, and so offers a unique insight into colonial life of this period.[115]

One proviso has to be borne in mind: although the *Lex Ursonensis* is a document specifically designed for one particular town, it contains many tralatitious elements within it. This can be seen, for example, from references to a *Lex Julia* in chapters 97 and 104.[116] If this is the case, it is legitimate to speculate to what extent these modified general laws coincid-

---

[114] Strabo, 8. 6. 23.
[115] E. Gabba, 'Rifflessioni sulla Lex Coloniae Genetivae Iuliae', in González and Arce (eds.), *Estudios sobre la Tabula Siarensis*, 157 ff. Contra M. W. Fredriksen, 'The Republican Municipal Laws: Errors and Drafts', *JRS* 55 (1965), 183–98.
[116] See Hardy, *Three Spanish Charters*, 8 f.

ed with the reality of the situation as found at Urso, and to what degree its provisions were, or could be, enforced there.[117]

The manuscripts of Pliny refer to Urso as 'Urso quae Genua Urbanorum'. 'Genua' is a corruption of 'Genetiva' and it has been held that 'Urbanorum' too is a corruption, of 'Ursonensium'. This reading has been challenged on the grounds that a *colonia* for the urban poor was set up at Corinth, as has been seen above, and that chapter 105 of the town's charter, allowing freedmen to hold municipal office,[118] makes it likely that Urso was another example of such a *colonia*.

Sutherland divides the Spanish *coloniae* into two types, military and civilian, suggesting that the civilian *coloniae* were Urso, Ucubi, Itucci, and Hispalis.[119] However, an inscription found at Urso, dating from the Caesarian period, records a 'L. Vettius C.f. centur(io) Leg(ionis) XXX, IIvir iterum c.c.C.Iul.' ('L. Vettius, son of Caius, centurion of the Thirtieth Legion, *duovir* twice of the colonists of the colonia Claritas? Iulia').[120] If the abbreviation of the town name was amended to read *c.c.G.Iul.*, a very minor correction, an expansion to 'c(olonorum) c(oloniae) G(enetivae) Iul(iae)', would be possible (this form of abbreviation appears at several points in the charter, e.g. chapter 65), in which case it appears that some veterans were settled at Urso. If the inscription is to be taken as it stands, the natural expansion is *c.c.* C(*laritatis*) Iul(*iae*), that is, Ucubi, another of Sutherland's postulated civilian colonies. At Hispalis, also believed by Sutherland to be a civilian colony, a dedication by the *coloni* and *incolae* to L. Blatius Ventinus, aedile, *duovir*, and military tribune of the Fifth and Tenth *Gemina* legions, has been found.[121] This could suggest a military component to the colonial body, although in this case perhaps Blatius was part of the Augustan deduction of Βαῖτις, discussed above, rather than of the original Caesarian deduction. In all events, however, it appears that colonial foundations were not neatly divided into military and civilian settlements as Sutherland suggests. This distinction is therefore not helpful. What can be examined, however, is the nature of the community established by the charter.

The *Lex* shows almost all the features of a Roman town discussed previously in Chapter 2. The town has local autonomy, and the machinery

---

[117] Even the provisions allowing freedmen to hold office appear to have had parallels elsewhere. A freedman *IIvir* is attested at Curubis in 45 BC (*CIL* 8. 977), and a freedman *praefectus jure dicundo* at Formiae in *c*.43 BC (*CIL* 10. 6104).

[118] Normally this would be regarded as a disqualification: *Lex Malacitana*, ch. 54.

[119] Sutherland, *The Romans in Spain*, 127.   [120] *CIL* 2. 1404.

[121] *CIL* 2. 1176.

of its system of local government is set out in the same terms as that found in Italy. It is governed by an *ordo* at whose head were two *duoviri* and under whom were two aediles. The *ordo*, however, retained a firm grip over the actions of these magistrates. Chapter 129 of the law lays down that they must obey the *decreta* of the *decuriones* at all times, and consultation with the *ordo* is required for a multitude of actions.[122]

One field where the magistrates of the town did appear to enjoy more freedom was jurisdiction, as is implied by the full title of the two senior magistrates, *duoviri iure dicundo*. This aspect of communal life is covered at length, and, not surprisingly as the law was drafted at Rome, follows entirely Roman practice. Our surviving fragment of the *Lex* begins with a chapter dealing with the Roman procedure of arrest, *manus iniectio*.

Both groups of magistrates were attended by *apparitores*. These officials are listed in the same order of superiority as at Rome, and parallel the *apparitores* of the magistrates at Rome. The pay and conditions of these minor officials are set out in chapter 62 of the law. No qualifications are stipulated by the law save that candidates had to be of free birth and fellow colonists, though we know from Fronto that at *Colonia Concordia* in Venetia scribes had to be of decurional rank.[123] This may have been true at Urso; the scribe's office is seen as an important one, being the only minor post requiring a public oath be taken on its inception. A fine of 5,000 HS was imposed on the relevant magistrate if he did not see to its administration.

The scribes' oath was to be taken 'nundinis in foro' ('on market-day in the town-square'). From this we can see that the *colonia* had a *forum* which was envisaged as an area for public business and for trade. The provision for such ceremonies to be held on market-days would have been made with the intention of ensuring that the ceremony would be witnessed by as many of the colonists as possible, but would also have had the incidental effect of having it witnessed by large numbers of natives, so familiarizing them with Roman practice.[124]

From the figures given, we can calculate that the *colonia* spent the figure of 16,200 HS per annum on the wages of officials. This seems a comparatively small sum and may reflect the restricted means of most colonists. This modesty in finances is reflected throughout the whole of the law. Perhaps this feature was present in all *coloniae* in Baetica. Many would have been composed, in the main, of ex-legionaries who would not

---

[122] See Hardy, *Three Spanish Charters*, 16, and F. Abbott and A. Johnson, *Municipal Administration in the Roman Empire* (1926), 67–8.
[123] Fronto, *Ad Amicos* 2. 7.   [124] *Lex Urs.*, ch. 81.

have had great personal resources. A growth in prosperity would have allowed charges to be increased in the wealthier *coloniae*, such as Corduba and Hispalis, with the passing of time. Many of the *coloniae* were on the sites of old towns which had contained *conventus* of wealthy Roman settlers; men of at least equestrian status are attested at Urso.[125] This raises the question of whether the members of the old *conventus*, particularly given their past Pompeian political affiliations, were granted membership of the new colonial citizen bodies, a point which will be discussed further below. The low charges could have been a way of ensuring that the colony did not wither soon after foundation. Another possibility is that they were low to act as an incentive to stay, and to counteract the type of drift away from new settlements described by Tacitus and mentioned above.

The chapter of the law dealing with *apparitores* also assumes that there was a *familia* of public slaves at the colony's disposal, allowing each aedile four such slaves.[126] Public slaves are also attested at other *coloniae*. Two are recorded at Astigi,[127] and a *familia publica* is mentioned at Corduba.[128] Such slaves were not restricted to *coloniae*; examples have been found at non-colonial towns, such as Munigua,[129] and are provided for in the Flavian Municipal Law.[130] It is not possible to know whether such slaves came from the local native population. If they did this would constitute a form of Romanization, albeit one that would be resented.[131] The habit of freeing such slaves, along with individually owned slaves, would help to add to the Roman community. The difficulties of performing a formal manumission beyond Rome might have led to problems in this regard;[132] however, the Flavian Municipal Law assumes that public slaves could be freed formally by local magistrates without any problems.[133]

The official religious life of the *colonia* reflects its administrative arrangements in also being established as a mirror of the religious practices at Rome itself. Chapter 66 provides for the setting-up of colleges of

---

[125] Ps. Caes., *B. Hisp.* 22. *Equites* are also attested at Hasta Regia, ibid. 26.

[126] C.f. *Lex Irnitana*, ch. 19: 'Eisque aedilibus servos communes municipium eius municipi, qui is appareant, limo cinctos habere liceto' ('And these aediles are to be allowed the public slaves of the town to serve upon them as *limocincti*').

[127] *CIL* 2. 1472, 2. 1480.   [128] *CIL* 2. 2229.   [129] *AE* (1972), 254.

[130] *Lex Irn.*, chs. 19, 72.

[131] Unless of course we accept Petronius as evidence that occasionally enslavement was seen as a way of eventually obtaining Roman citizenship (*Satyricon* 57). Ps. Caesar, *B. Hisp.* 34. 2, implies the enslavement of natives in the late republican period. Some natives must have been enslaved in the penal measures enacted by Caesar at the end of the Civil Wars, Dio 43. 39. 1.

[132] L. Halkin, *Les Esclaves publics chez les Romains* (1965), 142.

[133] J. González, 'The *Lex Irnitana*', commentary on ch. 72 of the law, p. 223.

pontifices and *augures*, whose members are to have the same privileges as those of the parallel *collegia* found at Rome.[134] These provisions are explicitly said to be the same for all *coloniae*, 'ponti[fi]ces eique augures . . . sunto, ita uti qui optima lege optumo iure in quaque colon(ia) pontif(ices) augures . . . sunt erunt' ('let priests and augurs be established who are to enjoy the fullest rights that priests and augurs enjoy in every colony'), again hinting that there was an archetypal plan underpinning the individual colonial laws. The religious officials are said to have been 'facti' ('created') by Caesar, or his deputies, in the first place, and later in the law the same is said of the *duoviri* ('factus creatusve').[135] Cicero, describing the *colonia* at Capua, notes that the commissioners concerned appointed all the initial *decuriones*.[136] It would not be surprising if this were also the case at Urso.

If the old *conventus* members were admitted to the body of the *coloni*, the nomination of the first list of *decuriones* might be seen as a safeguard to ensure that the ruling body of the *colonia* was 'politically correct'. Many *conventus* members seem to have been far wealthier than the new colonists, and had shown pronounced Pompeian sympathies in the past. Had they been allowed to compete for office on equal terms with the new colonists they might well have dominated the public life of the *coloniae*, something Caesar would have been anxious to avoid. The low prices recorded throughout the *Lex Ursonensis* may have been low for precisely this reason, namely to allow the new, loyal, but poorer, colonists to compete with the richer, but politically suspect, *conventus* members on an equal footing after the initial deduction. If so, similar low costs would have been the rule throughout the Spanish *coloniae*. As has been seen, one of the early *duoviri* at Urso may have been L. Vettius, a centurion of the Thirtieth Legion. Vettius could have been one of the first *decuriones*; but, at any rate, his presence as a *decurion* suggests that the administration of the *colonia* was in loyal hands.

Chapter 66 also refers to the public religious acts (*sacra publica*) of the *colonia*. These would have provided both an opportunity for the settlers to assert their Romanness, and a method, whether intentional or not, of introducing such practices to the native community. They were envisaged as taking place in public religious buildings, as is shown by chapter 128 of the law, instructing the *duoviri* to appoint *magistri* to oversee the *fana*, *templa*, and *delubra* (chapels, temples, and shrines) of the *colonia*.

---

[134] A minor difference in their creation is that, unlike at Rome, they were elected by the ordinary *comitia*, not a smaller, special body.

[135] *Lex Urs.*, ch. 93.   [136] Cicero, *De Leg. Agr.* 2. 34. 93.

At the end of chapter 66 provision is made for the religious officials of the *colonia* to sit amongst the *decuriones* at the 'ludos gladiatoresq(ue)' ('games and gladiatorial spectacles'). In chapter 70 the *duoviri* are required to hold 'munus ludosve scaenicos' ('games or theatrical performances') to the three Capitoline deities of Rome, Jupiter, Juno, and Minerva. To do this each *duovir* could spend a maximum of 2,000 HS of public funds, and a minimum identical sum out of his own pocket. Again these sums are not large, probably for the reasons discussed above. The aediles were required to hold similar games (chapter 71) for three days, and a further day's games in honour of Venus. Although they could draw only half as much from public funds as the *duoviri*, the required private-spending requirement was identical. Chapter 127 of the law refers to the right of sitting in the orchestra at the *ludi scaenici*, suggesting that a theatre existed. Such a structure has been found at Urso, cut out of the living rock. Unfortunately it is undated, but, given the provisions of the law, it may well have been built early in the *colonia*'s life. The absence of the adjective 'scaenicos' in chapter 125 of the law led Mommsen to conclude that *ludi* other than theatrical performances were meant here. This may have been so, the reference being to gladiatorial games or chariot racing.

The presence of the three Capitoline deities suggests that a *capitolium* existed at Urso, but no such temple has been found as yet. Such a temple does not seem to have been regarded as a necessity; Timgad, a *colonia* founded on a virgin site, where it would be expected that essential attributes would be laid out correctly, did not acquire a *capitolium* until late in its history, and then not in a central position. Nor do *capitolia* appear to have been exclusive to *coloniae*. At Belo, for example, three closely grouped temples standing above the *forum* appear to be a form of *capitolium*.

As has been seen, the holding of 'spectacula' was regarded as one of the standard features of a Roman town. Their provision, although it was for the *coloni* themselves, would have helped to diffuse aspects of Roman culture, albeit not of the highest kind, to the local inhabitants.

Colonial games were probably the stimulus for the games which began to be put on in non-colonial towns. Indubitably the largest cultural export in this field would have been gladiatorial games. The *ludi scaenici*, given the nature of the colonists, are more likely to have been pantomimes than high tragedy. In both cases native spectators would have picked up some Latin by their attendance. That natives were allowed to attend can be seen from the categories listed in chapter 126 of the law—*coloni, incolae, hospites, adventores*. This is a standard phrase (colonists, resident aliens, guests, and visitors).[137] There could be some dispute as to whom the *incolae* were, but the category of *adventores* seems to make it clear that natives, even if they were not *incolae*, could attend.

The law can tell us less about the private buildings of the *colonia*. Chapter 75 is a prohibition on unroofing buildings in the town. At first sight this might suggest that there was resistance to urbanization, or at least a lack of enthusiasm for it in Urso. However, in reality it appears to be a tralatitious element of the law which is also found elsewhere, and so is more a reflection on the problems of sustaining urbanization in the Roman world as a whole than an indication of particular problems at Urso.[138]

Perhaps of more interest is chapter 76. This prohibits tileries of greater than 300 tiles in the 'oppidum' of the *colonia*. If such a building exists, it is to become a *locus publicus*. The rest of the chapter is confused. Anyone may initiate an allegation, and a magistrate is to pay the equivalent sum into the public treasury. Something has dropped out of the law here. Hardy suggests that this would be a provision for the owner to pay compensation to avoid the 'municipalization' of his works.[139]

Can we use the chapter to determine anything about the demand for tiles in the *colonia* and hence perhaps the demand for building? Unfortunately the answer appears to be no. 'Figlinas teglarias maiores tegularum CCC tegulariumve' is a problematic phrase. Normally it is interpreted as referring to the ability to produce 300 tiles per day.[140] However, as tile kilns could only be used once a week at the most, since time is needed for cooling after firing, this seems to be incorrect. A tilery found at Canterbury, measuring 6 × 1 × 1 m., could produce a maximum of 1,680 tiles per firing.[141] This would be 240 tiles a day. However, this calculation does not allow for wasters, which could account for up to 50 per cent of the total produced. If the calculation is based on the production of unfired tiles per day, surviving workmen's records show that this number could be produced by a single workman.[142] This general lack of precision makes it impossible to use the chapter to deduce the demand for tiles in Urso, or to speculate on the level of urbanization envisaged.

A better explanation, as suggested by d'Ors, is to see the limitation

---

[137] See e.g. *ILS* 5671 (Interamnia), *ILS* 5672 (Praeneste), *ILS* 5673 (Urbinum).

[138] See *Lex Mal.* 62; *Lex Tar.* 1. 34; A. D. E. Lewis, 'Ne quis in oppido aedificium detegito', in J. González (ed.), *Estudios sobre Urso* (1989), 41–56.

[139] Hardy, *Three Spanish Charters*, 34.   [140] e.g. by Hardy, ibid. 34.

[141] F. Jenkins, 'A Roman Tilery and 2 Pottery Kilns at Durovernum (Canterbury)', *Antiquaries' J.* 36 (1956), 40–56.

[142] *EE* 2. 925, 928, 929.

on the production of tiles as referring to the size of the building concerned, the law being more concerned with the fire-risk of having a tilery within the town than with the size of tile-production.[143] This would explain why the ban is only for the *oppidum* of the *colonia*. The partial nature of the ban makes speculation on the need for tiles in Urso even more futile, as a high demand could have been served by large tileries outside the town itself. If the fire-risk is the point of the ban, various other aspects of the chapter would make more sense. The seriousness of the risk would explain the universal provision for a prosecution, and after becoming a *locus publicus* the land may have been sold to raise revenue. It would be this money that the magistrates were to deposit in the public treasury. This explanation is strengthened by the ban on burials and cremations within the town (chapter 73), although this could also have had religious motives.

The community envisaged by *Lex Ursonensis* is therefore a town conceived of, and run, in a strictly Roman fashion. This should come as no surprise as the *colonia* had been created for a Roman settler population. The charters of other *coloniae* were probably based on the same master document which lies beneath the *Lex Ursonensis* and would have had a similar Roman emphasis. However, was this Roman outlook reflected in the actual layout of these settlements? For example in the possession of large public buildings, which were commonly regarded as a sign of a classical town?

The physical appearance of the *coloniae* in Baetica is problematic: their sites are for the most part unexcavated, or overlaid with large modern cities. We know that Roman-style buildings had already existed in Corduba and Hispalis in the late republican period, but these may well have been destroyed in the sacking of these cities at the end of the civil wars. The sack of Corduba involved the city being fired, and, according to the author of the *Bellum Hispaniense*, the death of 22,000 people.[144] After the battle, Caesar killed the freed servile population which had resisted him, and sold into slavery the rest of the ἐπιχώριοι or inhabitants (it is unclear whether or not this term includes the members of Corduba's *conventus*). Dio's statement here must be an exaggeration since, as will be seen, some inhabitants of the town went on to prosper. Caesar is said to have acted in a similar manner at Hispalis.[145] There may well therefore have been very little to build on from the republican period.

The two best-excavated *coloniae* in Spain, neither of which, unfortunately, lies in Baetica, show a marked contrast in their development. At

[143] A. d'Ors, *Epigrafía jurídica de la España romana* (1953), 201 ff.
[144] Ps. Caes., *B. Hisp.* 34.   [145] Dio, 43, 39. 2–3.

Emerita Augusta in Lusitania there are clear signs of rapid, Roman-style urbanization. The wall of the *colonia* has been dated by Richmond to 23 BC; the town's theatre can be securely dated by epigraphy to 16 BC; the *colonia*'s drainage system runs beneath the theatre and must therefore predate it. Similarly the hexastyle temple and *forum* complex appear to be Augustan in date, as does the *circus*. It must be remembered however that Emerita, unlike the *coloniae* of Baetica, was a virtual greenfield site. Consequently it was built by, or under the guidance of, Roman architects, and so would have taken on a Roman guise almost automatically. Nevertheless there are some traces of native influence. The hexastyle 'temple of Diana', while being totally Roman in plan, contains in its *tympanum* a semicircular arch which is not Roman in conception.[146]

A stark contrast to this overwhelmingly Roman site is found at Ilici in Tarraconensis. Here the *colonia* retained the street-plan of the old Iberian town, and private housing also remained Iberian in design.[147] The pottery found on the site is overwhelmingly Iberian in both decoration and design. Non-Roman weights also appear to have been used well into the Roman period. There are some signs of Roman influence, such as the evident centuriation of the *colonia*'s *territorium*, and the coinage of the town, which is entirely Roman in conception, depicting on one issue a temple of a standard, classical, Roman form. Fragments of capitals which could have come from such a temple have been found on the site. The general impression, however, is of an Iberian site with a Roman overlay. This situation changes radically in the first century AD, when, after a destruction layer, dating to the reign of Claudius, the archaeological record shows the town taking on a much more standard Roman appearance in terms of the forms of houses found, and Roman cultural artefacts begin to predominate. The excavator attributes the destruction layer to civil strife in the *colonia*.[148] However, fire from accidental causes would have had similar devastating effects.

It may be that such a fire is the reason for the differences in urban development found at Emerita and Ilici. Emerita was a new site, and so could be constructed to a standard Roman plan. This plan may have been self-consciously Roman, as Emerita was to be the capital of a province and

[146] I. A. Richmond, 'The First Years of Augusta Emerita', *Arch. J.* 87 (1930), 98–116. A similar arch is found at a surviving temple at Augustobriga.

[147] R. R. Fernández, *La ciudad romana de Ilici* (1975), ch. 7, esp. pp. 163–4 and *El yacimiento arqueologico de la Alcudia de Elche* (1991), 44–64, where the period ending in the mid-1st c. AD, i.e. well after the foundation of the *colonia*, is styled not Roman, but 'ibero-romano'.

[148] Fernández, *La ciudad romana*, 183.

in one of the wilder areas of Spain;[149] or it could be that it was so constructed because this was the natural way for Roman engineers to build a
city. At Ilici, on the other hand, a town was already in existence, and it was
only after the destruction of the old town by fire, from whatever cause,
that a need to rebuild the city *de novo* arose.

Emerita and Ilici represent the two extremes of the possible layout of
the *coloniae*. Most appear to have at least some early Roman features, but
all too often there has been too little excavation to ascertain clearly where
the balance between the Roman and non-Roman lay. This balance might
have been thought to be affected to some degree by the nature of old
settlement. Yet, if this were the case, it would seem natural that Iberian
sites, being the form of settlement most divergent from Roman norms of
urbanization, would have received more attention than former Punic
towns, such as Carthago Nova. However, the case of Ilici suggests that this
was not the case. In general it would be best to assume that development
was largely influenced by factors purely local to the *colonia* concerned.

The bare physical necessities for a *colonia* would have been a place to
hold games, a *forum* (these two could have been one and the same), and a
place for the town council to meet, be it a temple or a *basilica*, for
administrative purposes. From our evidence it appears that all the *coloniae*
took on a Roman shape as time went on, but so did most major non-
colonial sites, and there is at present no way of telling which group of
settlements reached this stage first. Buildings would have provided a
stimulus to Romanization, but the most valuable contribution of the
coloniae in this respect was probably to implant into the native population
the idea of what a Roman town should be like. However, no fixed idea of
a specific form to which all Baetican *coloniae* conformed can be deduced
from our present evidence.

Apart from the form of the *coloniae*, another question of importance if
we are to ascertain the effects of the *coloniae* on the native population is
who lived in the *coloniae* and their *territoria*, apart from the colonists
themselves. Here the *Lex Ursonensis* comes to our aid. Chapter 98 of the
law lays down the provisions for carrying out *munera*, standardly assessed
at five days' labour per man per year. This liability applied to all those who
'in ea colon(ia) intrave eius colon(iae) fines domicilium praediumve habe-
bit neque eius colon(iae) colon(us) est' ('hold in the colony or the territory
of the colony their place of residence or an estate and are not a citizen of

---

[149] See J. C. Edmondson, 'Romanization and Urban Development in Lusitania', in T.
Blagg and M. Millett (eds.), *The Early Roman Empire in the West* (1990), 151 ff., at p. 169.

the colony'), that is, not just the *coloni* themselves. The passage makes the assumption therefore that neither the *colonia* itself nor its *territorium* will be exclusively populated by the *coloni*. A parallel can be seen in an inscription from Salpensa, referring to 'incolis viris et mulieribus intra muros habitantibus' ('resident aliens, both men and women, living within the town walls'), which shows that there were non-citizens living in both the town itself and in its *territorium*.[150]

However, unlike the Salpensa inscription, where such non-citizens are specifically referred to as *incolae*, the Lex *Ursonensis* avoids this term here, although it appears earlier in the law.[151] Is there any possible reason for this absence? Is it, for example, to ensure that those living within the boundaries of the *colonia*, but who were neither *coloni* nor *incolae*, remained liable for *munera*? If so, what status would such a group have enjoyed?

To solve these problems it is necessary to look more closely at the meanings of 'incola'. Although this word can have a general meaning of 'inhabitant of a place', its legal usage is more restricted. In the *Digest* the word is defined as meaning someone resident away from the place of his birth: 'incola est qui in aliquam regionem domicilium suum contulit' ('an *incola* is a man who establishes his place of residence in a region away from his place of birth/home').[152] An example of such an *incola* is the *Cordubensis* L. Lucretius Severus, who was made a *decurion* 'ex incolatu' at Axati.[153] As time went on, the possibility of native *incolae* of this type would have increased, particularly among the rich, mobile, section of the population. The idea underlying the *Digest*'s definition is that a man will be a citizen if he lives (has his *domicilium*) in the same town as the one in which he was born (his *origo*), whereas if he lives away from the town of his birth, he will be an *incola* where he lives, while remaining a citizen of the town of his birth. Such a distinction is simple, and would have held good for most communities in the empire. However, when a *colonia* was founded where there had been a prior settlement, problems would have arisen. The deduction of the *colonia* would have normally extinguished the existence of the old town. The inhabitants of this latter settlement would consequently have been left in an anomalous position. They would not be *coloni*, unless they had been enrolled specifically as such; nevertheless their *domicilium* was in the same place as their *origo*. Hence they would not be *incolae* of the *colonia* either, in the sense given above.

---

[150] *CIL* 2. 1282.   [151] In ch. 95, which deals with the appointment of *recuperatores*.
[152] *Digest* 50. 16. 239. 2 (Pomponius).   [153] *CIL* 2. 1055.

The best escape from this dilemma is to assume that the deduction of a *colonia* entailed a total extinction of any previous settlement in the eyes of the law. In this case the native inhabitants of the *colonia* would have their *domicilium* away from their *origo* (they would not in fact possess an *origo* in this case) and hence be *incolae*. One piece of evidence which suggests that the native population of a *colonia* were regarded as *incolae* is an inscription from Hispalis recording a native Iberian, Frutonius Brocci f., who is described as a *negotiator ferrarius* (trader in iron) and an *incola Hispalensis* (a resident alien of Hispalis).[154] However, this cannot be regarded as unequivocal proof. Frutonius was a trader, and, since Hispalis was the ἐμπόριον (market town) of the area, he may have been a native of another town who had had switched his *domicilium* to Hispalis and become an *incola* in this way. Better proof is forthcoming from an inscription found at Augusta Praetoria and dating from 23–20 BC, that is, only some twenty years or so at the most after the foundations in Baetica, and which shows that here the native population were regarded as *incolae* of the *colonia*.[155] It therefore seems likely that the same situation obtained in the *coloniae* of Baetica, and that the native inhabitants of previous settlements were treated as *incolae* of the new colonial foundations.

Apart from the native population and immigrant traders in the *coloniae*, another group which could, conceivably, have had the status of *incolae* are the members of the precolonial *conventus* settlements. In this way they would have been forced to contribute to the financial well-being of the *coloniae*, while being deprived of any chance to cause political upsets. Not all *conventus* members would have been so treated. The Elder Seneca's family, which was in Corduba at the time of the Civil Wars, does not appear to have lost its political rights under the new dispensation,[156] nor does that of his friend, Clodius Turrinus. Turrinus' family is said to have lost a great deal of wealth in the Civil Wars, 'civili bello attenuata domo'.[157] However, since his grandfather was Caesar's *hospis* in Corduba, perhaps during Caesar's quaestorship in the province in 68 BC, it is unlikely that they suffered from the foundation of the *colonia* (although the confiscation of some land for allotments is a possibility). Perhaps the reference is to loss of property in attacks by Pompeian supporters in the city in the faction fights which we know broke out there.[158] According to Griffin,[159]

---

[154] *CIL* 2. 1199.
[155] *ILS* 6753 = V. Ehrenberg and A. H. M. Jones, *Documents Illustrating the Reigns of Augustus and Tiberius* (2nd edn., 1955), no. 338.
[156] Seneca, *Controv.* 1 *pr.* 11.   [157] Ibid. 10 *pr.* 14–16.
[158] Ps. Caes., *B. Hisp.* 34.
[159] M. Griffin, 'The Elder Seneca and Spain', *JRS* 62 (1972), 1 ff., at p. 4.

Turrinus' name betrays native descent. If this is true, his family may have
been part of the group of 'select natives' who were included in the original
precolonial foundation by Marcellus in the second century BC.[160] In short
although there is no proof that the majority of old *conventus* members
suffered a loss of civic rights in this way, nevertheless it must be remembered that unless they were specifically enrolled as colonists, they would
not have been full members of the new foundations, and hence technically
would have been *incolae*.

If we assume therefore that the majority of the population of the old
native town of Urso became *incolae* of the new *colonia*, would this exhaust
the categories of inhabitants there? As noted above, the absence of the
word 'incola' in chapter 98 of the law suggests that this was not the case.
A clue to the existence of a further category is also provided by chapter
103. This empowers the *duoviri*, in times of emergency, to hold a levy of
the 'colon(os) incolasque contributos' ('colonists and resident aliens assigned to its jurisdiction'). As we know nothing of 'incolae contributi' it
seems reasonable to assume that a 'que' has dropped out of the text here
and that the original ought to read *incolae contributos*[que], giving us two
distinct groups: the *incolae* and the *contributi*. If this is the case who were
the *contributi*, if not the native population of Urso? The answer is probably
members of other smaller native settlements which lay within the *territorium* of the new *colonia*. Such communities appear to have retained some
vestigial political rights, but were subordinated to the overall authority of
the *colonia*.

It is possible that there had been communities politically dependent on
the Iberian town of Urso prior to the deduction of the *colonia*, and that
this arrangement was simply perpetuated after its foundation.[161] Alternatively, these communities could have simply been swallowed up to create
the necessary *territorium* for the *colonia*. We have little information on this
practice in Spain. Pliny notes that the tribe of the Icositani were attached
in this way to the *colonia* of Ilici in Tarraconensis. However, this tribe is
normally regarded as having been of Mauretanian origin, so this cannot be
regarded as a typical arrangement.[162] Lusitania, on the other hand, provides a purely Spanish example of two minor settlements, Castra Servilia

[160] Strabo, 3. 2. 1.
[161] For the possibility that Iberian society was stratified in this way, see J. Mangas,
'Servidumbre comunitaria en la Bética prerromana', *Memorias de historia antigua*, 1 (1977),
151 ff.
[162] Pliny, *NH* 3. 3. 19. It is unclear whether the tribe was transported to Spain or not. See
Mackie, 'Augustan Colonies in Mauretania', 332 ff.

and Castra Caecilia, as *contributi* of the *colonia* of Norba.[163] Both these examples probably predate the Flavian grant of the *ius Latii* to Spain. But it is unlikely that this is equally the case with the 293 'contributed' communities in Tarraconensis mentioned by Pliny.[164] These were probably placed in such a position as part of the implementation of the *ius Latii* rather than through the provisions of prior arrangements in the province. This subordination of native peoples by contribution may have been common, and perhaps was the reason why the Trinovantes of Camulodunum resented their colonization so bitterly. Alone amongst the tribal groups of Britain, no urban site forming the basis of an administrative centre has been found in their tribal area, supporting the supposition that the tribe was attributed to the *colonia*.[165] It must be remembered that in some cases, for example Cologne in Germany, natives appear to have been made colonists along with the deducted veterans,[166] but no evidence of this practice has been found in the *coloniae* founded at this period in Baetica.[167] Strabo lists three Spanish *coloniae* which are 'co-settled', συνῳκισμέναι, although he does not make it clear what he means by this phrase; he may imply that this process had a Romanizing purpose. The three are Emerita, Pax Augusta (*sic*), and Caesaraugusta, none of which is in Baetica.[168] However, given Strabo's views on the high state of civilization in the province, it is perhaps not surprising that he does not list any Baetican examples.

The law therefore envisages non-colonists living in and around the *colonia*. This would be necessary if the *colonia* proper, itself a community of only *c.*2,000–3,000 settlers, were to be viable. Most sites probably had some natives living in the town itself. The inclusion of natives in the citizen body of republican Corduba has already been noted. An inscription from this town, probably dating to the AD 20s, records honours given to L. Axius Naso by two *vici*, or town districts, the *vicus Forensis* and the *vicus Hispanus*.[169] As *vici* were normally named honorifically, or after gods, the nomenclature of these two *vici*, particularly the *vicus Hispanus*, probably reflects the ethnic composition of the *vici*.[170] This is borne out by the names of the other *vici* we know of at Corduba, which conform to the

---

[163] Pliny, *NH* 4. 22. 117.   [164] Ibid. 3. 3. 18.

[165] P. Salway, *Roman Britain* (1984), 115 n. 2.   [166] Tacitus, *Germ.* 28; *Hist.* 4. 65.

[167] This is in contrast to the inclusion of all willing natives in the *colonia Latina* created at Carteia and of τῶν ἐπιχωρίων ἄνδρες ἐπίλεκτοι in the informal settlement founded in Corduba in the second century BC.

[168] Strabo, 3. 2. 15.   [169] *AE* (1981), 495.

[170] 'Hispanus' as opposed to 'Hispaniensis' meant 'native Spanish' as opposed to simply 'of Spain'.

more usual pattern of nomenclature; a *vicus Augustus* is attested,[171] and possibly a *vicus Patricius*.[172] A tombstone listing the *caput cantere*, a *vicus* found in the thirteenth district of Rome, probably refers to the home of a Roman immigrant,[173] although we do know that some *coloniae*, for example Pisidian Antioch, did name their districts after areas in Rome.[174] Corduba was perhaps divided by a wall in the early part of its history,[175] and this too may reflect a racial divide in the *colonia*. A similar wall is found at the British *colonia* of Lindum (Lincoln).[176]

How long such a divide persisted is not known; the dedication to Naso suggests that it continued in some form until at least the Tiberian period. Some Iberians certainly lived in Corduba: for example L. Cornelius Caranto, who was presumably an enfranchised Iberian, although he, like Turrinus, may have been descended from Marcellus' select natives.[177] At Ilici, in Tarraconensis, there is a large house, dating from the early years of the *colonia*, with a mosaic depicting a stylized fortified town surrounded by the inscription: 'Satu(?) Acos, Acos et Sabini, Cor. Scrad. Acos.'[178] These names suggest that some wealthy Iberians, already with Roman pretensions, lived in the *colonia*. Poorer natives are also attested at Ilici; their presence is revealed by Iberian graffiti found on pots in this period. It is not clear what the status of either of these groups would have been. The poorer natives may have been either *contributi* or *incolae*. The wealthier group probably held the latter status, perhaps hoping by adopting Roman customs to gain access to the politically privileged group of the town, and to demonstrate their closeness to this group to their own people. At Urso the law gives no hint of separation, but this could have been taken as read, or included in a lost part of the law. If the site of the *forum* of the town has been correctly interpreted, it was flanked by some Iberian houses. However, there is no indication of the date of occupation of these buildings, which could have been demolished before the building of the *forum*. Alternatively the buildings could have been erected for Roman use using local labour and techniques.

We can see therefore that the *coloniae* would have had a mixed popu-

---

[171] *CIL* 2. 2208.
[172] J. F. Rodriguez Neila, 'Los vici de Hispania y Corduba', *Corduba*, 1 (1976), 101 ff., at p. 117.
[173] *CIL* 2. 2248a. See the comments of L. A. Curchin, '*Vici* and *pagi* in Roman Spain', *REA* 87 (1985), 327 ff., at p. 332.
[174] B. M. Levick, *Roman Colonies in Southern Asia Minor* (1967), 76 f.
[175] R. Knapp, *Roman Córdoba* (1983), 13, 54–5.
[176] J. Wacher, *The Towns of Roman Britain* (1974), 120–37 and fig. 29.
[177] *CIL* 2. 2286.   [178] *ILER* 2109.

lation. Political control would obviously have rested with the *coloni* themselves. There is little evidence that in Baetica this body incorporated the
native population along with the deducted settlers. Beneath the *coloni*
were the *incolae*, a heterogeneous group composed of immigrant traders
and probably the old native inhabitants of the precolonial town. Other
incolae perhaps included members of the old *conventus* of Roman citizens
found in many of the native towns where *coloniae* were subsequently
deducted. Below these appear to have been the *contributi*, attached to the
colonia, having no rights, but only obligations within it, and perhaps
enjoying residual political rights of their own.

Natives lived within the *oppidum* of the *colonia* itself as well as in its
territorium, as can be seen from the *vicus Hispanus* at Corduba, and
some such natives may have been wealthy individuals. However, it also
seems that the two communities, Roman and native, occupied separate
areas within the urban environment in some cities, at least for a period of
time.

Apart from the natives who lived under direct colonial jurisdiction,
another way of looking at the *coloniae*'s impact on the native population of
the province is to examine the relations that held between them and the
surrounding communities. The effects of centuriation and possession of
praefecturae have already been discussed. However, more light can be shed
on this subject by an examination of the so-called *hospitia* agreements
entered into by some colonies, and other settlements. Such agreements
seem at first sight to represent the introduction of a Roman convention to
a new area. Similar documents using the same formulae as the Spanish
examples quoted below have been found, for example, in Africa.[179] The
agreement was made between two unequal partners, who could be either
individuals or, as in the cases involving the *coloniae*, corporate entities.
The length of time concerned is invariably long; the arrangement was
intended to last for many generations, probably in the minds of those
entering into it for ever. The texts of these documents are enigmatic in
that they merely record the fact of the *hospitium* being made, without
spelling out the obligations involved on either side. However the weaker
partner, here the native community concerned, became a form of depend-
ant of the stronger of the two contracting parties, here the Roman *colonia*.
The *hospitium* made in the province between Q. Marius Balbus and,
probably, the Lacilbulenses in AD 5, speaks of the agreement involving

---

[179] e.g. *ILS* 6095, from Cortona, dating to AD 65; *ILS* 6103 from Hippo Regius dating to
AD 55.

fides and *clientela* (guardianship and debts of obligation).[180] This phraseology is paralleled by examples from other areas.[181]

The native site of Iptucci made a *hospitium* agreement with the *colonia* of Ucubi in AD 31,[182] as did the inhabitants of Baxo three years later.[183] At Astigi, a more doubtful stone records a dedication to Sextus Allius Mamercus by the *concili* [*sic*] *immunes Ilienses Ilipenses decuriones*.[184] This may conceal a *hospitium* agreement made with an individual.[185] The native communities involved in these agreements all use some form of Roman terminology. In both the *hospitia* mentioned above the native parties style themselves *senatus et populus*. Whether this shows a move towards an internal reorganization on Roman lines of the communities concerned is debatable. The phrase is invariably used of communities which lacked any Roman legal status, and may simply be a standard formula meaning the rulers and people of a given community.[186]

---

[180] The best commentary is A. d'Ors, 'Una nueva tabla emeritense de hospitium publicum', *Emerita*, 16 (1948), 64–5. See also *ILS* 6097=*CIL* 2. 1343: 'anno Cn. Cinnai Magn [i] L. [Messallae Volesi cos] XV K(alendas) Novembris . . . Q. Marius Balbus hosp[itium fecit cum] senatu populoque [Lacilbulensi sibi] liberisque eoru[m eosque liberos] posterosque eor[um in fidem] clientelamqu[e suam liberorum] posterorumq[ue suorum recepit. Egerunt leg(ati)] M. Fabius . . . C. Fabius . . .' ('in the consulate of Cn. Cinna Magnus and L. Mesalla Volaesus, on 18 October, Q. Marius Balbus made a *hospitium* agreement with the senate and people of Lacibula and their children and received into his trust their children and posterity and accepted their bond of loyalty to him. The agreement was made by the delegates M. Fabius . . . and C. Fabius . . .').

[181] e.g. *ILS* 6099 and 6099a from near Brixia, but dealing with African communities.

[182] *AE* (1955), 21: '[Publ]io Me[mmio Regulo et] L. Fu[l]cinio Trione c[os]. Senatus populusque Iptuccitanorum [hospitium] fecit cum colonis coloniae Clarita[tis Iuliae] Ucubi liberis posterisque eorum s[ibi liberis] posterisque suis. Egerunt C. Trebecius Luca[nus], C. Attius Seve[rus], L. Catinius Opt[atus]' ('In the consular year of Publius Memmius Regulus and Lucius Fulcinius Trio the senate and people of Iptucci made a *hospitium* agreement with the colonists of the *colonia* Claritas Iulia Ucubi, and between their children and descendants. The agreement was enacted by C. Trebecius Lucanus, C. Attius Severus, and L. Catinius Optatus').

[183] *AE* (1983), 530a: 'Q. Marcio Barea [. . .] T. Rustio Nu[mmio] Gallo [Cos]. Senatus populusque Baxonensis hospitium fecit cum colon[i]s coloniae Claritatis Iuliae ipsis liberis posterisque suis. Egerunt leg(ati) M. Fabius Qu. f. Rufus, C. Terentius P.f. Macer' ('in the consulate of Q. Marcius Barea and T. Rustius Nummius Gallus the senate and people of Baxo made a *hospitium* agreement with the colonists of the *colonia* Claritas Iuliae and with their children and descendants. The agreement was struck by the delegates Marcus, son of Quintus, Fabius Rufus and Caius, son of Publius, Terentius Macer'). For a detailed commentary, see J. F. Rodríguez Neila and J. Ma. Santero Santurino, '"Hospitium" y "Patronatus": Tabula de bronce de Cañete de las Torres', *Habis*, 13 (1982), 105 ff.

[184] *CIL* 2. 1475.

[185] Cf. the *patronatus* agreement made by the *concilium conventus Cluniensis* in AD 222 with the legionary legate of *Legio VII Gemina*, C. Marius Pudens Cornelianus (*ILS* 6109).

[186] See e.g. the agreement made between L. Domitius Ahenobarbus and the *senatus populusque civitatium stipendiariorum pago Gurzenses* in AD 65 (*ILS* 6095).

This distinction is illustrated by a further *hospitium* agreement made with Emerita in AD 6 by the 'Martienses qui antea Ugienses' ('the people of Martia previously known as the people of Ugia').[187] The Martienses use the form 'decuriones et municipes' ('councillors and townsfolk') rather than 'senatus et populus' ('senate and people'). This should indicate that they possessed a Roman legal status, most probably the *ius Latii*,[188] something supported by the Roman names of their *legati*. The Ugienses' change of name is also of interest; possibly it was a result of pressure from the *colonia*. Adopting a Roman-style name would make the community easier to deal with, and, probably, to locate from the Roman point of view, given that there were a large number of duplicate, or very similar, native names in Spain. The Ugienses probably lived in Baetica, and so the agreement reveals another instance of cross-provincial dealings.

However, despite their seemingly Roman pedigree, it would be a mistake to see the *hospitia* agreements as an example of the straightforward adoption of Roman customs by communities in Spain. This form of agreement had a long history in the pre-Roman history of the Iberian peninsula. The most well-known example is the *hospitium* agreement between two *gentilitates* of the Zoelae in the north-west of the country.[189] Diodorus Siculus mentions the phenomenon,[190] and probable examples of *hospitia* agreements written in Iberian script have been found.[191] The native custom on which the Roman practice appears to be founded was probably more Celtic/Celtiberian than Iberian proper. It is of interest therefore that Lacilbula, Iptucci, Baxo, and Ugia all lie in areas of the province that had a high Celtic population. Given this background, d'Ors is probably correct to conclude that the *hospitia* agreements of the Roman

[187] *AE* (1952), 49: '[M. Aemilio lepid]o L. Arrun[tio] Cos. Decuriones et Municipes Martienses qui antea Ugienses fuerunt, hospitium fecerunt cum decurionibus et colonis coloniae Augustae Emeritae sibi liberis posterisq(ue) eorum. Egerunt legati P. Mummius P. f. Gal. Ursus, M. Aemilius M.f. Gal. Fronto' ('In the consulate of Marcus Aemilius Lepidus and Lucius Arruntius the councillors and citizens of Martia which was previously called Ugia made a *hospitium* agreement with the councillors and colonists of *Colonia Augusta Emerita* for themselves, their children, and descendants. This was enacted by their ambassadors Publius Mummius Ursus, son of Publius of the Galerian tribe and Marcus Aemilius Fronto, son of Marcus, of the Galerian tribe').
[188] If the *legati* involved are Ugienses, their possession of Roman citizen rights should indicate that the town possessed at least the *ius Latii*. For a further discussion, see Ch. 5.
[189] *CIL* 2. 2633.
[190] Diodorus Siculus, 5. 34. A possible connected phenomenon is that of the *devotio Iberica*, where a group of individuals dedicated themselves to the death to a patron. See Plutarch, *Vit. Sert.* 14; Valerius Maximus, 2. 6. 11; Caesar, *BG* 3. 22. 1.
[191] J. Ma. Ramos y Loscertales, 'Hospicio y clientela en la España céltica', *Emerita*, 10 (1942), 308 ff.; A. Tovar, 'El bronce de Luzaga y las téseras latinas y celtibéricas', *Emerita*, 16 (1948), 75 ff.

period are a Romanized form of this native custom, rather than a purely Roman innovation in the life of the province.[192]

The adoption of a Roman *hospes* may have encouraged the native community concerned to adopt a Roman way of life,[193] but this cannot be automatically assumed to have been the case. The agreements, like the physical aspects of most *coloniae*, show a synthesis of Roman and native culture producing here something which is an interpretation of an essentially native institution in terms comprehensible to Rome.[194] The end result shows that both parties have retained their own conceptual world, and perhaps as a consequence of this each party may have had a slightly different idea of what was involved in such agreements.

As well as entering into agreements with the new settlements, some of the older communities may have been absorbed into the *coloniae* themselves. A common candidate suggested is the town of Carbula which it is alleged was absorbed by the *colonia* at Corduba. Carbula coined in the first century BC, and is listed by Pliny as a separate town, but then is no longer attested as an independent entity. A *pagus Carbulensis* of Corduba is, however, found.[195] This, it is argued, could indicate the extinction of Carbula as a separate entity, and its assimilation into Corduba as a district of that town. However, this argument is unconvincing. It is equally possible that our lack of attestation is fortuitous, and that the *pagus Carbulensis* was so called because it lay on the boundary of the two towns' *territoria*. The presence of a presbyter, Lamponianus, from Carbula at the Council of Elvira in the third century AD along with the bishop of Corduba, Osius, in a list of delegates, all of whom appear to come from self-governing towns, strengthens this second view.[196]

Other candidates for absorption are the 'vetus' sites mentioned by Pliny at Tucci and Astigi. These sites should have been situated near their homonymous *coloniae*, and so would have fallen within their *territoria*, and hence not have had self-government. However, Pliny lists old Astigi as an *oppidum liberum*. The town must therefore have had an independent life of its own, and presumably a *territorium*.[197] We have no way of knowing what relations were like with the neighbouring colonists, but it is likely that voluntary adoption of some Roman practices occurred.

The encouragement of such adoption, though in a passive sense, would have been the major contribution of the *coloniae* to changing the lifestyle

[192] A. d'Ors, 'Una nueva tabla emeritense,' 74.
[193] e.g. the name-change of the Ugienses discussed above.
[194] This intermingling of Roman and native political ideas will be discussed extensively in Ch. 6 with regard to the *Lex Irnitana*.
[195] *CIL* 2. 2322.   [196] J. Vives, *Concilios visigoticos e hispano-romanos* (1963), 1 ff.
[197] Pliny, *NH* 3. 1. 12.

of the province. As privileged communities colonies were bound to attract attention from the native population, who would absorb some of the customs and forms used there. The native aristoracy, in particular, would have been susceptible to this form of imitation, in order to demonstrate to their people that they were part of the highest stratum in society. The *coloniae* appear to have held games as a legal requirement of their existence, and this form of cultural export seems to have taken root. Such games would not have been performed with the same regularity in the old *conventus*, nor would the specifically Roman religious ceremonies which went with them. From the law of Urso we can see that markets were a feature of colonial life. These would again have drawn native traders, and familiarized them with Roman trading techniques and probably Roman weights and measures. The *conventus* would not have provided opportunities for trade on such a regular basis, and would have been content to use native customs in their trading. This familiarization with the Roman way of life would certainly have affected those natives living in the *coloniae*, or their *territoria*, whether they wished so or not. The centuriation of land would also have had a far-reaching effect on native land-use. The main difference between the *coloniae* and the old *conventus* was probably one of formality. The *conventus* operated from within native communities, and whereas they probably used Roman forms of administration, these would only have been binding on themselves. On the other hand, as has been seen, the *coloniae* were governed by entirely Roman law codes and administrative machinery. Their effect on provincial life therefore would have been much more far-reaching.

In the imperial period the *coloniae* did not uniformly become sites of importance. Some, such as Corduba and Hispalis, did rise to prominence, but, given their important trading positions and administrative functions, this is not surprising. Others, such as Asido, simply became average towns, or, as in the case of Itucci, declined from prominence to such a degree that their sites are now unknown.

Otho made a concession concerning citizenship to Emerita and Hispalis in AD 69, either extending the number of *coloni* there by granting citizenship to some of the *incolae* or *contributi* or sending extra families of settlers to these towns. This measure was designed for popularity, and suggests that even the larger *coloniae* experienced difficulties in prospering, at least in the Julio-Claudian period.[198]

---

[198] Tacitus, *Hist.* 1. 78: 'provinciarum animos adgressus Hispalensibus et Emeritensibus familiarum adiectiones . . . dedit' ('working on the minds of the provincials he added extra families to the citizen bodies of Hispalis and Emerita').

There are no clear indicators for either the decline or the prosperity of the *coloniae*, but one potential candidate for such a role is the presence of wealthy or prominent individuals who hailed from these settlements. Best represented in this respect, as might be expected, is the provincial capital, Corduba. This was the birthplace of Sextus Marius, described by Tacitus as 'ditissimus Hispaniarum' ('the wealthiest man in Spain'),[199] a mining magnate whose favourite party-trick was to pull down his neighbours' houses and then rebuild them at his own expense. However, he appears to have lived in Rome, as do Aemilius Aelianus who insulted Augustus,[200] and Aemilius Regulus, who was involved in an abortive plot to assassinate Caligula.[201] Seneca's fellow townsman, Turrinus, has already been mentioned. Seneca also records the names of other Cordubans, such as the poets Sextilius Ena and Statorius Victor, and the orator M. Porcius Latro.[202]

Other *coloniae* are less well represented in our sources. Ucubi appears to have been the home town of the Annii Veri;[203] we know of two wealthy merchants from Astigi, M. Iulius Hermesianus[204] and D. Caecilius Hospitalis;[205] and Italica appears to have produced at least nine senators in the second century AD. All these places owed their prominence to their wealth rather than their colonial status. Other wealthy towns which were not *coloniae* also produced figures of note; for example Iliberris was the home of Q. Valerius Vegetus, the suffect consul of AD 91,[206] and Gades that of L. Cornelius Pusio, a suffect consul in AD 90,[207] the literary figure Canius,[208] and the Pythagorean philosopher Moderatus.[209] But there is no comparable record from the smaller *coloniae* such as Itucci and Asido.

Despite the Roman form of the *coloniae*, cultural exchange between Roman and native does not seem to have been an entirely one-way process. To some degree it is legitimate to talk of the 'Iberianization' of the Roman *coloni* as well as the Romanization of the native population. The native appearance of parts of early Ilici has been mentioned above, and it appears that non-Roman weights and measures continued in use here. Macrobius records that the Accitani worshipped the native god Neto.[210] Schulten believed that the natives of Acci were meant here, but there is no

---

[199] Tacitus, *Ann.* 6. 19; Dio, 58. 22. 2.   [200] Suetonius, *Vit. Div. Aug.* 51. 2.
[201] Josephus, *Ant. J.* 19. 1. 3.   [202] Seneca, *Controv.* 1 pr. 16, 9 pr. 3.
[203] *SHA, Marcus* 1. 6.   [204] *CIL* 2. 1481 with *CIL* 6. 20742.
[205] *CIL* 2. 1474 with *CIL* 6. 1625b.
[206] *CIL* 2. 2074 (his mother), *CIL* 2. 2077 (his wife).
[207] *PIR* (2nd edn., 1933), ii. 352 n. 1425 with *AE* (1971), 175.   [208] Martial, 1. 61.
[209] Thouvenot, *Essai sur la province romaine de Bétique*, 672.
[210] Macrobius, *Sat.* 1. 19. 5.

reason why the colonists should not have honoured the local god, as the Romans were not a race of religious particularists. It is interesting to note too that, although the coinage of the *coloniae* displays their official names, it is only at Corduba and Hispalis in Baetica that these names occur in regular general use. At other sites it is the older, native names which are normally used.[211] In Tarraconensis, on the other hand, the new Roman names of Tarraco and Caesaraugusta entirely supplanted their Iberian predecessors, Kese and Salduba. This difference may well be a commentary on the more advanced nature and stronger staying power of Iberian civilization in the south of Spain. However, there is no evidence of the extensive acculturation in the Baetican colonies which Levick found in the colonies of Anatolia.[212]

The *coloniae* therefore were probably responsible for the widespread dissemination of Roman ideas of urbanization in Baetica, introducing for the first time formalized types of Roman towns, and drawing many natives into their orbit with a good deal of passive Romanization. In some aspects, for example in the sphere of law and, in the case of greenfield sites, architecture, they did imitate Rome as closely as possible. However, in other areas they appear to have been content to adapt native structures rather than destroy these and start again. Some acculturation of the colonists also occurred, but not to the extent found elsewhere in the empire, especially the Greek-speaking East. The *coloniae* did not, however, retain their position of pre-eminence simply by being *coloniae*. Those which went on to be major sites did so because of other factors, while others became only average or minor towns.

---

[211] e.g. at Astigi the normal adjective used by natives of the town is *Astigitanus* (e.g. *CIL* 2. 1473); there is only one possible example of the use of the town's official titles for the same purpose (producing *Firmana*, J. González, 'Miscelanea epigráfica andaluza', *A.e.A.* 55 (1982), 153 ff., at p. 156). This contrasts sharply with Corduba and Hispalis where *Patriciensis* and *Romulensis* are frequently found.

[212] B. M. Levick, *Roman Colonies in Southern Asia Minor* (1967), chs. 11 and 12.

5

From Caesar to Vespasian: Problems of City Status

As has been seen, in the republican period there were very few communities possessing a Roman legal status in the south of Spain. The number of such towns gradually increased from the time of Caesar onwards. Unfortunately our records of this development are small in number, the most extensive account being the Elder Pliny's summary of the types of community in the province.[1] This lists the total number of towns (*oppida*) as 175; a figure which included 9 *coloniae*, 10 *municipia civium Romanorum*, 27 (*oppida? municipia?*) *Latio antiquitus donata*, 6 free towns, 3 treaty towns, and 120 tribute-paying towns.

Pliny is usually believed to have drawn heavily on the surveys of Spain conducted under Agrippa when compiling these figures. If this is the case, the summary in the *Natural History* ought in the main to reflect the state of Baetica in the Augustan period. Unfortunately, however, Pliny seems occasionally to have amended his survey to take into account developments up to his own day; for example, the figure he gives for the number of colonies to be found in Tarraconensis is correct only if the two post-Augustan colonies of Clunia and Flaviobriga are included in the total. Flaviobriga is mentioned in the text, but Clunia is not. The most striking example of this conflation of several distinct chronological periods comes at the very end of the survey of the Iberian peninsula where, seemingly as an afterthought, Pliny mentions the Flavian blanket grant of *Latinitas* to these provinces, thus rendering redundant virtually everything he has previously recorded about the legal statuses of the Iberian towns.[2]

This tendency to mix apparently in an unsystematic way information presenting different chronological periods as if they were one is not the only problem we encounter when using Pliny's records. His survey is in itself avowedly partial in nature. Pliny, after stating the numbers of towns concerned, goes on to say that he will list only those towns which are worthy of record or easily pronounced in Latin, 'digna memoratu aut Latino sermone dictu facilia'. Given the subjective nature of these criteria,

---

[1] Pliny, *NH* 3. 1. 7.
[2] Ibid. 3. 1. 30, the nature of which will be examined in a subsequent chapter.

we might suspect that important information has slipped out of the record here; information which it is now impossible to restore with confidence.

Are any general checks available on Pliny's information? One possibility would be to use the Greek geographer Strabo for this purpose. Strabo states that 'Turdetania' (here comprising not only the Baetis valley, but also the surrounding highlands which went up to make the province of Baetica) contained allegedly (φασί) 200 *poleis*.[3] This appears to confirm Pliny's general accuracy since Strabo does not know the precise total of towns concerned, two hundred being the nearest round number. Like Pliny, Strabo relied on previous authors for his account. His source of information here was probably Artemidorus (*fl.* 100 BC). If so, Strabo's account shows that the numbers of towns in Baetica had not changed significantly from the beginning of the first century BC down to the Augustan period. Strabo does not record either a title or the status of any of the towns he mentions, probably because, like Pliny, he is merely relying on received information, amending it when personal knowledge makes this possible. Here, if his source is Artemidorus, neither title nor status would have been in existence at the time when the account was originally written.

Pliny lists all the colonies of Baetica. Of the other categories of town, two of the three treaty towns are mentioned, Epora[4] and Malaca,[5] and two of the six free towns, Old Astigi and Ostippo.[6] A further free town can probably be identified as Singilia Barba, which is styled as a 'Municipium Flavium Liberum' on two inscriptions. This title which makes no sense in itself is perhaps an attempt to draw attention to, and preserve the memory of, the town's privileged status before Vespasian's grant of *Latinitas* to Spain.[7] Singilia is mentioned by Pliny,[8] but he omits the second half of its name, 'Barba', which is often attested in epigraphy of the town, and any mention of free status. Singilia therefore offers a good illustration of the random nature of the criteria Pliny used in his survey.

No evidence allowing the identification of the other three free towns has yet come to light. This is also true in the case of the other treaty town. Knapp confidently asserts that this was Ebusus, stating that all towns of Punic origin were assigned to the *conventus* of Gades.[9] If this were true the

---

[3] Strabo, 3. 2. 1.   [4] Pliny, *NH* 3. 1. 10.   [5] Ibid. 3. 1. 8.
[6] Ibid. 3. 1. 12.
[7] *CIL* 2. 2025, and E. Serrano Ramos *et al.*, 'Varia arqueológica malacitana', *Jábega*, 11 (1975), 44 ff.   [8] Pliny, *NH* 3. 1. 10.
[9] In app. 7 of his *Aspects of the Roman Experience in Iberia*. This appendix attempts to identify all the towns possessing legal status in Baetica, but presents no good evidence for its conclusions.

problem would be easily solved, as Ebusus is attested as a treaty town.[10]
However, Knapp does not argue for his assertion, and Ebusus is normally
thought to have been part of the province of Hispania Tarraconensis,
which makes more sense in terms of its geographical location. Knapp's
underlying thesis seems simply to be wrong; towns with a Punic past
existed well outside the *conventus* of Gades, for example Salacia in
Lusitania, and so there is no good reason to posit that Ebusus was
allocated to the *conventus Gaditanus*.

Hübner, in his introduction to the inscriptions of Epora, suggested that
Ripa could be the third treaty town. His argument is based purely on
Pliny's text where Ripa immediately precedes Epora in Pliny's list, and is
marked off from its predecessors by 'mox' ('. . . Obulco quod Pontificense
appellatur, *mox* Ripa, Epora foederatorum, Sacili Martialium . . .'), leading Hübner to suggest that the two nouns are both governed by the
following genitive *foederatorum*. This solution has more to commend it
than Knapp's, but the grammatical argument certainly cannot be said to
be conclusive in itself.

It is perhaps significant that two cities listed as either free or in treaty
with Rome, Malaca and Ostippo, had strong Punic backgrounds. At
Ostippo a *decemvir* is attested, dating from the Tiberian period.[11] It has
been suggested that this office could be an approximate rendering of a
Punic municipal office, such as *suffete*, into Latin.[12] Even if this is not the
case, it does appear to be a native, rather than a Roman, form of magistracy.[13] At Marchena, close to the town, a series of *stelae* which may be
part of a Tanit cult have been found.[14] There is a high incidence of Punic-
type names, such as Saturnina and Fortunata, in the epigraphy of Ostippo, and Livy remarks in his history that the town always supported
Carthage, 'Carthaginiensium semper partis'.[15] Malaca, described in the
early principate by Strabo as 'Phoenician in appearance', ψοινικικὴ τῷ
σχήματι,[16] also issued coins of Punic design and with Punic legends at this

[10] Pliny, *NH* 3. 5. 76.   [11] *CIL* 2. 5048.
[12] T. R. S. Broughton, 'Municipal Institutions in Roman Spain', *CHM* 9/1 (1965), 126 ff.
[13] See the detailed discussion in Ch. 8.
[14] Discussed at length in Ch. 8. See J. A. Pérez, 'Un caso de pervivencia púnica durante
el imperio Romano, el municipio Bético de Ostippo', *Memorias de historia antigua*, 5 (1981),
95–102. But see contra, M. Blech, 'Esculturas de Tajo Montero', in J. Arce (ed.), *La religión
romana en Hispania* (1981), 97–109. The office of *Xvir* is now attested at La Rambla
(Cordoba), weakening its possible Punic origin.
[15] Livy, 28. 22. 2. It might be interesting to speculate whether Livy was generalizing from
historical records or perhaps making an inference from the Punic nature of the town in his
own day.
[16] Strabo, 3. 4. 2.

date. Singilia too possessed some irregular administrative features. Two town councils are attested, the *ordo Singiliensis*, and the *ordo Singiliensis vetus*.[17] This may indicate a double community, or perhaps the *vetus ordo* is the remnant of an inner council of elders of the kind that Aristotle mentions as existing at Carthage.[18] Rome may have been prepared to recognize the organization of the Punic towns as superior to that of the native Iberian ones, and so give them special rank, while not granting them a Roman status on the grounds that they were still too barbarian in outlook. Alternatively these towns perhaps preferred free or treaty status to that of being integrated fully into the Roman body politic. Certainly such statuses had an appeal; Cicero notes that some towns in Italy debated at great length whether to retain them or become *municipia* after the Social War.[19]

The other two towns known to have been in these categories have a less obvious claim to preferential treatment. Nothing is known of Old Astigi, presumably an Iberian centre of some importance, and, if it lay next to the newly established *colonia*, of strategic significance, commanding the head-waters of the River Singilis. At Epora a priest of Hercules is attested,[20] perhaps hinting at Punic influence and masking a cult of Melqart; but, given the general popularity of Hercules in the ancient world, this is by no means certain. The town's epigraphy also records a large number of Iberian names, such as Fulcina Attuna, Calpurnia Uprenna, and P. Attenius Afer.[21] It was, again, a strategically important site placed on a river, and lying on the main road from the province to the north.[22]

The town's most interesting feature, however, is an insciption dating to the reign of Claudius which, along with a further inscription, also of the first century AD, records that members of the town were enrolled in the Galerian tribe.[23] This suggests that Epora was given some form of Roman legal status before the reign of Nero, who almost invariably used the Quirine tribe in his new enrolments. Such a grant could explain the dedication to the 'Lupa Romana' ('the Roman she-wolf') by the *sevir*, M. Valerius Phoebus.[24] This form of dedication is unusual, and could be seen as an apt way of marking the acquisition of some form of citizen rights. This would bear important implications for Pliny's survey, suggesting that Epora was no longer a treaty town at the time when the *Natural History* was written. We have no way of knowing whether Pliny has

[17] *CIL* 2. 2026.   [18] Aristotle, *Pol.* 2. 11.   [19] Cicero, *Pro Balbo* 8. 21.
[20] *CIL* 2. 2162.   [21] *CIL* 2. 2160, 2159.
[22] As attested in al-Himyari, *Kitāb ar-Rawd al-Miṭār fī Habar al-Akṭār*, 56.
[23] *CIL* 2. 2158, 2159.   [24] *CIL* 2. 2156.

amended the number of such towns at the beginning of his survey to take account of this change, as he appears to have done in the case of the colonies of Tarraconensis. There is however, as will be seen below, a plausible way of explaining the occurrence of the Galerian tribe without assuming a grant of Roman legal status.

The ten *municipia civium Romanorum* listed by Pliny are also difficult to detect. One initial question is why Pliny chose to call the communities of Roman citizens in Baetica and Lusitania 'municipia', while elsewhere, for example in Tarraconensis, he calls them 'oppida'. Some scholars have seen a difference in status as being implied by this differentiation, 'oppida' denoting a less organized form of community than 'municipia'. This is to read too much into the wording of Pliny. Gades, for example, is one of the ten *municipia* of Baetica, as is shown by the large number of coins carrying the head of Agrippa with the legend 'Municipi Patronus' ('town patron').[25] Columella, a native of the city, also refers to his home town as a *municipium*.[26] Pliny, however, describes Gades as a township of Roman citizens called *Augustani* living in the city of *Iulia Gaditana*, 'oppidum civium Romanorum qui appellantur Augustani urbe Iulia Gaditana'.[27] Similarly several of the towns in Tarraconensis called *oppida c.R.* by Pliny minted coins describing themselves as *municipia*, for example Dertosa,[28] Bilbilis,[29] Calagurris,[30] and Ilerda.[31] Pliny therefore is merely using *variatio*. Another possibility is that Pliny's sources for Baetica and Lusitania used 'municipia', while his source for Tarraconensis used 'oppida', and since there was no difference in meaning the use of both phrases did not seem incongruous to Roman eyes.

Gades obtained its grant of citizenship from Caesar in 49 BC.[32] Prior to this, Caesar had given the town a new constitution, removing, Cicero implies, many of its Punic features.[33] Certainly by 43 BC *quattuorviri* and *comitia* are attested, showing that a reasonable Roman political veneer was in place.[34] The name of the town causes some problems. Pliny's account suggests that it was *Urbs Iulia Augusta Gaditana*; an inscription, dating from the Antonine period, refers to the *Municipium Augustum Gaditanum*.[35] *Urbs* is not an uncommon epithet for a town in Spain, occurring in the titles of three *coloniae*, Tarraco, Carthago Nova, and Salacia, but it does at first sight, given its feminine gender, seem an

[25] e.g. *MI* nos. 89. 90.
[26] Columella, *RR* 7. 2. 4.   [27] Pliny, *NH* 4. 22. 119.   [28] *MI* nos. 820. 821.
[29] *MI* nos. 546–50, 552.   [30] *MI* nos. 684–97.   [31] *MI* nos. 315–7.
[32] Dio, 41. 24.   [33] Cicero, *Pro Balbo*, 19. 43.   [34] Cicero, *Ad Fam.* 10. 32.
[35] *CIL* 2. 1313.

unlikely title for a *municipium*. Nevertheless there is a parallel for its use as a non-colonial *cognomen* from the town of Osca in Tarraconensis. Here coins dating to the Augustan period display the legend 'V(rbs) V(ictrix) Osca'.[36] One *quadrans* of the town bears the obverse legend 'Mun.' and 'Osca' on the reverse.[37] The only natural interpretation of the coin's legend is 'Municipium Oscense'. The town therefore had become a *municipium* by the reign of Augustus. Despite this the legend 'V.V. Osca' persists into the reigns of Tiberius and Caligula.[38] At Dertosa, coins with the legend 'Mun. Hibera Iulia' are attested.[39] Similarly at Bilbilis the legend 'Mun. Augusta Bilbilis' is present.[40] Names of a gender completely different from that of the status of the town therefore could be tolerated among its titles, a point which will become of increasing importance below.

The only other *municipium c.R.* securely attested is Regina, which Pliny explicitly states was of this rank.[41] The site of the town, placed in the *conventus* of Gades by Pliny, is uncertain. It has been identified with a variety of sites in the south of the province close to Hasta Regia,[42] on the assumption that Pliny's Regina was the source of the coinage bearing the bilingual Libyo-Phoenician and Latin legend, Turricina.[43] However, given their similarity in design to *asses* struck by Carisius at Emerita and the fact that some have been found overstruck with Emeritan countermarks, it appears that these coins were in fact struck by the town of Regina, sited at the modern village of Casas de Reina in Extremadura,[44] leaving the site of the more southerly *municipium*, Regina c.R., undetermined.

Apart from the cases above, there are no clear instances of *municipia c.R.* in the province. The best potential candidate for this rank is Italica, described as a *municipium* on its coins,[45] which date from the Augustan and Tiberian periods. But it is unclear whether this is a reference to a *municipium* with citizen rights, or to one assigned the *ius Latii*. Some inhabitants of Italica were Roman citizens,[46] but this need not imply that all the townsfolk enjoyed this status. Italica itself is mentioned by Pliny

---

[36] *MI* nos. 604–8.   [37] *MI* nos. 610.   [38] *MI* nos. 611–16.

[39] *MI* nos. 818.   [40] *MI* nos. 546–7.   [41] Pliny, *NH* 3. 1. 15.

[42] e.g. Cortijo de Casina.

[43] e.g. A. Beltrān, in *Curso de numismática* (1950), i. 306, and F. Chaves Tristan, 'Numismática antigua de la ulterior', *Numisma*, 30 (1980), 99–122.

[44] See O. Gil Farres, *La moneda hispánica en la edad antigua* (1966), 314, and E. Collantes Vidal, 'Reacuñaciones en la moneda ibérica', *Ampurias*, 31–2 (1969–1970), 255–7, esp. p. 256.

[45] *MI* nos. 1043–53.   [46] Ps. Caes., *B. Alex.* 52, 57.

merely in a list of the *oppida* of the *conventus* of Hispalis, with no distinguishing features, though his partial approach makes it impossible to draw any conclusions from this. The strongest argument against an immediate identification of Italica as a *municipium c.R.* from its coinage is that several towns in Tarraconensis which describe themselves as *municipia* on their coins are listed by Pliny as having Latin, not Roman, citizen rights. These include Ercavica,[47] Cascantum,[48] and Osicerda.[49]

Nevertheless Italica should have been a *municipium civium Romanorum* prior to its grant of honorary colonial status by Hadrian, since Hadrian can find no advantage for its citizens in being promoted to colonial status, something which there obviously would have been had the town possessed only the *ius Latii*. Hadrian calls the town a 'municipium antiquum',[50] and compares it to Utica, which received Roman citizen status from Augustus.[51] This suggests that Italica may have received this status at the same time, but it could have obtained it at any time prior to Hadrian's grant. González on the other hand believes that the town remained a *municipium iuris Latii* up to the time of this grant.[52]

It is impossible, therefore, to tell whether Italica was a Roman or Latin *municipium* at this period. Coins provide even more elusive hints concerning the status of other communities. Three towns, Ilipa,[53] Orippo,[54] and Iliturgi,[55] have their names as a neuter adjective on their coins. This may indicate that 'municipium' is understood as their governing noun. Nevertheless 'oppidum' cannot be ruled out, nor can the less likely possibility that 'aes' should be understood here, in which case the coins give no evidence about legal status. All date from the latter half of the first century BC.

Ilipa and Isturgi are given titles in Pliny's description of Baetica. Ilipa's is corrupt and reads 'Ilpa' (the correct reading is 'Ilia'),[56] Iliturgi's is *Forum Iulium*.[57] Orippo is mentioned without a title in a list of towns of the *conventus* of Hispalis.[58] If these towns were all of the same rank, a title does not appear to be a firm indication of possession of legal status. Again, if

[47] Pliny, *NH* 3. 3. 24, *MI* nos. 558–60, 562–5.
[48] Pliny, *NH* 3. 3. 24, and *MI* nos. 644–6.
[49] Pliny, *NH* 3. 3. 24, and *MI* nos. 809–11.
[50] Aulus Gellius, *NA* 16. 13.   [51] Dio, 49. 16.
[52] J. González, 'Italica: Municipium iuris Latii', *MCV* 20 (1984), 17 ff.
[53] *MI* nos. 883–94.   [54] *MI* no. 919.
[55] *MI* no. 839.
[56] Pliny, *NH* 3. 1. 11. For 'Ilia', see *CIL* 2. 1475 and the discussion in J. Millán León, *Ilipa Magna* (1989).
[57] Ibid. 3. 1. 10.   [58] Ibid. 3. 1. 11.

they were *municipia*, there is no way of telling if they enjoyed Latin or citizen status.

Another Baetican *municipium* may be attested by a coin bearing the legend 'Mun. Dipo(. . . ?)',[59] but its provenance is unclear, and our literary sources suggest that the town lay in Lusitania, not Baetica.[60] The coin is normally dated to the first century BC. If 'Dipo' was in Lusitania, it is another example of Pliny not amending his sources, as at the beginning of his account of Lusitania he names all the four *municipia* of the province he lists, but 'Dipo' is not among them.[61]

A further hint of a *municipium* comes from a fragmentary inscription found at Arunda, but rejected as a forgery by Hübner, reading 'Iulio Divo municipes . . .'.[62] Hübner gives no reason for rejecting the stone, and he may have done so simply because Arunda is mentioned without a title in Pliny;[63] hence Hübner may have assumed that the town could not have been a *municipium*. The dedication to Caesar after his death perhaps suggests that he granted municipal status to the town, or that it was granted in the Augustan period. Caution is needed; 'divus' normally precedes rather than follows its governing noun, and although this could merely be the error of a provincial stone-cutter, it could also indicate that the stone was forged.

A bronze tablet found at Emerita in Lusitania may provide evidence of a *municipium* in Baetica.[64] Dating to AD 6, it records how the 'decuriones et municipes Martienses qui antea Ugienses fuerunt' ('the councillors and citizens of Martia previously known as Ugia') made a *hospitium* agreement with the *colonia* of Emerita. The Ugia concerned has been identified as Ptolemy's Ugia in Baetica.[65] Attempts have also been made to link it with one of the two titled Urgias (Castrum Iulium) in Baetica, on the grounds that both titles have a martial content; but this is fanciful. The community involved may have been situated in Lusitania rather than Baetica, where all the known towns whose names approximate to Ugia are found in the south of the province, and hence far from Emerita; consequently a *hospitium* agreement with a *colonia* of this region, such as Urso or Hispalis, would seem more convenient for the Ugienses. Nevertheless, given the importance of personal contacts in the Roman world, the possibility of the Ugienses being in Baetica cannot be ruled out. Ugia should have had some form of legal status, as its envoys, P. Mummius Ursus and M. Aemilius Fronto, were both Roman citizens, enrolled in the Galerian tribe.

D'Ors suggests that the Roman settlement found at Azuaga in Extrem-

[59] *MI* no. 914.   [60] Livy, 39. 30. 2; *IA*, 418. 3; *Rav. Cosm.* 314. 8.
[61] Pliny, *NH* 4. 22. 117.   [62] *CIL* 2. 123*.   [63] Pliny, *NH* 3. 1. 14.
[64] *AE* (1952), 49.   [65] Ptolemy, 2. 4.

adura is the Ugia of the tablet.[66] Only the initial of this town, 'U', is known, but its geographical location, its apparent enrolment in the Galerian tribe,[67] and possible title of 'Iulium'[68] lend support to the hypothesis. However, if Azuaga was Ugia, it is strange that the title Martialis, of which the tablet makes so much, does not occur on the surviving inscriptions, many of which contain the town's name, and so the identification, while attractive, cannot be said to be certain. Nevertheless it does appear that there was an early privileged town at Azuaga.

If the town involved was Lusitanian, rather than lying in Baetica, it provides, along with 'Dipo', another warning about the nature of Pliny's description of Iberia, as there is no mention of the town in the Lusitanian section of his account. Once again we have an example of Pliny failing to amend his sources to bring them up to date.

An alternative approach to this problem would be to assume that Caesar, given the hostility to his cause in Spain, made individual rather than communal grants of Roman citizenship after his Munda campaign. In this case while some families at Ugia might have obtained citizen rights, the majority would have remained *peregrini*. This would have left Ugia simply a stipendiary community where some Roman citizens happened to live. This citizen group ought to have played a leading role in the town, explaining the selection of the ambassadors from it. If this was the case, it is easy to see why Pliny, given his criteria for inclusion, could have omitted the town as unimportant regardless of the province in which it was situated. This solution, too, is not without its problems: if it is correct, it implies that neither the phrase 'decuriones et municipes', nor the possession of a title, implies any special status for the community.

Our last attested *municipium* is Belo, where an inscription has been found which dates to the early second century AD and reads: 'Q. Pupio Urbico Gal. IIvir. MCB ex dec(reto) ordinis Q. Pupius Genetivus pater et Iunia Eleuthera mater piissimo filio posuerunt' ('To Quintus Pupius Urbicus of the Galerian voting tribe a *duovir* MCB by decree of the town council. His father Quintus Pupius Genetivus and mother Junia Eleutheria set up this monument to an exemplary son').[69] 'MCB' expands to 'm(unicipii) C(laudii) B(elonensis)'. Claudius seems, therefore, to have established a *municipium* at Belo. This would make good historical sense. Claudius' reign saw campaigning in Mauretania, the campaigns were supplied from Baetica, and Belo would have made an ideal base for this purpose.

[66] D'Ors, 'Una nueva tabla emeritense', 46–74.   [67] *CIL* 2. 5547.
[68] *CIL* 2. 5544: 'Divo Nervae D.D. *m.I.V.*P.I.E.D.'   [69] *AE* (1971), 172.

Further support for such a grant could be seen in the upsurge of
building activity at Belo in the Claudio-Neronian period, which might
have been sparked off by its acquisition of higher status, in the same way
as the later Flavian grant of the *ius Latii* appears to have heralded a major
increase of building in the province. The presence of the Galerian tribe
also implies a pre-Flavian grant of status.[70]

Albertini argued, admittedly without the knowledge of the above inscription, that Claudius established a *colonia* at Belo. His argument is
based on the fact that Belo is assigned the title 'Claudia' in the *Antonine
Itinerary*.[71] Central to this view is the belief that the gender of a town's title
must always agree with that of its status, but this is not the case; 'Claudia'
could agree with the gender of 'Belo' (this question of agreement is of
importance and will be discussed at length below); and the assumption
that a title implies status can also be legitimately doubted.

Attempts have also been made to identify Belo with the mysterious
colonia of Iulia Traducta mentioned by Pliny and Strabo.[72] However,
Mackie has demonstrated that this town should be placed in Mauretania
rather than Baetica. Moreover, even if Iulia Traducta is placed in
Baetica, there is no firm evidence to identify the town with Belo. Therefore this approach to securing colonial status for Belo must also be said to
fail.[73]

Apart from the above, one further piece of evidence has been used to
argue for a *colonia* at Belo. This is a highly fragmentary bronze inscription, dating to the late first century AD, found in the town's *capitolium*.
The fragment, which appears to be part of an imperial letter to the town,
has a fourth line which reads '. . .]co[. . .'. This has been restored as
'co[l](oni)', but it seems extremely unwise to base a claim for legal status
on such slight evidence.[74]

The evidence for the Galerian tribe at Belo, and hence its early acqui-

---

[70] Dio, 60. 24. 5, see also D. Nony, 'Claude et les espagnols, sur un passage de
l'Apocoloquintose', *MCV* 4 (1968), 51–71
[71] *IA* 407. 3, with E. Albertini, *Les Divisions administratives de l'Espagne romaine* (1923),
61–2.
[72] Pliny, *NH* 5. 1. 2 places the town in Mauretania, but Strabo 3. 1. 8., giving it the title
of Ἰουλία Ἰοζα, places it on the Mediterranean coast of Baetica. The latter is the location
preferred by Brunt, *Italian Manpower*, 591. Galsterer identifies Belo with Iulia Traducta,
Untersuchungen zum römischen Städtewesen, 32 ff.
[73] Mackie, 'Augustan Colonies in Mauretania'.
[74] The fragment as a whole reads '. . .]eam rump[. . . / . . .]st deficie[. . . / . . .]
abundequ[. . . / . . .]co[. . . / . . .]qu[. . .', A. d'Ors, 'El bronce de Belo', *Emerita*, 27
(1959), 367 ff. See the discussion in Galsterer, *Untersuchungen zum römischen Städtewesen*,
34 f. Galsterer, however, is unwilling to dismiss the argument entirely, remarking: 'vielleicht
Kolonie des Claudius' (p. 65).

sition of a Roman legal status, is also, unfortunately, problematical. The *cognomen* of Urbicus' father, 'Genetivus', could suggest he was a native of the *colonia* of Urso rather than Belo. In this case, the Galerian tribe may be present as one of the tribes in which citizens of Urso, not Belo, were enrolled. The only tribe presently attested at Urso is the Sergian, but several Baetican colonies contained colonists enrolled in two tribes, and in two of these, Hispalis and Corduba, the two tribes were the Sergian and Galerian.[75] If Urbicus' father was from Urso, our inscription can tell us nothing about the tribe allocated to Belo, and the argument for pre-Flavian legal status falls. Consequently Belo may have been simply a stipendiary town with the title 'Claudia' in the Julio-Claudian period.[76] However the balance of evidence, although not entirely conclusive, is that it did become a *municipium* in the Claudian period. If so, Pliny has not amended his text to take account of this change. When he lists Belo he describes it as an *oppidum*, making no mention of any title.[77] Again it is impossible to tell if Belo was a *municipium* with Roman citizen, or Latin, rights, or whether Pliny has included it as such in his summary at the beginning of his description of Baetica.

Finally, the town of Carteia probably enjoyed the status of *municipium iuris Latii* when Pliny's sources were compiled. The town had received the *ius Latii* as a *colonia Latina* in 171 BC with the title *colonia Libertina/orum*.[78] Carteia's coins initially bore legends containing the abbreviation 'S(enatus) C(onsulto)', but were later followed by series with the abbreviation 'D(ecreto) D(ecurionum)'. The change probably marks one in status from a *colonia Latina* to a *municipium iuris Latii*. However, there is no way of ascertaining when this took place. Pliny again fails to make any note of Carteia's legal status, confining himself to commenting that the town was the site of Tartessos.[79] Brunt holds out the possibility that Carteia may have been a beneficiary of the *Lex Iulia* of 90 BC, and hence become a *municipium civium Romanorum*.[80] It could therefore be added to the list of towns potentially possessing this status in the province, as well as to those having the *ius Latii*, but our sources offer no proof one way or the other here.[81]

---

[75] See J. González, 'Urso: Tribu Sergia o Galeria', in González (ed.), *Estudios sobre Urso*, 133–53.

[76] The view of F. Vittinghoff, *Römische Kolonisation und Bügerrechtspolitik unter Caesar und Augustus* (1951), 110.

[77] Pliny, *NH* 3. 1. 7.   [78] Livy, 43. 3. 4.   [79] Pliny, *NH* 3. 1. 7.

[80] Brunt, *Italian Manpower*, 206 n. 3.

[81] Galsterer, on the other hand, believes the town retained Latin colonial status: *Untersuchungen zum römischen Städtewesen*, 7 ff., 66.

A total of nine or ten possible *municipia* can therefore be identified in Baetica, four of which are clearly attested. Of these, Gades probably took this title on its grant of citizenship in 49 BC, and the coins of Italica provide a *terminus ante quem* for the use of the title. Ugia's (if it was a Baetican town) *hospitium* agreement provides a *terminus ante quem* for its acquisition of this status, and Belo's promotion to the rank of *municipium* appears to be indicated by its title Claudia. Of the others, only Arunda can provide a tenuous possible date for its acquisition of the title. Only two of these *municipia*, Gades and Regina, can be be securely attested as *municipia c.R.* It is unclear whether the remaining seven or eight ought to be included in Pliny's list of towns with Roman or Latin rights.

Attempts to determine the towns of Roman legal status in the province have normally centred on a search not for communities with Roman citizen status, but for those said by Pliny to have enjoyed Latin status. Only three, or perhaps four, of these are listed explicitly by Pliny: the town of Laepia, which had the title †Regia,[82] Carisa Aurelia, Urgia Castrum Iulium, and Urgia Caesaris Salutariensis.[83] The normal way of identifying the remaining Latin towns has been to use the titles given by Pliny in his survey of the province, although it is interesting that Pliny in the passage just discussed does not think that this in itself is sufficient to distinguish them. The standard analysis of this kind was carried out by Henderson,[84] who listed the following titles which she claimed had 'an unmistakable colonial ring':

Segida Augurina
Nabrissa Veneria Colobana [thus Henderson, but the text 'Nabrissa cognomine Veneria et Colobana' implies that Colobana was a separate town]
Seria Fama Iulia
Nertobriga Concordia Iulia
Segida Resituta Iulia
Ugultunia Contributa Iulia
Lacimurga Constantia Iulia
Tereses? Fortunales
Urgia Castrum Iulium sive Caesaris Salutariensis [A better reading is 'item' which would imply

Ulia Fidentia
Urgao Alba
Ebura Cerealis
Iliberri Florentini
Ilipula Laus
Artigi Iulienses
Vesci Faventia
Illiturgi Forum Iulium
Laepia Regia?
Carisa Aurelia
Calenses Aeneanici Urgia
Lucurgentum Iuli Genius
Sacili Martialium

[82] Pliny, *NH* 3. 1. 15; all *codices* read 'Laeparelia', the reading above is that proposed by Mayhoff.
[83] Ibid.
[84] M. I. Henderson, 'Julius Caesar and Latium in Spain', *JRS* 32 (1942), 1–13.

two towns of the same name but different titles   Osset Iulia Constantia
rather than one town with two titles.]

Henderson goes on to identify a further four neuter titles which she believes were colonial titles, but were altered when the towns concerned changed from colonial to municipal status.

Sexi Firmum Iulium	Obulco Pontificense
Ossigi Latonium	Isturgi Triumphale

Henderson believed that these titles were obtained after extensive grants of Latin rights in Baetica were made by Caesar, in the same way as he distributed such rights in Sicily and Gallia Narbonensis. This would have created a large number of Latin colonies, thus providing the reason for the feminine gender of the titles. Later, under Augustus, the status of these communities was changed to that of *municipium*; and this, in some cases, led to the previous title being put into the neuter gender. Henderson detects a notice of this grant in Dio.[85] When describing the aftermath of the Munda campaign, Dio says that Caesar τοῖς δὲ εὔνοιάν τινα αὐτοῦ σχοῦσιν ἔδωκε μὲν καὶ χωρία καὶ ἀτέλειαν, πολιτείαν τέ τισι, καὶ ἄλλοις ἀποίκοις τῶν Ῥωμαίων νομίζεσθαι, οὐ μὴν καὶ προῖκα αὐτὰ ἐχαρίσατο ('to those who had shown goodwill to him he gave land and immunity from taxation, to some Roman citizenship, and to others the right to be considered Roman colonists'). Henderson took the phrase 'to be considered Roman colonists' to refer to the grants of Latin status made by Caesar. González, on the other hand, while accepting the main thrust of Henderson's argument, thinks that it is the grants of πολιτεία which signify the grant of Latin status.[86] Of these two views that of Henderson must be preferred. There is no equivalent for Latin status in Greek, and when it is referred to, for example in Strabo's description of Nîmes,[87] it is transliterated. Πολιτεία always appears to signify the full citizenship, and Henderson was right to see this part of the sentence as referring to individual grants of citizenship or, less likely, grants of the status of *municipium c.R.* to whole communities.

Nevertheless, Henderson does appear to have misunderstood Dio here, as she believed that these grants of land and immunity, 'clearly refer to the Julian *coloniae immunes*, such as Urso and Ucubi' whereas the passage seems to be referring to the Spanish communities in the province. Immediately before the section on Caesar's grants, Dio notes how Caesar levied

[85] Dio, 43, 39.
[86] J. González, 'El ius Latii y la lex Irnitana', *Athenaeum*, 75 (1987), 317–33.
[87] Strabo, 4. 1. 12.

tribute, not even sparing the temple-offerings at Gades, took land from some communities and increased the tribute of others. This is the μέν passage which answers to the corresponding δέ passage quoted above, and so to preserve grammatical symmetry, it would seem that both sections should deal with Spanish communities. In this case the grants could be seen as individual. This would make sense for Caesar on a political level, as all the Baetican towns, save Ulia, had risen against him, but there were pro-Caesarian factions in most towns. By rewarding loyal individuals he would not only secure their continuing loyalty, but also strengthen their position within their respective communities, so lessening the chances of future revolt. The privilege of being regarded as a Roman colonist suggests that where new *coloniae* were created, Spanish loyalists were incorporated into the citizen body of the newly founded settlement, so avoiding being *incolae* who had no effective political rights in their communities. Given that the *coloniae* were established in previously pro-Pompeian communities, this interpretation of Dio has much to commend it. A grammatical point in its favour may be Dio's use of τοῖς not ταῖς in this passage, ruling out the possibility that the noun to be understood is πόλις.

Nevertheless drawbacks remain. From a grammatical viewpoint the masculine plural could be used here if the noun to be understood is δῆμος. A further alternative is that the τοῖς of the text is neuter not masculine and the noun to be understood is ἄστυ. In all events the grammar of Dio's account can be construed to allow Caesar's grants to be to communities, not individuals. Moreover the first part of the sentence, concerning Caesar's penalties, does refer to whole communities, which may suggest that the second half, to preserve symmetry, should do so too. Nevertheless the second half of the passage would fit more easily with an individual interpretation. Pliny does list thirty-seven privileged communities in the province, which implies that corporate grants took place at some time, though there is no positive evidence that Caesar made them at this time, or indeed at all. The occurrence of the adjective 'Iulius' in the title of some of the titled towns which have the Galerian tribe attested, and which therefore probably obtained their status prior to Vespasian's grant of *Latinitas*, suggests that Caesar made the grants, but equally other titled towns show no evidence of this tribe, making it possible that the titles predated the grant concerned. Dio's evidence therefore would make sense if applied to communities or individuals. Perhaps the evidence is marginally in favour of individual grants.

Henderson, to support her position, suggested that the titles of the *coloniae* reflected aspects of Caesar's family history: for example, Aurelia was the name of his mother, Venus the supposed divine ancestor of the

Julian house, Aeneas the name of her son. This interpretation has been adopted enthusiastically by Henderson's modern supporters, such as González and Hoyos,[88] who propose further correspondences such as 'Augurina', referring to Caesar's augurate, 'Pontificense', to his becoming *Pontifex Maximus*, 'Alba', to Alba Longa, and 'Regia', to a noble house on his mother's side.

This is an overcomplex and oversubtle solution to the problem. If Caesar allotted the titles to praise himself, it would have been inept to make such obscure references to his own past history, particularly as many in the province, especially the native communities so named, would have had no idea to what these titles referred. Some of the offices involved, especially the augurate, seem, on dispassionate observation, too trivial to name towns after. Moreover, there are grammatical problems with this approach. 'Augurinus' is not attested in Latin, except as a proper name. The normal adjective to describe the augurate is 'auguralis' or very occasionally 'augurius'. Similarly 'Aeneanicus' is not found as an adjectival form. 'Alba' could be more easily interpreted as having a geographical reference. Such descriptions are found in Ptolemy's account of Lusitania, for example Πύργοι Λευκοί and Κατρὰ Λευκός.[89] 'Regia', too, if such it is, this section of Pliny's text being very corrupt, could more easily be taken as referring to the town's once being the seat of a petty prince, rather than to a branch of the Roman nobility.

Many of Henderson's titles are not obviously 'colonial' at all. Some have more natural interpretations which are readily apparent, for example Laepia Regia, and others could be based on quasi-transliterations of the tribal names of the town's inhabitants. This could be the root of 'Augurina', 'Aurelia', and 'Aeneanici'. A religious interpretation of some *cognomina* is also plausible. 'Latonium', 'Cerealis', 'Veneria', and 'Martialium' could refer to the local gods worshipped at these sites. We know, for example, that the local god Neto was identified with Mars.[90] Similarly 'Pontificense' could suggest that Obulco was an Iberian religious centre. 'Cerealis' could have a similar derivation, or refer to the fact that the town concerned, Ebura, was in a fertile area, which would be a distinguishing feature given its location in the uplands of the north-east of the province. Others, like Castrum Iulium and Forum Iulium, carry implications which are not grand enough for a *colonia*. *Castra* are attested in Spain, but they are small settlements, frequently attributed to larger ones. *Fora* were one of the standard forms of settlement recognized in the

[88] González, 'El ius Latii y la lex Irnitana'; B. Hoyos, 'The Elder Pliny's Titled Baetican Towns', *Historia*, 28 (1979), 439–71.
[89] Ptolemy, 2. 5. 6.   [90] Macrobius, 1. 19. 5.

republic,[91] but were very small and lacked self-government. *Fora* could grow and take on higher statuses, while retaining the original title of Forum, but it would be unlikely that such a title would be given at the moment of granting colonial status.

Another major problem with Henderson's analysis is its underlying assumption that the feminine gender of the titles must be governed by a feminine status-noun, such as 'colonia'. One immediate problem for such a position is that some of the titles involved, such as 'Fidentia', 'Laus', and 'Constantia' are nouns, and so would have to have remained in their prescribed gender whatever the status of the town concerned. Adjectival titles on the other hand appear to agree with the name of their town, not its status, for example: 'Segida QUAE Augurina cognominatur' and 'Iliturgi QUOD Forum Iulium (cognominatur)'. This can be seen from examples of towns possessing titles which were of a different gender from that of their status. At Dertosa, for example, coin legends bear the title 'Mun. Hiber*A* Iuli*A*' and 'M.H.I. Ilercavoni*A*',[92] while at Bilbilis legends read 'Mun. August*A* Bilbilis'.[93] Here the feminine gender of the adjective must agree with the town name, not the status of the town. Henderson was prepared to admit that such 'ungrammatical' practices did go on, but saw them as showing a previous colonial status. However, the evidence from Bilbilis is particularly difficult for such a position, as Henderson envisaged Augustus transforming the Spanish Latin *coloniae* into *municipia*. Bilbilis has its title, 'Augusta', in the feminine gender, and clearly received it in the reign of Augustus. No prior colonial status can therefore be invoked, and so it seems that the title must agree with the town's name, not its status as Henderson postulated.

Adjectival titles were able to accommodate themselves to whatever gender was required in the circumstances. At Urgavo a Hadrianic inscription refers to the town as the 'municipium Albense Urgavonense', which seems to support Henderson's contention that there was a shift in status at Urgavo, and that the title was changed to reflect this. Nevertheless an interesting counter-example occurs at Conimbriga in Lusitania. Conimbriga received Latin rights from the grant of Vespasian and so had the title *municipium Flavium Conimbrigense*, but on a dedication to the town and its lares, we find the feminine form *Fl(aviae) Conimbricae*.[94] The adjective here agrees with the feminine gender of its governing noun. The inscription from Urgavo would follow this natural gender-rule: its governing noun is *municipium*, with both the town's name and title being

[91] See Lex Rubria (Lex de Gallia Cisalpina), *FIRA* i. 19, i. 21.
[92] *MI* nos. 818–20.   [93] *MI* nos. 545–9.   [94] *AE* (1969/70), 247.

relegated to adjectives. Town titles could thus flagrantly disagree with the gender of the judicial status of the town and also be accommodated to fit a natural gender. The titles of towns therefore cannot give us any insight into the nature of their legal status.

One of Henderson's strongest supporters, González, has brought forward three other arguments.[95] The first goes beyond Henderson in assuming that Ossonoba Aestuaria was granted Latin colonial status by Caesar. Henderson specifically excluded Ossonoba from her list on the grounds that the title sounded more like a geographical description than a colonial title. (This concession by Henderson is in itself a blow to her overall thesis as it concedes that titles which contained no necessary reference to legal status could be given to Spanish towns, strengthening the idea that some of her 'obviously' colonial titles could refer to geographical or local features, e.g. Alba and Regia.) González uses an ingot of copper found in a shipwreck off the south of France to put forward his case for Onuba's status.[96] This reads: 'Imp. Antoni./Primuli (et) Silonis/ CCXCVII/ pro(curator?) Col(oniae?) Ono/bensis'. This interpretation has been generally accepted in the past. Nevertheless it poses major difficulties, as there is no known instance of a *procurator* being in charge, or being one of the officials, of any self-governing Roman community.[97] It is possible that 'Col' ought to be interpreted as *col(legii)*, but mining firms invariably styled themselves *societates* not *collegia*, so there are problems here too. Given the extremely corroded state of the ingot, perhaps the best solution is to read the last two words as one, there being no clear evidence of a break. This would produce *pro(curator) Colonobensis*. We know from Pliny that a town called Colobana (variant, Conobana) existed on the Baetis estuary. The Iberian habit of reduplicating syllables, and the large number of near-homonymous towns in Baetica, makes such a correction possible, and the heterodoxy of the standard reading is in its favour. Another alternative has been proposed by Euzennat.[98] This reads the final two lines of the inscription *pr(ocurator) Ossonobensis*, eliminating the title *colonia*, and changing the provenance of the piece to the modern Portuguese town of Faro. It is highly doubtful therefore whether Onuba can be shown to have been a Latin *colonia*.[99]

[95] González, 'El ius Latii y la lex Irnitana'.   [96] *AE* (1963), 109.

[97] The reading is e.g. accepted by Galsterer, *Untersuchungen zum römischen Städtewesen*, 21, 67.

[98] M. Euzennat, 'Lingots espanols retrouvés en mer', *Études classiques* (1968–1970), 83–98.

[99] For further readings, see C. Domergue, *Les Mines de la péninsule ibérique dans l'antiquité romaine* (1990), 286–7.

González's second piece of evidence concerns Iliturgi. Here a fragmentary inscription, rejected as a forgery by Hübner, reads 'Imp C . . . Had . . . P.P. Tr . . . *Coloniae* Fo . . . Iliturgit. D . . .'.[100] Hübner rejected the inscription because Pliny did not list Iliturgi as a *colonia*. This is a weak argument, but the inscription still remains problematical. It is unlikely that Iliturgi would have retained the right to style itself a *colonia* when other towns had been forced to accept the rank of *municipium*, as can be seen from the inscription of Urgavo discussed above, and is also the case at other titled towns, for example Osset,[101] Iliberris,[102] Sacili,[103] Isturgi,[104] and Ulia.[105] There is no known imperial connection to make such a favour likely, so Hübner's assumption that the stone is a forgery is probably correct. Both Tovar[106] and Galsterer,[107] however, are prepared to accept the inscription as genuine: they see it as a sign that the town later received full Roman-citizen colonial status, rather than as an indication that it had once been a *colonia Latina*. Although this approach seems more appropriate to the evidence, it must be remembered that there is nothing to support it. In all events it appears that there is no good evidence that Iliturgi enjoyed Latin colonial status in the Julio-Claudian period.

González's third piece of evidence is two coins said to have borne the legends: 'Iulia Constantia *Col* Osset' and '*Colon* Iul. Constantia Osset'. Unfortunately these coins have been lost. The first was reported in the seventeenth and the second in the eighteenth century, so there must be doubts over their readings; neither legend is of a standard form, a fact which can only increase fears that they have indeed been misread. It cannot be said therefore that these coins establish the colonial status of Osset. The only other evidence for a privileged status at Osset is an inscription said to have been found at San Juan de Aznalfache, the traditional location of Osset, recording a benefaction to a L. Caesius Pollio by the *municipes* of the town.[108] However, the inscription cannot be dated, and consequently it is best to assign it to after the Flavian period when the town would have become a *municipium Flavium*. In any case the inscription provides evidence only of a Julio-Claudian *municipium* at Osset, not of a Latin *colonia*.[109]

[100] *CIL* 2. 190*.   [101] *CIL* 2. 1256.   [102] *CIL* 2. 1572.   [103] *CIL* 2. 2186.
[104] *CIL* 2. 2121.   [105] *CIL* 2. 1535–7; *AE* (1974), 373.
[106] *Iberische Landeskunde*, i. *Baetica* (1974), 110
[107] *Untersuchungen zum römischen Städtewesen*, 13, 66: 'Kolonie spätestens seit Hadrian'.
[108] *CIL* 2. 1256
[109] For the possibility that Osset was enrolled in the Galerian tribe, which would imply it received a privileged status prior to Vespasian's grant of the *ius Latii*, see *ILS* 1101 with R. Wiegels, *Die Tribusinschriften des römischen Hispanien* (1985), 52.

Occam's razor therefore can safely be applied to the hypothesis that some towns in Baetica enjoyed the rank of *coloniae Latinae* at some point in their existence. There is no positive attestation of such a status, and the feminine titles of the towns recorded by Pliny do not seem to preclude their having been *municipia*. The notion of Latin *coloniae* probably arose because towns of Latin status were called *coloniae* in Gaul, the most famous example being that of Nemausus. One reason for this difference in nomenclature may be that while in Baetica there were towns already established, which would naturally be called *municipia* on a grant of legal status, in Gaul on the other hand many towns had to be created *de novo*, leading to their being called *coloniae*, with its implication of foundation, in Latin.[110]

At this point the underlying principle on which we are considering Pliny's titled towns, namely that the very fact that a town possessed a title implies that it also possessed a certain legal status, needs to be examined. This was not the case in the East of the empire, where many towns without colonial status had titles.[111] Examples include Φλαυία Νέα Πόλις,[112] Καισαρεῖς Τράλλεις,[113] and Καισαρεία Γερμανική.[114] In addition to such instances of stipendiary towns with titles, the East is full of towns with imperial names, such as Sebaste, or Sebastopolis. The Carian town of Stratonicea took the name of Hadrianopolis on its refoundation by this emperor, but no promotion in its legal status is known. Similarly a town without status in Paphlagonia had the title 'Caesarea Hadrianopolis'. Moreover, even *canabae* or the informal settlements outside army forts and of even lower status than stipendiary towns are known to have possessed imperial names.[115] Town titles, or grandiose town names, therefore do not necessarily imply that the town concerned enjoyed a special legal status.

Against this, it could be argued that it is not legitimate to assume that the same conditions held in the West of the empire. Here the names in Baetica do stand out in contrast to other provinces, and the fact that in Lusitania all three communities with Latin rights do have titles suggests that these are a marker of legal status. Similarly, in Baetica, it could be argued that the fact that the only three, or possibly four, towns specifically

---

[110] See Strabo, 4. 1. 11, on Vienne and N. J. DeWitt, *Urbanization and the Franchise in Roman Gaul* (1940), 23.

[111] For a full listing, see B. Galsterer-Kroll, 'Untersuchungen zu den Beinamen der Städte des Imperium Romanum', *Epigraphische Studien*, 9 (1972), 44–145.

[112] Justin, *Apology* 1. 1.   [113] *IG* 14. 2499.

[114] *BMCGC, Galatia, Cappadocia and Syria* (1899), 115.

[115] *ILS* 2475, the *Canabae Aeliae* of *Legio XI Claudia* at Durostorum in lower Moesia.

said to have had Latin rights, Laepia, Carisa, and the two Urgias, are titled again strongly suggests that a title was a legal-status indicator.[116]

In the case of Lusitania, we know of the title of only one of the Latin towns, Myrtilis, from Ptolemy.[117] Pliny therefore did not think the title of any note, which is strange if it was a status indicator, as he specifically refers to Myrtilis as a Latin town.[118] Myrtilis' title 'Iulia' also differs from the other titles previously discussed. All these are longer than a single adjective: for example, the other two Latin towns of Lusitania had the titles *Urbs Imperatoria* (Salacia)[119] and *Liberalitas Iulia* (Evora).[120] If the title did denote rank, why did Myrtilis have such an attenuated title compared with her fellow Latin cities?

In Baetica itself only a maximum of four out of over twenty titled towns are specifically listed as of Latin status, implying not that titles were a status marker, but rather the reverse. A parallel can be found in Tarraconensis where Pliny records a tribe called the Segisamiulienses in the *conventus* of Corunna.[121] There is no evidence that this tribe was other than stipendiary, and its location, in the north of Spain, supports this view. However, in Ptolemy the tribe has a titled town, Segisama Iulia,[122] which, if the title/legal-status equation is correct, would give it as much claim to Latin status as Myrtilis. An easier explanation of the title is at hand; Florus and Orosius record that this Segisama was where Augustus established a camp in one of his campaigns in the north-west of Spain.[123] The title should reflect this event rather than a grant of legal status. Other examples could include Iliturgi and Urgia, whose titles of Forum and Castrum Iulium seem too small to identify a town of colonial status, but would aptly commemorate brief activity by Caesar there.

A stipendiary town could therefore possess a title. Evidence for this assertion can be found in Baetica itself at the town of Cortes de la Frontera. Here three inscriptions have been found from a community called Saepo.[124] The first is a dedication to Hadrian by the *Res P(ublica) V(ictrix) Saep(onensis)*, the second a similar dedication to Marcus Aurelius and the third a record of the erection of a statue to a municipal benefactor by the *ordo splendidissimus Municipi Victric(ensis) Saeponensium*. Pliny lists a Saepo, in Baetica, which could be the town in question.[125] Significantly it is in a list entirely composed of non-titled towns which follows a list of titled towns in the same area and so would, according to Henderson's

---

[116] Pliny, *NH* 3. 1. 15.   [117] Ptolemy, 2. 5. 5.   [118] Pliny, *NH* 4. 22. 117.
[119] Ibid. 4. 22. 116.   [120] Ibid. 4. 22. 117.   [121] Ibid. 3. 3. 26.
[122] Ptolemy, 2. 6. 50.   [123] Florus, 4. 12; Orosius, 6. 21. 3.
[124] *CIL* 2. 1339, 1340, 1341.   [125] Pliny, *NH* 3. 1. 14.

theory, be a stipendiary town. Pliny lists another town, Usaepo, which could also perhaps be identified with our Saepo. As the title 'Victrix' precedes the name of the town in our inscriptions, Pliny, or his source, possibly wrote it, or its abbreviation, in this place in his text, producing U.Saepo, and consequently this could have been miscopied as Usaepo; or perhaps the error started with Pliny himself. If our Saepo is Pliny's Usaepo this is of crucial importance, as it is one of the few towns to which Pliny allots a specific status, and that status is stipendiary.[126] The case of Saepo, taken with those of Segisama and Ugia examined above, strongly supports the position that titles were not given solely to towns with a Roman legal status.

This is confirmed further by Pliny himself. When writing about Baeturia, he states: 'Celticos a Celtiberris ex Lusitania advenisse manifestum est sacris, lingua, oppidorum vocabulis *quae cognominibus in Baetica distinguntur*' ('that the Celtici come from Celtiberia in Lusitania is obvious from their religious practices, language, and the names of their towns which are distinguished by titles in Baetica').[127] The implication here is that there are two groups of towns, one in Baetica and one in Lusitania, one of which is distinguished from the other by the use of *cognomina*. A further passage describing Lusitania states that 'stipendiariorum quos nominare non pigeat *praeter iam dictos in Baetica cognominibus*' ('of the stipendiary towns it is worth mentioning apart from those already listed among the titled towns of Baetica'),[128] implying that there were towns in Baetica of stipendiary status with *cognomina*. At first the group listed after the first passage discussed here seems to correspond to the stipendiary titled towns mentioned in the second, but this is not the case. Most of the first set of titled towns have citizens enrolled in the Galerian tribe, suggesting that they obtained legal status at an early period. These include Seria,[129] Nertobriga,[130] Siarum,[131] Contributa,[132] and 'U'/Azuaga.[133] Various solutions to this problem could be proposed. First, that the towns concerned obtained their rights after Pliny's sources were compiled, and so he did not know of their enhanced status; secondly, that 'dictos . . .' in the second passage does not agree with the preceding 'stipendiarios'; so, while there are towns with the same names in both Lusitania and Baetica, the status of those in Baetica is undetermined, allowing some of them to

[126] Ibid. 3. 1. 15.   [127] Ibid. 3. 1. 13.
[128] Ibid. 4. 22. 118.   [129] *EE* 8, p. 520, no. 303.   [130] *AE* (1980), 562.
[131] J. González, 'Interrex y occisus est a latronibus', *Actas 1 Congreso andaluz de estudios clásicos* (1982), 223 ff.
[132] *CIL* 2. 1029.   [133] *CIL* 2. 2342 = 5547.

be of Roman legal status; or, finally, that Pliny's selective criteria have led him to miss out some titled stipendiary towns in Baetica as being of no importance. Of these it is the final solution which seems most likely. The first would require large-scale Latin grants late in the reign of Augustus or later, which seems unlikely, and the second requires a very strained reading of Pliny's Latin.

The question now arises: what was the reason for these titles, if not to mark legal status? The best solution is the one suggested by the passages themselves, but dismissed out of hand by Henderson, namely to distinguish the large number of homonymous, or nearly homonymous, towns of the province from one another. As has been seen, two Saepos were sited close to each other; Pliny's list implies that his two titled Urgias were neighbours; and, as Ptolemy's Ugia (possibly the Ugia Martialium discussed above) does not seem to have been either of these, a third near-homonymous town also existed in the province. Pliny's titled towns also include two Segidas. To these can be added the separate towns of Tucci, Itucci, and Iptucci, those of Osca and Osqua (with a further Osca in Tarraconensis), those of Ilipa and Ilipula. In addition one of the *coloniae* of the province was called Astigi, one of the titled towns Artigi, and there were two rivers called the Maenoba. Other towns in the province, such as Iliturgi and Iliturgicola, provide examples of near-homonymous names by the use of suffixes and reduplicated syllables. The attestation of a *centuria* Isurgut (cf. Isturgi) hints that the common place-names of the area were also used for much smaller holdings of land as well.[134] Given this plethora of similar names, the creation of titles would help the Roman authorities to distinguish the communities involved more clearly and avoid administrative difficulties. Singilia Barba may be another example of this process. 'Singilia' seems to be an adjective referring to the River Singilis, while 'Barba' appears to be the name of a native town. A fragmentary inscription possibly recording a further town named Barba has been found in the province,[135] so 'Singilia' should be a distinguishing title of one of two homonymous towns.

That some, though by no means all, of our titles reflect Julian propaganda is probably a result of the fact that Caesar did campaign here and not elsewhere in Spain. Even in the furthest parts of Tarraconensis imperial titles occur if there had been an imperial presence. Tribal distin-

---

134 *CIL* 2. 1064.
135 *CIL* 2. 1695, '. . . M(unicipium?) Barb(a?)' from near Martos (Jaén). See R. Atencia Páez, *La ciudad romana de Singilia Barba* (1988), 115–34.

guishing titles were probably used less frequently in Baetica than elsewhere in Spain simply because Baetican society was more advanced and
there were fewer tribal names to use. This is reflected in the ancient
geographers, who refer to fewer than six tribes when dealing with Baetica.

The titles may also reflect another problem mentioned by Pliny, namely
the unpronounceability of Iberian names for a Latin speaker. A title here
could have provided a useful substitute for the name of the town. One
possible example of this has already been mentioned: the Martienses
previously called the Ugienses who made a *hospitium* agreement with the
colonia of Emerita. Further examples which might be suggested are the
town of Regina c.R. where the original name of the settlement might have
seemed so barbarous to Rome that its title came into common usage
instead, and the town of 'Ripa'. Given that 'Ripa' lay on the banks of
the Baetis, here too we could have an example of a pronounceable title
supplanting an unpronounceable or confusing native name.[136]

If the titles of towns cannot help us to locate the towns which possessed
legal privileges in Baetica in the Julio-Claudian period, are any
other methods available to us? Probably the best way of approaching the
problem is to look at the tribes into which communities were enrolled.
The Quirine tribe was used by Vespasian, though also by Nero, and
occasionally Claudius, and it is reasonably safe to assume that towns
enrolled in it were beneficiaries of Vespasian's grant of *Latinitas* to the
Iberian peninsula. The Galerian tribe, on the other hand, was used by
Caesar, Augustus, and Claudius (possibly also by Tiberius and Caligula).
Communities enrolled in this tribe therefore are likely to have obtained
their privileges earlier than Vespasian. On a survey of Baetica, we find
twenty-three communities so enrolled. These are Nertobriga,[137] Carmo, a
major town of the province which is not mentioned by Pliny at all,[138]
Epora,[139] Iulipa,[140] Iliturgicola,[141] Arsa,[142] Belo,[143] Baesippo,[144] Barbesula,[145]
Baria,[146] Carisa,[147] Celti,[148] Ilipa,[149] Iliturgi,[150] Isturgi,[151] Ossigi,[152] Sacili,[153]
Seria? (the modern Jerez de los Caballeros, although here the attestation is
from a legionary who could have obtained citizenship, and consequently
his tribe, on recruitment to the army, in which case nothing would be

---

[136] Pliny, *NH* 3. 1. 10, 'circa flumen ipsum . . . Ripa'.
[137] *CIL* 13. 6853, 6854, 6865.   [138] *CIL* 2. 1380.
[139] *CIL* 2. 2158, 2159, but see the discussion above.   [140] *CIL* 2. 2362.
[141] *CIL* 2. 1648.   [142] *ILER* 6845.
[143] *AE* (1971), 172, see the discussion above.   [144] *IRPC* 73.   [145] *CIL* 2. 1941.
[146] *ZPE* 49 (1982), 186.   [147] *CIL* 2. 1367.   [148] *AE* (1980), 558.
[149] *CIL* 2. 1090.   [150] *AE* (1965), 101.   [151] *CIL* 2. 2121.
[152] *CIL* 2. 3350.   [153] *CIL* 2. 2188.

implied about the status of his home town),[154] Siarum,[155] 'U'/Azuaga,[156] Ulia,[157] Urgavo,[158] and perhaps Osset.[159]

Some of these cases, such as that of Belo, are problematic, and have already been discussed. The interest of the list is that it shows some correspondence (eleven are found on the above list), but not a total agreement, with the list of titled towns. Carmo is a noteworthy discrepancy. As one of the most important towns in the province, and, as the inscription listed above shows, with Roman *equites* living there, it would not be surprising if it had received privileged status, but Pliny does not even mention it. Others of these towns are mentioned by Pliny, but no hint is given of their status. Arsa is listed as an 'oppidum non ignobile' ('no mean city'), along with Mellaria[160] (for geographical reasons this cannot be the same Mellaria earlier described as a *vicus* by Pliny,[161] and is another example of homonymity in the province), Mirobriga Regina, Sosintigi, and Sisapo. There is no indication whether this statement has any reference to status. Baria is mentioned, but again there is no hint of its possible status.[162] The same is true of Celti.[163]

It appears therefore, that some towns with legal status had titles, but others did not. The results of the tribal survey only go to confirm the rest of the evidence that town titles can, in themselves, tell us nothing about a town's legal status.

Of most interest, however, are those towns which seem to have changed status since Pliny's sources compiled their information. Epora, a treaty town, has already been discussed, but two towns, described specifically as stipendiary by Pliny, Barbesula[164] and Baesippo,[165] seem to have been enrolled in the Galerian tribe. This should indicate that there was development in the province beyond the initial set of grants and before Vespasian's universal grant of the *ius Latii* to the Iberian peninsula. Alternatively, perhaps some individuals in the town obtained personal grants of citizenship in a community which remained unprivileged. It is not valid to argue that attestation of such individuals would be unlikely to survive, as they would have been the wealthiest and most influential members of the communities concerned and as such the most likely to appear in our epigraphic record.

At Barbesula, there is counter-evidence against Galerian enrolment: an

---

[154] *AE* (1980), 562.   [155] J. González, 'Interrex y occisus est'.
[156] *CIL* 2. 1029.   [157] *AE* (1961), 343, (1974), 373.   [158] *CIL* 2. 2105.
[159] *ILS* 1101, with R. Wiegels, *Die Tribusinschriften des römischen Hispanien*, 52.
[160] Pliny, *NH* 3. 1. 14.   [161] Ibid. 3. 1. 3.   [162] Ibid. 3. 3. 19.
[163] Ibid. 3. 1. 11.   [164] Ibid. 3. 1. 15.   [165] Ibid.

inscription recording a *duovir* in the Quirine tribe.[166] Nevertheless a further inscription, also of a *duovir*, this time enrolled in the Galerian tribe, has also been found. One of these two individuals should be an immigrant, but it is impossible to tell which. Another interpretation would be that the Quirine tribe's attestation shows that while Caesar made some individual grants in Barbesula, the town obtained Latin rights only under Vespasian. This interpretation perhaps is the more likely as it has the advantage of combining all the evidence from the town in a unitary whole.

If Caesar did make individual grants of citizenship after Munda, a tribal survey, like one of titles, will be useless for determining which towns had legal status, as we could never be sure whether we were dealing with recipients of personal grants, or those who had gained the citizenship from being citizens of a town which had Latin or citizen rights. The tribal survey is also limited in that we cannot tell from it what kind of status the towns concerned possessed, if they did in fact have one.

In conclusion, we unfortunately know less about the towns of Baetica in the first half of the first century AD than orthodoxy suggests. The number of status-bearing towns which can be identified with confidence is small, comprising only the citizen colonies, two *municipia c.R.*, and three towns of Latin status. The title of the last set of towns is is unclear, but may have been *municipium*, as this is the only title attested epigraphically. Other towns can be suggested as likely candidates for various ranks, but in no case is the matter certain. In particular the titled towns do not appear all to have been of one rank, and some towns listed without titles appear to be strong candidates for having possessed legal status. Some changes may have occurred in the period, such as possible grants of Latin status to Epora, Baesippo, and Barbesula. However, the epigraphic evidence that leads to this conclusion can be explained in an equally plausible way which would avoid such problems.

If it was kept up to date until Vespasian's grant of Latin status to the Spanish peninsula (something which is by no means certain), Pliny's survey of town numbers and their statuses would show that at the time of its writing over 68 per cent of Baetica still consisted of unprivileged communities and over 73 per cent of towns lacked Roman legal status. If we assume that there were developments between its composition and Vespasian's award, even the most generous interpretation of our available

---

[166] *CIL* 2. 1940.

evidence suggests that the speed of growth into Roman legal status was slow. Baetica, therefore, despite its reputation as a 'Romanized' area of the empire, remained mainly peregrine, in terms of legal status at least, in the Julio-Claudian period.

6

The Flavian Municipal Law: *Peregrini, Cives Latini,* and *Cives Romani*

ANY discussion of the extent of Roman-style urbanization and practices in Baetica in the early imperial period must centre to a large degree on an examination and assessment of Vespasian's grant of the *ius Latii* to *Hispania* and its consequent impact on provincial life. Our evidence for the grant is twofold: literary and epigraphic. Unfortunately, despite the importance of the event, our only literary record is a brief afterthought at the end of Pliny's account of the Iberian peninsula which ironically renders redundant most of what he has said previously about the legal status of the various communities there.[1] Nevertheless Pliny's notice does show us that the grant gave a right which had previously been enjoyed by very few towns in the region to all communities there.

Vespasian's action poses a large number of important questions. Pliny gives no reason why the emperor thought fit to make the grant or when he did so. A further problem is the fact that the very nature of the *ius Latii* itself is a controversial matter. Added to all these difficulties is the methodological problem: whatever our answers to the above questions, can these tell us about the sort of life which was actually led in the province of Baetica rather than that which was envisaged or intended by Vespasian and the drafters of the law?

What reasons would Vespasian have had for making such a grant? Three different possibilities immediately come to mind: that the grant was a reward for the previous adoption of Roman practices in the area,[2] that it was an incentive to encourage this process in the future,[3] or that it was granted as a concession when Rome was under some form of pressure. If the last option is the case, two further points arise: why did communities in the Iberian peninsula want the *ius Latii* and which part of the local

---

[1] Pliny, *NH* 3. 30.
[2] The view of J. S. Reid, *The Municipalities of the Roman Empire* (1913), 241.
[3] See H. R. Graf, *Kaiser Vespasian* (1937), 84, who speaks of a 'flavischen Urbanisierungspolitik in den Provinzen', and R. K. McElderry, 'Vespasian's Reconstruction of Spain', *JRS* 8 (1918), 53 ff., at p. 61.

community was the grant aimed to assuage—the whole population, or just the ruling classes?

The above considerations cannot be divorced from a discussion of the timing and geographical scope of Vespasian's action. If the *ius Latii* was granted in a time of peace, one of the first two reasons for making the grant, outlined in the previous paragraph, would seem most appropriate; however, if the grant was made in a time of tension, the final solution would appear more likely to have been the case. Pliny's phrase 'universa Hispania' is vague; the Iberian peninsula comprised three provinces not one, and is often, though not consistently, referred to collectively as the Spains, 'Hispaniae', in classical sources, including Pliny himself.[4] Does Pliny mean that the grant was made to the whole of the peninsula, or just one province within it? As the development of the three provinces towards urban life differed radically, the answer to this question must bear heavily on why it is thought that the grant was made in the first place.

Our epigraphic evidence for the grant is much more extensive than the meagre literary note found in Pliny. The end result of the grant was the promulgation of a municipal law and we are fortunate to possess several extensive fragments of copies of the charter, engraved on bronze, embodying the substance of this law. The largest of these is that from the town of Irni, complete, save for the first eighteen chapters and a central lacuna, which is fortunately filled partially by a second fragment from the town of Malaca.[5] Further fragments have been found from the charters of Salpensa, Ostippo, Villonensis, perhaps more controversially from the present-day site of Cortegana in the province of Huelva (ancient name unknown) or from Italica; and finally an unprovenanced piece probably found in Hispalis but not originally from this town.[6]

---

[4] e.g. Tacitus, *Hist.* 3. 53; Mela, 3. 1. 10. For Pliny's use of this convention, see *NH* 4. 20. 110.

[5] Irni: J. González, 'The *Lex Irnitana*'; Malaca: *FIRA* 1. 24.

[6] All the charter fragments with the exception of the lost piece from Hispalis are conveniently collected in J. González, *Bronces juridicos romanos de Andalucía* (1990). For individual fragments, Salpensa: *FIRA* 1. 23; Ostippo: A. Marcos Pous, 'La ley municipal de Ostippo', *Cordoba*, 12 (1988), 43 ff.; Villonensis (previously misread as Basilipo, e.g. A. d'Ors, 'La ley municipal de Basilipo', *Emerita*, 73 (1985), 31 ff.): F. Fernández Gómez, 'Nuevos fragmentos de leyes municipales y otros bronces epigráficos de la Bética en el museo arqueologico de Sevilla', *ZPE* 86 (1991), 121 ff.; Cortegana: for the debate surrounding the provenance of this fragment, see J. González, 'Italica, municipium iuris Latii', *MCV* 20 (1984), 17 ff. and 'More on the Italica fragment of Lex Municipalis', *ZPE* 70 (1987), 217 ff., and contra A. Canto, 'A propos de la loi municipale de Corticata, Cortegana, Huelva, Espagne', *ZPE* 63 (1986), 217 ff.; Hispalis: *EE* 9. 261. See also H. Dessau, 'Zu den spanischen Städtrechten', *Wiener Studien*, 24 (1902), 240 ff. The piece is now lost. As the fragment contains the word 'Mun[icipii]' it is clear it cannot be part of the charter of Hispalis which

The overlap of the almost complete charter from Irni with the other surviving fragments shows that there was, at root, one 'master' municipal law, applied over the whole area of the grant, with minor local variations and modifications added where necessary.[7] Unfortunately our surviving charter fragments give us no clues as to why Vespasian decided to grant the *ius Latii* to the Iberian communities nor when this process was begun. Nevertheless the content of the law might be thought to give some evidence as to what such a grant entailed for the recipient communities, and hence the reason for its promulgation.

The law embodied on our charters is highly Roman in form, and its provisions appear to assume that the workings of the towns it deals with will operate in the same way as if they were to be found in Italy.[8] This ties in with the standard interpretation of the nature of the *ius Latii*; namely that a grant of this status to a town created a group of individuals, *cives Latini*, whose rights stood somewhere between those of a simple *peregrinus* and those of a full-fledged *civis Romanus*. Crook describes this group as being in a ' "half-way" position, not Roman citizens, but possessed of some of the citizen rights . . . but what exactly that included is by no means clear'.[9]

Such individuals were known as the *Latini coloniarii*, and their rights were modelled on those of the *prisci Latini*, but seem to have been less extensive than those of this earlier group.[10] They appear to have had the right of *suffragium*, and hence could vote at Rome, though not hold office there, and that of *commercium* and hence access to the *ius civile*.[11] On the other hand they did not have the right of *conubium*, that of making a lawful marriage with a full Roman citizen, except in special cases.[12] In addition to this group of rights, those who held local magistracies in such communities, in the case of the *ius Latii minus*, and all members of the local council,

---

was a *colonia*. The engraving of the piece suggested a 1st-c. date, ruling out any possible link with the more well-known Cortegana/Italica? fragment which dates to the 3rd c.

[7] Some fragments of such a master copy of the law exist in the archaeological museum in Seville: see F. Fernández Gómez, 'Nuevos fragmentos de leyes municipales', esp. 125–7. Unlike the other charter fragments the text is not arranged in columns. The surviving fragments contain parts of chs. 67–71 of the law.

[8] See the provisions of ch. 72.

[9] J. A. Crook, *Law and Life of Rome* (1967), 43–4.

[10] See J. A. C. Thomas, *Textbook of Roman Law* (1976), 405–6.

[11] See in this respect the provisions of ch. 93 of the law that all actions not specifically covered by the charter should be dealt with according to the *ius civile*.

[12] Gaius, *Institutes* 1. 56; Ulpian, *Reg.* 5. 4. The letter appended to the end of the *Lex Irnitana*, dealing with marriages which have been made contrary to the provisions of the law (most probably between *cives Romani* and *cives Latini*), also appears to bear this out.

in the case of the *ius Latii maius*, along with varying numbers of their relatives, became full *cives Romani*.

In the most important commentary on the *Lex Irnitana*, González makes several stronger claims for the nature of the rights which devolved on individuals from a grant of the *ius Latii*. These include the view that the legal undertakings of all the citizens of the town would have been governed by the Roman legal concepts of *manus*, *mancipium*, and *patria potestas*. This is inferred from chapters 21 and 22 of the law, which state that after the magistrates of the town receive the Roman citizenship this should not affect the aforementioned relationships they already had, that is, prior to being *cives Romani*, and hence while still *cives Latini*.[13] Similar provisions are found concerning the notion of *tutela* in chapters 28 and 29. From chapter 86, which deals with the enrolment of *iudices* in the town, González deduces that *cives Latini* had the *tria nomina*, and were enrolled in the citizen tribes of Rome. The possession of this combination of rights would make the *civis Latinus* virtually indistinguishable from the full *civis Romanus*.[14]

If there were large numbers of provincials possessing such individual Latin rights, similar in many respects to those of full Roman citizenship, and being governed by the forms of Roman law, the natural implication is that Baetica, and perhaps Spain as a whole, will have contained a far larger proportion of individuals leading a substantially Roman way of life than might otherwise have been expected, and that this fact will in turn have been reflected in a highly Roman style of municipal life.

If this is the case, the award of the *ius Latii* should be seen as a reward for reaching such a stage of evolution. This would imply that the area had developed, voluntarily, classical urban structures on a major scale in the Julio-Claudian period. Alternatively it might be supposed that the charters and the granting of their ensuing rights were used as a method of prompting such urbanization by on the one hand compelling the local population to use Roman structures, while, on the other, granting them the privileges which went with such an adoption.

Some commentators have argued that Roman law was indeed a major factor in changing the customs of communities with whom Rome came into contact.[15] However, such a view raises several serious methodological

[13] González, 'The *Lex Irnitana*', 147 ff.

[14] Ibid. 149: 'the position of a *civis Latinus* was in many respects close to that of a *civis Romanus*'.

[15] See e.g. J. Edmondson, '*Instrumenta Imperii*: Law and Imperialism in Republican Rome', in B. Halpern and D. W. Hobson (eds.), *Law, Politics and Society in the Ancient Mediterranean World* (1993).

points. Our evidence suggests that Rome, rather than attempting to impose the full forms of Roman law on peregrine communities, was prepared to compromise with native practices when drafting legal solutions to problems, as can be seen in Spain from the acceptance of non-Roman legal forms in the *Tabula Contrebensis* from the republican period and the various *hospitium* agreements dating from the republican and imperial periods. Such compromises suggest that Roman law was not used as a deliberate instrument for the spreading of Roman practices. The second question is whether local magistrates on whom Rome relied to uphold the law would have had enough knowledge of Roman law, or indeed Latin, to enforce the law as it had been envisaged.[16] If they did not, the Roman nature of the law would be compromised whether or not this had been intended.

A stark alternative to the standard view of *cives Latini* outlined above, is the 'minimalist' position proposed by Millar.[17] This holds that the *ius Latii* in the imperial period entailed merely the right of the magistrates of the town concerned to obtain Roman citizenship on the completion of their office, in the case of a grant of *Latium minus*, or, if the grant concerned was one of *Latium maius*, the right of the whole town council to receive Roman citizenship. These are the only rights concerned with such grants which are listed by Gaius in his discussion of their nature, and explicitly mentioned by the other literary references which we have to the *ius Latii*.[18] Asconius, discussing Pompeius Strabo's grant of *Latinitas* to Transpadana, states 'ius dedit Latii, ut possent habere ius quod ceterae Latinae coloniae, id est ut petendo magistratus civitatem Romanam adipiscerentur' ('he granted them the Latin right, that they should have the same privilege that the rest of the Latin colonies had: namely that they might obtain Roman citizenship on holding local office').[19]

Possibly Asconius is merely listing the one salient privilege out of many here, but this is an unnatural reading of the Latin. 'Id est' implies that it is the nature of the grant as a whole that is being talked about. Similarly Strabo, in his account of the Gallic town of Nemausus, states that it had obtained τὸ καλούμενον Λάτιον, ὥστε τοὺς ἀξιωθέντας ἀγορανομίας καὶ ταμιείας ἐν Νεμαύσῳ Ῥωμαίους ὑπάρχειν ('the so-called Latin right, giving the result that those who had been elected aedile or *quaestor* in Nîmes obtain Roman citizenship').[20] The corollary to this minimalist

[16] For a controversial but generally persuasive account of literacy in the ancient world, see W. V. Harris, *Ancient Literacy* (1989).
[17] F. G. B. Millar, *The Emperor in the Roman World* (1977), app. 4, pp. 630ff.
[18] Gaius, *Institutes* 1. 96.   [19] Asconius, *In Pison.* 3.   [20] Strabo, 4. 1. 12.

interpretation of the *ius Latii* is that apart from those who were entitled to obtain Roman citizenship, the rest of the population of the town remained simple *peregrini*, possessed of no special rights. This leads to the hypothesis that there were no individual free-born *Latini* in the empire, producing a much more pessimistic view of the spread of Roman customs in the provinces than that of the 'standard' position. Only the upper classes of the communities concerned would have been affected in depth by the grant, leaving the vast bulk of the population in much the same state it had previously enjoyed.

However, we do appear to have two unambiguous references to free-born *Latini coloniarii* from the imperial period. Ulpian lists the group as one which had the right of *mancipatio*.[21] Gaius too refers to the *Latini coloniarii*, when dealing with the provisions of the Lex Aelia Sentia of AD 4.[22] These references do seem to indicate that the *Latini coloniarii* persisted as a status-group into the imperial period. This conclusion is borne out by various parts of the Flavian law. The early chapters of the law strongly suggest that the citizens of the towns concerned possessed a variety of strictly Roman legal rights, in particular that of *patria potestas*, which is singled out by Gaius as a distinguishing mark of a Roman citizen, before receiving, individually, Roman citizenship under its provisions.[23]

More significant are the chapters dealing with the manumission of slaves in the communities concerned. The chapter concerned with individuals manumitting their own slaves makes it clear that the resulting freedmen are to be 'optum[o] iure Latini Libertini'.[24] If we assume, as we must, that the standard rule for manumission, namely that the manumittee, on gaining his freedom, acquired the same status as his liberator, applied in Irni, it appears that the citizens of the town must be *cives Latini*.

---

[21] Ulpian, *Liber Singularis Regularum* 19. 4: 'mancipatio locum habet inter cives Romanos, Latinos coloniarios, Latinos Iuniosque, peregrinos quibus commercium datum est' ('*manicipatio* is possible between Roman citizens, *Latini colonarii*, informally freed slaves, and foreigners who have the right of legally binding commercial undertakings with Romans').

[22] Gaius, *Institutes*, 1. 29: 'si uxores duxerint vel cives Romanas vel Latinas coloniarias' ('if they marry Roman citizen women or one from the *Latini colonarii*').

[23] Gaius, *Institutes* 1. 55: 'quod ius [i.e. *patria potestas*] proprium civium Romanorum est. Fere enim nulli alii sunt homines [presumably the small number of "alii" includes "cives ·Latini"] qui talem in filios suos habent potestatem qualem nos habemus' ('this law is peculiar to Roman citizens. For almost no other people have such power over their sons as we have'). See also *Institutiones Justiniani* 1. 9: 'Ius autem potestas, quod in liberos habemus, propium est civium Romanorum: nulli enim alii sunt homines qui talem in liberos habeant potestatem, qualem nos habemus' ('The right of control we have over our children is peculiar to Roman citizens: for no other men have have the kind of power over their children that we have').

[24] Ch. 28.

It could be argued that the phrase 'Latini Libertini' here refers to the category of informally liberated slaves created by the provisions of the *Lex Iunia Norbana* of 17 BC or AD 19, and that the whole chapter is dealing with the process of manumission to be carried out by this group. However, this appears improbable; if it were the case, it would follow that there would be no room in the charter for a chapter dealing with the manumission process to be carried out by ordinary *municipes*, which seems unlikely.

Moreover the chapter's provisions concerning the freedmen's property rule this out. A Junian Latin, like a slave, possessed a *peculium* which reverted to his master upon death,[25] whereas the freed *Latini* of the charter are said to have a fully alienable *hereditas*, which is the mark of a free man, and consequently, in this case, of a *Latinus coloniarius*, not a *Latinus Iunianus*.[26]

Millar made the further point that in extant epigraphy no *colonia* was described as a *colonia Latinorum*, but an adjectival form was always used instead. However, this has changed with the discovery of the *Tabula Siarensis*.[27] This document, also found in Baetica, describes various funerary honours to be paid to Germanicus, and refers to '[magistratibus qui i(ure) d(icundo) in] municipio aut colonia Latinorum' ('the magistrates who hold jurisdiction in Latin municipalities and colonies') (frag. 2. 1). Here we seem to have a direct reference to communities not simply possessed of a right, the *ius Latii*, but apparently composed of individual *Latini*. This interpretation is supported by Pliny, who, when listing towns of Mauretania,[28] describes one town, Arsennia, as 'composed of *Latini*', 'Latinorum', and immediately calls another, Tipasa, 'given the *ius Latii*', 'Latio dato'. There appears to be no difference in status between the two towns. Pliny is probably simply using *variatio* here to break up a monotonous list. The possibility that 'Latinorum' could be used as a way to refer to such a town most naturally implies that the citizens of the towns concerned enjoyed the status of *cives Latini*.

If we accept that individual *cives Latini* existed, and that González's inferences about the privileges they possessed are correct, it would at first seem more reasonable to assume that the grant of *ius Latii* was a reward for

---

[25] Gaius, *Institutes* 3. 56 and Ulpian, *Institutes* 3. 7. 4 both use the ambiguous phrase 'iure quodammodo peculii' ('by a sort of law of *peculium*') for this process. However, the *Codex Theodosianus* 2. 22. 1 explicitly states that a Latin has a *peculium*. See also Thomas, *Textbook of Roman Law*, 406, 526.

[26] Ch. 72, the freedman is previously said to be 'Liber et Latinus'.

[27] J. González, 'La Tabula Siarensis, Fortunales Siarenses et Municipia civium Romanorum', *ZPE* 55 (1984), 55 ff.

[28] Pliny, *NH* 5. 1. 20.

previous Romanization rather than an incentive to encourage this process in the future. The extent of the privileges granted is so close to an award of the full Roman citizenship that it would be natural to assume that the *ius Latii* would be given only to developed areas of the empire. The concessions involved seem too great to grant on a mere hope of future widespread change in lifestyle, and would in the meantime enflame conservative political opinion at Rome. The strength of this can be seen from the prolonged outrage caused by Claudius' admission of thoroughly assimilated nobles from Gallia Comata to the senate.[29]

At this point Pliny's statement that the grant was made 'universae Hispaniae' becomes important. This appears to imply that the grant was to the whole of the peninsula. If so, a problem is caused, as the obvious backwardness of much of north-western Spain and Lusitania shows that the award of the *ius Latii* here cannot have been for previous developments in urbanization. However, as noted above, Latin authors frequently speak of 'the Spains', 'Hispaniae', as there were several provinces in the peninsula, not a *provincia Hispaniensis per se*. It could be argued, therefore, that Pliny is not referring to the whole of the peninsula, but to the whole of a single province within the peninsula, and that the province concerned is Baetica, where all our surviving municipal charters have been found.[30] Another alternative is to suggest that Pliny's use of 'tribuere' should be taken to mean 'offered' rather than 'gave', and so, although the grant was made to all of Spain, many of the more backward communities would not have taken up the offer of the *ius Latii*.[31] It is hard to sustain such a position. 'Tribuere' is used of the rights given on discharge to the troops of the Praetorian Guard, which were certainly not merely offered. It is also difficult to envisage part of the native nobility not taking up an offer which would allow at least some of them to obtain Roman citizenship. Indeed refusal to do so could have been regarded as an indication of disloyalty and hence be dangerous. Similarly, widespread refusal could have been a spark for rebellion and therefore the offer would not have been contemplated by Rome. Given the ambiguity of this passage of Pliny, and the importance of determining the scope of the grant in order to ascertain its purpose, it is necessary to look closely at any possible evidence we possess which might suggest that the scope of Vespasian's grant extended beyond Baetica.

One approach is to look at towns which took the title 'Flavius' in some

---

[29] Reflected most bitterly in Seneca. *Apocolocyntosis* 3.
[30] Galsterer, *Untersuchungen zum römischen Städtewesen*, ch. 5, pp. 37 ff.
[31] This appears to be the view of S. Keay, *Roman Spain* (1988), 58.

form in Lusitania and Tarraconensis: examples include Conimbriga in Lusitania,[32] and Aquae Flaviae in Tarraconensis. Although the adoption of these titles may well have been voluntary, it could have been provoked, as it was in Baetica, by Vespasian's grant of the *ius Latii*.[33] In Lusitania the Alcantara bridge inscription, dating from the reign of Trajan, provides us with further evidence for the grant extending beyond Baetica.[34] Here eleven communities, describing themselves as 'municipia provinciae Lusitaniae', joined together to build a bridge. The inscription has been rejected as a forgery by Galsterer on the grounds that these communities were not *municipia*.[35] Of those listed, five, the Lancienses, the Medubricenses, the Tapori, the Colarni, and the Interamnienses, are listed as stipendiary *civitates* by Pliny.[36] This is not fatal to the argument, as the inscription dates to after Vespasian's grant of *Latinitas*, and so the status of the communities could well have changed. The Aravi however, are attested as a *civitas* in the reign of Hadrian, after the building of the bridge.[37] This at first sight appears a more serious objection to the authenticity of the inscription, but again is not necessarily fatal. *Civitas* could be used by any community within the empire, including those which were technically higher in rank. Given the slight evidence against it, the Alcantara bridge inscription is best taken as genuine. If so, it provides some of the strongest evidence that Vespasian's grant was not solely restricted to Baetica, for although it is impossible to determine securely if the rank of *municipium* was reserved for towns/communities which had obtained a grant of *Latinitas*, it is hard to find an example of the word used in the context of a community which had no status higher than that of a stipendiary *civitas*. An edict of Claudius gives some support to this rather circumstantial evidence.[38] In it Claudius lays down instructions for 'colonias et *municipia* non solum Italiae, verum etiam provinciarum, item civitatium' ('the colonies and municipalities not only of Italy but also the provinces and also the other settlements there'). *Municipia* here appears to be a clearly defined status-group. If this is the case, the *municipia* of the Alcantara bridge inscription will have had the *ius Latii*, and, since Pliny records almost half of them as of definitely stipendiary status, at least in the reign of Augustus, if not later, it is reasonable to assume that they

---

[32] *AE* (1969/1970), 247.

[33] See the letter of Vespasian to the Saborenses, *CIL* 2. 1423 = *ILS* 6092.

[34] *CIL* 2. 760.

[35] Galsterer, *Untersuchungen zum römischen Städtewesen*, 62 ff. Contra B. Hoyos, 'In defence of C.I.L. 2. 760', *Athenaeum*, 56 (1978), 390 ff.

[36] Pliny, *NH* 4. 118.   [37] *CIL* 2. 429; *AE* (1954), 87.   [38] *ILS* 214.

owed their new status not to gradual individual evolution, but to Vespasian's grant.

A final argument is provided by Pliny's wording itself. Immediately prior to his notice of Vespasian's grant, Pliny states that all of Spain is rich in mineral ores. In making his point he divides the peninsula into 'Baetica' and 'Hispania Citerior'. Having just made this distinction, it is unlikely that he would immediately switch to using 'universa Hispania' to apply to only one of the two categories he has just used; he must be using it as a convenient shorthand for both of them.

The argument for restricting the grant of *ius Latii* to Baetica, on the grounds of relative urban development, is even more deeply flawed than might at first seem the case. For the province, although possessing some of the sections of the peninsula most exposed to Rome, also spanned extensive highland regions where there were many backward communities.[39] It appears therefore that Vespasian's grant was to the entire Spanish peninsula. A general survey of the areas to which the *ius Latii* was granted *en bloc* would seem to bear this out; these all seem to have been areas of low urbanization.

If we accept the above arguments it appears that the grant of the *ius Latii* cannot have been made as a reward for the adoption of Roman customs. Was it then intended to encourage this process rather than to reward it? If the grant is seen as an act of statesmanship, this interpretation could be valid. Nevertheless, on a survey of other areas which had previously been granted Latin rights *en bloc*, there appears to be no discernible tendency towards this practice stemming from the award.

The Transpadani obtained a grant of *Latinitas* from Pompeius Strabo in 89 BC.[40] Nevertheless this award does not seem to have provided any stimulus for the adoption of Roman customs. Moreover, unlike the grant to Spain, where our charter stipulates that there shall be Roman-style magistrates, there appears to have been no such requirement that the Transpadanes should use Roman forms of magistracy immediately after obtaining this privilege. Cicero, writing to Atticus in 51 BC, says, 'erat rumor de Transpadanis, eos iussos IIIIviros creare' ('there was a rumour about the Transpadanes that they had been ordered to create municipal magistracies').[41] This implies that the Transpadani had not had such magistrates before; and yet, at the time of Cicero's writing, they had possessed the *ius Latii* for over thirty years.

---

[39] See Pliny's comments on Baeturia, *NH* 3. 1. 13.   [40] Asconius, *In Pison.* 3.
[41] Cicero, *Ad Att.* 5. 2. 3.

Nor does this lack of an insistence on Roman forms seem limited to the republican period. Lepcis Magna in North Africa may have possessed Latin rights in the Flavian period, although the use of 'municipium' as a title is our only evidence for this.[42] If the town did possess the *ius Latii*, it is striking that this did not affect the form of local magistracy there. Lepcis in this period was governed by *suffetes*, a traditional Punic office, rather than by the normal *duoviri* or *quattuorviri*.[43] Similarly when Nero gave Latin rights to the Maritime Alps in AD 64, no perceptible increase in the use of Roman forms of civic organization in this area followed.[44] In the Western Alps the title *municipium* is not attested until the mid-second century AD; however, the epigraphy from this region is sparse, and to infer that the settlements here did not call themselves *municipia* is a dangerous argument from silence. Examples of such towns calling themselves *civitates* or *respublicae* equally do not rule out the possibility that they were officially *municipia*, as these forms were perfectly legitimate for towns of any rank within the empire to use. Nevertheless the area does not appear to have been one where the growth of Roman practices was widespread.[45]

It also seems that a grant of the *ius Latii* need not have entailed strict autonomy. Pliny, listing the Alpine tribes who had been given this status, notes that among them are the Trumplini and 'conpluresque similes finitimis adtributi municipiis' ('many similar groups assigned to the authority of neighbouring towns').[46] An inscription from Tergeste, dating from the time of Antoninus Pius, shows how this arrangement would have worked.[47] The stone records the honours given to Fabius Severus by the Tergestini for persuading the emperor to give the Carni and Catali, who were attributed to the town by Augustus, the right that 'per aedilitatis gradum in curiam nostram admitterentur ac per hoc civitatem Romanam apiscerentur' ('that on being elected aedile they should enter our senate and as a consequence obtain Roman citizenship'). The town is thankful for this, as it means that the Carni and Catali will now be liable to the *munera* of the town as well as obtaining its privileges. This form of attributed *ius Latii* is probably what Strabo has in mind when he states that Nemausus ὑπηκόους γὰρ ἔχει κώμας τέτταρας καὶ εἴκοσι τῶν ὁμοεθνῶν ... συντελούσας εἰς αὐτήν, †ἔχουσα† καὶ τὸ καλούμενον

---

[42] A. Birley, *Septimius Severus* (2nd edn., 1988), 16 ff. See the use of the title 'patronus municipii', on *IRT* 342 and *IRT* 346 dating to AD 77/8 and 82/3 respectively.
[43] *IRT* 347, 348, 412.
[44] Tacitus, *Ann.* 15. 32: 'Caesar nationes Alpium maritimarum in ius Latii transtulit' ('Caesar granted the peoples of the Maritime Alps the Latin right').
[45] See A. N. Sherwin-White, *The Roman Citizenship* (2nd edn., 1973), 367 ff., esp. p. 374.
[46] Pliny, *NH* 3. 20. 134.   [47] *ILS* 6680.

Λάτιον ('controls twenty-four villages inhabited by people of the same stock . . . contributing towards its exchequer. The town itself possesses the Latin right').[48] The use of κώμας here shows either the small size of the settlements concerned or their non-urban nature.

The singular ἔχουσα in the quotation above is Corais's amendment of two manuscript traditions which read ἐχούσας,[49] and ἔχουσαν[50] and has been accepted by all subsequent editors. The singular suggests that it was only Nemausus itself which had the Latin right, but Pliny in his survey of the area includes amongst the towns with the Latin right 'XXIV Nemausensibus adtributa' ('the twenty-four under the jurisdiction of Nîmes'), showing that the attributed communities also enjoyed this privilege.[51] In the same passage he also notes that there are a further nineteen 'ignobilia' *oppida* with the Latin right. These presumably held the same relationship to other cities as the twenty-four did to Nemausus. The attributed areas were technically ruled from the centre to which they were attributed. This would not be too problematic in the case of Nemausus, and Strabo's comment that the people of the κῶμαι were ὁμοεθνεῖς suggests that this was a pre-Roman arrangement which persisted under Roman rule.

In the case of the Alpine tribes it is more difficult to see this arrangement working as smoothly. The attributed tribes were invariably mountain-dwellers, and the towns to which they were attributed situated in the valleys below. The tribes must have been governed in most respects by their own local bodies with little interference from these towns. The tribes' nobles would have been able to satisfy their own political ambitions through involvement in the town's *ordo*. Such involvement would have opened up the chance of obtaining Roman citizenship and hence enhancing their standing amongst their own tribe. Without such an outlet this search for prestige might well have taken the form of raiding the lowland towns or attacking travellers journeying through the Alpine passes. By the grant of the *ius Latii*, therefore, Rome tied in the interests of the highland nobles with its own, so stopping a potential threat to the lowland towns of north Italy and helping to make the passage of the Alps more secure. The grants made in the republican period also had the effect of creating new *clientes* for the originator of the legislation. The most notable example of this is the Transpadane *clientela* built up by Pompeius Strabo. These grants therefore had a clear purpose, but this was not to civilize the Alpine tribes, and the adoption of the blessings of Roman civilization was ex-

---

[48] Strabo, 4. 1. 12.   [49] A, *B1*.   [50] C.

[51] Pliny, *NH* 3. 4. 37; perhaps one of the manuscript readings of Strabo (A, *B1*) reflects this.

tremely slow in these areas. It will be argued below that Vespasian's grant of the *ius Latii* to the Hispanic provinces was similarly motivated by self-interest.

It is unclear if all the tribes who obtained Latin rights, but were not attributed in the manner described above, had an urban centre created for them. Some did. Pliny notes that the Convenae 'in oppidum contributi' ('who were brought together into a town')[52] had the Latin right, but immediately before this passes over without comment the Auscii who also possessed the *ius Latii* and had probably received it at the same time.[53] It is impossible to tell whether Pliny singles out the Convenae who had been gathered together in a town, because this was unusual, and thus implies that the other tribes were not organized in urban units, or whether the Convenae are mentioned because it was only on the grant of *ius Latii* that they finally gained an urban centre, and this is what made them unusual. The Roman authorities may not have been concerned about the trappings of urban life if they had a fixed group with which they could have dealings on their own terms; and the *ius Latii*, by creating a small élite of Roman citizens, would secure just such a group.[54]

One aspect of local political life which would have been controlled after the grant of the *ius Latii* was the question of who was to hold office in any one year. The Flavian Municipal Law lays down strict criteria as to how many individuals, and which ones, can be created Roman citizens in any one year.[55] We have no indication of how such regulations were enforced in a non-urban context; nevertheless it would not have been impossible to devise some system to implement them. This form of control would have been of great use to Rome: it would define the ruling body of the tribe, while satisfying the ruling classes' ambitions, and at the same time making their rule seem dependent on Roman forms, and hence weakening any 'nativistic' appeal they might have to the rest of their tribe.

The only conclusion which can be drawn from the above survey is that there is no prima-facie case for the view that the *ius Latii* was normally used to reward a group for adopting a Roman way of life, as it was granted to backward areas; nor, conversely, that it was used to stimulate the growth of Roman civic customs in such areas; if it was, it must be regarded as a device which, for whatever reasons, failed consistently to achieve its purpose. No town of Latin status in Spain appears to have progressed

[52] Pliny, *NH* 4. 108.   [53] Strabo, 4. 2. 2.
[54] For groups within the empire devoid of urban centres, see the discussion of the Bituriges of central Gaul and similar cases in Ch. 2.
[55] Ch. 21.

further in status even to *municipium civium Romanorum*, let alone to *colonia civium Romanorum*.[56] The privilege appears to have been highly flexible, being granted to both developed and non-developed, possibly even to non-urban, communities. In general there does not seem to have been any single reason why the right was granted, and so each instance ought to be examined separately, rather than being seen as part of an overarching scheme. There is therefore no good reason to reject the natural force of Pliny's comments, which imply that Vespasian's grant was made to the entire Iberian peninsula, not merely to the province of Baetica.

If we rule out the two options above, it remains to ask whether the grant of *ius Latii* was made as a concession rather than as an act of positive statesmanship. An important consideration here is the date at which the grant was made. Pliny's notice reads: 'universae Hispaniae Vespasianus imperator Augustus iactatum procellis reipublicae Latium tribuit' ('the emperor Vespasian Augustus granted to all Spain the Latin right which had been battered by the storms of state').[57] Neither the statement nor its context gives any clue to the date of the award. An inscription from Igabrum dating from Vespasian's sixth consulate (i.e. AD 75/6), and talking of 'beneficio Imp. Caesaris Aug. Vespasiani c.R. c(onsecuti) cum suis per h[onorem]', provides us with a firm *terminus ante quem*.[58] Standardly the grant has been assigned to Vespasian's censorship of AD 73/4. Such a date, well into the emperor's reign, would imply that the grant was an act of statesmanship; but, as has been seen, none of the reasons given for such an act seems appropriate.

The reason for dating the grant to AD 73/4 is itself merely a conjecture, which rests on the fact that some inscriptions from Baetica mention Vespasian's censorship. At Munigua, for example, two posthumous dedications to 'divo Caesari Aug. Vespasiano Censori' have been found.[59] This has in turn led to the suggestion that Vespasian's censorship was regarded as an event of great importance in the province and the natural reason for this would be that it was while *censor* that the emperor made the award of the *ius Latii* to the area. The weakness of this line of argument is immediately apparent. We have no firm link between the censorship and the grant, only an inference. Moreover, Vespasian in general placed great emphasis on his censorship, and inscriptions referring to him by this title are found even in Rome dating to well after his assumption of the

---

[56] Reid offers no justification for his statement: 'probably the majority of these [the *municipia* of Spain], if not all, acquired Roman privileges before the general enfranchisement was carried out by Caracalla', *The Municipalities of the Roman Empire*, 241.

[57] Pliny, *NH* 3. 3. 30.   [58] *CIL* 2. 1610.   [59] *CIL* 2. 1049, 1050.

office.[60] Consequently our Baetican inscriptions should be seen as merely reflecting a general imperial trend, rather than marking out a specific Iberian sensibility. Furthermore there is no essential need for Vespasian to have held the office of *censor* when he made the grant. The timing of such an action appears to have been entirely at the emperor's discretion. Nero was not *censor* when he gave the *ius Latii* to the Maritime Alps in AD 64, and Seneca implies that the emperor theoretically could give the Roman citizenship to a whole province if he so wished.[61]

If the grant of the *ius Latii* need not be linked to Vespasian's censorship, can a better alternative date be found? The present reading of Pliny's text is strange. It is difficult to see how an abstract concept such as *Latium* could be 'tossed by the storms of state'. This form of pathetic fallacy does not appear regularly in Latin until a much later period. A better reading is to amend the text to read 'iactatus', a minority manuscript tradition,[62] allowing the adjective to refer to 'Vespasianus', instead of 'Latium'.[63] This produces a much clearer sense. It is easy to see how Vespasian could have been battered by the storms of state, particularly in the early days of his reign, when Civilis' rebellion in Germany and Sarmatian incursions into Moesia had not yet been quelled. Vespasian's support came mainly from the East of the empire, and although Spain had quickly joined his cause,[64] this could have seemed like mere fickleness at the time, as the Iberian provinces had also been eager to side with both Otho and Vitellius when they had appeared to have been in the ascendant.[65] All Vespasian's immediate successors had some connections with the peninsula. Galba had been the governor of Hispania Tarraconensis when he began his rebellion against Nero. He appears to have been a popular governor[66] and obtained religious sanction for his actions from the (native?) prophetess of Clunia.[67] Galba probably raised this town to colonial status, which would have further increased his local popularity.[68] He also recruited a legion, the

[60] e.g. *ILS* 252.   [61] Tacitus, *Ann.* 15. 32; Seneca, *De Benef.* 6. 19. 2.
[62] *Codex Riccardianus*, accepted by Sillig.
[63] See A. Bosworth, 'Vespasian and the Provinces: Some Problems of the Early 70s AD', *Athenaeum*, 51 (1973), 49 ff.
[64] Tacitus, *Hist.* 3. 44.   [65] Ibid. 1. 76.
[66] Plutarch, *Galba* 4; Tacitus, *Hist.* 1. 49; and more grudgingly Suetonius, *Vit. Galbae* 9.
[67] Ibid. 9. 2.
[68] See Hübner, *CIL* 2. 383 and A. García y Bellido, 'El nacimiento de la legión VII Gemina', in A. Viñaya González (ed.), *Legio VII Gemina* (1970), 303 ff., 319. Galba struck *sestertii* at Rome with the legend 'Hispania Clunia Sul.' which may refer to a colonial grant (Mattingly and Syndenham, *RIC* (2nd edn., 1984), i., Galba, no. 469). The town had certainly obtained colonial status by the time of Hadrian, as is attested by *CIL* 2. 2780 (see also Ptolemy 2. 6. 55, Κλουνία κολωνία).

Seventh Galbiana, from the natives of the province.[69] It is possible that he also made grants to towns further south in the peninsula during his brief reign. Anticaria in Baetica, for example, may have received the title 'Sulpicia', and hence possibly the *ius Latii*, from him.[70] Otho too had been a popular governor of an Iberian province (Lusitania).[71] He courted further popularity in the peninsula by adding more families to the *coloniae* of Hispalis and Emerita (this probably meant raising some wealthy native families to the citizenship) and placing various Mauretanian cities under the jurisdiction of Baetica.[72] His successor, Vitellius, also probably sought popularity in Spain (he is said to have lavished grants of *Latinitas* on the empire and it is probable some of these were in Spain[73]). Given this recent past history, Vespasian, who could not have risked a rising in the peninsula, but needed to denude its garrisoning force of two of its three legions in order to obtain reinforcements to fight Civilis,[74] may have thought it prudent to provide benefactions of his own to the area.[75]

There is a strong case therefore for adopting Bosworth's position that the *ius Latii* was granted to Spain much earlier in Vespasian's reign than has previously been thought,[76] and for believing that the grant was made for pressing reasons of state, rather than as a reflection of or an attempt to change the cultural ambience of the Iberian provinces.

If this is the case, we need to examine the reasons why the concession of the Latin right would have been seen as something which would have appealed to the native population, and seemed to them worth possessing, at least as much as considering why Rome thought it appropriate to award it to the region. As has been seen, Vitellius certainly thought that he could win popularity in this way.

---

[69] Suetonius, *Vit. Galbae* 10. 2: 'e plebe provinciae'. One consequence of this would have been various natives obtaining Roman citizenship. Such grants may have extended to the auxiliary regiments recruited from the same source at the same time, if Alföldy is correct to read 'Alae [S]ulpiciae c.R.' for 'Alae . . . †viriclaror†' in *CIL* 2. 2637 ('Ein hispanischer offizier in Niedergermanien', *MM* 6 (1965), 105 ff.).

[70] See Thouvenot, *Essai sur la province romaine de Bétique*, 196 with *CIL* 3. 1196, the tomb of a veteran of the 14th Legion, C. Sentius Flaccus, from Sulp(icia?) Antiq(uaria?). The stone was found at Apulum.

[71] Tacitus, *Hist.* 1. 13: 'comiter administrata provincia' ('the province had been governed in a popular fashion'); Suetonius, *Vit. Oth.* 3: 'provinciam administravit . . . moderatione atque abstinentia singulari' ('he governed the province . . . with moderation and a marked lack of exploitation').

[72] Tacitus, *Hist.* 1. 78.   [73] Ibid. 3. 55.   [74] Ibid. 4. 68, 5. 14.

[75] The importance of the area is hinted at when the Vespasianic commander, Antonius Primus, refers to the peninsula along with Gaul as the 'validissimam terrarum partem' ('the most powerful area of the globe') (Tacitus, *Hist.* 3. 53).

[76] Bosworth, 'Vespasian and the Provinces'.

The major appeal of the *ius Latii* would have been its provision that the *magistri* of the towns concerned along with their families were given access to the Roman citizenship *per honorem*.[77] Nevertheless the rest of the population would also be assuaged by being raised to a status-level higher than that of other *peregrini*. Moreover, for the merchant classes of these towns, who would have been particularly numerous in the lowlands of Baetica and eastern Hispania Tarraconensis the right of *commercium*, allowing them to enter into business contracts as equals with Roman citizens, would have been invaluable. In addition to these factors, in the extremely status-conscious world of antiquity, the grant would have been a desirable status symbol, allowing the communities concerned to demonstrate their closeness to the ruling power, and perhaps to some degree to feel partners with it, rather than mere subjects. In some respects therefore the granting of the *ius Latii* may represent the reverse of a desire by Rome to 'Romanize' the Iberian peninsula; namely a concession that would not otherwise have been granted, being thought too advanced for at least the majority of communities concerned, which was extracted from Rome in a period of stress. In this case, although it is quite plausible that Spanish communities wished to have a Roman-style law code, there still remain a large number of questions as to what practices this brought about in reality.

So far it has been established that a grant of the *ius Latii* gave to individual members of the recipient community a set of rights in many ways similar to those of the *civis Romanus*; and that in the case of Spain this grant probably was made early in Vespasian's reign, and to the entire peninsula rather than merely a part of it. However, Vespasian's grant of *ius Latii* was not in itself the final chapter in the process of conferring Latin status on the Spanish provinces. The Flavian Municipal Law, as we can see from our surviving fragments, dates to the reign of Domitian, not to that of Vespasian.[78] This is made clear by Chapters 19, 20, 22, and 23 of the law, which speak of those ex-magistrates who have obtained Roman citizenship under the provisions of the law, or under those of the *edicta* of Vespasian, Titus, or Domitian. The *edictum* of Vespasian must be that making the initial grant of the *ius Latii*. Those of Titus and Domitian are probably confirmations of it on their own accessions to power.[79] The

---

[77] As is shown by the singling-out of this feature by Strabo and Asconius.

[78] The absence of the title 'Germanicus' suggests that it was created prior to Domitian's adoption of this title in AD 83/4.

[79] Galsterer, *Untersuchungen zum römischen Städtewesen*, 38 nn. 13, 16; Millar, *The Emperor in the Roman World*, 405 n. 60, 414 n. 16.

dichotomy between these *edicta* and the *Lex* shows that this latter was a separate enactment.

Why did Domitian think it necessary not merely to confirm his father's *edictum*, but also to devise a new law to embody it? Normally it is assumed that Vespasian's *edictum* was only the first step towards granting Latin status to the Iberian peninsula: it may have comprised no more than the grant of the status of *municipium* to the towns concerned; the individual rights granted to their inhabitants which went with this; and a set of brief instructions, perhaps like the order to 'IIIIviros creare', as had been the case with Transpadana, but without the creation of a complex law regulating all aspects of civic life. This view envisages that in the meantime a more all-embracing law was in the process of being drafted. The Flavian Municipal Law is seen as the end-product of this process, and thus as the culmination of Vespasian's designs for the province.

One problem with this hypothesis is the time-scale involved. The production of copies of a municipal law for the peninsula would have been a major undertaking: if we use Pliny's figures there must have been a requirement for at least 129 charters in Baetica alone, and the rest of Spain would have needed a minimum of another 172 copies.

However, these difficulties are concerned with the physical production of individual copies of the law, not with its initial creation. As will be seen, the Flavian Municipal Law contains many tralatitious elements, and it is difficult to imagine that its genesis, as opposed to its publication, took ten years. Given that this is the case, it is best to assume that the Flavian Municipal Law was not the end result of a long process, but rather a replacement for whatever arrangements had been put into place by Vespasian's *edictum*.

This in turn raises the question of whether the grant of the *ius Latii* necessarily entailed the creation of a detailed municipal law such as that found on our Spanish charters. The view that this was the case is normally accepted, although it has been doubted by Millar.[80] The case of Lepcis Magna, if it did receive the *ius Latii*, might suggest that such a charter could be more flexible than the Flavian Municipal Law in terms of accommodating previous local tradition. Do we possess any concrete evidence for a legal charter predating the Flavian Municipal Law in the case of Spain? Unfortunately the answer to this question must be no. However, there is a suggestive reference to an unspecified *lex* in the imperial letter

[80] See Sherwin-White, *The Roman Citizenship*, 375 ff.; contra Millar, *The Emperor in the Roman World*, 405.

appended to the end of the *Lex Irnitana*. This *lex* included provisions about which marriages in the community possessed *conubium*. It seems likely that the *epistula* is referring to a municipal charter embodying the grant of *ius Latii*. If the letter was issued at the same time as the *Lex Irnitana* proper, as González believes, the *lex* referred to must predate the *Lex Irnitana* and can most naturally be seen as a Vespasianic predecessor to it.[81] Nevertheless this cannot be regarded as beyond all doubt. The date of the letter cannot be established with complete confidence. It is possible that it postdates the *Lex Irnitana* proper and consequently refers to it, not to a prior piece of legislation.

However, if the letter is dealing with a *lex* consequent to Vespasian's *edictum*, such a law could still have dealt simply with the creation of *duo/quattuorviri*. Some provisions dealing with *conubium* would have been necessary as a part of such a law, as the magistrates created by it would have become *cives Romani* on leaving office, and hence the problem would have arisen of whom they could marry with *conubium*, and whether their previous marriages took on this status.

A hint that modifications to Vespasian's first settlement had been made prior to the creation of the Flavian Municipal Law is perhaps found in Chapter 20 of the law, which speaks of the *quaestores* created by the *Lex*, and by not only the *edicta* but also the *decreta* and *iussa* of Vespasian, Titus, and Domitian. The last two possibly imply that Vespasian's initial law was later modified on more than one occasion. This does suggest that Vespasian's settlement was not as detailed as the Flavian Municipal Law, and may have been of the minimal kind outlined above. This possibility is made all the more likely if the grant was made as an emergency measure towards the beginning of the emperor's reign. Despite this, there is no positive evidence to suppose that Vespasian did not intend his arrangements to be final; and, as has been seen, his *edictum* seems to have been embodied in a *Lex Municipalis* of some sort. Two reasons suggest themselves for modifications to this initial law. The first is that it was inadequate in coping with the administrative necessities of the Iberian communities. This possibly led to the *ad hoc* creation of quaestors in some communities.[82] The other is that the law was being abused. Such abuses would be of particular concern in the field of the acquisition of Roman citizenship.

If the process of appointing magistrates and the grants of Roman citi-

---

[81] See González, 'The *Lex Irnitana*', 238. Also J.-L. Mourgues, 'The So-Called Letter of Domitian at the end of the Lex Irnitana', *JRS* 77 (1987), 78 ff.

[82] González, 'The *Lex Irnitana*', 201.

zenship to ex-magistrates had not been firmly regulated, one potential field of abuse would have been an attempt to increase the number of Roman citizens created by inflating the numbers of magistrates in the towns, and shortening their period of tenure. Domitian's letter at the end of the *Lex* shows that some form of abuse, whether intentional or not, had taken place with regard to marriages which possessed *conubium*. Nor need the scope for abuse have rested solely with the native population. Governors and other Roman officials may well have been able to exploit the situation by demanding bribes for the recognition of Roman citizenship, granting it to some who were not qualified for it and withholding it from others who were so qualified.

In short there is nothing to suggest that Vespasian had not intended his settlement for Spain to be a long-lasting one. But it still may be the case that it was soon found to be inadequate and open to abuse: a situation that gradually became worse over the ten years of its operation. It would not be surprising if Domitian, a strict constitutionalist, had ordered a major revision of local city law in Spain, if he believed that this was necessary. The emperor is known to have taken a keen interest in provincial matters, and it would be perfectly in character had he ordered such a course of action, especially given the size of the provinces concerned.[83] Certainly some Spaniards felt indebted to Domitian rather than Vespasian for the grant. At Cisimbrium, Q. Annius Niger states that he was 'c.R. consicutus [*sic*] per honorem IIvir. beneficio Imp. Caes. Domitiani'.[84] This, could, of course, just be politeness to the ruling emperor. Nevertheless it is significant that this attribution does not occur in our extant epigraphy, except to Vespasian and Domitian. It is of interest that the *Lex Ursonensis*, in other words the charter of a *colonia*, whose legal status would have been unaffected by Vespasian's grant of *ius Latii* to the peninsula, also dates, in the form we now possess it, to the reign of Domitian. The coincidence of these dates may be just that, but it does suggest that the emperor thought that some form of major and systematic action was required in Spain on these questions.

Part of the problem with Vespasian's settlement may have stemmed from a lack of a provision that his arrangements be systematically displayed. Chapter 95 of the Flavian Municipal Law not only charges the *duoviri* to publish the law on bronze as soon as possible, but also to do so in a manner which would allow the charter to be read from ground level. It seems that this order may also have been applied to towns which were

---

[83] Suetonius, *Vit. Dom.* 8.   [84] *AE* (1981), 496.

not included in Vespasian's grant. This would explain why the *colonia* of Urso also republished its law at this time, incorporating in it small revisions required by developments since its first charter was drafted just after the death of Caesar.

Theoretically it would be possible to argue that the Flavian Municipal Law, as we now have it, did not apply to all of Spain, and that parts of the peninsula would have continued to use whatever settlement was provided under Vespasian's original enactment. It is true that all our fragments of the Flavian Municipal Law have come from Baetica, and the majority of these from the lowland area. Nevertheless the notion that exceptions to the Flavian Municipal Law were permitted is unlikely. While the *Lex* does deal with ex-magistrates created under past legislation, these provisions seem merely to guarantee their rights for the future, and do not envisage more magistrates being created in this way. Second, if Domitian did reform his father's settlement because he thought it inadequate, it is most unlikely he would have allowed such arrangements to persist. Some evidence that the law was enforced even in the more backward areas of Spain comes from a fragment of the law found in the village of Cortegana in the province of Huelva.[85] This area of Baetica was far less subject to Roman influence than the Baetis valley, with elements of Celtic culture persisting for a long period of time.[86] The law was therefore in force here, and the provision that it was to be displayed in bronze was complied with, presumably at some cost to the local community.

The Flavian Municipal Law which we possess is therefore the culmination of a process which began with Vespasian's grant of *ius Latii* to Spain. This grant appears to have been found gradually more and more unworkable, leading to its modification in the reign of Vespasian himself and those of his sons, and finally under Domitian to its replacement by the law which we now possess. The law appears to have been a part of a major restatement of city law in the region, which affected, to some degree, even towns which had obtained Roman citizen status prior to Vespasian's grant of the *ius Latii*, as the republication of the city law of the *colonia* of Urso at this time shows. The new law appears to have been enforced throughout Baetica. It may equally have been enforced in Lusitania and Tarraconensis, since these fell under the scope of Vespasian's grant of *ius Latii*.

[85] See R. Cagnat, *CRAI* (1904), 177, and Canto, 'A propos de la loi municipale de Corticata'. See contra, however, González, 'More on the Italica Fragment of Lex Municipalis', who argues that the fragment originated in Italica.
[86] For a general survey of the province of Huelva in antiquity, see M. Almagro Basch, *Huelva: Prehistoria y antigüedad* (1974).

Unfortunately, however, we have at present no way of knowing if this was the case or not as no fragments of municipal law have been recovered from these provinces.

What sort of town, therefore, was envisaged by the Flavian Municipal Law? The answer is one which would be run in a highly Roman manner. Virtually no concessions are made to past pre-charter practice.[87] González is right to remark that Chapters 84 to 96 of the law are entirely Roman in conception. The administrative and judicial arrangements for the towns, as explicitly listed by the law, are all Roman in form, and Chapter 93 makes it clear that all legal questions not specifically dealt with are to be treated in terms of Roman law. Thus, no law is available to the *municipes* but the *ius civile* of Rome. At first sight therefore the grant of *ius Latii* created a highly uniform group of communities subject to the strictures of Roman law. This uncompromising approach, and the almost complete uniformity of the individual town charters, seems to contradict the remarks of Hadrian concerning *municipia* recorded by Aulus Gellius.[88] According to Gellius, the emperor expressed surprise when his home town of Italica petitioned him to be raised to the rank of a *colonia* from that of a *municipium*; he drew the Italicenses' attention to the fact that while their town was a *municipium* they were allowed to use their own laws,[89] whereas promotion to colonial status would result in their being bound to use Roman law.

There appears to be a head-on clash here, and certainly a major problem is presented for those who, like González[90] and d'Ors,[91] believe that a fragment of a charter embodying the Flavian Municipal Law, now in a private collection in Seville,[92] was found at Italica. Such a charter could not be described as showing that Italica enjoyed individual 'mores legesque'; yet Hadrian, as a native of the town, ought to have been well informed as to the nature of its municipal law. This particular problem can nevertheless be resolved. First, there is no need to believe that this fragment of the charter came from Italica, rather than from the village of Cortegana in the province of Huelva, as stated by its original publisher, Cagnat.[93] Consequently there is no certain way of telling what Italica's

---

[87] Ch. 31 allows the number of *decuriones* to remain at its pre-charter number (at Irni, sixty-three), and ch. 81 allows the arrangement of honorific seating at municipal games to remain the same.

[88] Aulus Gellius, *NA* 16. 13.

[89] The emperor remarks that *municipia* 'suis moribus legibusque uti possent'.

[90] González, 'Italica: Municipium iuris Latii'.

[91] A. d'Ors, *Epigrafía jurídica de la España romana* (1953), 345, 460.

[92] *AE* (1964), 80; the fragment is in the Casa Lebrija in Seville.

[93] Cagnat, *CRAI* (1904), 177, and Canto, 'A propos de la loi municipale de Corticata'.

constitution was like at the time of Hadrian's remarks. Second, Hadrian may have been speaking as an antiquarian. He loved to show the depths of his learning to his court, and Gellius comments that he spoke 'peritissime' ('very learnedly') on this occasion. Given this love of abstruse erudition,[94] perhaps the emperor was demonstrating his antiquarian knowledge by noting that the advantage of enjoying individual laws belonged to *antiqua municipia*, placing stress on 'antiqua' here. It is likely that *municipia* which had been given this status individually and at an early date did obtain individually tailored charters which reflected their old customary practices. The coins of Italica carry the title 'munic.' in the Augustan period,[95] and Utica, the other town mentioned in Hadrian's speech as a 'municipium antiquum', probably also received municipal status at this time.[96] Later towns received less individualized grants, and Hadrian may have been demonstrating his knowledge of this change.[97] Moreover, the block grant of the *ius Latii* to Spain would probably have made the creation of individual charters administratively impossible, even if this was still regarded as desirable.

We must bear in mind the problems of how closely such a highly Roman document suited the communities to which it was granted; how far such communities were able to implement it; and to what degree it was simply a theoretical blueprint for a community, drawn up at Rome without reference to the specific situation in Spain.

One of the most strikingly Roman aspects of the Flavian charter which runs against Hadrian's dictum, is found in chapters 21 and 22: namely the implication that all *municipes* enjoyed the rights of *manus*, *mancipium*, and *patria potestas*.[98] Here the law states that all these relationships which have held before the acquisition of Roman citizenship are to continue to hold in the same way after Roman citizenship has been granted. Great care is taken to transfer entire family units from Latin to Roman status. This is to avoid a breakdown in family structure. Gaius makes it clear that the *potestas* relationship cannot hold between those of different legal status.[99] This total transfer was still not enough, though, to preserve stability. Even if both father and son were given Roman citizenship, a *potestas* relationship between them would not automatically obtain, but required a special request to the emperor to bring it into force.[100] Although this would not be

---

[94] *SHA Hadr.* 16.   [95] *MI* nos. 1045–6.
[96] Dio, 46. 16, and Brunt, *Italian Manpower*, 604.
[97] See Sherwin-White, *The Roman Citizenship*, 362–3.
[98] The power of *patria potestas* is here described as *potestas parentium*. Although this at first suggests a different right, Gaius (*Institutes* 1. 55) uses the same phrase to mean *patria potestas*, so it is best taken as having this meaning here too.
[99] Gaius, *Institutes* 1. 128.   [100] Ibid. 1. 93, 2. 135a.

a problem in individual instances, in a community where men would regularly be created Roman citizens this lack of rights would cause major disruptions in the families concerned, and leave them in a somewhat anomalous position. In addition to the lack of rights normally enjoyed by other Roman citizens, some social stigma could have been attached to them, as emancipation from *patria potestas* normally appears only to have happened for criminal or disreputable reasons.[101] Therefore Gaius' normal rule, if applied to the towns given the *ius Latii*, would have caused a great deal of social disruption in the very ruling class that was being relied on to provide stable government there. Given this situation, it is not surprising that Gaius adds a special chapter qualifying his remarks on when the *potestas* relationship is to hold for those obtaining the citizenship, which excludes those who have obtained the citizenship by the *ius Latii* from the general principles he has listed. This qualifying chapter reads: 'Alia causa est eorum qui Latii iure cum liberis suis ad civitatem Romanam perveniunt; nam horum in potestate fiunt liberi' ('The case concerning those who obtain Roman citizenship along with their children through the Latin right is different. For the children of such men become subject to their power').[102] This immediately removes all the problems that the general law would have caused if it had been applied to towns with the *ius Latii*. The provisions of our law about these matters can be seen as a specific example of Gaius' general rule about *potestas* relationships where the *ius Latii* is being put into practice, ensuring that there is a permanent provision to the effect that Roman legal obligations always hold for those given the citizenship under its terms and that special imperial dispensation for this is not required.

The law does seem to imply that all *municipes* enjoyed these rights, something reinforced by the provision of Chapter 93 that Roman law be used in the town in general. There is no attempt, however, to define how these rights were to devolve on the inhabitants of the Spanish towns when the law was first promulgated. Presumably, previously existing native relationships were hardened for legal purposes into these Roman categories. The slight possibility exists that the past tense is used in the relevant extant chapters of the law in a retrospective manner, and is assimilating previously held native rights, analogous to the Roman categories of *patria potestas* and the like, to their Roman equivalents, on the grounds that now that those concerned are Roman citizens it is correct to talk as if such Roman relationships had obtained in the past. Therefore

---

[101] Crook, *Law and Life of Rome*, 110.   [102] Gaius, *Institutes* 1. 95.

although it seems reasonably clear that the *cives Latini* of Irni did enjoy these relationships, we cannot be entirely certain that this was so. The general tenor of the paragraphs concerned is to ensure that the acquisition of Roman citizenship does not interfere with the web of rights and obligations already in place in the native community. In this it is paralleled by cases where those concerned are *peregrini*, most notably in that of the *tabula Banasitana*, which records two grants of citizenship to the chiefs of the Zagrenses and their families, but notes that this is to be done 'salvo iure gentis' ('preserving local practices').[103] In the same way the third edict from Cyrene makes it clear that a grant of Roman citizenship in no way affects the obligations of the recipient under the local law.

Similar instances of trying to preserve communal stability, particularly among the upper class, are found in the two concessions to pre-charter practice found in the law. One allows the *ordo* of the new *municipium* to remain at the same size as the previous governing body of the town.[104] What is at stake here is the possible disruption of the ruling class by the introduction of a new body, and Rome's determination to avoid this. The new *ordo* under these provisions would have been nothing more than the old ruling body perpetuating itself under a new name. The officials of these new bodies would now have had to fit into the pattern of Roman local magistracies; and the seeming lack of non-iteration clauses shows that perhaps even hereditary chieftains would have been able to accommodate themselves into the new system without difficulty.[105] The other concession to previous customs, that the same set of honorific seating-arrangements at *spectacula* should be kept, would again allow the ruling class to keep its traditional privileges, and is probably also for this purpose.[106]

The chapters of the law discussed above deal with problems directly related to Latin *municipia*. They are all concerned with questions of interest to the ruling class of the town. On the other hand when the law is dealing with more general issues its creators appear, on at least one

---

[103] A. N. Sherwin-White, 'The *Tabula Banasitana* and the *Constitutio Antoniniana*', *JRS* 63 (1973), 86 ff.

[104] The *ordo* of sixty-three at Irni seems very idiosyncratic, perhaps masking a local tribal system built around the number seven. It is difficult to know how small an *ordo* would have been permitted. The anonymous 3rd-c. imperial letter to Tymanda (*ILS* 6090), if it is not merely considering local circumstances, may suggest a minimum of fifty members.

[105] Rome was in general well disposed to oligarchic rule. The provision of ch. 51 of the *Lex Malacitana* show that competition for office was not envisaged as a problem.

[106] It is interesting to see, however, that it is cast in these terms which presuppose a purely Roman context.

occasion, not to have thought through with the same case the status of the communities for whom they were legislating. This can be seen in the provisions for the appointment of *iudices*, found in chapter 86 of the law. Here the magistrate concerned with the enrolling of *iudices* is enjoined to have their 'praenomina nomina item patrum praenomina et ipsorum tribus cognomina' (*'praenomina, nomina*, their fathers' *praenomina*, and their tribes and *cognomina'*) inscribed on a tablet. The *iudices* are to be chosen from the decurions who have no other duties in the year concerned and from other 'ingenui' (free-born) *municipes*. There is no explicit statement that possession of Roman citizenship is required of the *iudices*. It appears therefore that all the *municipes* of Irni possessed full Roman nomenclature and filiation, and were enrolled in a Roman voting tribe. This position is enthusiastically supported by González.[107]

However, would this have been the case? Enrolment in the tribes of Rome seems unlikely, as neither the republican *cives sine suffragio*, nor the republican *Latini coloniarii*, on whom our *cives Latini* were modelled, were so enrolled. This negative assumption is borne out by a survey of the tribes found in Spain. If González's argument were correct, we should expect the *tribus Quirina*, normally regarded as the one into which new citizens were enrolled during the Flavian dynasty, to be the region's predominant tribe. The tribe is widely attested in Spain, occurring 179 times in *CIL* 2, that is, 25 per cent of the total number of tribal attestations. Nevertheless it is not the tribe with the largest number of attestations: the Galerian tribe occurs 343 times, or 49 per cent of the total. It could be argued that simply examining the tribal affiliation of individuals is unsound, as towns with a large epigraphic record will distort the results unacceptably. But even if the survey is conducted on a town-by-town, rather than an individual, basis the *tribus Quirina* still does not predominate. Out of a total of 202 towns surveyed by Wiegels, the Quirine tribe appeared 78 times, or 38 per cent of the total, while the Galerian tribe appeared 82 times, or 40 per cent of the total.[108] A survey based on the tribal affiliations of known individuals does therefore seem to produce a distorted result; however, this distortion appears only to be one of degree rather than to change the picture completely. The only Iberian province where the *tribus Quirina* is the most attested tribe is Lusitania, which contributed the smallest number of towns to Wiegels's survey, and hence is likely to have produced the least reliable result.

---

[107] J. González, 'Las leyes municipales Flavias', in J. Mangas Manjarrés (ed.), *Aspectos de la colonización y municipalización de Hispania* (1989), 133 ff., esp. p. 145.

[108] Wiegels, *Die Tribusinschriften des römischen Hispanien*.

If González were right, these results would be extremely difficult to explain. However, if *cives Latini* were not enrolled in the Roman tribal system, as seems likely, the pattern found above is entirely explicable, as only the ex-magistrates of towns who had received Roman citizenship *per honorem* will have become liable for tribal affiliation. Moreover it is likely that these posts would have been monopolized by a small number of families in each town, further reducing the number of citizens created over a period of time, as the new magistrates on many occasions would have already obtained the citizenship through their father or grandfather holding office.[109] Again, if there were a *cursus honorum* among these offices, only those who held the aedileship or quaestorship would qualify for Roman citizenship *per honorem* each year, the *duoviri* already having done so by virtue of being aediles; and as it is possible that the aediles concerned would have been of the same family as previous magistrates, they would already have been Roman citizens on taking up office, and thus have no need to qualify for it *per honorem*. Consequently in some years no new Roman citizens would be created in the Flavian *municipia*, and so the numbers of individuals with Flavian names and tribal affiliation would not grow rapidly. The *Lex* itself makes it clear that a maximum of only six new Roman citizens could be created in any one year.[110] On the other hand, in the *coloniae* and *municipia c.R.* created before Vespasian's reign, there would be a large body of Roman citizens enrolled in different tribes. This body would have outnumbered the new citizens created by the Flavian grant for a considerable period of time, as is reflected in the figures assessed above.

González's inference concerning the *tria nomina* is equally suspect. The provisions of chapter 86 are used, along with Claudius' ban on the usurpation of the *tria nomina* by *peregrini*,[111] to argue that the *municipes* of Irni used this form of nomenclature and that it was exclusive to *cives Romani* and *cives Latini*. However, Claudius' ban is against the usurpation of Roman *gentilitates*: 'vetuit usurpare Romana nomina dum taxat gentilicia' ('he forbade them to usurp Roman names at least the family ones'). This is unlikely to have been a ban on the use of the *tria nomina per se*, but rather on the use of the names of noble Roman families to gain a false appearance of nobility. Nor does there seem to be any evidence that the *tria nomina*

---

[109] A good example of this family dominance of office is attested from Augustoritum, in Gaul, where an inscription records that Tiberius Taurius Taurianus, described as a *IIvir* of the *civitas Lemovicum*, erected a tombstone for his father, Taurius Silvanus, also a *IIvir* of the *civitas. AE* (1961), 56.

[110] Ch. 21.   [111] Suetonius, *Vit. Claud.* 25.

were universally used in Latin towns.[112] Amongst the Alpine tribe of the Triumplini, who Pliny tells us had obtained Latin rights,[113] the standard form of peregrine nomenclature, a single name followed by filiation, is common.[114] It might be argued that this tribe was too backward to prove a general point, but instances occur also at more 'civilized' towns with the Latin rights, for example at Nîmes,[115] and Carpentras.[116] Similar instances occur throughout Spain, even in towns with Flavian titles, where according to González's theory the *tria nomina* should be universal, for example at Aquae Flaviae in Tarraconensis,[117] at Flavia Conimbriga in Lusitania,[118] at *municipium Flavium Cananiense*,[119] and at *municipium Flavium Arvense*,[120] both in Baetica.[121] Unfortunately none of our examples from Baetica can be dated accurately, so it might be replied that they predate Vespasian's grant. This argument, however, cannot be used against the evidence from Carteia, which became a Latin colony in the republican period.[122] If González is correct, its inhabitants would have used the *tria nomina*. However, on the town's coinage no magistrate uses this form.[123] Instead two names are used even on coins which postdate the original grant of the *ius Latii* by over a hundred years.[124] Elsewhere in Spain a similar picture appears. At Conimbriga, for example, an inscription dating to the mid-second century, well after Vespasian's grant of the *ius Latii*, records an Albinus Arconis f. and his two sons Arco and Aecandus.[125]

---

[112] González equivocates on this issue, stating that 'los municipes de Irni tienen filiacion completa . . . poseían *tria nomina*' ('Las leyes municipales flavias', in Managas Manjarrés (ed.), *Aspectos de la colonización y municipalización de Hispania*, 145), while elsewhere conceding that this would not have come about immediately ('The *Lex Irnitana*', 148 n. 4).

[113] Pliny, *NH* 3. 20. 134.

[114] Examples include Strenus Brisiae f., *CIL* 5. 4912; Clado Cariassi f., *CIL* 5. 4924; Niger Salvi f., *CIL* 5. 4925; and Huimenus Lubiani f., *CIL* 5. 4929.

[115] Gratus Celeris f., *CIL* 12. 3117; Sextus, *CIL* 12. 3145.

[116] Aesilus Savi f., *CIL* 12. 1160; Vinuleius Vinici f., *CIL* 12. 1165; Rufus Sacconis f. *CIL* 12. 1176.

[117] *CIL* 2. 2484, 'Camalus Burni f.'; see also G. Alföldy, 'Notes sur la relation entre le droit de cité et la nomenclature dans l'empire romain', *Latomus*, 25 (1966), 37 ff.

[118] *ILER* 4845, 'Albinus Arconis f.'

[119] *CIL* 2. 1080, 'Septumius'; *CIL* 2. 1077, 'Apollinarius'.

[120] *CIL* 2. 1071, 'Saturninus Rufi f.'

[121] Further Baetican examples include a Rufinus Rufi f. at Ostippo, *CIL* 2. 1463; and a C. Memmius C.f. at Epora, *CIL* 2. 2174.

[122] In 171 BC, Livy 43. 3. 1–4.

[123] For a general survey of Carteia's coinage, see F. Chaves Tristan, *Las monedas hispano-romanas de Carteia* (1979).

[124] Examples include names such as C. Vib., Tristan Chaves, ibid. 138, placed in 50 BC; and M. Falcidius, ibid. 142, placed in 40 BC. Other officials use two names and filiation such as C. Maius C.f., ibid. 142–3, placed in 35 BC.

[125] *ILER* 4845.

A further problem with González's view is the lack of Flavian-based names found in the peninsula. Dio notes that Claudius insisted on his name being taken by new citizens.[126] If this was not just an idiosyncrasy, it follows that as Vespasian's grant of *Latinitas* turned all Spaniards into *cives Latini*, they, or at least their children, would have adopted new names of the *tria nomina* form, incorporating a Flavian element. Flavian *nomina* and *cognomina* therefore should have predominated in the ono-mastics of the peninsula. However, this is not the case. Of the *nomina* listed in *CIL* 2 there are only 95 *Flavii* as opposed to 404 *Iulii*, 121 *Iunii*, 113 *Aelii*, 197 *Fabii*, 143 *Sempronii*, and 365 *Valerii*. This lack of Flavian names occurs even in towns which we know had the title of *municipium Flavium*, albeit the epigraphy is often sparse. The same pattern appears with *cognomina*. Tranoy believes he has detected a high number of such *cognomina*, which he considers show the influence of the *ius Latii* on the north-west of the peninsula.[127] However, of the sixty-two examples Tranoy lists only four are in fact examples of 'Flavius' as a *cognomen*. The overwhelming majority of Tranoy's examples are instead the name 'Fla-vus' (41 i.e. 67 per cent) or derivatives of this adjective. The conflation of 'Flavus' with 'Flavius' is methodologically suspect, as the former name could easily be a reference to hair colour rather than a receipt of Latin rights. This doubt is strengthened by the fact that the area concerned was a predominantly Celtic area and is also suggested by the fact that the second most popular *cognomen* in north-west Spain is 'Rufus' (Flavus being the most popular), which clearly refers to this characteristic. If the 'Flavus' examples are dropped from Tranoy's list, far from being the most popular *cognomen* in the area, 'Flavius' becomes the least popular.

A final test of nomenclature, if Vespasian's grant was made to the whole of Spain, is to look at the names of Spanish auxiliary troops, who ought, from the late first century onwards, to have had names of the *tria nomina* form. A large number of the existing stones do have this style of name, but most of our inscriptions are from the tombs of auxiliaries who obtained Roman citizenship on discharge, and who would have assumed the *tria nomina* as an indication of this status. However, there are exceptions. Albonius Tacili set up a votive offering at Collippo, in Lusitania, for his son who was serving with the army and was simply called Saturninus.[128] This inscription, dating to the late first or early second century, shows that Saturninus did not have the *tria nomina* while serving, and came from

---

[126] Dio, 60. 17. 7.
[127] A. Tranoy, *La Galice romaine* (1981). The *cognomina* are tabulated on p. 364 with commentary on p. 205.
[128] *CIL* 2. 338.

a community where peregrine-style nomenclature and filiation were still being used. From a diploma dating to AD 103 we learn that a decurion of *Ala I Pannoniorum Tampiana*, described as a *Hispanus*, had the name of Reburrus Severi f.;[129] and a further diploma dating to AD 107 records the name of another Spaniard as Lovessius Maximi f.[130] If these names were kept after discharge, as the diploma implies, not all Roman citizens seem to have thought the *tria nomina* worth assuming. This seems to be borne out by evidence from the town of Rider in Dalmatia, which received Latin rights under the Flavians, or possibly under Hadrian, and has a large epigraphic record. Here the *tria nomina* form of nomenclature only appears amongst the magistrates of the town after Caracalla's grant of universal citizenship in AD 212. Prior to this the townsfolk, including the curial class, used native forms of nomenclature.[131]

Obviously the provisions for the recording of *iudices* found at Irni could not have been carried out to the letter in Rider, as there would not have been enough candidates with *tria nomina* to enrol. It is unlikely, however, that the qualifications for being a *iudex* at Rider differed greatly from those at Irni. This inevitably leads to the problem of why, if González's inference from the provisions of the charter is wrong, the regulations for the town were drafted as they are, with the assumption that all its citizens had the *tria nomina*. The first possibility is that *iudices* were to be drawn only from those citizens of the town who were Roman citizens. We know from the first Cyrene edict that this was certainly the case at Cyrene before these edicts were issued by Augustus. However, the statement that the *iudices* are to be drawn from 'ingenui municipes' as well as the *decuriones* (who themselves would not all have been Roman citizens) makes this unlikely, especially as a minimum age-limit of 25, 'non minores quam XXV annorum', rules out participation by the sons of those who had obtained Roman citizenship *per honorem*, and had consequently obtained the citizenship themselves, but were too young to embark on a political career of their own. The only other 'ingenui municipes' who were Roman citizens, and possibly not decurions, would have been the parents of those who had obtained their citizenship *per honorem*, and it is likely that many of these would have belonged to the curial class. It seems unlikely that this group alone is being referred to by the phrase 'ingenui municipes' and thus it is reasonable to assume that other *iudices*, who were not Roman citizens, were appointed.

---

[129] *CIL* 16. 48.   [130] *CIL* 16. 56.
[131] e.g. Aplis Lunnicus Triti f., *CIL* 3. 13989; and the *decurion* Apludus Staticcus, *CIL* 3. 2773.

The solution to this problem is twofold. First, it must be remembered that there would have been Roman citizens in Irni, the products of the creation of *cives Romani per honorem*, as provided for in the law, to whom these regulations could be applied. The law stipulates a property qualification of at least 5,000 HS to qualify as a *iudex*. This, in a small and poor community such as Irni, would mean that the *iudices* were most likely to be drawn almost entirely from the curial class, who were precisely those who were likely to have obtained Roman citizenship *per honorem*, and to have obtained tribal affiliation as a consequence of this. In the case of other *iudices* the law would merely indicate that their names were to be set down as fully as possible. Moreover, if the charter was drawn up at Rome, as seems to have been the case,[132] this small group of *cives Romani* would, by their very possession of Roman citizen status, have been seen as the most important group within the town, and legislation would have been tailored to meet their needs, rather than those of the rest of the inhabitants. In this case the provisions for recording *iudices* in the Flavian Municipal Law would have worked perfectly for Roman citizens who possessed the *tria nomina*, and at the same time have made it clear that in the case of the enrolment of *iudices* who were *Latini*, the full name of the *iudex* and the name of his father was to be recorded. In other words the spirit of the law is clear even if its letter would have been on occasions inapplicable.

What appears to have happened is that the charter has been drawn up as a general blueprint for how legal procedure ought to carried out in the Spanish *municipia*. In this respect it represents a bench-mark of correct procedure which was officially expected to prevail, but which must in most cases have been something to aim at, rather than be implemented immediately. Instead of being designed directly to Romanize the Spanish communities to whom it was to be applied, the law is rather a vision of what the Roman lawyers who drew up the charter believed life would, or should, be like in a town whose citizens enjoyed a status close to that of Roman citizenship, and for which they drew on other pieces of municipal law already to hand and familiar to them. It appears from the provisions of chapter 86 that some of these were laws dealing with communities of *cives Romani*, where these provisions would have worked perfectly, rather than drawn from other *municipia iuris Latii*. Further examples of this can be seen in chapter 72 of the charter, where the *municipia* of Italy, which would have been of Roman-citizen, not Latin, status, are cited as an

---

[132] See González, 'The *Lex Irnitana*', 214, 238; a view now accepted by H. Galsterer, 'Municipium Flavium Irnitanum: A Latin Town in Spain', *JRS* 78 (1988), 78 ff., 89, and n. 59.

example to follow. The mis-engraving of 'colonos' for 'municipes' in chapter 79 suggests that colonial law, again most probably from a *colonia civium Romanorum*, has been drawn on. Echoes of other Roman laws can also be detected.[133]

This generality means that we do not gain the same insight into the particular municipal life of Irni, or any other town to which the charter applied, as we would have if the charters had been tailor-made for each community. The problem is made worse in so far as the law applied to communities which would have differed greatly from one another in terms of their development towards a Roman model of urbanization. This spectrum of difference is shown most strongly when comparing the settlements of the Baetis valley with those of north-west Spain; but an equally broad spectrum existed in Baetica itself between the lowland sites and those found in the highlands on either side of the Baetis valley.

Some of these communities would have had a long way to go before the provisions of the law could be implemented as envisaged by its creators. Although chapter 95 of the law requires the local magistrates to place a copy of the charter in the most prominent place in their town, and where it could be read from ground level, there must be a question over whether there would have been sufficient literacy in Latin in some towns of the province for their inhabitants to understand the highly technical legal Latin of the charter.[134] Nevertheless the display of bronze tablets would have been of use to the central authorities as a demonstration of the power and wealth of Rome.[135] They would also, conversely, have provided the local community, and in particular its ruling element, with a concrete display of its status and the 'Romanness' with which they wished to be associated.[136] As long as the sections of the law controlling the succession to the local magistracies and regulating the powers of these offices were understood and adhered to, it is likely that the rest of the law could then be subject to local interpretation, as discussed below, without any objection by the central authorities.

[133] González, 'The *Lex Irnitana*', 150.

[134] Literacy in antiquity has become the centre of considerable debate; for powerful doubts about its extent, see W. V. Harris, *Ancient Literacy* (1989).

[135] The remarks of Celsus (*Digest* 1. 3. 17) that to understand the law what is necessary is not to understand its 'verba', but to grasp its 'vis' and 'potestas', may refer to this phenomenon.

[136] This aspect of the charter should not be overlooked. The bronze tablets of the *Lex Irnitana* stood almost 2 ft. high, and placed end to end would have extended some 30 ft., making an impressive visual spectacle. A related question of interest is who would have paid for the tablets. Their creation would have needed a considerable financial outlay by the poorer communities in the province if they had to pay for them by themselves.

Throughout the charter there is an assumption of an extensive knowledge of Roman law. The crux of the problem of how to use the charters
to interpret the nature of society in Baetica is this: how accurately did this
assumption reflect the reality found on the ground in Baetica, rather than
that of the lawyer's *scriptorium*? Would the average *municeps* of Baetica
know what was technically meant by the highly Roman nature of the
categories of law concerned? Gaius, for example, singles out *patria potestas*
as something characteristically, almost uniquely, Roman;[137] so, even if he
were willing to do so, would our typical provincial have been able to
implement the law correctly?

This seems highly unlikely. Rome would have had to undertake a large-
scale attempt to educate the population, or at least the curial class, as a
whole. This project would have been impossible even had the will to carry
it out existed. A more likely interpretation is that although these concepts
were highly Roman in the form laid down by the law, there were almost
certainly previous native arrangements which dealt with the same general
areas. Consequently, as the number of officials in the provinces with
knowledge of Roman law was very small, and a reference work on the
subject was notoriously lacking before the second century AD, it is likely
that the Roman legal concepts of the charters would frequently have been
interpreted in the light of circumstances and previous peregrine legal
practice, a process which Galsterer has called '*interpretatio peregrina*'.[138]

As has been noted above, the regulations concerning the creation of
Roman citizens probably did not suffer from this problem, simply because
they were the most important part of the law as far as both the local
population and the Roman authorities were concerned. The other area of
paramount concern to Rome, the make-up and functioning of the local
council, is precisely an area where compromises are made, a concession
which augurs ill for the general understanding of other provisions of the
law.

Would such ignorance, if it existed, have significantly affected the
smooth running of the towns of Baetica? The answer to this question is
probably no. Apart from access to the Roman citizenship, most of the
other rights granted by the charter would have been of marginal importance to many inhabitants of the province. The majority of their dealings

[137] *Institutes* I. 55.
[138] H. Galsterer, 'Roman Law in the Provinces: Some Problems of Transmission', in M.
Crawford (ed.), *L'Impero romano e le strutture economiche e sociali delle province* (1986), 13 ff.
Although see contra M. Crawford, 'The Laws of the Romans: Knowledge and Diffusion', in
González and Arce (eds.), *Estudios sobre la Tabula Siarensis*.

would have been internal to their communities, and of no interest to the Roman authorities. It is hard to see, for example, what benefits possessing the *ius commercii* brought to a peasant farmer in Baeturia. Many Baeticans would probably have continued to live exactly as they had before, applying new Roman terms to old practice. The only group in the province who stood to gain substantially were the merchants of the Baetis valley and Gades, who had frequent dealings with Rome. But, while these were a financially important group, they would not have made up a substantial proportion of the province's population. In other words, more often than not the provisions of the charter would have been fitted to native arrangements rather than vice versa. It is quite possible, for example, that what a *municeps* of Irni understood by *manus*, or *tutoris nominatio*, would differ considerably from what was understood by the Roman lawyers who drafted the law. This would allow the spirit of the law to be preserved in cases where its letter would simply seem inapplicable to the town. At the same time proper Roman regulations would be provided for those Roman citizens who were in the town, and who would be regarded as the most important section of it by the drafters of the law. The end-product would therefore be a compromise between native practice and Roman law, with native practice probably predominating, if only by default. This phenomenon would have been of different strengths in the different regions of the province. In the towns of the lower Baetis valley, where trade had led to extensive contact with the wider Roman world, a great deal of orthodox Roman law was probably understood and practised, and so local interpretations of it would have been few. However, it is difficult to see this being the case in the more isolated communities found in Baeturia and Bastetania. Here, in contrast, the level of *interpretatio peregrina* was probably extremely high.

The nature of the legal activity undertaken would also have affected the phenomenon. Minor cases would have been in the hands of local officials from the town concerned, who would themselves have had no grounding in Roman law, and here the scope for local interpretation of the law would have been enormous. This would especially have been so when the case was one not specifically covered by the charter. Such cases ought, by the provisions of chapter 93 of the law, to have been settled according to the practice at Rome. However, it is likely that on many occasions no one knew what this was, and the gravity of the offence concerned will not have seemed sufficient to make it worth while sending to the governor to find out. Here geography would have played a significant role; the more inaccessible a community was from the centre, the more cases would have fallen into this category. In such cases native law would have been used by default. On the other hand where appeal to the governor was thought worth while, or where he otherwise became involved, such cases would be tried by Roman law. The participants in such cases, who would normally have been from the upper classes, and hence have been responsible in some degree for the administration of justice in their home communities, may then have carried back this knowledge of correct procedure to their own towns and introduced its practice there.[139]

Another source of diffusion would be the possible power that knowledge of the correct forms of law might bring in local politics; where an appeal to a correct procedure, or demonstration that an opponent had acted incorrectly, might bring personal advantages. One example of this may lie behind the letter appended to the end of the *Lex Irnitana*, dealing with marriages which had been made against the provisions of the law. The letter shows two things; first, that the regulations concerning *conubium* had been misapplied, and second, that this had been brought to the notice of the authorities and needed rectifying. As Rome tended to be reactive in its approach to government, the letter could well have had its genesis in an internal political dispute in Irni, or perhaps a legal case involving an inhabitant of Irni and a member of a different *municipium*.

The letter suggests that such misunderstandings were corrected as they came, randomly, to light. Such misinterpretations probably increased the further one travelled from the central lowland core of the province. Distance would also mean that the rate of correction here would have been much lower. One aspect of the charter may itself show how a lack of firm communications allowed such variation to come about. On the *Lex Malacitana* Domitian's name has been erased as a consequence of his *damnatio memoriae*, whereas on the *Leges Salpensana* and *Irnitana* it has been allowed to remain. The best reason for this discrepancy is that Malaca, a major port, enjoyed good communications with the Mediterranean world. Salpensa and Irni, on the other hand were less immediately accessible, and so the erasure order would have been more difficult to carry out here.[140]

[139] Here it is of interest that the four *conventus* capitals of the province, where the governor would have given judgement, Corduba, Hispalis, Astigi, and Gades, are all in the lowland area of the province. Therefore those communities who needed most help with the interpretation of the law, the highland communities, are precisely those who would find access to the governor's court most difficult.

[140] Alternatively Domitian's name may have been allowed to stand at Irni, because of his letter, appended to the town's charter, the provisions of which would have been important to the local aristocracy. Nevertheless it seems unlikely that this was the case at Salpensa as well.

The importance of geographical location and communication means it would probably be wrong to see the phenomenon of *interpretatio peregrina* as a form of active native resistance to Rome. Rather, it would have been an inevitable consequence of the lack of any means of diffusing knowledge of Roman law. This is not to rule out the possibility that on occasions the charter was deliberately misinterpreted to gain either personal, or group, advantages. On the other hand, the general nature of the charter also makes it unlikely that the Flavian law was intended to bring about an immediate and complete change in the way of life of the communities who had been granted the *ius Latii*. Instead it provided a blueprint of a town towards which it was assumed the towns of the province would evolve. Such evolution would be gradual, as the deviation from the law would only come to light, and be corrected, gradually. On the other hand it would have assuaged conservative opinion at Rome by ensuring that the *cives Romani* and *cives Latini* of Iberia were living, in theory at least, under the forms of Roman law. Its provisions that the *ius civile* was to be used at all times would also have been administratively convenient for the governor and his advisors, who would not have had to concern themselves about the vagaries of native law.

What, then, would have been the effects on the life of an average *municeps* of Vespasian's actions? Apart from generating a certain pride in the acquisition of a superior status, they may have been less far-reaching than at first might seem to be the case. On the lowest level there does not appear to be any evidence that every *municeps* was enrolled in a Roman tribe, or had been given the right to, or compelled to use, the *tria nomina* form of nomenclature.

The rights of *patria potestas* and the like which devolved on him would have had the power to alter his family relationships, but it is unclear whether they would have been sufficiently understood to be implemented in depth. It is this transfer from peregrine to Latin status, assumed by the law to have already occurred, which poses the greatest problems for modern interpretation. How was this handled, especially in communities with little knowledge of Roman legal practice? If the initial transfer from peregrine to Latin status was carried out in the Spanish towns with the same thoroughness with which the Flavian Municipal Law handles the transfer to Roman from Latin status of ex-magistrates, it seems that care would have been taken to ensure that there was no disruption to family relationships which had existed prior to the grant of the *ius Latii*. This in turn may have led, especially in isolated communities, to a belief that these old practices were the same as their Roman successors, and so retarded the full implementation of the Roman legal practice.[141] Other general rights which an inhabitant of the Iberian provinces would have obtained as a *civis Latinus*, such as the *ius commercii*, would have been of little relevance in his everyday life.

As regards his wider political life, the old ruling body of his town would have been perpetuated in the same form, at least numerically, in the new municipal *ordo*. The élite of the community would have preserved their position above him by securing the superior status of *civis Romanus*. If, as seems to be the case, there was no *conubium* between *cives Latini* and *cives Romani*, the old élite would have been even more firmly entrenched than perhaps they had been previously. Consequently the passing of the Flavian Municipal Law, would, in many respects, have been a case of *plus ça change, plus c'est la même chose*.

We cannot therefore infer immediately that Baetican towns pursued a Roman way of life from the fact that they possessed a legal charter expressed in terms of Roman law. The degree of Roman practice would have varied from place to place, and have depended greatly on the geographical location of each, and on the contact this afforded them with the wider Roman world. Baetica probably exhibited a wide spectrum of degrees of absorption of Roman law and legal practices.

If the grant of *ius Latii* did not herald the introduction of communities which conformed exactly to the provisions of Roman law and the norms this embodied, did it have any other effects? One appears to have been an upsurge in building. In the town of Munigua, for example, the Flavian period was witness to a major development of the town centre on Roman lines. Beyond the province, in neighbouring Lusitania, the town of Conimbriga also rebuilt its *forum* area in a more grandiose way. Nevertheless this response to the grant seems to have been a spontaneous reaction by the native population, rather than something intended by the Roman authorities. This can be seen from Vespasian's qualified enthusiasm in his reply to the petition of the Saborenses to move their town in AD 77. Although Vespasian gives them the permission they seek, and the right to title their town after him, he is far less eager to grant the Saborenses extra powers to raise taxes, presumably afraid that this will affect their ability to pay their imperial ones.[142] This extra revenue would most likely have been

---

[141] This phenomenon would probably have been less marked in the Baetis valley. Also, Celtic native practices may not have seemed too incongruous to Roman eyes; Gaius, when looking for a parallel to Roman *patria potestas*, finds a near equivalent in the customs of the Celtic Galatae (*Institutes* 1. 55).

[142] This wish to adopt the title 'Flavium' is purely voluntary and should be typical of how the title came to be adopted in many Baetican communities.

spent on new buildings in the town, and the nature of Vespasian's reply shows a greater preoccupation with revenue than 'Romanization'. The date of the letter, AD 77, shows that this was the case even if the grant of *ius Latii* was not made at the beginning of his reign, but several years later. If so, the debts referred to in Titus' letter to the town of Munigua could also have been incurred in this process.[143] Again Titus' less than friendly reply suggests that such works were the response of the local population to the grant, rather than that the grant was a deliberately intended stimulus for urbanization. A further example of the grant possibly leading to a town financially overextending itself is found at Cartima, where an inscription dating from the late first century records that the *pontifex* of the town, L. Porcius Saturninus, paid off 20,000 HS of municipal debt from his own pocket.[144]

In conclusion it is difficult to assess the effect of Vespasian's grant of *ius Latii* in Baetica. The grant, made to the whole of the peninsula, may have been made as almost an emergency measure at the beginning of the emperor's reign, and possibly needed major reinstatement by Domitian. The Flavian Municipal Law which he then promulgated is a general, though highly Roman document, which would have been applied to a wide variety of very different communities. If it was made to assuage the population, the grant appears to have succeeded. The title *municipium Flavium* seems to have been assumed voluntarily, and at least fifteen *civitates* in Baetica have been found with this title. There also seems to have been an upsurge of building in the province. The measure's popularity would have centred above all on the means it gave for local native aristocracies to attain the Roman citizenship, and possibly on the feeling of 'Romanness' which it gave to the rest of the population.

However, apart from these effects, the impact of the law must have been highly varied. As has been seen, the extremely Roman form in which it was granted does not necessarily mean that it was implemented in this way. The effects of *interpretatio peregrina* would have led to the adoption of a whole spectrum of degrees of Roman practice in the province, ranging from the complete or near-complete in the Baetis valley to the minimal in the highland regions. This degree of variation would have depended not only on the willingness of local communities to adopt Roman practice, but also on their ability to discover what these were, on the one hand, and perhaps, on the other, the degree of activism practised by individual provincial governors in weeding out misinterpretations of the law. Of-

---

[143] *AE* (1962), 288.   [144] *CIL* 2. 1957.

ficially the province could be said to be governed by Roman law, but this official fiction, while holding reasonably good in some areas of the province, and being administratively convenient, would have been a shallow veneer in others. The result is that the Flavian law, although giving us a potential insight into the workings of the Roman legal mind, as a document of social interpretation still leaves a large question mark over what life was really like on the ground in Baetica.

7

The Physical Remains of Baetican Towns and their Interpretation

AFTER surveying constitutional developments in the province, it remains to examine the physical effects of these changes. Did urban centres take on a more Roman appearance in the early imperial period?

A study of the growth of a classical urban mentality should start with a survey of the development of the public buildings and amenities which were regarded as essential for town life.[1] However, an examination of the spread of private Roman-style buildings will also be of use, as it will reveal, to some degree, the extent to which Roman mores penetrated into the private, as well as the public, urban life of Baetica. Finally the shape and location of towns as a whole, apart from their constituent elements, will be considered. For ease of reference each of these categories will be dealt with under separate subheadings.

In all these areas various factors need to be taken into consideration. The first is the motivation for the erection of the buildings, which may not be a simple reflection of a wish to urbanize by the local population. A related question is the time at which the structures were built: why did some periods appear more auspicious for building than others? The distribution of buildings within the province is also important. As has already been seen, Baetica comprised several distinct regions: were these geographical differences reflected in the distribution of Roman buildings?

Unfortunately the Roman remains of the south of Spain have in the past been much under-studied and underexcavated. Few sites have seen substantial excavation, many others sadly often provide only fragmentary pieces of information.[2] To supplement the extant remains, the existence of some other structures can be deduced from epigraphic evidence. This is of two kinds: that referring directly to buildings, and that which deals

---

[1] See the discussion in Ch. 2.

[2] See e.g. Stylow's anguished remark: ' "Córdoba callada"? Si!, es que no la dejan hablar.' A. U. Stylow, 'Apuntes sobre el urbanismo de la Córdoba romana', in W. Trillmich and P. Zanker (eds.), *Stadtbild und Ideologie: Die Monumentalisierung hispanischer Städte zwischen Republik und Kaiserzeit* (1990).

with events, such as gladiatorial contests, which can perhaps be inferred to have taken place in specific buildings, such as, in the example given, an amphitheatre; but this second type of evidence is not without problems, as will be seen below.

FORA

As the *forum* was the political heart of a Roman town, a consideration of the *fora* of the province provides the ideal starting-point for the examination of the public buildings found in Baetica. A total of sixteen *fora* can be identified in the province.

Fora at Corduba and Hispalis are attested in the late republican period. The *forum* at Hispalis appears to have been colonnaded, and a *basilica* is mentioned at Corduba in this period, which ought to be associated with the *forum*.[3] As previously mentioned, there is no indication of the size, or monumentality, of these buildings, which could have been quite small, and may well have been destroyed in the Civil Wars period, when both towns were sacked.[4] These early *fora* do not imply the widespread adoption of Roman customs, and were probably used for trading by the *conventus* settled in these two towns, and in the case of Corduba by the provincial governor for provincial, rather than municipal, matters.

Given the fragmentary nature of much of our evidence, caution must be exercised in assuming that any paved area uncovered in excavations is a part of a *forum* complex. After all, many Roman towns possessed more than one open space. Added to this problem is the fact that even native towns tended to possess an open public space.[5] Here of course the problem is compounded as we are forced to rely on Roman literary sources for our evidence. Can we be sure that a reference to a *forum* is not merely the author importing classical terminology into a native context?

These problems of interpretation are well illustrated at Corduba, where the situation is further complicated: being a provincial capital, the town should have possessed, like Emerita and Tarraco, two *fora*, colonial and provincial. The site of one of these is normally accepted as the area of purple and black marble paving found by Santos Gener between the

[3] Hispalis: Caesar, *BC* 2. 20; Corduba: Cicero, 2 *Verr.* 4. 25; basilica: Ps. Caesar, *B. Alex.* 52.
[4] Ps. Caesar, *B. Hisp.* 32–4; Appian, *BC* 2. 104; Dio, 43. 28, 38–9; see the discussion in Ch. 3.
[5] See e.g. Livy 28. 3. 13 for the mention of a 'forum' at the native town of Oringis in 206 BC.

Calles Cruz Conde and Gongora.[6] Another section of paving has also found to the east, at the corner of the Calle de Eduardo Quero, which may by part of a continuous whole. Santos Gener dated the remains to the republic, but more recent work would assign them to the Augustan period.[7] The identification of the area as a *forum* rests on the large number of civic dedicatory inscriptions found here. It is unclear whether this area, if it is part of a *forum*, belonged to the provincial or city *forum*, although the city *forum* seems the more likely candidate.[8] But the site may not be a *forum* at all. The greater part of Santos Gener's excavation uncovered a large bath complex onto which the paved area abutted. The connection between the two was through an 'atrium' measuring 10 × 11 m., leading immediately to the main plunge-bath of the bath complex. This is an unusual arrangement for an entrance to a Roman bath-house, where the changing rooms and heated rooms would be expected to precede the plunge-bath. It might be possible to see the paved area described by Santos Gener connected to the bath complex as a *palaestra* or *gymnasium* rather than as a *forum*. Added to this problem is the fact that bath-houses were not normally constructed adjacent to *fora*. At this point, however, it becomes difficult to account for the dedications found in the area. Problems exist therefore with any obvious interpretation of the remains: we still do not know the exact extent of the paved area, or the precise layout, or orientation of the bath-house.

Stylow believes that he has detected the provincial *forum* in the area of the modern Calles Jesus y Maria and Angel de Saavedra. Again the deduction is based on epigraphic finds—a cluster of inscriptions dedicated to provincial *flamines* have been found in this area.[9] The presence of a large column capital, over a metre high, suggests that a major temple, possibly that dedicated to the provincial imperial cult, was located here. The remains appear to date to the Flavian period.

A *forum* complex was erected at Carteia in the Augustan period. Excavations at the site have uncovered an area of paving in front of a monumental stairway.[10] At Hispalis, Campos and González believe that they

    [6] S. Santos Gener, *Informes y memorias*, 31 (1955).
    [7] Stylow, 'Apuntes sobre el urbanismo de la Córdoba romana', 273; J. L. Jiménez Salvador, 'El templo romano de la calle Claudio Marcelo en Córdoba', *Cuadernos de arguitectura romana*, 1 (1991), 119–32, at p. 129.
    [8] This is the view, *inter alia*, of Stylow, 'Apuntes sobre el urbanismo de la Córdoba romana', 272–82.
    [9] Ibid. 274–9.
    [10] The initial reports, Woods, 'Carteia and Tartessos', 251–6; Presado Velo *et al.*, *Carteia*, i suggest a late republican date for the finds. On the other hand, J. J. Sayos Abengochea in Menéndez Pidal (ed.), *Historia de España* (2nd edn., 1982), ii, ** ch. 5., proposes a Julio-Claudian, date.

have located two *fora* dating from the imperial period: a 'civic' *forum*, centred on the area now occupied by the Iglesia del Salvador, and a 'mercantile' *forum*, centred on the site of the present-day cathedral, and hence by the course of the Baetis as it was in antiquity. Although these suggestions are plausible, the fragmentary nature of the evidence, mainly the find-spots of inscriptions, mean that the hypothesis can have only the status of a reasonable conjecture.[11]

However, in general it appears that development in the province occurred at a slightly later date in the Julio-Claudian period. The *forum* complex at Celti dates from around AD 20. Prior to this the site was occupied by Iberian-style houses. The complex itself did not last long; it was overbuilt in the late first or early second century AD by a large peristyle house. Presumably a new *forum* complex replaced the Tiberian one, and it could be suggested that such new construction was inspired by the grant of the *ius Latii* to the province by the emperor Vespasian.

The most thoroughly excavated *forum* in the province is that of the coastal town of Belo. An open *forum* area seems to have been built in the Augustan period, but it was the reign of Claudius that saw a major renewal of interest and monumentalization of this part of the town. The *forum* measures 33 × 30 m.: too square to fit the Vitruvian ideal proportions of 3 : 2. It is paved, and bounded on the north side by a wall on which stands a *capitolium* of three temples in one of which a fragmentary statue of Juno was found, to the south by a *basilica*, and on the east and west by porticoes.

The most interesting feature of this complex is the wall and three-temple *capitolium* at its northern end. The initial design comprised the wall and the three temples above it. In the centre of the wall lay a raised square block of masonry, probably intended as a *tribunal*. Access to the temples was by two stairways flanking the wall. This terraced arrangement was dictated mainly by the topography of the area, but is also paralleled by sites in Africa, for example Lixus and Tingi. A further African parallel can be seen in the three-temple *capitolium* at Sufetula in Africa. However, it must be emphasized that this postdates the Belo complex by about a century. There is, nevertheless, a parallel in the old *forum* at Lepcis Magna, which is bounded at one end by three separate temples (albeit not a *capitolium*) and a *basilica* at the other. There does, therefore, appear to be an African link in the structures at Belo, the reasons for which will be discussed further below.

The wall underwent extensive modifications at an undetermined time after its construction. The *tribunal* was subsumed into a new lower ter-

---

[11] J. Campos and J. González, 'Los foros de Hispalis, colonia romana', *A.e.A.* 60 (1987). 123 ff.

race. The centre of the wall at this new level was cut back into a semi-circular *nymphaeum* with a monumental fountain, draining into conduits leading around the edge of the *forum*. Access to the new terrace was again by stairways at each side of the wall. This development can be seen as an attempt to embellish the town as wealth increased, and the design of the *nymphaeum* shows that an effort was made to present a pleasant façade. However, the underlying reason for the modifications was more practical. The *capitolium* had been built on a natural line of drainage, the consequences of which would have caused structural damage had a drainage point not been provided. This apparent carelessness in choosing a site for building is paralleled at Italica, suggesting that aesthetic reasons may have overridden practical considerations on some occasions, perhaps strengthening the parallelism between Belo and various African sites. On the other hand, it may simply reveal that Roman architects were more incompetent, or ignorant, than is often assumed.

The northern wall of the *forum* underwent further changes when a temple was built on the western end of the fountain terrace and a smaller shrine at its eastern end. This rendered both access-stairways useless, although they seem to have survived, and two new staircases were built on the axes of the ends of the *nymphaeum* semicircle. The northern end of the *forum*, therefore, was continually developed both for practical, and later aesthetic, reasons. There was a strong emphasis on symmetry, the *nymphaeum* being aligned with the central of the three temples, and the two lower temples with the corresponding upper ones. Nevertheless the disproportionate size of the two lower temples will have broken this symmetry to some degree, and these buildings, depending on their height, may have obscured the view of the *capitolium* envisaged in the original plan. The three temples of the *capitolium* all date from *c*.AD 40–60. The central temple appears to have been built slightly before the other two. All are prostyle in form, built of local stone, and stuccoed. Stratigraphic soundings suggest that there was nothing on this site prior to their erection.

On the south side, the *forum* was bounded by a *basilica* which possessed a colonnaded portico facing the *forum*. Three doors gave access to the *basilica* from this portico, the rear wall of which was stuccoed. The stratigraphy of the structure suggests again that it was built in the early years of Claudius' reign. The building extended along the *forum*, was 20 m. deep, and was divided into a broad nave and two aisles by two colonnades of eight pillars. At the western end lay a *tribunal* reached by ten steps. Its interior was decorated with painted stucco-work. Fourteen of the capitals from the internal colonnades survive. Seven are Ionic, another seven a crude form of composite capital, owing something to local, native, traditions. All are of local stone and stuccoed. Two statue bases were also found, along with a headless togate statue with a cornucopia at its feet. This has been interpreted as being a statue of Claudius, although it could be of any dignitary. A bust of the emperor Trajan was also found. There are traces of an earlier building beneath the *basilica*, dating to the last quarter of the first century BC.

To the south of the *basilica* lies another paved area, running down to the *decumanus maximus* of the town. Its existence serves to remind us of the care which must be taken in assuming that any paved area discovered in isolation in a town is its *forum*. In this square on the western side, a building of 9.5 × 10.1 m. abuts onto the *basilica*. This originally had at least one upper storey, as is revealed by two internal staircases. These begin at the northern, or basilican, end of the building, whereas access to it is by a doorway 3 m. wide in the centre of its south face, preceded by a vestibule supported by two pillars. On its western side is a narrow colonnaded lane leading to the *forum*. The building has been interpreted by its excavators as a temple with two pillars *in antis*. The staircases are, however, problematic, and a previous interpretation suggesting that the building was a library, or archive, is preferable. Again the stratigraphy suggests a Claudian or Neronian date.

The western side of the *forum* also had a monumental aspect. In the north-western corner is a building measuring 14.5 × 9.5 m. This should be another temple; a statue base was uncovered at its rear and the main *cella* is preceded by a small anteroom 2 m. deep, best interpreted as a *pronaos*. Adjacent to the temple is a further monumental structure, possibly the town's *curia*, or senate-house. Again this building appears to have been built in the Claudian period, superseding an earlier Augustan structure. Adjoining this are traces of a monumental arch. Compared with the grand structures on the west side, the eastern side of the *forum* presents a stark contrast. Here the portico floor was only of hardened earth. Its rear is occupied by a number of small shop buildings, irregular in size, though of approximately the same dimensions. These date from the late Augustan, or Tiberian, period and later fell into disuse. The *basilica* encroaches on this portico at its southern end and its foundations block the portico's original drain. The decline of the shops is best explained by the building of the *basilica*, which will have made access to the *forum* difficult, not only for prospective buyers, but also for the shopkeepers to bring in their wares. The *macellum*, built on the *decumanus* to the west of the southern paved area, may have been built, in part, to provide a new area for traders to operate in. Its date is again Claudian, or early Flavian, which would tally with this theory.

The *forum* complex at Belo therefore was constructed mainly in the Claudian period, when a concerted effort was made to give the town a monumental centre. It is significant, however, that the town was unable to afford, or saw no reason, to import marble for use in the construction of its public buildings. Instead these are of local stone stuccoed to give the appearance of marble. The Claudian date for the expansion is best explained by the wars fought in Mauretania in Claudius' reign. Grain was supplied to the Mauretanian army from Baetica,[12] and Belo would have been the ideal place from which to channel such grain. Pliny notes that the passage to Tingi from Belo is the shortest crossing to Africa and Strabo comments on her trade with Mauretania.[13] Belo probably became a depot town at this time, the extra wealth this introduced being used to adorn the city. The town's epithet, 'Claudia', also suggests that this period was one of importance in its history; the presence of the Galerian tribe here at this period suggests, as was seen in Chapter 5, that the town may have received the *ius Latii* at this time. Such a grant may well have been a stimulus for the town to build a more monumental centre in order to demonstrate in physical form its new higher status.[14] Some form of Augustan centre had existed previously, but this seems to have been devoid of major monumental buildings.

The African echoes in Belo's architecture can easily be explained by its proximity to that continent. Some of the buildings are constructed in the style known as *opus Africanum*, where irregular courses of stone are flanked by stone uprights. This method of construction is Punic in origin. In the late empire bricks from Mauretania appear to have been used at Belo. Lamps and other pottery of African manufacture are also found.[15]

The dating of the *forum* complex at Belo has recently been challenged, and a late republican date proposed.[16] The challenge is based in part on a critique of the accepted stratigraphy of the site, but rests mainly on the fact that the capitals of the temples on the *capitolium* have a form which predates, stylistically, that found in Claudian Rome. However, it would

---

[12] Dio, 60. 24. 5, AD 44.   [13] Pliny, *NH* 5. 1. 2; Strabo, 3. 1. 8.

[14] *AE* (1971), 172. For a general argument that growth was stimulated by Claudius' campaigns, see D. Nony, 'Claude et les espagnols, sur un passage de l'Apocoloquintose', *MCV* 4 (1968), 51 ff.

[15] It is only fair to note that the raised *podium* also occurs at Bilbilis.

[16] M. Pfanner, 'Muster republikanischer Städte in Spanien' and 'Struktur und Erscheinungsbild augusteischer Städte', in Trillmich and Zanker (eds.), *Stadtbild und Ideologie*.

not be surprising if provincial architecture lagged behind that of the imperial, or even the provincial, capital.[17] Moreover, though less likely, given Claudius' archaizing tastes, antique capitals may have been an attempt to follow imperial trends. The Claudian date also fits better with the rest of the town's stratigraphy. The new dating, although worthy of note, needs more secure evidence if it is to be proved correct.

The *forum* complex at Munigua postdates the *forum* at Belo, being built in the Flavian period, and is completely different in plan. It is built on an artificial terrace on the eastern slope of a hill which is dominated by a large temple complex. The *forum* provides an architectural link between the town below and the temple above. It is an almost perfect square of 20 × 20 m. so again flouts the proportions laid down by Vitruvius, but unlike the *forum* at Belo, contains a major building, a temple, at its centre. The temple (measuring 15 × 10 m. including its colonnade) is too large to have allowed commercial activity in the *forum*, whose use must therefore have been civic in nature. On its north side lies a portico with a central shrine. This contains a granite base for a statue of a horse with an inscription describing the dedication of an *equus* and an *aed(es) equilis* by L. Aelius Fronto, to Dis Pater.[18] The unusual choice of deity probably represents a syncretic Iberian cult.[19] The complex dates to the Flavian era, and was part of a conscious attempt to give Munigua a monumental centre at this time. The neighbouring temple, its processional way, and the bath complex also date from this period.

Unfortunately no firm date can be given to the *forum* complex uncovered at Iliberris. This was paved with local brown marble, and had a width of 26.5 m. and an indeterminate length. On its south side lay a monumental gallery, decorated with pilasters, leading to a stuccoed stairway. To the north two marble steps led up to a small podium supporting stuccoed limestone pillars perhaps forming part of a portico. Remains of Ionic, Corinthian, and composite capitals were found, along with traces of statue bases, around the edges of the paved area.[20] Also discovered was a fragment of a lintel bearing a broken inscription recording that Ser. Persicus, to celebrate his sevirate, adorned some part of the town's *forum*

[17] This was certainly the case at Corduba and Tarraco: Jiménez Salvador, 'El templo romano de la calle Claudio Marcelo', esp. pp. 126–7 and n. 28.

[18] W. Grünhagen, 'El monumento a Dis Pater de Munigua', in *Segovia: Symposium de arqueologia romana* (1977), 201–8.

[19] Ibid. 201 ff.; J. Ma. Blázquez, *Diccionario de las religiones prerromanas de Hispania* (1975), 90.

[20] F. Molina González and J. M. Roldán Hervás, *Historia de Granada* (1983), i. 245–8, lam. 10. The account is almost entirely based on M. Gómez Moreno, 'Monumentos arquitectónicos de Granada', *Miscelaneas, Historia—Arte—Arqueologia* (1949), 347–90.

and *basilica* '. . . fori et basilicae . . . †baecliis† et postibus exornatas'.[21] The inscription, described by its nineteenth-century excavators, has subsequently been lost. 'Baeclis' is either a *hapax legomenon*, or corrupt. Other versions read 'biicis' and 'ibviciis'. Various restorations have been suggested: for example, 'incensis iterum subliciis et postibus' and 'subiectis ei postibus'. There is no realistic method of choosing between the rival versions, nor of dating the inscription, although a surviving, more fragmentary, version has been dated to the second century AD, giving us a probable *terminus ante quem* for the building of the *forum*. Again a Flavian date might seem an obvious time for such construction. The *forum* must have been an imposing public space in its heyday. If built to Vitruvian principles, it would have been approximately 39 m. long. Iliberris, the modern Granada, grew in importance in the Roman period, and this *forum* may be seen as an indication of this. Nevertheless it appears that the town was not rich enough to import marble, but utilized local marbles and stucco-work The remains of the town must have been totally effaced by the medieval period, as the Muslim historian, al-Himyari, who is eager to note ancient remains, describes Granada as a modern foundation.[22]

Other archaeological remains of *fora* are less conclusive. An area paved with large marble flags was found in 1903 at Urso between the remains of the theatre and the modern unmade road known as the Vereda de Granada. This could be part of the *colonia*'s *forum* but equally it could simply be part of a plaza serving the theatre, such as the one to be found at Italica. One possible argument in support of the area being the *forum* is that the bronze tablets of the *Lex Ursonensis*, which were presumably displayed in the colony's *forum*, were found nearby. Similarly, at Acinippo there are brief reports of a *forum* area, built in the early Augustan period; but the incompleteness of the site's excavation must lead to caution here.[23]

Other *fora* in Baetica are known only from inscriptions. At Cisimbrium we learn that C. Valerius Valerianus dedicated a *forum*, *aedes* (plural), five *signa*, and five *statuae* of the gods at his own expense. Valerius was *duovir* and *pontifex perpetuus* of the town at the time of the dedication. If he did donate everything he states, the expenditure involved would have been considerable, even for a modest *forum*. Unfortunately the inscription cannot be dated.[24] On a similar dedication from Iliturgicola L. Porcius Quietus and his son, Titus, record their dedication of a 'templum et signum et forum', adding that the land was 'solum suum'. If this land was in the centre of the town, as would be expected with a *forum* complex, it

[21] *CIL* 2. 2083.   [22] Al-Himyari, *Kitāb ar-Rawḍ*, 19.
[23] *Arqueologia '81* (1982), no. 170.   [24] *CIL* 2. 2098.

suggests that small *municipia*, such as Iliturgicola, possessed remarkably little public land. Again, the dedication appears to be of a whole *forum* complex, which included a temple. Whether the plan of the *forum* was similar to that at Munigua, with a central temple, or a more standard one, with the temple at one end, there is no way of telling. In any event it represents a major act of euergetism by Quietus and his son and perhaps indicates the degree to which one or two wealthy families would have dominated the political life of some small Baetican towns.[25]

Hints of improvements to a *forum* can be seen at Naeva, where L. Aelius Aelianus and his wife, Egnatia Lupercilla, held *spectacula* after dedicating 'omnes statuae quae in his portic (is) . . . sunt' ('all the statues found in these porticoes'). Perhaps the porticoes in question were not in the *forum* but elsewhere, especially given the heat of the region. However, it would seem natural for a town to have porticoes in the *forum* if nowhere else. The inscription dates to the mid-second century AD, and may, therefore, form a *terminus ante quem* for the *forum*.[26] Similar hints are found at Canania, where L. Attius Vetto erected *porticus lapideae marmoratae*, again 'solo suo'. The monumental porticoes may not have been in the *forum*, but it would seem a natural place to provide them if they did not already exist here. The phrase 'solo suo' raises questions about municipal land, and may tell against the porticoes having been in the *forum*. Vetto is described as a *duovir* of the *municipium Flavium Cananiense*, giving as a *terminus post quem* the reign of Vespasian. The mention of marble is interesting, given the large amount of stucco-work found in the province. It is likely to have been local rather than imported.[27]

At Cartima, among other acts of beneficence, Iunia Rustica dedicated a bronze statue of Mars in the *forum*. This inscription dates to the Flavian period. At Nescania, L. Postumius Stico dedicated a bronze *signum* in the *forum*.[28] At Arunda, a statue was dedicated to L. Iunius Iunianus in the *forum*,[29] and similarly at Saepo a statue was dedicated in the *forum* to Pomponia Roscia.[30]

The physical remains of *fora* in the province show that in some towns at least, such as Belo and Munigua, they took a predominantly Roman form, albeit there frequently seems to have been some continuation of native culture intermingling in this overall Roman framework, as is shown by the Iberian-influenced sculpture found in the *basilica* at Belo, and the cult of Dis Pater at Munigua.

---

[25] *CIL* 2.1649.   [26] *ILER* 1735.   [27] *CIL* 2. 1074.
[28] *CIL* 2.1956, 2. 2006.   [29] *CIL* 2. 1359.   [30] *CIL* 2.1341.

Our epigraphic evidence, although it can reveal nothing about the physical shape of the *fora*, shows that even in the smaller towns of the province they were used in a thoroughly Roman way: namely for the advertisement of acts of euergetism and the erection of statuary honouring local dignitaries. Most of our evidence comes from the lowland areas of the province. It is difficult to ascertain whether highland settlements also had *fora*. One slight indication that this may not have been the case is that chapter 95 of the *Lex Irnitana* instructs the magistrates of the towns concerned to place a bronze copy of the *lex* not in the *forum*, but merely in the 'celeberrimus locus' ('the most frequented place') of the town.

In conclusion it can be said that large settlements in Baetica possessed Roman-style *fora*, but very little is known about their specific details. The stimulus to build such centres is difficult to ascertain. Most of the evidence dates from the Flavian period or later. In some cases it is clear that the stimulus to build was peculiar to the town involved, for example the Claudian military activity and/or the possible grant to the *ius Latii* at Belo, and hence cannot be used to demonstrate a general trend in the province. Smaller settlements may have possessed such *fora*, but even if this was not the case, the public square in such a town certainly seems to have played some of the roles of a *forum*.

BATH-HOUSES

If the *forum* was the centre of civic life in a Roman town, the baths were the centre of social life, and were taken as an index of Roman, and more specifically urban, behaviour.[31] Bath-houses are the most commonly attested monument in Baetica, with a possible twenty-nine towns showing evidence of them.

The provincial capital, Corduba, as would be expected, possessed a monumental-sized bath-house. This was situated along the present-day Calle Conde Cruz, where Santos Gener excavated a building measuring at least 60 × 20 m.[32] At one end lay a large *piscina*, divided into two plunges by a central wall. To one side of this an *atrium* led to a paved area, believed

---

[31] See Seneca, *Ep.* 86 and esp. *ILS* 5720 and 5721. These inscriptions, from country estates, boast: 'lavat(ur) more *urbico*, et omnis humanitas praestatur' ('here we wash in the style of the city with all civilization requires') and: 'more *urbico* lavat(ur) [et] omnia commoda praestantur' ('here we wash in the style of the city and all necessities are available'). For a general survey of the role of the bath-house in Roman culture, see K. Dunbabin, 'Baiarum Grata Voluptas: The Pleasure and Danger of Baths', *PBSR* 44 (1989), 6 ff.

[32] S. Santos Gener, *Informes y memorias*, 31, 72 ff.

by Santos Gener to have been the town's *forum* (the difficulties of this interpretation have been discussed above); on the opposite side lay a series of rooms, some heated by hypocausts, and many decorated with mosaics, including a well-known mosaic of Pegasus. Large amounts of painted stucco were found, suggesting a richly decorated interior. The *piscina* appears to have been surrounded by a monumental portico which used a large number of finely moulded bricks in its construction. This, along with the fact that much of the building is built in the *opus quadratum* style, led Santos Gener to propose a late republican date for the building, and to suggest that it was destroyed in the sack of the city at the end of the Civil War. This date seems far too early. The Pegasus mosaic dates, stylistically, to the second century AD,[33] and at least one other mosaic shows artistic parallels to an Ostian mosaic of the same date. The division of the plunge-bath can be paralleled from the Hadrianic baths of Italica. It is hard to believe that a *conventus*, however rich, would erect such a monumental, public structure. It seems better to postulate a Flavian, or later date, for the construction of the complex. This monumental set of baths was not the only one to be found in the town; de la Torre discovered traces of a further set in the Calle de la Concepción. Again this situation is not peculiar and can be paralleled in any large town in the empire.

The largest baths in the province are the so-called Baths of the Moorish Queen in the *nova urbs* at Italica. These measure 75 × 62.5 m., and are entered through a portico leading to a colonnaded patio, whence led off the bath chambers proper. The complex is the size of two normal *insulae*, and was designed to show the scale of imperial munificence bestowed on Italica. Hence, like the *nova urbs* in general, it is of little use in assessing the general urge or ability to construct Roman buildings in the province. A further large public building which may be another bath-house has been revealed by the recent geophysical survey of the *nova urbs*, but as yet has not been excavated. A smaller bath-house, symmetrically designed and perhaps of the same date, found in the *vetus urbs* represents the size of building that the community could afford without imperial assistance.

The remains in the other *coloniae* of the province are fragmentary. At Hispalis a major bath-house, interpreted by Caro as a Roman labyrinth, lay beneath what is now the archiepiscopal palace.[34] At Urso, a *piscina*, meas-

---

[33] J. M. Blázquez, *Corpus de Mosaicos de España*, iii. *Mosaicos romanos de Córdoba, Jaén, y Málaga* (1981), 33–4.
[34] R. Caro, 'El labirinto de Sevilla: Sus reliquias', in *Adiciones al libro de las antigüedes y Principado de Sevilla*, published as *Memorial historico-español de la Real Academia de la Historia* (1851).

uring 5 × 3.3 m, has been found to the west of the theatre with five steps leading down to it. Five composite capitals were discovered in it, along with remains of column shafts worked in local stone and stuccoed, a large amount of stucco, and quantities of tiles and bricks. The size of the find suggests a public building.[35] At Astigi, an inscription, now lost, records the building of a *lacus X cum aeramentis* by the *IIvir* [. . .] Longinus. *Aeramenta* were tools such as strigils used in the bathing process.[36]

The baths at Munigua abut onto the *forum* complex, but are on lower level than the *forum* itself. They are modest in size and rectangular in plan, dating from the Flavian period. Below the bath-house traces of earlier settlement have been found, which show that the area, prior to the erection of the baths, had been used for iron smelting. This appears to have gone on until the Flavian period, again suggesting that an attempt was made at this period to give the town a more monumental and 'Roman' centre.

Traces of a bath-house have also been found at Iliberris near the *forum*. It is unclear, however, whether these are the remains of a Roman structure, or of a later Arabic one which reused a substantial amount of Roman material. Arabic baths certainly did exist: they are attested by the geographer al-Himyari. This author mentions bath-houses at many sites in Baetica in the Arabic period, but there is no good evidence that these were reused Roman buildings.

At Arva, remains of a bath-house have been found under a modern iron-works. They comprise a colonnaded *frigidarium* lined with marble, and a semicircular *piscina* adjoining it.[37] A further set of baths has been found at Las Torrecillas, approximately a mile from the town. These may be a public building, lying outside Arva proper, but they could equally have formed part of a villa or industrial complex. The former solution is perhaps supported by the fragmentary traces of a bath-house which have been found on the Camino de Brenes, approximately 1 mile from the town gates of Carmona.[38] While it might be thought that the risk of fire would lead to the siting of baths outside the town, this does not appear to have been a normal constraint on their erection.[39] Possibly the reason should be sought in a shortage of land.

Within Carmona itself a concrete stuccoed reservoir measuring 46 ×

[35] P. Paris, *Promenades arquéologiques en Espagne* (1910), 151.   [36] *CIL* 2. 1478.

[37] J. Hernández Díaz *et al.*, *Catalogo arqueológico y artistico de la provincia de Sevilla* (1939–55), i. 120. G. Bonsor, *The Archaeological Expedition along the Guadalquivir* (1931), 28 ff. and figs XVIII–XIX.

[38] Ibid. 92.   [39] Though it was the normal practice at military sites.

13 m. has been found. It was surrounded by a stone balustrade, with steps down to the pool proper, and was decorated with marble statuary. Such a structure could have been the *piscina* of a bath-house, but it is more likely to have been a monumental *nymphaeum* or water cistern.[40] Nearby at Canania are the domed remains of a *laconicum*, known locally as 'La Bola'.[41] In the same area there are also traces of a bath-house at Villartilla, Bonsor's suggestion for the site of Oducia.[42] Traces of bath-houses have also been discovered at Obulcola, where remains of marble wall-lining were found. Unfortunately the excavator does not indicate if this came from the area of the bath-house.[43] Early antiquarians report traces of bath-houses at Lacipo[44] and Mellaria,[45] though the value of these early accounts is debatable. Further traces exist at modern Gerena (ancient name unknown).[46] The baths here were constructed of *opus testaceum* around a clay core, and should date to the second century AD.

At Las Bóvedas (ancient name unknown) are traces of a bath-house constructed with a central room from which sets of rooms radiate.[47] This building probably dates to the third century, and should therefore be contemporary with the small set of baths known at Belo, which are constructed on the remains of a substantial house of the first century AD. At Carteia, a hypocaust pavement with associated lead piping has been tentatively identified as a bath-house.[48] At Acinippo, a series of *piscinae* or stepped cisterns, arranged on a rectangular plan, along with a hypocaust-heated floor, and probably belonging to a large public bath-house, have been found.[49] Tenuous reports exist of bath-houses at two small sites near Corduba, La Torre,[50] and Majada,[51] the latter being described by its excavator, Santos Gener, as a 'población romana'. Neither account offers a description of the finds. More recent excavation reports speak of baths at La Luisana[52] and Orippo,[53] but again offer no description of findings.

---

[40] Hernández Díaz *et al.*, *Catalogo arqueológico y artistico de la provincia de Sevilla*, iii. 91.

[41] G. Bonsor, *Los pueblos antiguos del Guadalquivir y las alfarerias romanas* (1902), 19–20; *The Archaeological Expedition along the Guadalquivir*, 42–3.

[42] Ibid. 44.

[43] J. A. Ceán Bermúdez, *Sumario de antigüedades romanas que hay en España* (1932), 320.

[44] Ibid. 230.   [45] Ibid. 363.

[46] Hernández Díaz *et al.*, *Catalogo arqueológico y artistico de la provincia de Sevilla*, iv. 166.

[47] S. Giménez Reyna, 'Las Bóvedas', in *Memoria arqueologia de la provincia de Málaga = Informes y memorias*, 12 (1946), 93 ff.

[48] Woods, 'Carteia and Tartessos', 253.   [49] *Arqueologia '83* (1984), p. 51, no. 1. 53.

[50] Márquez Trigueros, *NAH* 2 (1953), p. 231, no. 730.

[51] S. Santos Gener, *NAH* 2 (1953), p. 233, no. 743.

[52] *Arqueologia '83* (1984), no. 1. 58. The excavator has suggested that these were medicinal, rather than ordinary municipal, baths.

[53] *Arqueologia '81* (1982), no. 252.

The major problem with many of these minor reports is the fragmentary nature of the finds concerned, and, in the case of antiquarian reports, the question of whether the structures have been correctly identified. It is possible, for example, that the raised pavement of a hypocaust-heated room in a private house, or even a similar floor of a granary, has been mistaken for a bath-house. In addition there is the difficulty of determining whether the bath-house, if such it is, is a public or private structure. This is a major stumbling-block, given the fragmentary evidence which prevents a complete understanding of many of the buildings described above. All reports from rural sites have been excluded from the above list, but this does not rule out the possibility that some of the listed examples may not be part of wealthy town houses.

A good example of this problem is provided by the bath complex found at Nertobriga in the north of the province.[54] This site comprises a vestibule, a large rectangular *piscina*, followed by a *laconicum, calidarium*, and *tepidarium*, the last being decorated in blue marble. However, the small size of the chambers, and the number of adjoining rooms, has led some commentators to believe that these are the baths of a large house and not a public building.

The province also boasts a set of medicinal baths dating to the first century AD which are again located in the north of the province at Cabeza del Buey. Unlike similar sites elsewhere (Bath, England, provides an obvious point of comparison), the building of the spa site does not seem to have stimulated urban growth. The reason for this seems to have been the extreme isolation of the site.[55]

Other bath-houses are known only from inscriptions. At Malaca, L. Granius dedicated a *lacus* (swimming-pool) at his own expense, suggesting an expansion to a pre-existing bath-house.[56] At Setefilla (ancient name unknown) a Saturninus also provided in his will for the building of a *lacus* and the supply of *aeramenta* (bathing equipment).[57] At Burguillos, (ancient name unknown) a town *curator*, G. Aufidius Vegetus, built a bath-house.[58] This inscription dates from the mid-second century AD. At Lucurgentum, a *sevir*, M. Helvius Anthus, gave, amongst other things, a 'balineum gratis' to the women.[59] The best interpretation of this is that

---

[54] J. R. Mélida, *Catalogo monumental de España. Provincia de Badajoz* (1925), i. 397, no. 1604.

[55] J. A. Calero Carretero, 'El complejo termal romano de "La Nava" (Cabeza del Buey, Badajoz) cuatro campañas de excavaciones', *Extremadura Arqueologia* (1979–83), i. 155 ff.

[56] *CIL* 2. 1968.   [57] *CIL* 2. 1071.   [58] *CIL* 2. 5354.   [59] *AE* (1953), 21.

Helvius paid for a day's entrance to the bath-house for women. The inscription dates to the early third century AD, providing a *terminus ante quem* for the bath-house. The form of benefaction is unique in the province.

Two inscriptions record the donation of a bath-house and money for its subsequent upkeep. At Tagili, Voconia Avita donated a bath-house and a lump sum of 2,500 *denarii* for its upkeep in either the late first or early second century AD.[60] Whereas at Murgi, a *sevir*, L. Aemilius Daphnus, undertook to give 150 *denarii* each year of his life for the maintenance of the bath-house he had provided.[61] If the rates are equivalent in each case, Avita's money would last seventeen years, corresponding roughly to a lifetime. Finally, at Cartima Iunia Rustica rebuilt the 'porticus publicos vetustate corruptos' ('public porticoes fallen into disrepair through old age') and added a new *porticus* 'solo suo' ('on her own land') with a *piscina* and *signum* of Cupid.[62] This inscription is Vespasianic in date, and implies that the baths had been in existence for a considerable period of time. An Augustan date could be suggested for their original building, although the phrase 'vetustate corruptos' could be a euphemism, as is often the case in the late empire. It might, however, suggest a flagging of enthusiasm for Roman mores which was then rekindled by the grant of *ius Latii* to the province. The phrase 'solo suo' again raises questions of land-ownership in the settlements of Baetica.

Bath-houses, therefore, are widespread in Baetica. Nevertheless it is striking that the vast majority of the examples above lie along either the Mediterranean coastal strip of the province, or the Baetis valley. There is little evidence of their presence in other areas. Those that can be dated appear to have been built in the Flavian period or later. Given that they were closely linked to the Roman style of life, Vespasian's grant of the *ius Latii*, giving to the inhabitants of the province a status similar in many respects to that of *civis Romanus*, may have been a spur to the construction of this Roman institution *par excellence*. However, it must be borne in mind that many of our reports are fragmentary and undatable, so this can only be a provisional conclusion. There is no attestation of the rank of *gymnasiarch* or any such official specifically charged with the upkeep of baths and the provision of equipment. It appears from the *Lex Irnitana* that this was the duty of the town aediles.[63]

---

[60] *AE* (1979), 352.   [61] *CIL* 2. 5489.   [62] *CIL* 2. 1956.   [63] Ch. 19.

GYMNASIA

Connected to bath-houses are the related structures of *gymnasia*.[64] Unlike the bath-house, which, as has been seen, is widely attested in the province, there are few physical traces of *gymnasia* in the province. Our best evidence is supplied by the geophysical survey of the *nova urbs* at Italica which has revealed a large *gymnasium/palaestra* adjacent to the Baths of the Moorish Queen. A further example may be the area of paving adjacent to the bath-house in Corduba discussed above. Apart from this physical evidence we have two firm epigraphic references to *gymnasia*. A clay votive boat found at Canania has an inscription reading: 'Manus Aureli Pacatiani filius possessor leopardor(um) denudator gimnasius Arescu'.[65] The inscription is highly problematic, but it seems that the dedicant was connected to the *gymnasium* in some way. The first solution which springs to mind is that a *denudator* ought to be some form of changing-attendant, but this seems to jar badly with the previous title of *possessor leopardorum*. At Lucurgentum the *sevir*, Helvius, mentioned above, gave a *balineum gratis* to the women, while at the same time giving a *gymnasium* to the men.[66] Presumably this was the free provision of oil etcetera, for a day.

Two other possible references to *gymnasia* are known. At Nescania an inscription dating to AD 153 refers to two 'curatores iuvenum Laurensium', L. Calpurnius Gallius and C. Marius Clemens.[67] *Collegia iuvenum* had their genesis in the Hellenistic world as associations of upper-class youths and were centred on *gymnasia*. They were introduced to Rome by Augustus and spread throughout the western empire. However, their nature is unclear. They appeared to have performed *lusus iuvenales*, which may have been athletics displays normally performed in a *gymnasium*.[68] Another possibility is that these *lusus* were paramilitary parades, which would obviously not require such a building.[69] The description of the two *curatores* as 'Nescanienses' and the *collegium* as of the 'Laurenses' perhaps hints that the *collegium* was not situated in Nescania, but elsewhere—whether in the province or not is impossible to say. A final reference to *gymnasia* is an inscription from Malaca, albeit rejected by Hübner as a forgery, recording the restoration of a *gymnasium*.[70]

[64] See e.g. the plaza adjoining the Corduban bath-house discussed above.
[65] *CIL* 2. 6328.   [66] *AE* (1953), 21.   [67] *CIL* 2. 2008.
[68] A *iuvenis* of Aquae Sextiae is described as 'bene doctus harenis', which suggests that this was the case (*CIL* 12. 533).
[69] For a general overview of these groups, see S. L. Mohler, 'The iuvenes and Roman Education', *TAPA* 68 (1937), 442–79.
[70] *CIL* 2. 171*.

AQUEDUCTS

Again related to bath-houses, but also having independent value in the Roman conception of a town, were aqueducts and sewers.[71] Both are widely attested in the province. Understreet drains can be traced in Naeva and Astigi; such a system also existed in Regina in Baeturia. All the streets in the *nova urbs* at Italica possess drains, which are also found from the Augustan period onwards in the *forum* area of Belo. Further understreet drains are attested in Olontigi.

At Arva an aqueduct runs a distance of 1 km from the La Mezquita spring to the baths. At Iliberris an aqueduct brings water to the town from 30 km. away. At Celti an aqueduct, partially carried on arches, ran for 3.5 km. The main aqueduct of Belo is 5.7 km. in length, running from the Fuente de Palomas. It is carried on arches three times over a drop of 10 m. in some parts (El Arroyo Churriano) and brought some 6,000 gallons of water a day to the town. A large amount of this was presumably used in the manufacture of garum. Its excavator suggests a third-century date for the aqueduct, which is finely worked in the local grey stone, but its parallels with the aqueducts of Emerita make a first-century date more appropriate.[72] To the west of the town a monumental *nymphaeum* with painted and stuccoed internal walls has been found. Another aqueduct carried on arches is attested by Wiseman near Sexi.[73] In Sexi itself the Muslim geographer, al-Himyari, states that there was an ancient quadrangular construction which tapered towards the top. On two sides there were grooves in the face of the structure, and on one of these sides (that facing the sun) was a large reservoir, fed by an aqueduct running from a kilometre away over numerous arches built of hard stone. This aqueduct is probably the same as Wiseman's, and al-Himyari should be describing the remains of a monumental *castellum aquarum*, or *nymphaeum*, of the Roman town.[74] Another feature of the town's water-system which still survives is the cistern complex, now known as 'La Cueva de siete palacios'. The complex is very similar to those found at Carthage, and perhaps, given the Punic background of the two sites, reflects a common Punic heritage.[75] Al-Himyari also mentions that there were two aqueducts at Acinippo and one at Onuba. The geographer's twentieth-century trans-

[71] See Pliny, *NH* 36 104 and Frontinus, *De Aquis* 16.
[72] A. Jiménez, 'Los aqueductos de Belone Claudia', *Habis*, 4 (1973), 273–94.
[73] F. W. Wiseman, *Roman Spain* (1956), 200.
[74] Al-Himyari, *Kitāb ar-Rawḍ*, 179.
[75] Gómez Moreno, 'Monumentos arquitectónicos de Granada', 379–80.

lator, Levi-Provençal, notes that the latter was still being used when he visited the site.[76] Aqueducts can also be traced running to Italica from Aznalcazar and Isturgi, but the Caños de Carmona in Hispalis is now accepted to be Arabic work. At Carmona itself a monumental fountain has been found on the Paseo del Arrahal. Such a structure would have needed an aqueduct to feed it.

Epigraphy provides evidence of other aqueducts. Public aqueducts are mentioned in the *Lex Ursonensis*,[77] and references to public drains are also found here and in the *Lex Irnitana*.[78] At Ipolobulco a *sevir*, C. Annius Prasius, dedicated statues of Marcus Aurelius, Verus, and Commodus in honour of his sevirate, and restored to the town the free use of water, which had been frequently been denied in the past, 'gratuitus aquae usus quem saepe amisimus redditus'. This implies that there was a municipal aqueduct and that revenue was derived from its use.[79]

At Mellaria, G. Annius Annianus, the town's *pontifex perpetuus*, paid for an *Aqua Augusta* in his will.[80] The name of the aqueduct is of interest, as at nearby Igabrum another *Aqua Augusta* was paid for by M. Cornelius Novatus Baebius Balbus. Balbus was a provincial *flamen*, which provides a *terminus post quem* for the aqueduct of the reign of Vespasian.[81] Given the proximity of these last two towns, and the common name of the *Aqua Augusta*, perhaps there was one large aqueduct which neighbouring towns were compelled to maintain. The purpose of such an aqueduct is hard to see; it could have been to supply the upper Guadajoz valley and the *colonia* of Ucubi. On the other hand 'Augusta' here could just be the use of a common honorific name. This thesis is supported by a further aqueduct with a similar name, Aqua Nova [[Domitiani]] Augusta, attested at Corduba.[82]

TEMPLES

Temples prove more difficult to assess than the buildings previously discussed, for, particularly in the case of epigraphic evidence, we cannot be sure that the temples referred to were of a Roman form. The motivation for their erection will also have varied. The temple of the imperial cult, for example, would probably always have been of a classical design, but this shape may have been as much a result of pressure from the

[76] Al-Himyari, *Kitāb ar-Rawḍ*, 34, 79.   [77] Ch. 99.
[78] Urso, ch. 77; Irni ch. 19.   [79] *CIL* 2. 1643.   [80] *CIL* 3. 2343.
[81] *CIL* 2. 1614.   [82] *AE* (1986), 335.

Roman authorities as a spontaneous adoption of Roman architectural forms.

Unfortunately, at Corduba the putative provincial *forum* which would have been the focus of the provincial imperial cult has yielded only one Corinthian capital. However, its size, over a metre in height, suggests that a temple of monumental size was located here. The capital suggests a Flavian date for its construction. Much more substantial remains of a major temple are to be found on the modern Calle Claudio Marcelo. García y Bellido suggested that this building would have had a podium measuring 32 × 16 × 3.5 m., columns 9 m. high, and a total height of 18 m. To its front, in a paved area, 77 m. wide, are the remains of a square altar, each face measuring 4.5 m., somewhat resembling the *Ara Pacis* at Rome. The temple is built from a white marble, which probably originated from the Spanish quarries of Alto Paso. Stratigraphic soundings beneath the temple have found a sealed chamber under the *podium* containing pottery from the Julio-Claudian period. Similar results have been found from soundings beneath the *pronaos* and the paved area around the altar.[83] The building therefore has its *terminus post quem* in the Flavian period.[84] The overall picture of this temple is of a monumental Roman prostyle structure very much on the lines of the Maison Carrée in Nîmes, but exceeding this latter temple's dimensions. The complex is located outside the walls of the *colonia* on a slope which would make it visible many miles away. One chance find in this area is of a stone ship's prow, designed to fit onto another structure at its rear. Presumably this formed part of the decoration of the complex. Its interest lies in the fact that the *proembolium* of the ship is carved as a lion in the traditional native manner, showing that local aesthetics survived at some level even in this highly Roman environment.[85] The purpose of the complex and the deity to whom it was dedicated unfortunately remain unknown. Its Flavian date may suggest a connection with the grant of the *ius Latii* to the peninsula, when it appears that colonial charters were revised.[86] It is highly likely that

---

[83] A. García y Bellido, 'Hallazgos ceramicos del templo romano de Corduba', *Anejos del Archivo español de arqueologia*, 5 (1973).

[84] García y Bellido's conclusions have been endorsed by more recent excavations conducted by Jiménez Salvador, 'El temple romano de la calle Claudio Marcelo', and by the studies of the style of Corinthian capitals in the peninsula, e.g. A. Díaz Martos, *Capiteles corintios romanos de Hispania* (1985), no. C11; M. A. Gutierrez Behemerid, 'Sobre la sistematización del capitel Corintio en la peninsula Ibérica', *BSAA* 48 (1982), 25 ff., at p. 32.

[85] A. Blanco Freijeiro, 'Vestigios de Corduba Romana', *Habis*, 1 (1970), 109 ff. The suggestion here that the carving formed part of a *rostrum* seems implausible.

[86] If the temple is connected with Domitian, a dedication to Minerva would seem a strong possibility, given the emperor's devotion to this goddess (Suetonius, *Vit. Dom.* 15).

Corduba possessed other temples, but none has survived to leave identifiable traces.[87]

A similar temple of monumental size was erected in the *nova urbs* of Italica on the most dominant site in the city. The temple complex, like that described at Corduba, was located on the crest of the ridge dominating the local area. It measures 125 × 100 m., is colonnaded on all four sides, and has a monumental entrance. The rear wall of the colonnade contains rectangular and semicircular *exedrae*. In the centre is a large octostyle, prostyle, temple of a standard layout, constructed predominantly of concrete and brick, covered in stucco and marble of the highest quality, which may well have been imported. The complex, named by its excavators the *Traianeum*, occupies the space of two normal *insulae* and, like the rest of the *nova urbs*, is an expression of imperial wealth and munificence.[88]

Apart from the *Traianeum*, a three-roomed structure built on a prominent rise in the *vetus urbs* has been suggested as a republican *capitolium*. However, this seems increasingly unlikely, and the building may well have been commercial rather than religious. It dates to the second century BC, and was destroyed by fire in the succeeding century.[89] Another temple is implied by the terracotta *acroterion* depicting a female nature goddess, a πότνια θηρῶν, found in this area, and dating to the early first century BC, although the nature of the depiction, which is Punic, may suggest a building non-Roman in style as its source. The *podium* of another temple, probably dating from the imperial period, has been detected under the houses of the village of Santiponce, the site of the *vetus urbs*, but has not been excavated.

Even the *Traianeum*, however, would not have been able to overshadow the most spectacular temple in the province, the Sanctuary of the Terraces found in the town of Munigua. This building takes on even more significance when it is remembered that, unlike the two major temples previously discussed, it would have received no official support. The sanctuary was built on a hill overlooking the town, and overlying an Iberian settlement which lasted throughout the Julio-Claudian period. The artificial terrace on which the main edifice was built measures 42.5 ×

---

[87] Stylow, 'Apuntes sobre el urbanismo de la Córdoba romana,' 271–2, cites a highly fragmentary inscription mentioning a temple dedicated to Tu[tela], but no remains of the temple itself remain.

[88] P. León Alonso, 'La zona monumental de la nova urbs', in León Alonso (ed.), *Italica = EAE* 121 (1982), 97 ff.

[89] M. Bendála Galán, 'Excavaciones en el cerro de los palacios', in León Alonso, *Italica*, 31 ff.

22.5 m.; its central semicircular shrine and *cella* measure 15 × 15 m. The whole is closely modelled on the republican shrine to Fortuna Primigenia at Placentia, dated to *c*.125–100 BC. The building at Munigua was constructed of concrete and sheathed in at least five different kinds of marble. The stratigraphy of the site indicates a Flavian date for its erection. A more recent suggestion, based on a stylistic consideration of the capitals found on the monument, argues for a late republican date. It is not clear, however, how this can be reconciled with the stratigraphy of the site, and a natural lag between fashions and/or technique in Rome and the provinces may account for the perceived stylistic anomalies.[90] The reason for such a major structure in a relatively minor town is difficult to explain. Presumably it is a major work of euergetism by a wealthy notable, perhaps inspired by a trip to Italy. The scale of the work may suggest that the instigator was aiming to impress a province-wide, rather than just a municipal, audience. One possible candidate for building part of the structure is Valerius Firmus. He is recorded, on two fragmentary inscriptions, as dedicating [*templu*]*m forum* [*exed*]*ra* [*ta*]*bularium*[91] and *bis templ.* [*p*]*orticus ex*[*edram tabu*]*larium s.p.*[92]

Below the Sanctuary of the Terraces, but above the *forum* complex, a further temple, 'the Temple of the Podium', was built, at a slightly later date, the beginning of the second century AD. Its construction again involved the erection of an artificial terrace. Beneath this terrace have been found traces of a private house with stuccoed and painted walls demolished to make way for the new temple. The temple's *podium* measured 15 × 10 m., and the terrace itself 20 × 15 m. The late first and early second centuries saw major changes at Munigua, a determined effort being made to develop the centre of the town into a major monumental complex. It is possible that this zeal led the townsfolk into financial trouble, and this is at root the problem to which the rebuke in Titus' letter to the town refers.[93]

At Hispalis there remain on the Calle de Marmoles three monolithic columns. These have often been taken as the remains of a large temple, this tradition dating back as far as the Arabic geographer al-Himyari, who speaks of 'majestic porticoes' in Hispalis, and takes these to be evidence of former temples.[94] In fact the columns which are of granite, unfluted, and

---

[90] M. Pfanner, 'Muster republikanischer Städte in Spanien' and 'Struktur und Erscheinungsbild augusteischer Städte', in Trillmich and Zanker, *Stadtbild und Ideologie*. For problems with stylistic dating, see Jiménez Salvador, 'El templo romano de la calle Claudio Marcelo'.
[91] *AE* (1972), 268.   [92] *AE* (1972), 269.   [93] *AE* (1962), 288.
[94] Al-Himyari, *Kitāb Ar-Rawḍ*, 14.

which resemble in style those of Hadrian's Pantheon in Rome, are more likely to be all that remains of a large colonnade.[95] Their bases also show affinities to those of the Pantheon. Two further columns now found in the Alameda de Heracles originate from this building. The capitals of these last two, while being Roman, appear not to have been original to the columns. They are marble, and of extremely high quality, paralleling the capitals of Hadrian's villa at Tivoli. It has been suggested that they were worked by the same group of craftsmen and imported to Hispalis. However, there is a simpler solution. The building of the *nova urbs* at Italica at this period would have necessitated the arrival of building craftsmen, quite possibly in imperial employ. The colonnade and the building from which the Alameda capitals originated (the bath-house beneath the archiepiscopal palace?), may have been a product of their work. Hispalis, given its size, maritime connections, and proximity to Italica, would have been the base for many of them. The town could easily have taken advantage of this fortuitous occurrence. The buildings therefore may well be a reflection of opportunism rather than an indication of a consistent policy of urban development.

At Belo, the capitoline temples have already been discussed. They are orthodox prostyle temples worked in local, stuccoed, stone. Their capitals are perhaps too heavy for the classical canon of this order. To the east of the *capitolium* complex lies a further temple, identified by inscriptions found *in situ* as a temple of Isis.[96] The building is not of a standard temple form, but perhaps this is to be expected with such a deity. Unfortunately it cannot be dated. Another small shrine to Isis has recently been uncovered in Italica, built into a porticoed square behind the theatre. An inscription from Igabrum perhaps contains a reference to the cult of Isis; it mentions a *colleg[ium] illychiariorum*, a form of *lampadarii*, an office in the cult of Isis. Perhaps therefore there was a further temple or shrine, of whatever form, to the goddess here.[97]

The seventeenth-century antiquarian M. Farinas uncovered a 'temple' structure at Acinippo. This is described as having a circumference of 49 m., and as being paved with grey jasper. Within the structure were rooms measuring 6.65 × 4.15 m., divided by sleeper walls. Absence of further information makes it impossible to interpret what must have been

---

[95] I. Rodríguez Temiño, 'Algunas cuestiones sobre el urbanismo de *Hispalis* en época republicana', *Habis*, 22 (1991), 157 ff.

[96] J. Bonneville *et al.*, 'La Dix-huitième Campagne de fouilles à Belo', *MCV* 20 (1984), 439 ff.

[97] Igabrum, *AE* (1972), 272.

a major structure. It is difficult to understand what Farinas is describing; in particular the reference to the jasper flooring seems problematic.[98] There are further references to a temple of Flora at Sisapo, and of 'Augustus' (= Trajan?) and Plotina at Urgavo.[99] These reports cannot be successfully assessed. One danger which must be borne in mind is that those concerned may have found a dedicatory inscription and inferred a temple from this.

At Carteia the remains of a temple, or certainly some major public edifice, have been found in the *cortijo* 'El Rocadillo', where the remains of massive columns have been discovered, along with two protomes and parts of an architrave. The work was executed in the local conchiferous limestone and heavily stuccoed and it should date to the Augustan period. Tiles bearing the name of M. Petrucidius, an official of either the late republic or early empire, have been found here, but there is no evidence either to associate, or to dissociate, him with the erection of this building.[100] The remains are of interest, as they show two notable anomalies. The first is the use of Corinthianizing rather than Corinthian capitals. This style, which involved rendering the volutes of the capital in a more 'vegetable' way than on a normal Corinthian capital, and altering the decoration at the base of the column, using lily patterns here, increased in popularity in the early empire and suggests an early imperial date for the monument.[101] The second is that the two protomes are worked in the form of crouching bulls, carved in an Iberian style, displaying similarities to those found at Urso. It seems therefore that at Carteia native aesthetics were not entirely dead in the early empire.

Non-Roman temple design certainly did survive at Gades, where the temple of Melqart persisted into the late empire. Unfortunately we are offered no sustained description of the temple, but given the Punic rites of the priests, it is reasonable to infer that the structure, too, was Punic in conception.

A large number of medieval Arabic geographers give a description of a so-called temple at Gades. This structure is described as quadrangular and four-tiered in plan, with each side of the lowest tier measuring between 40 and 100 cubits. The following two tiers each decreased in size, possibly being one-third of the size of the tier below. The fourth tier

[98] M. Farinas, *Las antigüedades de Ronda* (1650), 317.
[99] S. Morales Tafero, *Anales de la ciudad de Arjona* (1965).
[100] Woods, 'Carteia and Tartessos', 253.
[101] M. A. Gutierrez Behemerid, 'El capitel corintizante: Su difusión en la peninsula Ibérica', *BSAA* 49 (1983), 73–104.

tapered to a base 4 cubits square on which stood a statue holding a key, or, in our only eyewitness source, a baton in its hand. The total height of the monument was 24 cubits of which the statue comprised 6 or 8. The monument was destroyed in a vain search for treasure by Ibn Maimun in AD 1145. Despite its normal description as a temple, the earliest Arab geographer to describe this structure, an anonymous Almerian of the tenth century AD, whose work is preserved with that of al-Zuhri, and who is our only eyewitness, takes care to distinguish it from the temple, referring to it as a lighthouse. This attribution should be partially correct, given the shape of the building, which closely parallels that of Roman lighthouses, and the importance of Gades as a port. Other Arabic sources insist that the building was solid, and so the structure was probably a warning landmark rather than a lighthouse proper. Given the size of the building and its absence from the accounts of Strabo and Pliny, its construction probably postdates these two authors. The Antonine age, when the province's trade with Rome and its prosperity were at its height, would seem a reasonable conjecture for the date of the building.

A temple of Ba'al Hammon is also attested in the town in the second century AD and this, too, may have been of Punic design.[102] On the other hand, Gades is likely to have had classical-style temples as well as those recalling its Punic past. An inscription records that a *marmorarius*, P. Rutilius Philippus, donated a *theostasis* in the temple of Minerva in the town. It is possible, of course, that the Minerva referred to is a syncretic Punic deity who could have had a non-classical temple.[103] Two coastal cities of Punic origin, Malaca and Abdera, display temple façades on their coinage, which dates from the late republican/early imperial period. In Abdera's case, two coin types, firmly dated to the reign of Tiberius,[104] show a classical tetrastyle, or in one case, a pentastyle, temple façade.[105] These could represent classical-type temples which existed in these towns; on the other hand, as in many cases in Africa, they might merely depict the classical façade of an entrance to a temple which itself was non-Roman in conception. The variation in the number of columns depicted on the Abderan coins also raises suspicions. Are two separate temples being depicted, or did the die-engraver simply make a mistake? A further

---

[102] The relevant sources are quoted by A. García y Bellido, 'Iocosae Gades', *BRAH* 129 (1951), 73 ff.
[103] *CIL* 2. 1724.
[104] *MI* Malaca, no. 111; Abdera, nos. 119, 120, Tiberian, nos. 123, 124.
[105] Ibid., no. 119.

alternative is that a temple was seen as a good motif for the coinage of the city, and no reference is intended to the city's monuments at all. The latter interpretation is strengthened by the fact that on one of the coins two tunny fish are substituted for the central two columns of the temple.[106] It is possible, therefore, that there were classical temples in these cities in the early empire; but, on the other hand, their temples may have been Punic in conception or there may have been no temples at all.

Inscriptions also provide evidence for further temples. The dedication by the two Quieti of a temple with a *forum* at Iliturgicola has already been mentioned, as has a similar dedication at Cisimbrium by Valerianus. At Nescania, the *curatores iuvenum Laurensium*, L. Calpurnius Gallius and C. Marius Flaccus, erected an 'aedes et tetrastylum' to Jupiter Pantheus in AD 153.[107] At Arucci, Baebia Crinita, the *sacerdos* of Turobriga, dedicated a temple worth 200,000 HS to Apollo and Minerva.[108] This is the largest civic donation known from peninsular Spain. The size of the benefaction is all the more surprising, as Arucci is in the Sierra Morena in the north of the province, away from its most prosperous regions. At Barbesula, S. Fulvius Lepidus and his wife Fulvia dedicated an *aedicula* to [H?]amon.[109] This inscription is Trajanic in date. 'Aedicula' implies something smaller than a full-scale temple, perhaps a structure like the small shrine to Dis Pater in the *forum* at Munigua. Here another similar monument stands in a monumental portico on the processional way up to the Sanctuary of the Terraces, behind the *forum*. The presence of Hamon at Barbesula may be explained by the town's coastal position. Another *aedicula* was possibly dedicated by a *sevir*, C. Titius Sophon, at Osqua.[110] The only other temple known in the province is a temple of Athene, recorded by Posidonius, via Strabo, at the town of Odysseia. This town is a mystery. Strabo implies that it was situated in the Andalusian Corderilla and that its temple enjoyed some fame. It has, however, never been located. The temple itself, if it existed, is more likely to be a Punic or Iberian foundation than a Roman one.[111]

In general, therefore, Roman-style temples appear to have been the preserve of major urban sites. The presence of some of these, such as the *Traianeum* and the temple for the imperial cult in Corduba, may reflect official pressure more than a native impulse to urbanize. On the other hand we do find Roman temples in areas where their presence must be due

[106] Ibid., no. 123.   [107] *CIL* 2. 2008.
[108] *CIL* 2. 964. We have no indication of the form of the temple, however.
[109] *CIL* 2. 1939.   [110] *CIL* 2. 2031. The reading of the stone is dubious.
[111] Strabo, 3. 4. 3.

entirely to municipal wishes. The most spectacular example of this is clearly the Sanctuary of the Terraces at Munigua.

Beyond the religious and administrative life of a town, public entertainment played a major role in urban life. Did the province see a growth in this form of classical building during our period?

CIRCI

Despite the mention of a *circus* in the *Lex Ursonensis*,[112] no material remains of such a structure have been found in the province. Various early antiquarian writers refer to a large oval or semicircular building at Cádiz between the Ermita de Santa Catalina and La Casa Folgo, but the nature to this is unclear.[113] Canto has proposed that a *circus* existed at Italica. Her argument is based on the interpretation of aerial photography, but the assertion seems dubious and has not yet been published.[114] Of all the allusions to *circi* on inscriptions, only one, dating to the late empire, at Zafra (ancient name unknown) mentions a *circus* building; here reference is made to the building of the *podium* of a *circus*.[115] This could represent the renewal of a *circus* building, but in fact appears to be a reference to the initial phase of building.[116] All other references are to *ludi circenses*, not *circi* proper. Given the lack of substance of Roman *circi*, their loss, if they existed, may not be too surprising. The majority of recorded games were held by eminent local dignitaries either to celebrate their acquisition of some office, or their gift of a building to their home town. Games held as a legal requirement of office are not recorded epigraphically at all. There may have been some prohibition against this or perhaps, given their compulsory nature, they were simply thought unworthy of mention.

At Astigi, the *sacerd*[os], Aponia Montana, held *ludi circenses* to celebrate her acquisition of a priesthood. A further set, held by P. Numerius Eupator, are recorded on a late first-century inscription.[117] At Corduba, L. Iunius Paulinus held *circenses*, along with other games, to celebrate his

[112] Chs. 71, 128.
[113] J. R. Ramirez Delgado, *Los primitivos nucleos de asentamiento en la ciudad de Cádiz* (1982), ch. 6.
[114] See J. H. Humphrey, *Roman Circuses* (1986), 380–1 and n. 51. Canto's article listed as forthcoming in *A.e.A.* 57 (1984) by Humphrey was not in fact published.
[115] *CIL* 2. 984.   [116] Humphrey, *Roman Circuses*, 381.
[117] *CIL* 2. 1471, 1479.

acquisition of a provincial flaminate. This inscription dates to the late second century AD.[118] At Tucci, *circenses* were again held, along with other spectacles, to celebrate the acquisition of a priesthood. This grant appears to have been given in the second century AD. A second set are also attested from this *colonia*; these were held by M. Valerius Marcellus, along with *ludi scaenici*, to mark his donation of a *horologium* to the town.[119] It is not unreasonable to infer that at these colonial sites, in particular at Astigi and Corduba, given their wealth, permanent *circi* existed. Support for the presence of such buildings comes from the *Lex Ursonensis*, where the aediles are required to hold their mandatory games in either the *forum* or the *circus*.[120]

Ludi circenses are also attested beyond the ambit of the *coloniae*. At Ossigi, they were celebrated in conjunction with a public feast by a *sevir*, S. Quintius Fortunatus;[121] other examples are those held for two days at Ilipula,[122] those at Arunda,[123] and those at Ulia, which were held in the reign of Caracalla.[124] At Tagili, Voconia Avita held *circenses* to celebrate her donation of a bath-house, already discussed above, in the late first century AD.[125] Finally at Murgi, L. Pedanius Venustus and his sons held games to honour their dead wife/mother in the second century AD.[126]

The low attestation of *circi* in the province is surprising given this spread of inscriptions, and the fact that *ludi circenses* were the Roman form of entertainment *par excellence*, surpassing even the popularity of gladiatorial combat in Rome. Perhaps some of the towns above had permanent *circi*, but as games were held on individual initiative and were sporadic, and because *circi*, unlike theatres or amphitheatres, could not easily serve any other purpose, it is more likely that such games were held on areas of level land near the town concerned, with temporary stands erected when necessary. Against this, it could be said that the provision of buildings, too, was carried out by individuals and that the argument above assumes too much central direction and purposive thought in their erection. Even so an individual donor would probably obtain more gratitude and publicity from his fellow townsmen by erecting a building which would be used more frequently than a *circus*, such as a bath-house, or which could be used for more than one purpose, such as a theatre, or amphitheatre. Consequently *circi* were probably not a common choice for acts of euergetism.

[118] *CIL* 2. 5523.   [119] *CIL* 2. 1663, 2. 1685.   [120] Ch. 71.
[121] *CIL* 2. 2100.   [122] *CIL* 2. 954.   [123] *CIL* 2. 1360.   [124] *CIL* 2. 1532.
[125] *AE* (1979), 352.   [126] *CIL* 2. 5490.

AMPHITHEATRES

There is much more substantial evidence for the presence of gladiatorial games, the other major form of Roman entertainment, in the province. The physical remains of several amphitheatres have been found in Baetica. The largest are those of the amphitheatre which formed part of the *nova urbs* in Italica. This was part of the whole development of the *nova urbs*, and therefore dates to the Hadrianic period. It could hold *c*.30,000 spectators, and was the fourth largest amphitheatre in the entire empire. However, it must be remembered that this monumentality is due to its having been part of an imperial gift, and not as a result of the wealth or size of population at Italica. The building is constructed to make use of two hillsides along its long axis, access to the upper tiers being by monumental external staircases. Unfortunately, although this arrangement saved much material and effort, it placed the amphitheatre on a natural line of drainage which has led in modern, and presumably in ancient, times to regular flooding, a problem solved by the erection of a dam only in the last twenty years.[127]

The other surviving amphitheatres of the province are more modest in size. That at Carmo was built outside the city walls near the necropolis. Again it is built into the neighbouring hillside to save material. The upper part of the seating was made of wood; sockets have been found which would carry supports for such an arrangement. Perhaps surprisingly, no attempt was made to replace this wooden superstructure with stone at a later period. Stucco-work was found on the lower seats carved from the hillside. Given its archaic design and the finding of a *denarius* of 27 BC, its excavators have proposed an early Augustan date for its construction.[128]

At Astigi, the amphitheatre lies under the present-day bullring. It measures 133 × 106 m., making it approximately the same size as those of Tarraco and Emerita.[129] At Ucubi traces of an amphitheatre, with an internal diameter of 35 m., survive.[130] Thouvenot has a picture of a surviving amphitheatre at Acinippo, but gives no details of its size or possible date of construction.[131] Traces of a curved building with an internal diameter of 35 m. exist at Carteia, but these may be the remains of a

---

[127] The flooded amphitheatre still features on the older postcards of the site on sale in Seville. It was romantically described by the 19th-c. traveller A. J. C. Hare in *Wanderings in Spain* (n.d.), 125.

[128] C. Fernández Chicarro and A. Olivella, 'Informe sobre las excavaciones del anfiteatro romano de Carmona', *NAH* 5 (1977), 119–29.

[129] S. Ordóñez Agulla, *Colonia Augusta Firma Astigi* (1988), 60.

[130] Thouvenot, *Essai sur la province romaine de Bétique*, 457.   [131] Ibid. 458.

theatre.[132] Similar traces were found under the hospital of Santa Ana in Malaca, and since the town's theatre has been traced elsewhere, these seem likely to be the remains of an amphitheatre.[133] At Corduba similar traces of an elliptical building were discovered during the building of the Casas Consistoriales and the cloister of the convent of San Pablo in the eighteenth century.[134] Finally, various Gaditanian antiquaries note the presence of an elliptical structure 610 metres in circumference near the Porta de Torre in Gades.[135] This could be the remains of an amphitheatre, as traces of a further curved building, interpreted as a theatre, have been found on the Calle de Silencio in the town.

Other possible amphitheatres are suggested from inscriptions. These mainly record gladiatorial contests, or are the tombs of gladiators. One at Hispalis, however, may give evidence of an otherwise unknown amphitheatre. Found in the Calle de la Alfalfa, it appears to record reserved placcs in some building for the decurions, veterans, and an individual.[136] This could refer to the vestiges of an amphitheatre, but a theatre is also a possibility.

Inscriptions give strong support to the existence of an amphitheatre at Corduba. Indeed it would be unthinkable if the provincial capital did not possess such a building. L. Iunius Paulinus has already been mentioned for his production of *ludi circenses* to celebrate his provincial flaminate; in addition to these, he also held a 'munus gladiatorum' and two *lusiones*.[137] Corduba possesses the largest number of gladiatorial tombstones in the western empire.[138] These include the more exotic types of gladiator, such as the *essedarius*, many being members of *vernae* from beyond the province.

Gladiators are also attested on tombstones at Gades,[139] and perhaps Hispalis, where the abbreviation TRP appears on a fragmentary tombstone to L. Vivi . . . [Fl]avino, and is followed by another fragment, 'in

---

[132] Ibid. 457–8.

[133] P. Rodríguez Oliva, 'Malaca, ciudad romana', in *Symposium de ciudades augusteas*, 2 (1976), 53 ff., at p. 61.

[134] For a general discussion of the possible sites of Corduba's amphitheatre, see Knapp, *Roman Córdoba* (1983), 63–4, and A. Ibañez Castro, *Córdoba Hispano-Romana* (1983), 327 ff., esp. 336. A building uncovered and sadly destroyed during the recent construction of the AVE railway line, although at first thought to be an amphitheatre, has now been shown to be part of a late Roman *praetorium*.

[135] e.g. J. Suarez de Salazar, *Grandezas y antigüedades de la isla y ciudad de Cádiz* (1610), 128. For a general discussion see Ramirez Delgado, *Los primitivos nucleos de asentamiento*, ch. 6.

[136] *CIL* 2. 6283.   [137] *CIL* 2. 5523.   [138] *AE* (1962), 45–55, (1971), 178–9.

[139] *AE* (1962), 57–8; *CIL* 2. 1739.

ludis hispal'. Hübner regarded the latter fragment with suspicion, and suggested that the first was the standard abbreviation for 'T(e) R(ogo) P(raeteriens)'. An alternative proposal reads the abbreviation as TR.P or 'TH(raex) P(osuit)'. The second fragment would then make sense. The 'ludus Hispalensis' mentioned could have been a school of gladiators based at Hispalis. On the other hand it could refer to the *ludi* (i.e. games) *Hispalenses*. The tombstone would then make perfect sense as referring to a Thracian gladiator who fought in the official games at Hispalis. This reading would also constitute our only epigraphic reference to official games which were required to be held.[140] We have one literary reference to such games, namely Columella's allusion to the fact that wild beasts were imported to Gades from Africa for *munerarii*.[141] No epigraphic references to *venationes*, or wild-beast hunts, survive. Hispalis, as a *colonia*, presumably required its magistrates to hold games, as did its fellow colony, Urso.[142] This would almost certainly mean that a permanent amphitheatre existed at Hispalis. A stone from Jerez de la Frontera records the presentation of twenty pairs of gladiators by a *quattuorvir*, L. Fabius. These games were held in honour of a 'Vic. Augg.', indicating a mid-second-century date at the earliest.[143] A hint of gladiatorial games also survives on a fragmentary inscription from Ostippo.[144]

One other inscription merely mentions *ludi*. Given the qualification of other forms of games as 'scaenici' or 'circenses', it is reasonable to assume that this refers to a gladiatorial contest. This inscription comes from Urgavo, where a *duovir*, A. Cantilius, put on such *ludi* twice.[145]

Inscriptions recording *spectacula* are more problematic. The word appears to be generic, and to cover all kinds of games. Those recorded therefore could be gladiatorial contests, chariot races, theatrical performances, other forms of entertainment, or a mixture of all of these. Aelianus and Lupercilla, on dedicating their porticoes at Naeva, put on games described as 'speculares et vela'. Part of this benefaction may have been a theatrical performance, as implied by *vela*. However, it seems more likely that what is being referred to is a gladiatorial contest where an awning was

---

[140] *CIL* 2. 1190 with P. Piernavieja 'Dos notas sobre los antiguos "ludi" españoles', *12 CNA* (1973), 579–82.

[141] Columella, *RR* 7. 2. 4.   [142] *Lex Urs.* ch. 70, for *IIviri*, ch. 71 for aediles.

[143] *CIL* 2. 1305, (the provenance from Asido depends on expanding M.C. to M[unicipii] C[aesarensis], but an expansion to M[unicipii] C[eretensis], the ancient name of Jerez, must surely be preferable).

[144] *CIL* 2. 1441.   [145] *CIL* 2. 2113.

provided for shade.[146] At Cartima, Iunia Rustica too held *spectacula* to mark her benefactions.[147]

A final sign of interest in gladiators is the discovery of two terracotta toy gladiators at Belo.[148] However, this need not imply that contests were held here, and what was once thought to have been been an amphitheatre outside the town walls has now been shown to have been a *nymphaeum*.

There is, of course, no certainty that a reference to gladiatorial contests implies an amphitheatre. The greater part of our evidence, however, does come from colonial or wealthy sites, suggesting that these contests, a source of considerable expense, were normally held in major centres where amphitheatres were available. Alternatively, poorer towns could have used their *fora* to hold gladiatorial games, as Vitruvius implies, or have erected temporary amphitheatres for this purpose.[149]

Another possibility is that the smaller towns had humble arenas, perhaps earthworks, to stage all kinds of entertainments. At Siarum, M. Quintius Rufus built 100 'loca spectaclorum [*sic*] a solo saxsis [*sic*]' ('seats for spectacles built from the naked rock').[150] Similar structures are referred to at Aurgi, in the part of Tarraconensis bordering the north-east of Baetica, built by two *seviri* in the time of Trajan.[151] The structures concerned may have been all-purpose arenas as suggested above, and Rufus' inscription perhaps hints that his use of stone as a building material was exceptional.

THEATRES

The presence of theatres too may be seen as showing the acceptance of Roman cultural values. There is, of course, no evidence as to what sort of plays were performed here, but they were presumably in Latin. This may suggest a degree of competence in the language, although it must be remembered that the spectacle could still be thought enjoyable by a spec-

---

[146] Clearly a major advantage in Andalusia where such an awning is a standard feature of bullrings. For the presentation of such *vela* as an additional attraction at gladiatorial games, see K. M. Coleman, 'Fatal Charades: Roman Executions Staged as Mythological Enactments', *JRS* 80 (1990), 44 ff., at p. 56.

[147] *CIL* 2. 1956.

[148] S. Doudaine, 'Deux poupées gladiateurs', *Habis*, 14 (1983), 239–44.

[149] Vitruvius, 5. 1. 2. A modern parallel for temporary arenas is provided by the temporary bullrings erected for local festivals in many Spanish towns.

[150] *AE* (1972), 249.   [151] *CIL* 2. 3364.

tator who could not understand what was being said. Further caution also needs to be exercised. In Gaul, for example, theatres are found in non-urban contexts, and appear to have had a religious purpose.[152]

Against this, theatres in Baetica, like amphitheatres, are mainly concentrated in the large towns of the province. However, unlike the amphitheatres, they are small in size, markedly so compared to those of southern Gaul, or the larger towns of Africa. This may in turn suggest that theatrical performances were not a popular form of entertainment, and this again may reflect on the degree of Latinity and general level of Roman culture found in the province.

One exception to this distribution is the theatre of Regina in the north of the province, with a diameter of 37 m., dating from the Flavian period. The rest of the theatres are found in the province's 'core', but the Regina theatre warns us that conclusions as to the distribution of buildings are very much hostage to chance survival.

The earliest attested theatre in the province is that at Gades. The letters of Cicero show that it was in existence by 43 BC.[153] Recent excavations on the Calle de Silencio have uncovered the possible remains of a theatre, equipped with sockets for a *velarium*, which could be the traces of this theatre.[154] The building was probably part of the new town built by Balbus at Gades.[155] Balbus had political ambitions at Rome, and the construction of a theatre may reflect these rather than a general high state of Romanization in Gades.

At Malaca there are remains of a theatre built into the Alcazaba hill. Although this was previously dated to the Augustan period, a more recent study suggests that a late first-century or early second-century date would be more appropriate.[156] At Singilia Barba traces of a theatre with a diameter of 30 m. exist.[157] At Acinippo the *scaena* wall of a theatre remains with a stage measuring 30 × 7.5 m. Thouvenot states that, judging from the remains, it ought to have been richly decorated. The building appears to have been constructed in strict accordance with Vitruvian principles.

[152] J. F. Drinkwater, *Roman Gaul* (1983), 179 ff. and fig. 8.3. These are the so-called *conciliabula* sites.

[153] Cicero, *Ad Fam.* 10. 32.

[154] *Arqueologia '81* (1982), 74; *Arqueologia '83* (1985), 1. 12.   [155] Strabo, 3. 5. 3.

[156] B. S. J. Isserlin, 'Report on the Archaeological Trial Excavations Undertaken at Malaga in 1974', *Actes du IIᵉ Congrès de l'Etudes des Cultures de la Méditerranée Occidentale* (1978), 65 ff.; M. F. González Hurtado de Mendoza and M. Martín de la Torre, *Historia y reconstrucción del teatro romano de Málaga* (1982).

[157] R. Atencia Páez, *La ciudad romana de Singilia Barba, (Antequera-Málaga)* (1988), 49–64.

Dates given for the building vary from the period of the second triumvirate to the second century AD. At Urso, the theatre has a diameter of 32.5 m. Paris records 'rich and elegant' stuccoed Corinthian capitals here, and a large number of fragmentary inscriptions appertaining to seat reservations. He also says that two pieces of statuary were found, the bust of a woman, and a torso of an ephebe: the theatre appears to have been lavishly decorated. Unfortunately Paris gives no indication as to its date. Again, like the theatre at Malaca, it is built into a hillside.[158]

A richly decorated theatre exists in the *vetus urbs* at Italica. An inscription of L. Blattius Traianus Pollio and C. Fabius Pollio runs across the *orchestra* recording their donation of it, the *proscaenium, itinera, arae*, and *signa*. The two describe themselves as 'pontif(ices) prim[i creati] Augusto'.[159] This creates problems for dating. Normally it is assumed that this is a reference to the provincial imperial cult which was instituted by Vespasian, giving a *terminus post quem*, and probably a firm date, to this period. However, if the date of the cult's inception is disputed, as it is by some, then a Tiberian date would seem in order. The theatre has, beneath its marble exterior, a more modest phase, of local sandstone. This would date to the Julio-Claudian period, if the usual dating is accepted, or to the Augustan or late republican period, if the inscription is dated to the Tiberian period. The building should predate the development of the *nova urbs*; for if a theatre had not already been in existence, one would have been provided here.

It is interesting that the provision of a theatre appears to have predated that of an amphitheatre. This may be because an amphitheatre was beyond the financial means of Italica and there was one nearby at Hispalis; or, if Italica was a town for the wealthy traders of Hispalis, an amphitheatre may have been regarded as too vulgar a construction to provide on a monumental scale. The provision of a theatre, on the other hand, would tend to promote a much more cultivated image of the town's inhabitants. Another possibility is that an amphitheatre did exist, but only on a modest scale. Even so, it is interesting that priority was given to the theatre.

The theatre at Belo dates from the Claudian period, and should be seen as part of the major development which took place in the town at this time. Again, it is modest in size, having a diameter of 17.8 m., and built into a hillside. Vitruvian canons are broken in order to give the building a sound foundation, but even so the drainage from the site is poor. The building, designed for economy, is of local stone which has been stuccoed, and is

---

[158] Paris, *Promenades archéologiques en l'Espagne*, 150–2.   [159] *AE* (1978), 402.

built with semicircular concentric galleries of seating, as found in the theatres of Gaul, rather than the continuously radiating galleries found at Rome. It underwent a rebuilding at an undetermined date. Its most impressive feature is the *pulpitum* with alternating rectangular and semi-circular niches covered in fine mortar and stuccoed. The stucco-work is painted to resemble marble and has added plant motifs. At the base of the niches are marble-lined pools fed from fountains above, carved in the form of recumbent male figures and Sileni. These are of provincial work-manship. The theatre, therefore, while being modest in scale, does at-tempt to be monumental within these constraints.

The other theatres of the province are less well known. Thouvenot refers to possible traces of a theatre at Hispalis in the Bocinegueria, but they were recorded almost two hundred years ago and so cannot be trusted.[160] At Corduba, there are traces of concave seating or steps, under the present-day archaeological museum, and of paving at the bottom of this structure, but their interpretation is unclear, given their fragmentary state.[161] A curved building exists at Carteia, but, as mentioned above, this could be the remains of an amphitheatre.

As with amphitheatres, our existing remains can be supplemented by epigraphic evidence, recording the holding of *ludi scaenici*. It must be remembered, however, that such performances need not imply a theatre, but could have been held in the *forum*, or perhaps in *loca spectaculorum*. Such games were held by Vetto at Canania to mark his donation of the porticoes mentioned above,[162] at Lucurgentum by Helvius Anthus over four days,[163] at Isturgi by the *duovir*, A. Terentius Rusticus, to mark his dedication of a *signum* of Mars in the Antonine period,[164] at Osset on a fragmentary stone recording a dedication to the town,[165] and twice at the *colonia* of Tucci, once to celebrate the acquisition of a priesthood in conjunction with *circenses*, mentioned above, and others, also held in conjunction with *ludi circenses* mentioned above, to mark the gift of a *horologium* to the town.[166] At Italica the *sevir*, L. Caelius Saturninus, put on *ludi scaenici* to celebrate his acquisition of the sevirate. In this case, it is certain that they would have been held in the theatre, as the inscription dates from the Trajanic period, well after the theatre's construction.[167]

[160] Thouvenot, *Essai sur la province Romaine de Bétique*, 426.
[161] See Knapp, *Roman Córdoba*, 63, and Ibañez Castro, *Córdoba Hispano-Romana*, 326 ff.
[162] *CIL* 2. 1074.   [163] *AE* (1953), 21 (3rd c. in date).   [164] *CIL* 2. 2121.
[165] *CIL* 2. 1255.   [166] *CIL* 2. 1663, 2. 1685.   [167] *CIL* 2. 1108.

OTHER STRUCTURES

The province also possessed other Roman buildings, notably town walls as at Carmona, but these seem to be an inheritance of their Iberian or Punic past rather than a new phenomenon. However, at Ilipa we have a record of an individual named Urchail building *portae fornic* [*?es?*] (possibly [*?icatas?*] is preferable), probably the gates of the defensive wall of the town.[168] The inscription is undated, but the Iberian name, plus other Iberian terminology in the inscription, suggests an early date. The inscription may refer to repairs done after the damage of the Civil Wars. A similar early, fragmentary, inscription from Hasta Regia, dated by its lettering to the late republican period, records the donation of something 'sua pecunia', by a '[. . .]aebi ser. t[. . .]'. Hübner reconstructed the inscription by envisaging four *quattuorviri* rebuilding the fortifications of the town. This seems too fanciful. We do not know that such officials existed at this date, and there is no evidence of what was dedicated. It could have been a small object, and although the dedicant may have been a Roman citizen of the Sergian tribe, the fragmentary nature of the stone makes the alternative reading [. . .]aebi ser[vus] equally plausible.[169]

At Belo, to the west of the *forum* complex, on the *decumanus maximus*, is a *macellum*. It is a standard building of this type, with ten inner shops and four on the street front. The inner area was designed as an ellipse with a central shrine measuring 3.05 × 1.3 m., such a centrepiece again being a standard feature of these buildings. Some attempts at a decorative effect were made, the dividing walls of the inner chambers having Corinthian pilasters. The building is Claudian in date, built over preceding Augustan structures, and probably intended as compensation for shop-owners when the construction of the *forum*'s *basilica* made this area unsuitable for trade. Although it is the only building of this kind discovered in Baetica, such structures may have been a common feature of Baetican towns, as provision for a *macellum* appears in the Lex Irnitana;[170] but it is also possible that the notice merely refers to a market-place and not a building as such.

The donation of a *horologium* at Tucci has already been mentioned. At Lacipo, the *pontifex* and *quinque?vir*, Q. Fabius Varus, dedicated a *crypta hypaetrus* to the deified Augustus. This should date to the reign of

---

[168] *CIL* 2. 1087.
[169] E. Hübner, 'Inscripción de Hasta Regia, anterior del imperio romano', *BRAH* 13 (1888), 18.
[170] Ch. 19.

Tiberius.[171] At Abdera, a similar building may be attested in conjunction
with a *basilica*.[172] At Malaca, a block of marble, measuring 0.9 × 0.4 m.
with two volutes and a *nike*, has been interpreted as part of a triumphal
arch erected to celebrate the repulse of the Moorish invasions in the mid-
second century AD; but this is only implausible speculation. At Celti, in
the fields known as La Monerva, a large amount of Roman material has
been unearthed, including large Corinthian capitals, and column shafts of
reddish marble. At Villartilla, the probable site of Oducia, Bonsor records
that the landowner told him that he had removed a large amount of
Roman 'rubbish' from his land.[173]

At Obulco, remains of a building with at least seven columns worked in
local stone have been found at the Ermita de San Benito. An inscription
from the town records the building of a *posthorreum* and *tabernae*, by a
Quintus Hispanus, who traces his ancestry through five generations. As
well as holding all municipal offices, he had been a *census adsessor* in
Baetica and Gaul and the (pro?)curator of the River Baetis. It is strange,
therefore, as he must have been a wealthy man, that the inscription notes
that these buildings were built on land bought by the town, 'solo empto ab
republica'. This suggests either a form of town planning, or simply a lack
of generosity on the part of the donor. If the latter, however, it is odd that
he should record it for posterity.[174] The building seems to have been a
public one. Perhaps the best suggestion that can be made is that it was a
warehouse for a local *annona* with shops to sell the subsidized grain placed
in front of it.[175]

Finally, at Carchena (ancient name unknown), several buildings of *opus
caementicum* have been uncovered. These appear to be warehouses, and
not linked to any town. The excavator has suggested that they are official
warehouses for the provincial *annona*, and dates them to the Augustan
period.[176]

PRIVATE BUILDINGS

Although, unlike public buildings, private houses were not regarded as
prime indicators of a town's standing in antiquity, their development can

[171] *AE* (1981), 504.   [172] *CIL* 2. 1979.
[173] Bonsor, *The Archaeological Expedition along the Guadalquivir*, 44.
[174] *CIL* 2. 2129.
[175] See J. F. Rodríguz Neila, 'Notas sobre las "Annonae" municipales de Hispania',
Hispania Antigua, 5 (1975), 315 ff.
[176] P. J. Lacort Navarro, 'Sobre los construciones romanos del Carchena', *Habis*, 13
(1982), 171 ff.

provide us with some index of the rate of changing tastes in the province. Traces of wealthy town houses dating from the Augustan period have been found in the *vetus urbs* at Italica. A large mosaic dating from this period contains a reference to a M. Traius who it has been suggested is an ancestor of the emperor Trajan whose family is known to have hailed from Italica. However, the most well-known town houses of Italica and the province in general are to be found in the *nova urbs*. These are large, spacious, and built to the peristyle plan, which became popular in the late republican period. The House of the Exedra is so large it has been thought to be a *schola* or club-house rather than a private dwelling-place. However, there is no evidence other than the size for this view which neglects the special circumstances of imperial patronage which led to the creation of the *nova urbs*. Nevertheless these buildings do not appear to have been occupied for long, despite their sumptuous size and surroundings. The shifting clay on which they were built soon began to cause structural problems. These are apparent in the entrances on the porticoed pavements blocked by pillars to keep the buildings standing. The House of Neptune has an unsightly pillar in its eponymous mosaic inserted to keep the roof up, and the Mosaic of the Planets has holes in it to hold wooden supports. The drift back to the *vetus urbs* may have started within a generation.[177] The *nova urbs* at Italica was clearly an imperial showcase. meant to impress with its grandeur, rather than being built with an eye to the future.

At Corduba, traces of peristyle houses have been found in the Plaza de Corredera, on the Calle de Ramirez de Casas Deza, and the Calle Conde Cruz.[178] In the Plaza de la Corredera are the remains of a central peristyle, paved with a black and white mosaic. Off this opens a large room, normally interpreted as a *triclinium*, containing a mosaic of Polyphemus and Galatea, which should, stylistically, date to *c.* AD 200. A small *impluvium*, measuring 1.8 m. square, adjoins the main peristyle, surrounded by an irregular-shaped black and white mosaic depicting marine life. Such mosaics enjoyed a vogue at Ostia in the second half of the second century AD (a further mosaic of Eros and Psyche found nearby is normally thought to come from a separate, neighbouring, house, and dates to the fourth

---

[177] J. M. Luzón Nogué, 'Consideraciones sobre la urbanistica de la ciudad nueva de *Italica*', *Italica* = *EAE* 121 (1982), 75 ff. The article contains a graphic picture of the effects of soil subsidence on present-day buildings.

[178] For a general discussion with bibliography of archaeological reports, see Knapp, *Roman Córdoba*, 63, and Ibañez Castro, *Córdoba Hispano-Romana*, 353 ff.

century). This may provide a date for the house, a view strengthened by the lack of a floor beneath the mosaic. In the Calle de Ramirez de Casas Deza, parts of a colonnaded peristyle of six Doric columns survive. The columns are made of local limestone and stuccoed. Between them runs an intercolumnal wall, again stuccoed, painted red with yellow decorative motifs, and rounded at the top. A break in this wall left access to the central patio garden over a grey marble threshold. Around the edge of this area is a channel constructed of marble slabs acting as an *impluvium*. The house found under no. 22 Calle de Conde Cruz is less well preserved. Again there are traces of a peristyle with large rooms at the side. One room has a polychromatic mosaic of Bacchus, encased in an octagon with allegorical figures radiating from each side. This piece shows affinities to a mosaic of Bacchus at Italica, dating to the second half of the second century AD. Another room contains a marine mosaic, tending to confirm a late second-century date. The ambulatory of the peristyle possesses a polychromatic mosaic, in its drainage channel, of Eros riding a dolphin.[179]

This evidence points to the existence of rich Roman-style houses at Corduba in the later high empire. Unfortunately we know nothing about their occupants. The wealthy Corduban aristocracy is an obvious answer, but members of the governor's entourage are also possible candidates. There is some evidence for earlier wealthy houses in the city. Martial records a 'notissima domus' ('famous house') where the 'platanus Caesariana' ('Caesar's plane tree') grew.[180] Martial makes it clear that the plane tree was planted by Caesar himself, and his description of it as 'mediis in aedibus' ('in the middle of the house') suggests a peristyle house, although the building could have been altered since Caesar's day. Its survival into the imperial period suggests that the sack of Corduba may not have been as severe as has been commonly assumed. The house could have been owned by a sympathetic member of the republican *conventus*. A supporter receiving confiscated property is another alternative. This evidence clashes with that of Varro, who, it must be remembered, served in the province: he notes the extreme conservatism of Spanish houses.[181] Presumably the peristyle house of Martial, if such it was, was a rare innovation at the time of its erection, but nevertheless a sign of things to come. Our major gap in the knowledge of Corduban housing is the same as that we encounter at all sites, namely a lack of information concerning the housing of the poor. We cannot tell if they continued to live in houses of

[179] For a full discussion of all mosaics, see J. M. Blázquez (ed.), *Corpus de mosaicos de España*, iii and iv (1981, 1982).
[180] Martial, 9. 61.   [181] Varro, *LL*, 5. 162.

Iberian design, or changed to Roman-type housing, and without this knowledge it is impossible to say whether the towns of southern Spain were predominantly Roman in appearance, or remained native with more Roman-style upper-class sectors.

Peristyle houses also existed at other sites. At Celti a large private house of this type was built over the site of the Tiberian *forum* at the end of the first century AD. A rectangular *impluvium* with a fountain found at La Pared Blanca, approximately 2 m. square and lined with white marble, provides evidence of another similar house here.[182] At Astigi traces of such a house were discovered on the corner of Calles Cervantes and Maritorija. Its remains comprised a small peristyle, or Vitruvian Corinthian *atrium*, off which opened a room with walls sheathed in marble, normally interpreted as a *triclinium*. The majority of mosaics found in the remains were black and white, but the *triclinium* possessed a polychromatic mosaic of the 'triumph of Dionysus', depicting the god in a tiger-pulled chariot. Its date should be Severan, but, as stylistically it postdates the other mosaics, the construction of the house may be earlier.[183]

At Carteia, a street with at least two peristyle houses has been found in the area known as La Torre Cartagena. A large amount of stucco-work was used in their construction and a hypocaust-heated pavement has been uncovered. The dating of these structures is, however, uncertain and they probably belong to a late imperial phase of the town's life.[184]

This is also true of the two houses in the lower town at Belo, excavated by Paris.[185] These face each other across a porticoed street, also of a late imperial date. Both had upper storeys. The staircase is in the entrance hall and so residents upstairs may have been tenants of the buildings' owners. Both also had colonnaded peristyles, one displaying a rounded intercolumnal wall like that found in Corduba. They were decorated with painted stucco, which on the abandonment of the buildings was covered with obscene Latin graffiti and drawings of chariots and gladiators. Both, especially the House of the Sundial, make use of reused architectural features, most notably reversed column capitals to form the base of peristyle columns. Two large houses have been found to the east of the *forum* complex: the so-called Great House, to the east of the southern paved area, and the north-eastern house to the south of the temple of Isis; neither

[182] Bonsor, *The Archaeological Expedition along the Guadalquivir*, 20 and fig. XII.

[183] See Blázquez, *Corpus de mosaicos de España*, iv. *Mosaicos romanos de Sevilla, Granada, Cádiz y Murcia* (1982), 13 ff. The mosaic is displayed in the Archaeological Museum in Seville.

[184] Presado Velo *et al.*, *Carteia*, i.   [185] P. Paris, *Les Fouilles de Belo* (1923), i. 120.

has been fully excavated. Both date from the Claudian period. Despite their size, they show no sign of a classical layout. Another partially excavated house lying to the west of the town on the *decumanus maximus* has non-connecting shops built onto it on its street side and again shows no sign of classical ordering in its arrangement of rooms. Some of these are paved with local stone, but others appear to have had floors of hardened earth.

It is significant that these houses date to the same period as that of the erection of Roman-style public buildings in the town. There does not appear to have been the same urge to copy Roman styles in private as there was in public architecture, suggesting that the native aristocracy actively imitated Roman habits only where there was a perceived gain in doing so, but in other areas retained their old customs. The low priority that the classical world put on private housing would, if this were the case, naturally lead to the dichotomy seen in Claudian Belo. Later, as the native aristocracy became more integrated into the Roman élite, private architecture would also begin to change, and we see this occurring in the late imperial houses in the lower town. Unfortunately we do not know if lower-class housing underwent the same metamorphosis. At Rute, there is a brief report of a Roman site containing fifteen houses, constructed of large stone blocks. Unfortunately no further information is available on what is the only report of housing of moderate means in the province.[186]

At Munigua, several houses are known.[187] House Three was built against one of the ramps leading to the Sanctuary of the Terraces and so is cramped in plan. House Two, dating to the Flavian period, was built along one of the *forum* terrace retaining walls. It had a second storey and was a working house; traces of an oil-press have been found, along with a vat for storing oil. To the east of the *forum* retaining wall are traces of a peristyle house, House One, also of Flavian date. In a small room adjoining the peristyle is a well into which a bust of the emperor Domitian had been thrown. Adjoining this house and sharing a wall with it is House Six, built to a more traditional design. An entrance hall opens on to an *atrium* with a central *impluvium*. The roof of this room was supported by four brick columns which would have been stuccoed. This led to a *tablinium*, measuring 9.2 × 6.66 m. The *tablinium* was the central room of the house, with further chambers arranged on either side of it. It had an *opus signinum* pavement and was decorated with moulded stucco-work; a small private

---

[186] S. Santos Gener, 'Rute (Zambra)', *NAH 1* (1952), 229.
[187] T. Hauschild, 'Informe preliminar sobre las excavaciones en casa 1 y casa 6 a Munigua', *NAH* 23 (1985), 235 ff.

bath-house may have existed in the south-east corner of the building. The house overlies other remains dating from the late first century AD, which show that the area was previously used for smelting iron and pressing oil. The house itself dates to the early second century AD, and so, although of earlier design, postdates its neighbour, House One. Perhaps here we see an example of the conservatism described by Varro, as this style of house ceased to be fashionable in Rome in the late republic. At Munigua, unlike at Belo, the change to Roman-style housing occurs at the same time as the town gained a classical monumental centre. On the other hand there was no attempt to organize the town into a grid of streets, which is a feature of the latter town. Consequently the perception of what were the important factors in presenting a Roman façade to the world, beyond the provision of public buildings, varied from place to place.

A final group of Roman peristyle houses have been found at Regina in the far north of the province. These fit in well with the general morphology of this site which is thoroughly Roman in appearance. Given the town's location, this is somewhat surprising, and underlines the possibility that general conclusions about the province may well have exceptions, which will increase as the areas covered by detailed excavation grow.

Our information on the extent of wealthy houses is supplemented by reports of mosaic finds. These were often lifted for preservation in the past when other remains were destroyed. As long as it can be ascertained that they come from an urban site, and not from one of the province's many wealthy villas, it is a reasonable assumption that they were originally part of wealthy private houses.

At Carmo, two major mosaics have been found: one from the Plaza de Abastos, with geometrical designs and a figure of spring, normally dated to the second century AD, and one depicting the four seasons with the head of the Medusa as its centrepiece, found in the Calle Pozo Nueva. This dates to the late second or early third century AD.[188] At Astigi, a large mosaic, measuring 6.25 × 2.2 m., depicting the death of Dirce, was found under the Calle de Merced. Blázquez would date the work to the beginning of the fourth century, but Hernández Díaz prefers a second-century date.[189] At Cartima, a polychromatic mosaic depicting the birth of Venus, measuring 7.5 × 4.5 m., was uncovered in the Calle González Marino de Abajo. Venus is enclosed in an octagon from which radiate squares containing pictures of birds. A late second-century date is assigned to this

---

[188] Blázquez, *Corpus de mosaicos de España*, iv. 31 ff.
[189] Ibid.; Hernández Díaz, *et al.*, *Catalogo arqueológico y artistico de la provincia de Sevilla* (1939–55), s.v. Ecija.

piece. A slightly later date is given to another mosaic depicting the labours of Hercules, found on the Calle dela Concepción.[190] At Canania, a large polychromatic geometric mosaic has been found, dating to the late second century. At Orippo, fragments of mosaics depicting a lion and heads of spring and autumn, and dating to the same period, have been preserved.[191] At Celti, a black and white marine mosaic has been found in the Calle de San Pedro. Finally there are reports of mosaic fragments on the Calle San José in Urso.[192] It is clear, therefore, that by the second century the wealthy houses of the major towns of the province had taken on a Roman form. The depiction of episodes of classical mythology on some mosaics argues that there was also some understanding of classical culture by this time.

How deeply rooted urban life was is unclear. The *Leges Irnitana* and *Ursonensis* both contain clauses forbidding the demolition of buildings in the town, with heavy fines for non-compliance.[193] This might suggest that urbanization was tenuous, but if so, the problem was empire-wide, as a large number of general provisions against this practice show.[194] The legislation could alternatively be designed to stop property speculation and the loss of rented poor accommodation, which would lead to internal unrest in the towns. The appearance in Belo of private housing of non-classical style at a time when classical public buildings were being erected is also suggestive and hints that at least in some areas a change to Roman public buildings does not necessarily indicate a wholesale adoption of Roman notions of classical life.

DUAL COMMUNITIES

It is now time to examine aspects of the general morphology of the province's towns, as distinct from the character of separate groups of buildings within them. It has already been noted that it is impossible to ascertain the form of housing used by the lower classes in the towns, and so to determine whether the towns of the province were predominantly native or Roman in appearance. One factor having a bearing on this problem is the possible existence of 'dual communities' within the

---

[190] Blázquez, *Corpus de mosaicos de España*, iii. 85 ff.   [191] Ibid., iv. 21 ff.
[192] Thouvenot, *Essai sur la province romaine de Bétique*, 645.
[193] *Lex Irn.*, ch. 62; *Lex Urs.*, ch. 75.
[194] *Digest* 1. 18. 7 (Ulpian), 18. 1. 52 (Paulus); *SHA*, Hadr. 18. 2. See also A. D. E. Lewis, '*Ne quis in oppido aedificium detegito*', in González (ed.), *Estudios sobre Urso*, 41 ff.

province. Such sites, which contained parallel Roman and native sectors, are best known from Africa. One such community was the Trajanic *colonia* of Timgad. Here P. Iulius Iunianus Martialianus is described as the patron of both the *colonia* and the *municipium* of Timgad.[195] This inscription dates from the reign of Alexander Severus, and shows that a merger of the two groups would not necessarily occur swiftly.

Some examples of such communities are also found in the other two *provinciae* of Spain. At the *colonia* of Pax Iulia in Lusitania a fragmentary inscription may record a gift given by a Iulius to two *sen[atus]*. However, possibly, and perhaps more plausibly, what is being recorded is simply a gift of a day's free bathing to each sex.[196] Much less plausibly it has been suggested that the honours given to M. Porcius Terentianus at the *municipium* of Dertosa in Tarraconensis by the 'universal' *ordo*, imply the existence of more than one such body in the town.[197] Similarly at the *colonia* of Valentia in the same province two governing bodies seem to have been in simultaneous existence. A fragmentary inscription speaks of the two *ordines* of the town, 'uterque ordo Vale[nti]norum'.[198] These two groups are probably to be identified with the 'Valentini veterani et veteres' found attested on a series of inscriptions from the town, including a joint dedication to the mother of Alexander Severus.[199] This latter stone again shows that the institution persisted into the late empire. It is, however, unclear who these two bodies were: one may have been native, the other Roman; but it is equally possible that both were Roman.[200] A similar inscription from Turiaso, recording a dedication by the 'Turiasunenses veteres et iuni [sic]', must, however, be a fake.[201]

In Baetica, Pliny's mention of an Astigi Vetus, as well as the *colonia* of

---

[195] *CIL* 8. 2392.

[196] *CIL* 2. 52: 'C. Iulius C.f. [. . .] IIvir bis prae [f. fabrum]/[. . .] utrique se†n†[. . .].'

[197] *CIL* 2. 4060: 'M. Porcio M. [f.] Terentia[no] huic universus [ordo] d(ecurionum) c(oloniae) D(ertosae) aedilicios et du[umvir]ales honor(es) de[crevit] M. Porcius Theop[ompus] pater . . .' ('To Marcus Porcius, son of Marcus, Terentianus. To this man the "universal" *ordo* decreed the privileges of aediles and *duoviri*. Marcus Porcius Theopompus his father . . .'). An alternative interpretation would be to see 'universus' as merely indicating a particularly high, or perhaps complete, turn-out of the town's *ordo* to vote for this honour; see *ILS* 6579 for an example of the use of 'universus' in this sense.

[198] *CIL* 2. 3745.   [199] *CIL* 2. 3733.

[200] See Brunt, *Italian Manpower*, 591–2, and also for further bibliography, J. Richardson, *Hispaniae* (1988), 161 n. 22.

[201] Recorded, although not transcribed, by F. Mateu y Llopis, 'Las monedas romanas de ⟪Valentia⟫', *Numisma*, 3 (1953), 9 ff. The dedicatee C. Livonianus is said to be a *sevir* of the town, yet to have been awarded Roman citizenship by Q. Caecilius Metellus Macedonicus, governor of Hispania Citerior in 142/1 BC. The chronological discrepancy clearly shows that the stone is a forgery.

Astigi, and a similar arrangement at Tucci, may suggest a dual settle-ment.[202] The title of the *colonia* at Tucci, *Gemella*, is normally taken to indicate that veterans of two legions were settled here, but could perhaps refer to a dual arrangement.[203] Against this it could be replied that Astigi Vetus, a town of some importance (it is described as an *oppidum liberum* by Pliny), could not have been such a close neighbour of the *colonia*, as it would have required its own *territorium*. However, it must have been in the area to merit the name Astigi, and no likely alternative site has been found.

It is still believed that at Corduba a wall bisected the *colonia*,[204] and that this division reflected a racial divide within the city. Such a partition of the town, if it existed, could have resulted from fortifications erected for Marcellus' original settlement. A similar arrangement occurs in Britain, where the *colonia* of Lincoln was divided by the old walls of the legionary fortress which were left in place.[205] Knapp has tried to show that more 'official' inscriptions come from one side of the division than the other, and so to demonstrate that there existed a native and Roman side to the partition. However, given the chance nature of our finds, and lack of knowledge about the proportionate size of our epigraphic sample, this approach is unacceptable. Better evidence for a divide comes from two stones, both honouring L. Axius Naso. One was dedicated by the *vicus Forensis*, the other by the *vicus Hispanus*. This latter title is unusual, as *vici* normally take geographical names or the name of a tutelary deity. This suggests that there was a native–Roman divide in Corduba, as does the fact that two stones were erected. Normally one stone would suffice for a dedication to a single individual. Thus we see citizens and *incolae* making joint dedications at many sites, including Corduba. The two stones show a certain guarding of independence, or perhaps simple snobbery on the Roman side.[206]

There is no indication if, or when, the two groups at Corduba merged. It would be a fair inference, though, that the native quarter, at least initially, would have had a less 'classical' appearance than the Roman

---

[202] Pliny, *NH* 3. 1. 12 (Astigi Vetus), 3. 1. 10 (Tucci Vetus). For Astigi, see S. Ordoñez Agulla, *Colonia Augusta Firma Astigi* (1988), 55.

[203] See J. M. Serrrano Delgado, *La colonia romana de 'Tucci'* (Cordoba, 1987).

[204] See e.g. A. Blanco Freijeiro and R. Corzo Sánchez, 'El urbanismo romano de la Bética', in *Symposion de ciudades augusteas* (1976), 137 ff., at p. 140, and the discussion in Knapp, *Roman Córdoba* (1983), 13, 54–5.

[205] C. Colyer, *Lincoln: The archaeology of an Historic City* (1975), 11–19.

[206] *AE* (1981), 495, with C. Castillo, 'Hispanos y Romanos en Corduba', *Hispania Antiqua*, 4 (1974), 191–7.

areas. The genesis of a dual community in a *colonia*, where a new Roman population had been imposed on a pre-existing town, is easy to understand. Was this phenomenon also found in towns where such settlement had not taken place? In Tarraconensis the town of Emporiae had separate Greek, Roman, and possibly Iberian quarters, but its history as an entrepôt for the north-west of Spain may have made it exceptional in this respect. As we have seen, the *municipium* of Dertosa, which was not in such a position, also may have had such an arrangement.

Similarly we have hints of 'dual communities' existing at non-colonial sites within Baetica. At Singilia Barba, the *Ordo Singiliensis* honoured the freedman C. Sempronius Nigello by making him a citizen of the town with the maximum number of privileges allowed to a *libertinus*. These honours were then confirmed by a second, independent body, the *Ordo Singiliensis Vetus*.[207] The nature of this second *ordo* is mysterious. Perhaps it was some form of honorific body, or, perhaps, though less likely, a Carthaginian-style council of elders. On the other hand it is possible that this is an example of the two *ordines* of a dual community working in concert.

Perhaps a further hint of a dual arrangement is to be found at Arucci, where an inscription records a dedication to M. Alterius Paulinus for services rendered to the town 'in tumultuario Baeticae bello' (presumably the Moorish incursions of the second century) by the 'Aruccitani veteres et iuvenes'. The phraseology of the inscription is, however, very strange, and Hübner was probably correct to reject it as an antiquarian forgery.[208] If the inscription is genuine, it shows some parallelism in terminology

---

[207] *CIL* 2. 2026: 'C. Sempronio Nigelloni [. . .] VI Aug in col. Patricia item in municipio Singil. VIvir Aug. perpetuo d.d. municipi municipium Singil. Honorem accepit impensam remisit. Huic ordo Singiliensis recipiendo in civium numerum quantum cui plurimum libertino decrevit, item huic ordo Singiliens. vetus eadem quae supra in universum decreverat suo quoque nomine decrevit' ('To Caius Sempronius Nigello . . . priest of Augustus in the colony of Patricia [Corduba] and by decree of the councillors of the townsfolk of the municipality of Singilis lifelong priest of Augustus in the municipality of Singilis. He accepted this honour and defrayed its expenses at his own cost. The council of Singilis on making him a citizen of the municipality gave him as many rights as can be given to a former slave. The old council of Singilis granted him in its own name the same things above which had been given in the name of all of Singilis').

[208] *CIL* 2. 100* = *AE* (1978), 398: 'M. Aterio Paulino M.f. qui tumultuario Baeticae bello assurgente multa pro repub(lica) bello retinenda fortissime gesserat. Arucitani veteres et iuvenes op(timo) civi' ('To Marcus Aterius Paulinus, son of Marcus who carried out most bravely the many things required by the state in war when war suddenly arose in Baetica. The inhabitants of Arucci, both new and old (or the elders and youth of Arucci) have erected this to the best of citizens'). The only modern commentator to accept the authenticity of the inscription is Blázquez.

with the two *ordines* attested at Singilia Barba: again we have an independent group which is seen as 'older' in some respect than the other section of the community. Again it is of interest that at Valentia as well one of two *ordines* is described as 'vetus'.

At neither Singilia Barba nor Arucci is there sufficient archaeological evidence to discover whether the political divide hinted at on the inscriptions just considered was reflected in the physical structure of the town. On the other hand we do have evidence of such a physical divide at the mining town of Sisapo in the far north of the province. Strabo notes that there was an old and new settlement here.[209] The site itself is situated on two hills. On one of these traces of Gallic and Spanish *sigillata* pots, tiles, and ashlar masonry have been found; in contrast on the other there are the remains of a large number of what appear to be round huts and there is a complete absence of Roman pottery.[210]

It seems therefore that a dual community could manifest striking physical differences between its two constituent parts. Although it must be borne in mind that Sisapo was a mining town, and therefore unlikely to be highly receptive to Roman customs, the contrast found here is extremely marked. There appears to have been no attempt to imitate the Roman urban or cultural model in the native area. The best way of explaining this phenomenon is that, as lower-class natives, the miners of Sisapo would never have been able to advance in Roman society and consequently saw no advantage in copying that society's mores, assuming of course that they would have been able to pay for such changes in the first place. Such an attitude might well have prevailed in the poorer areas of many towns.

There does, therefore, seem to be evidence for the existence of dual communities at non-colonial sites in the province.[211] The precise political implications of such arrangements are not clear. Their effects on the growth of classically planned towns is also uncertain, but it appears from the evidence found at Sisapo that they would have been a conservative force and would have slowed down the development of towns towards the classical model.

---

[209] Strabo, 3. 2. 3: Σισάπονα, τόν τε παλαιὸν λεγόμενον καὶ τὸν νέον ('Sisapo: the part called "old" and the new part').

[210] P. Sillières, 'Sisapo: Prospectations et découvertes', *A.e.A.* 53 (1980), 49 ff.

[211] A final suggestion of a dual community in the republican period is made by Corzo Sánchez, who proposes that in its earliest stages Italica was such a site. However, given the paucity of literary and archaeological data, this can only be speculation. In all events Corzo Sánchez believes the two communities fused rapidly: R. Corzo Sánchez, 'Organización del territorio y evolución urbana en Italica', in Léon Alonso (ed.), *Italica*, 306–10.

STREET-GRIDS

Another feature which would have had a significant effect on the appearance of the town would have been the presence or absence of an orthogonal street-grid. Unfortunately, most of the evidence in the province has to be extrapolated from modern street-plans, which cannot provide firm evidence. Grids have been deduced at Astigi,[212] Corduba,[213] and, less convincingly, at Hispalis[214] in this way.

It is noticeable that all the sites mentioned above are *coloniae*. Given that it was at such sites that the element of classical urban planning was most marked, perhaps we ought not to be surprised at the presence of a regular layout of streets there. However, this aspect of Roman urban morphology does not appear to have been insisted on even in all *coloniae*. The *colonia* of Ilici in Tarraconensis, for example, retained into the Julio-Claudian period the precolonial street-plan of the old Iberian town upon which it was deducted.[215] Consequently we cannot simply assume that all the *coloniae* of Baetica had an orthogonal street-grid.

Putting the *coloniae* aside, the evidence for street-grids in the rest of the province is varied. Some towns, including wealthy ones such as Malaca, do not appear to have adopted a gridded plan. In contrast others such as Belo, Obulcula, and Iptuci (Tejada Nueva), did so. In some cases the adoption of an orthogonal system of street-planning appears to have been provoked by special circumstances. The town of Caura, for example, adopted this system when it expanded from its original hilltop site.[216] Its adoption at Belo was probably part of the general development of the town at the time of the Mauretanian Wars. Perhaps its use hints that military builders were used in the town's redevelopment.

In general it seems that the grid plan was adopted only when a town underwent major redevelopment. Good examples of this are provided by the two Baetican towns discussed above, and the *colonia* of Ilici in Tarraconensis, which finally adopted a grid pattern when large parts of the town were rebuilt after a disastrous fire in the Julio-Claudian period. In this respect it seems that the adoption of a grid pattern would have been, especially for smaller towns, a conscious effort to give the community

---

[212] Hernández Díaz *et al.*, *Catalogo arqueológico y artistico de la provincia de Sevilla*, iii. 66 ff.

[213] See Knapp, *Roman Córdoba*, 55.

[214] See e.g. A. Blanco Freijeiro, *Historia de Sevilla*, i. *La ciudad antigua* (3rd edn., 1989), 129, fig. 12.

[215] R. Ramos Fernández, *La ciudad romana de Ilici* (1975), 163–4.

[216] Blanco Freijeiro and Corzo Sánchez, 'El urbanismo romano en la Bética', 158–9.

concerned a more Roman appearance. However, it also appears that in general the creation of a street-grid was not actively regarded as a priority, but something to be done if an opportunity arose. Even so this opportunity was not always taken. There was no attempt, for example, to impose a gridded plan at Munigua even when the town was extensively remodelled in the Flavian period to accommodate the Sanctuary of the Terraces and its associated buildings. Here an axial plan, reminiscent of those found at some Gallic sanctuaries,[217] was preferred in order to emphasize the monumentality of the temple building.

The recent work of MacDonald has suggested that a gridded street-pattern was not as essential to the classical city as has often been assumed.[218] The evidence we have from Baetica appears to bear out this hypothesis. The street-grid appears very much to be an optional, rather than an essential, part of the overall layout of a classical city.

DISTRIBUTION OF BUILDINGS

A general overview of the buildings reviewed above shows one extremely marked fact. This is the almost total absence of public buildings from the northern area of the province in the Sierra Morena. Only three public bath-houses have been identified in this area, one of which owed its existence not to a town, but to the occurrence of natural springs. Another, that at Nertobriga, may not even have been a public building at all. Only one of the *circi*, that at Zafra, comes from this area, and the theatre at Regina is the only known building of its kind found in the region. Similarly the temple at Arucci is the only major religious building attested here. Moreover, if the site of Turobriga lay close by to Arucci,[219] the dedication may owe more to Arucci's proximity to the centre of the cult of Ataecina, than to a more general wish to erect a classical building.

The north of Baetica therefore seems not to have been much changed architecturally in the Roman period; this view is reinforced by the fact

---

[217] G. C. Picard, 'Les Centres civiques ruraux dans l'Italie et la Gaule romaine', in *Architecture et société de l'archaisme grec au fin de la république romaine* (1983), 415 ff.

[218] W. L. MacDonald, *The Architecture of the Roman World*, ii (1986), esp. ch. 2, 'Urban Armatures'.

[219] Turobriga appears out of order in an otherwise entirely alphabetic list of towns in Pliny (*NH* 3. 1. 14). This implies that the site may have been close to Arucci. M. Almagro Basch, *Huelva: Prehistoria y antigüedad* (1974), 286–7, 304–7, suggests that Turobriga was located at the site of La Ermita de San Mames, just outside the modern town of Aroche, where there are substantial Roman remains.

that absence of major Roman buildings in the area is paralleled by an equal lack of Roman statuary[220] and epigraphic finds.[221] In addition to this lack of positively Roman features, large numbers of 'recintos', pre-Roman sites which retained many native characteristics, persisted in the Sierra Morena area well into the imperial period.[222] Nevertheless it must be borne in mind that the data used for our survey are inevitably hostage to chance and archaeological preferences. The town of Regina, for example, not only has a theatre, but also a gridded street-plan, understreet sewers, and classical peristyle housing. On the other hand we must remember that the town lies beyond the most mountainous regions of the Sierra Morena, in a thin strip of upland plains which border the province of Lusitania. Its position therefore is not typical of many of the settlements of this area.

To the south of the Baetis valley, the other major upland section of the province, the Andalusian Corderilla, is also poorly represented in terms of Roman buildings found there. Monuments are clustered in major towns of the area, such as Iliberris and Acinippo, but beyond these few specifically Roman remains have been found.

Combined, these two upland regions comprise over half of the area of Baetica. The apparently higher degree of resistance to Roman urban forms here is a product of several factors. The most important would have been the geography of these regions. Both are composed of broken hill country, which is difficult to cross and would have led to natural isolation and logistic difficulties in supplying building materials, even if the will to create a classical-style town had been present. It is noticeable that the towns in these areas which do exhibit a significant adoption of Roman forms, such as Iliberris and Regina, tend to lie on the major routes which pass through the regions. Another factor is the poverty of the soil. This would have meant that these areas would be much less likely to attract Roman settlement, would produce fewer surplus products for trade beyond their own locality, and would consequently be less exposed to Roman ideas of urbanization. Finally the racial make-up of these regions should be borne in mind. The inhabitants of the highland areas of the province were mainly Celtic, and so, unlike the Iberians of the lowland areas of the province, lacked an urban tradition. This too helps to explain the lower rate of urbanization here.

---

[220] H. G. Niemeyer, 'Aspectos de la escultura romana de la peninsula ibérica', *14th CNA* (1977), 915 ff.

[221] For the relative density of epigraphic finds in the province, see J. Untermann, *Elementos de un atlas antroponímico de la Hispania antigua* (1965), 18, map B.

[222] See the discussion in Ch. 8.

In contrast the Baetis valley and the Mediterranean coast of the province are characterized by a high incidence of classical buildings. Out of the twenty-nine bath-houses surveyed, twenty-one are located in these two areas. The same pattern is repeated with other buildings. Of twelve *circi*, nine are located in the two 'core' areas, one in the north, one at Arunda in the Andalusian Corderilla, and one at the *colonia* of Tucci, in the north-east of the province. It must be remembered, however, in this case, that the firmest attestation is at Zafra in the Sierra Morena. Of eleven theatres, eight are in the 'core' areas, two in the Baetican Corderilla, and one in the north. Out of six references to *ludi scaenici*, four are from the Baetis valley and two from the area around Tucci in the north-east. Of references to amphitheatres and gladiators, only the amphitheatre at Acinippo lies outside the 'core' areas. Temples exhibit the same pattern. Of our twenty examples, fourteen lie within the 'core' areas, one in the north-east, four in the Andalusian Corderilla and two in the north, one of which, at Sisapo, is not attested clearly. The Baetis valley contains all the examples we have of rich town houses, with the exception of those found at Regina.

The lowland area of the province therefore seems to have been much more affected by the Roman presence than the highlands which lay on either side of it. Nevertheless even within this area some noticeable patterns of distribution occur. Almost half the amphitheatres found belong to colonial sites and the remainder are at large wealthy towns. Evidence for large numbers of monuments in any one town also tends to be restricted to such sites. Clearly at sites such as *coloniae* there would be much more pressure to create a Roman environment, and such pressure would have been even greater at the provincial capital, Corduba.

Smaller towns appear to have had a less Roman appearance, perhaps with a general-purpose *locus spectaculorum* for the purpose of putting on games and with the most likely Roman building having been, on present evidence, a bath-house. Perhaps here a parallel can be drawn with Roman Britain. Here too we find that Roman features are clustered in the *coloniae* of the province and the so-called civitas capitals. In contrast few major public buildings are found in the smaller towns of the province, the vast majority of which also lack any form of organized street-planning.[223] This pattern, where Roman features are, in the main, found in the larger settlements of a region, seems to be paralleled more or less in Baetica. Of

---

[223] B. C. Burnham and J. Wacher, *The 'Small Towns' of Roman Britain* (1990), ch. 3, 'Internal Morphology'.

course one simple reason for this is that it is precisely in the larger settlements that individuals wealthy enough to construct public buildings would have been found.

THE LOCATION OF TOWNS

Although it is often believed that Rome, as a matter of course, moved native settlements on hilltop sites to new lowland locations for security reasons, this does not appear to have been the case in Baetica. Large numbers of towns remained on strategically important points throughout the imperial period. These included Italica, Sisapo, Ilurco, Nertobriga, Carmo, Osqua, Cisimbrium, Ugia, Iptuci (Tejada Nueva), and Lacipo. Towns which did change location appear to have done so of their own volition. The best example of this process is provided by the town of Sabora. The Saborenses petitioned the emperor Vespasian to be allowed to move to a lowland site, described as a 'planum', where they intended to build a new town, an 'oppidum', in Vespasian's name, 'sub nomine meo'.[224] This important document shows that the motivation for the move came not from Rome, but the local inhabitants themselves, and so implies that Rome had no active interest in moving the sites of Baetican towns. Various reasons could be suggested for the wish arising. One, which will be discussed further below, is that the grant of the *ius Latii* to Spain may have provoked an upsurge in building. Another is that the site had become too cramped for further development, and hence a move to a new site became necessary. This seems to have been the reason for the town of Caura moving to a new lowland site. Unfortunately in this case the date of the move cannot be established.

THE CHRONOLOGY OF DEVELOPMENT

At a number of sites, the adoption of Roman-style buildings appears to have taken place not as a gradual process, but at a single period in time. The most obvious examples of this are the building of the νέα πόλις at Gades by Balbus, and of the *nova urbs* at Italica under imperial patronage in the reign of Hadrian. However, other examples are also plentiful. A

[224] *ILS* 6092.

similar process appears to have taken place at Belo in the Claudio-Neronian period, and at Munigua, and, by inference from the inscription discussed above, at Sabora in the Flavian period.

At Belo, wider political circumstances, namely the outbreak of war in Mauretania, gave rise to the chance to develop the town. But how are we to account for the other instances? There can be no doubt that the action taken in these cases was thoroughgoing. At Munigua, for example, a monumental centre was suddenly created, whose construction involved the demolition of many existing workshops and houses. One reason for development at this time could have been Vespasian's grant of the *ius Latii* to Spain, which could have ushered in a period of civic pride. Such a stimulus, however, would have been purely incidental to Vespasian's intentions when making the grant, as the tone of his letter to the Saborenses makes clear. The view that the grant of the *ius Latii* did have this side-effect is strengthened by evidence from neighbouring Lusitania, where the *forum* at Conimbriga also underwent a major redevelopment at this time.

Another reason for sudden upsurges in building is more practical: it concerns the availability of suitable craftsmen to perform the necessary work involved. The fact that a major temple appears to have been built in Hispalis while the *nova urbs* at Italica was under construction has been mentioned above. An inscription recording the existence of a *statio serrariorum Augustorum* at Italica dates from the same period.[225] Similarly, Díaz Martos in his study of Corinthian capitals in Spain notes that the pillars from several sites in the Hadrianic period show a marked affinity to one another.[226] He suggests that the origin of these capitals is the workshop which produced those for the *scaena* of the theatre of Emerita, which underwent a renewal in this period; but the workshop concerned could equally have been based in Baetica. Surges in building therefore could indicate an increased presence of craftsmen in the area at that time.

THE FUNDING OF BUILDING

In his letter to the Saborenses, Vespasian, although he is willing to allow the town of Sabora to move site, is much less willing to allow the Saborenses to raise new local taxes. This request suggests that there may well have been a desire to develop the town, but that money was required to do

---

[225] *CIL* 2. 1131.
[226] Díaz Martos, *Capiteles corintios romanos de Hispania*, sect. E.

so and that in the eyes of the Roman state the payment of taxes was more important than such urban development.

Therefore, even if a local desire to reconstruct a town on more Roman lines grew up, it appears that this could be thwarted by the Roman authorities themselves. This problem would of course increase in intensity the smaller the town was. This in turn may account for the lack of Roman buildings found on many small sites, and in the poorer, highland areas of the province.

Although the Saborenses' request to Vespasian suggests that some municipal moneys could be used for public works, we have little independent evidence as to the scale of such collective action. Although there are many examples of *municipia* paying for honorific statues of local worthies, evidence of more extensive municipal constructions being paid for by public funds is rare. Even in the case of statuary, on many occasions the individual honoured paid for the resulting statue himself to increase his prestige, an agreement which was surely reached in many cases prior to the award of the statue in the first place. At Obulco the *municipium* appears to have bought the land on which a private benefactor subsequently built a public *posthorreum*. However, this is our only firm instance of municipal action on this scale.

Nor does there appear to have been any imperial intervention, if we except the *nova urbs* at Italica, which was in reality motivated by entirely personal considerations on the part of the emperor Hadrian. The normal source of revenue for building appears to have been wealthy individuals performing acts of euergetism—a pattern reflected throughout the Roman empire as a whole.[227] Again such dependence on wealthy benefactions would inevitably lead to a clustering of public buildings in the major cities, the home of the majority of the wealthy of the province. This problem would have been amplified by the fact that the larger towns appear to have exercised a magnetic effect over the wealthy citizens of smaller settlements, attracting them to themselves and so depriving their towns of origin of much-needed potential benefactors.[228]

In general, therefore, there appears to be no discernible policy of encouraging the building of Roman monuments. Building took place as the opportunity arose, or when special circumstances inclined a certain in-

---

[227] For a general discussion of this aspect of antiquity, see P. Veyne, *Bread and Circuses: Historical Sociology and Political Pluralism*, trans. O. Murray (1990).

[228] See A. García y Bellido, 'Dispersión y concentración de itinerantes de la España romana', *Archivium*, 12 (1963), 39 ff. This process has been studied in relation to Roman Greece by S. E. Alcock, 'Archaeology and Imperialism: Roman Expansion and the Greek City', *Journal of Mediterranean Archaeology*, 2/1 (1989), 87 ff., at pp. 111–16.

dividual to take action in this respect. The only time a general stimulus might be said to have existed was immediately after the grant of the *ius Latii* to the province, and it appears that this was not at all the intention of Vespasian when he made the award.

TOWN SIZE

The towns of the province are small in the main. Corduba reached a size of 70 hectares, but this is overshadowed by the sizes reached by the towns of Gallia Narbonensis, such as Nîmes and Vienne, measuring 220 and 200 hectares respectively. Roman London, too, at 134 hectares, was larger. Even the 'second cities' of the province fare badly in comparison. Carmo measured 47 hectares and Acinippo around 50. In contrast, in Britain, a province normally thought of as less urbanized, Verulamium started at the same size as Carmo in the Julio-Claudian period, but grew to 91 hectares by the Antonine period. Cirencester too, reached a similar size at the height of the early empire.

Various explanations can be offered for these, perhaps surprising, results. One is that the compact form of urbanization preferred by the Iberians may have led to a pattern of a large number of small towns. Another could derive from the fact that the province's wealth lay in the production of oil. This would probably have led to many wealthy provincials, while obviously having a town as their legal *origo*, spending much of their time on their estates, rather than in the towns where their presence would have generated more development. The large number of wealthy villa sites which existed in the province lends support to this view, as does the fact that Africa, a province deriving its income in a similar way, exhibits a similar pattern of large numbers of small towns.

GENERAL CONCLUSIONS

It can be seen that the early imperial period did lead to a growth of Roman structures in Baetica, but that this growth was uniform neither in spatial extent, nor in terms of its chronology. There is a sharp division in the distribution of monuments, corresponding, more or less, to the geographical divisions of the province: the lowland areas of the province possess a large number of Roman-style features, while these seem to be almost totally absent from large parts of the highland regions.

Even in the lowland regions, some division is apparent. Our evidence suggests that major groups of Roman monuments were found, in general, at the larger sites; and while it is clear that this is, in part at least, because more archaeological work has taken place here, it should also be partially due to the fact that smaller towns would not possess sufficient municipal resources nor wealthy citizens to construct new buildings.

The possible presence of internal divisions within cities also means that it is unclear whether most towns would have presented a Roman appearance beyond their upper-class quarters and public monuments. Some of these monuments, as has been seen, retained some native decorative features, which may suggest a persistence of some local aesthetics, and hence a qualified rather than an entirely wholehearted acceptance in either an active or a passive sense of a general Roman urban framework. Alternatively, it may simply show a lack of suitable craftsmen to carry out the work in a classical style. In either case Baetican towns would look slightly 'provincial' to a Roman visitor. The building of non-Roman-style housing at Belo when its public buildings were being redeveloped in a classical style perhaps also shows that the physical environment of the classical town was not, even in lowland examples, entirely accepted.

The majority of towns remained small, even in comparison to those of a province, Britain, often thought to be more backward than Baetica, and they retained, in the main, their hilltop sites. It is at the larger sites that the majority of Roman features are found. This again is not surprising and reflects the pattern found in other provinces, for example, Britain or Gaul.[229]

Overall it seems that the Roman notion of urban existence only took a strong hold in the lowland areas of the province. Roman features are most prominent in the large towns of these regions, and probably in their richer rather than their poorer districts, and decline as the size of the town concerned decreases and its distance from the lowland 'core' of the province increases.

The chronology of urbanization is also devoid of uniformity. However, there appears to have been little activity before the Flavian era, although special circumstances, such as those found at Belo, did lead to isolated flurries of activity. Vespasian's grant of the *ius Latii* may have acted as a stimulus to build Roman structures, as the overwhelming majority of buildings found in the province are from the Flavian period or later. However, this hypothesis needs to be qualified, as this period was pre-

---

[229] Burnham and Wacher, *The 'Small Towns' of Roman Britain*, esp. ch. 3.

cisely that when the empire as a whole was at the height of its wealth, and so a larger number of buildings might be expected. Moreover it seems that the grant, if it did provide such a stimulus, did so entirely unintentionally. No uniform trend of urbanization can be discerned, which may support the assertion made in Chapter 2 that the existence of a deliberate policy of urbanization is a hypothesis which requires further demonstration if it is to be accepted.

Finally, it is of interest to consider once more the provisions of the Flavian Municipal Law, which presuppose an entirely Roman environment in the towns covered by the grant of *ius Latii*, in the light of the above survey. The list of the duties of the town aediles in chapter 19, for example, would not have been applicable in all towns. Once again it is clear that the state of affairs envisaged by the law would have been for many towns something to aim at, rather than to apply immediately in all its aspects, and that it would, on occasions, have been necessary to have recourse to an *interpretatio peregrina* of the law; albeit the difficulties caused in this respect would have been far fewer than the legal problems discussed in Chapter 6.

The urban background assumed by the law may have provided a guide-line for future urbanization in the less well-developed communities of the province, by giving such groups a conceptual framework of what sort of urban centre they ought to aim to create at some time in the future. In this sense the law can be seen as a stimulus to further urbanization, and more specifically to have propagated classical urban ideals within the province; albeit if we accept the conclusions of the preceding chapter, this function would have occurred accidentally rather than having been the initial intention of the drafters of the law in Rome.

Given the results of the above survey, it would have been the same areas of the province which would have found difficulties in implementing both these aspects of the law. We can see therefore that there was a general correlation between a broader knowledge of Roman civilization and an adoption of its physical trappings. In Baetica these influences appear to have radiated out from the Baetis valley, where both were in general understood, with ever-decreasing force into the highland areas of the province; here the Lusitanian bandit-chief Viriatus, had he been able to revisit the province at the end of our period, might have found much that he could recognize.

8

The Survival of Non-Roman Cultural Forms in Baetica

As has been seen, the link between urbanization and the adoption of one or more Roman customs by a non-Roman community is a complex one. Understanding this relationship is made all the more complex in the case of Baetica because the two largest indigenous population groups in the province, the Punic and Iberian, already possessed their own urban traditions prior to the arrival of Rome. The mere fact of urbanization alone therefore cannot be used as a marker of acculturation towards a Roman way of life by these groups. Instead it is necessary to look at how contact with Rome changed the nature of urban settlement in the region, and to determine in what areas such changes occurred and the depth to which they penetrated native society. Two potential models present themselves: the first is that Rome took active steps to change the structure of native towns, in which case we would expect a low rate of survival for non-Roman customs; the other model suggests that a much looser approach was employed, with Rome's concerns centring more on the need for efficient revenue-raising, administration, and the use of towns for these purposes—more because this was the unit with which she had habitually dealt in these areas than because she felt an ideological imperative to impose her own pattern of urban life on subject groups. This latter model would suggest that far fewer Roman customs would have been adopted and that native cultural patterns would have persisted in many areas of life. Moreover it would further imply that most aspects of cultural change would have occurred through a process of voluntary imitation of Roman customs by the native population in areas where this was seen to bring positive advantages, such as those giving prestige and chances of rising through the social hierarchy. We would therefore expect to find a partial rather than a complete adoption of Roman habits, centring on those areas regarded by Rome as necessary for 'civilization', whereas in other fields native customs will have continued longer; although a more gradual acculturation would probably have taken place.

The Punic occupation of Spain began at the latest in the eighth century BC, with some sources putting the foundation of Gades (the Latinized version of the Punic name Gaddir or 'fortified place') as early as 1,100 BC.[1] The earliest archaeological traces of occupation in the town date from the eighth century BC, but it must be borne in mind that the occupation of the site by the modern town of Cádiz has severely restricted the amount of excavation possible, so the earlier foundation date could be correct.[2]

Hannibal is said to have transported 30,000 settlers from Africa to Spain in the Barcid period, the so-called 'Blastophoenicians' who provided the core of the Punic population which persisted down to the Roman imperial period.[3] The proximity of Spain to Africa and the wishes of the settlers to keep family ties would have preserved the strong links between the two areas. The impact of this settlement can be seen in Strabo's remarks that the Iberians became so subject to the Phoenicians that τὰς πλείους τῶν ἐν τῇ Τουρδετανίᾳ πόλεων καὶ τῶν πλησίων τόπων ὑπ᾽ἐκείνων νῦν οἰκεῖσθαι ('the majority of the towns and neighbouring places in Turdetania are now inhabited by Phoenicians').[4]

There are some difficulties with Strabo's account. The geographer never visited the province himself, and we do not know whether he is relying on contemporary information (although he appears to be well informed on the *census* figures of his time) when he makes this comment, or simply depending on his standard sources for the area, Artemidorus and Posidonius. If the latter is the case, the νῦν ('now') of the passage cited above will refer to the time of these writers, and so is not a reliable guide to the situation in the imperial period. What is meant by 'majority' here is also open to interpretation. Although Artemidorus and Posidonius had travelled in Turdetania, we do not know what sort of visit they made; a short tour on which only select, wealthy individuals were encountered would have given a false picture of the ethnic make-up and urban development of the region.[5]

Fortunately, Strabo is not our only source of information about the extent of Punic influence in Baetica. The Elder Pliny remarks that Agrippa had considered the whole Mediterranean coast of the province

---

[1] Ps. Arist., *De Mirab.* 134; *Vel. Pat.*, 1. 2.

[2] For an early dating of Phoenician artefacts in Spain, see W. F. Albright, 'Some Oriental Glosses on the Homeric Problem', *AJA* 54 (1950), 176. Contra P. James, *Centuries of Darkness* (1991), 44 ff.

[3] Appian, *Ib.* 56.   [4] Strabo, 3. 2. 13.

[5] As a comparison, see the comments of Villari on how the ethnic make-up of early 20th-c. Macedonia could be mistaken as being predominantly Greek by a visit of this sort. L. Villari, 'Races, Religions, and Propagandas' in Villari, *The Balkan Question* (1905).

to be Punic;[6] and the Gallaecian Orosius writing in the late Roman period states that not only historians, but also architectural monuments reveal Carthage's former empire in the peninsula.[7] The value of Pliny's testimony is that he shows that the Punic element in the south of Spain was still large and influential at the beginning of the imperial period; while Orosius hints that Punic-style buildings were still to be seen in his day, the fifth century AD, although it is unclear whether these buildings are merely remains from the Barcid period or subsequent buildings of the same style.

That towns of a predominantly Punic outlook did continue to exist well into the Roman period is suggested by Strabo's comments on the town of Malaca.[8] He remarks that although some geographers have confused Malaca with the Greek town of Maenace, the ruins of this latter site in fact lie some distance from Malaca and have kept the characteristics of a Greek city, τὰ δ'ἴχνη σώζουσα Ἑλληνικῆς πόλεως, while Malaca has a Punic appearance, Φοινικικὴ τῷ σχήματι. The passage implies that for Strabo's contemporaries it was easy to tell the difference between the layout of a Phoenician and a Graeco-Roman city.

Unfortunately this ability has been lost with the passage of time and it is now difficult to tell how the two kinds of town are to be distinguished. One factor involved may be that Malaca lacked an orthogonal street-grid, and that Strabo took the existence of such a grid to be a standard characteristic of a Hellenic town.[9] Whether the town possessed other Phoenician features, such as a *cothon*, or artificial harbour, or placed its *forum* near to this harbour—elements which Isserlin believes were typical of Punic towns—is impossible to say, given the limited archaeological data available.[10] García y Bellido suggested that the description of Malaca's city wall by the Arabic historian, al-Himyari, as built out of large stone blocks showed that this was a Punic structure. Although Punic architecture did utilize this style of building more than Roman techniques, the evidence must remain inconclusive.[11] Some Egyptianizing blocks have been found built into the Roman theatre. This may suggest that Punic monuments were not uncommon in the town, and, as the theatre appears to date from

---

[6] Pliny, *NH* 3. 1. 8.   [7] Orosius, 7. 2. 6.   [8] Strabo, 3. 4. 2.

[9] However, pre-Roman Carthage appears to have had some form of orthogonal layout, so this style of town-planning was not entirely alien to the Punic mind; see S. Lancel *et al.*, 'Town Planning and Domestic Architecture of the Early Second Century BC on the Byrsa, Carthage', in J. Griffiths Pedley (ed.), *New Light on Ancient Carthage* (1980), 13 ff.

[10] B. S. J. Isserlin, 'Some Common Factors in Phoenician/Punic Town Planning' *RSF* 1 (1973), 135–52.

[11] A. García y Bellido, 'Un importante texto arabe valioso para nuestra historia', *A.e.A.* 16 (1943), 303–17, esp. 315.

the late first century BC, that perhaps some of these survived into at least the Julio-Claudian period.[12]

Malaca's status as a federate city until Vespasian's grant of *ius Latii* could also suggest that it was governed in the Punic manner before this point in time.[13] The Punic form of government was similar enough to that of the classical world to be recognized as a legitimate political system; indeed Aristotle finds points to praise in the Carthaginian constitution.[14] However, such a viewpoint is highly speculative; it perhaps seems unlikely to have been the case when we consider that other Punic towns, such as Sexi and Abdera, did not enjoy this status, and that the only other such town listed by Pliny which did, Epora, was not Punic.

At the end of the first century BC a substantial number of towns in Baetica were still striking coins. Given that such activity would be regulated by the local council, a study of the iconography of these coins can help us to see what image of themselves the communities concerned wished to project. A number of towns of Punic origin were among the coining towns of Baetica. One was Malaca, whose coinage was certainly Punic in appearance. The images carried on the town's coins are the head of the Punic goddess Tanit and that of a form of Vulcan—a version of the Punic god, Chusor, who appears to have been much worshipped in Punic Spain.[15] Unfortunately there is no way of dating this coinage securely; it could equally well be assigned to the late republican or early imperial period.

Sadly this lack of firm dating affects virtually all the coins with Punic legends from the province. These include those of Sexi, which display the head of the Punic god Melqart, and the tunny fish from which the town derived its wealth;[16] those of Asido, again displaying Punic legends and symbols (the town became a *colonia*, which should rule out an imperial date for these coins, although Guadan assigns them to the reign of Augustus);[17] and those of Lascuta, which have examples with both Libyo-Phoenician and Latin legends, the Latin legend being on a coin depicting the head of the Punic god Melqart.[18] A coin from Oba has a bilingual Latin and Libyo-Phoenician legend, but cannot be dated securely.[19] Guadan

---

[12] González Hurtado de Mendoza and Martin de la Torre, *Historia y reconstruccion del teatro romano de Málaga* (1982).

[13] Pliny, *NH* 3. 1. 8.   [14] Aristotle, *Pol.* 2. 11.

[15] *MI* nos. 106–11. Vulcan: Cicero (*De Nat. Deor.* 1. 84.) notes that there is a difference between the Roman and the Spanish Vulcan, and is almost certainly referring to this god.

[16] *MI* nos. 112–18.   [17] *MI* nos. 285–7.

[18] *MI* nos. 290–2.   [19] *MI* no. 293.

puts a coin from Vesci with a Libyo-Phoenician legend in the reign of Augustus, but gives no reason.[20] Other coins from the town are bilingual, and Vives in his catalogue declines to date them. Finally at Belo, Guadan assigns two coins which display Punic symbolism, one carrying a bilingual Latin and Libyo-Phoenician legend, to the Augustan period, again without giving any reasons for his dating.[21]

There are only two Punic towns in the province whose coins can be securely dated to the imperial period. These are Abdera, which Strabo notes as a Punic foundation,[22] and Gades. In both cases the towns also coined before the imperial period. It is noticeable that the issues from the imperial period are far less Punic in form than those struck during the republic. In the case of Abdera, its coinage, probably dating from the late republican period, carried both Punic symbols, in the shape of busts of the god Melqart, and Punic legends.[23] A temple, variously depicted as tetra- and pentastyle, was also displayed. This could be a representation of the temple of Melqart in the town, and need not indicate a wholly classical building, but merely a classical entrance to a Semitic-style shrine; such buildings are commonly found in Roman Africa. The imperial coins are from the reign of Tiberius and display his bust and the legend 'Ti Caesar divi Aug f.' on the obverse.[24] On the reverse the temple still appears with the legend 'Abdera' written in Punic script on its *tympanum*, while in one case the Latin legend 'Abdera' is written between the columns. The development of Abdera's coinage suggests that the coins of other towns not displaying imperial iconography should date from the late republican period. However, it does not follow that the imperial period saw a concerted effort to remove Punic icongraphy. Although the obverse of Abdera's coins took on a Roman appearance, their reverses retained both Punic iconography and script. It is unclear whether the remodelling of the obverse of the coins was due to an edict that the emperor be depicted, or as a voluntary attempt by the town's authorities to curry imperial favour. Whatever the case might have been, the shift in coin design shows an accommodation to new circumstances on the part of the minters rather than a total change in cultural outlook.

At Gades a similar, but more complex, process occurred. Some Gaditane coins simply display Latin legends and Roman iconography, for instance the *sestertius* issued in honour of Gaius and Lucius Caesar, or that

---

[20] *MI* no. 294.
[21] *MI* nos. 288–9. J. P. Bost *et al.*, *Belo*, iv. *Les Monnaies* (1987), 101, proposes a more reasonable late-republican dating.
[22] Strabo, 3. 4. 3. [23] *MI* nos. 119–22. [24] *MI* nos. 123–4.

honouring the town's patron, Agrippa.[25] Others, however, still contained
Punic elements; a *sestertius* commemorating Balbus' pontificate, while
bearing on the reverse the Roman symbols of a knife and *simpulum* with
the Latin legend 'Pont. Balbus', retained on its obverse the traditional
bust of Melqart which had been used during the republican period.[26] This
bust was also retained for a *dupondius* with an entirely Roman reverse
bearing a winged thunderbolt and the legend 'Augustus divi f.'[27] Although
these coins used Latin rather the Punic script, on occasions a counter-
clockwise rather than clockwise legend is found, indicating either that the
population of the town still felt more at ease reading Latin in the same
direction as their native script, or that on occasions the town minters
mistakenly engraved Latin legends this way because they were used to
writing from right to left. In either case these legends show that aspects of
Punic culture were still strong in Gades at this period. Moreover a series
of *asses*, identical to those of the republican period, displaying the bust of
Melqart on the obverse and two tunny fish on the reverse with the Punic
legend 'MBAL A AGDR', could date to the Julio-Claudian period.[28]
If so, we can see the town issuing low-denomination coins for its own
population in a form and with a language which they understood, while
at the same time issuing other higher-value coins for wider circulation
which proclaim the town's newly acquired status of *municipium civium
Romanorum*.

Gades was by far the largest Punic town in the province and had been
built, as had many Punic settlements, not on the mainland but on a small
offshore island. Strabo remarks on the small area of the original town.[29]
Towards the end of the republican period Balbus, the town's most famous
son, enlarged Gades by building a new quarter known as the νέα πόλις.
These two sections then combined, the joint town being known as
Διδύμη. It would have been interesting to know whether the two quarters
differed in their layout. Balbus had extensive interests in Roman politics
and so may have built his new quarter to a more Roman plan than that
found in the original town. Unfortunately our lack of archaeological information makes this impossible to trace and deprives us of a prime opportunity to test the degree of importance given to Roman-style building by
both opinion at Rome and those who sought to enter Roman society from
the outside.

Balbus also built a port for the town on the mainland, and other

---

[25] Gaius and Lucius, *MI* no. 88; Agrippa, *MI* no. 89.   [26] *MI* nos. 84–6.
[27] *MI* no. 87.   [28] *MI* nos. 80–4.   [29] Strabo, 3. 5. 3.

Gaditani lived on a fertile island between the main island of Gades and the mainland (probably La Isla de León). Although according to Strabo the inhabitants of this island felt that they had made it a rival to Διδύμη, he noted that very few of the Gaditani overall lived there or on the mainland. He gives the circumference of Διδύμη as 20 stades, remarking that it was not crowded—οὐ στενοχωρουμένην. Despite this he goes on to say that it would not fall short in population of any city but Rome, mentioning that in a recent, καθ'ήμᾶς, *census* 500 *equites* had been recorded in the city, more than in any Italian town save Patavium. In his account of Patavium Strabo refers to the figure given for its population in a recent *census*— Ἧ... νεωστὶ τιμήσασθαι.[30] This is presumably the *census* of AD 14, and the reference to Gades should derive from this same *census*, dating Strabo's figures for the Gaditane population to the Augustan period.

The small physical size of the city should have led to a great deal of crowding. Strabo's statement that the city was not crowded should refer to gaps within the city boundary, implying either a luxury quarter of the city (La Isla de León?), or that the built-up area was even smaller than the boundary, resulting in a very dense urban settlement.

It seems likely, therefore, that multi-storey buildings were common in Gades; such buildings were a typical feature of Punic and Phoenician cities. Strabo notes this feature in Tyre, and both Appian and Diodorus Siculus mention it at Carthage.[31] Although this is suggestive it is not conclusive evidence about Gaditane topography—tenement blocks were also a prominent feature at Ostia and Rome itself. Nevertheless Horace feels he can refer to Gades as a Punic town without the risk of confusing his readership, suggesting that it was commonly regarded as such in his day.[32]

Given Gades' Punic appearance, history, and reputation, it would seem likely that its population contained a substantial Punic element. However, it is more important to attempt to analyse how such a putative population behaved than merely to demonstrate its genetic existence. Unfortunately this is a difficult area to assess. One approach would be to examine the nomenclature found on inscriptions from the town. The Phoenicians often used names with religious connotations which were frequently translated into their Latin equivalents. Names such as Abdbaal, for exam-

---

[30] Strabo, 5. 1. 7.
[31] Tyre: Strabo, 16. 2. 23; Carthage: Diodorus Siculus, 20. 43–4; Appian, *Libyca* 128.
[32] Horace, *Odes* 2. 2. 11: 'si Libyam remotis Gadibus iungas et uterque Poenus serviat uni' ('if you were to join Libya with far-flung Gades and make each group of Phoenicians serve one Lord').

ple, would become Saturninus, Saturn being the classical god normally identified with the Punic Ba'al.[33] Others names meaning 'favoured by the gods' or 'granted by the gods' were translated as Fortunatus, Felix, Donatus, Concessus, and so on. There are, however, great difficulties in this form of analysis, as many of these names could have been acquired without any Punic influence at all. However, at Gades some 28 per cent of the names recorded in *CIL.* 2 have hints of Punic origin; and given the rest of the evidence for the town this should be taken as showing a persistent Punic stratum in the community. Nevertheless the lack of non-Latin names which are found, for example at Lepcis Magna, shows that the population had at least partially adopted Roman patterns of nomenclature.

The presence of rock-cut tombs found in a cemetery located just outside the town and used until at least the first century AD[34] suggests that Punic funerary customs also continued into the early imperial period at Gades. Unfortunately the locations of later cemeteries, which might show that these customs persisted longer still, remain to be discovered.

The most renowned Punic survival at Gades, however, was its celebrated temple of Heracles. The temple was in fact dedicated to the Punic god Melqart, who was syncretized in the classical world with Heracles. Outside the temple were two bronze pillars,[35] a Punic feature paralleled most famously by the Temple of Jerusalem, itself built by Phoenician craftsmen.[36] Philostratus tells us that these pillars were engraved with characters in a script which was neither Egyptian nor Indian. Possibly the language concerned was neo-Punic, but it would be surprising if Philostratus was not aware of this script. The most likely candidate is a form of archaic Punic no longer spoken in imperial times and dating from the temple's foundation. Philostratus states that the priests would not tell him what the inscriptions meant. It is unclear whether this reluctance derived from religious scruple, or was intended to disguise the fact that the writings were unintelligible even to the priests. These latter, as described by Silius Italicus, dressed in Semitic fashion with long linen robes, had shaven heads, and went barefoot.[37] The priesthood was hierarchical, with a high priest at its head,[38] and required celibacy.[39] According to Strabo there was a spring which allowed ritual ablutions to be performed in the

[33] M. Leglay, *Saturne africain* (1966).
[34] A. García y Bellido, *Fenicios y Carthaginenses en occidente* (1942), 282 ff.
[35] Strabo, 3. 5. 5.
[36] 1 Kgs. 7: 15–22.; 2 Chr. 2: 15–17; Josephus, *Ant. J.* 8. 3. 4.
[37] Silius Italicus, 3. 24–8.   [38] Porphyry, *De Abstin.* 1. 25.
[39] Silius Italicus, 3. 28.

court of the temple.[40] Pliny gives a slightly different account, saying that the spring was near the temple rather than located within its grounds.[41] However, he may have been confused by the large amount of empty space found in Semitic temple complexes in relation to the size of the temple buildings themselves.

Within the temple itself, in accordance with Semitic custom, there was no image of the god.[42] Philostratus says that there were two unengraved, ἀσήμοι, bronze altars to Egyptian Heracles (i.e. Melqart), and a stone altar in honour of Theban (i.e. Greek) Heracles, carved with depictions of his labours.[43] Sacrifices were offered daily to the god, again a common Semitic practice,[44] and the victim offered was often a dove,[45] a bird regarded as sacred in the Near East.[46] Pigs and women were barred from the sanctuary.[47] The Semitic nature of the rites continued throughout antiquity; Appian notes that in his day they were performed φοινικικῶς (in a Phoenician manner),[48] as does Arrian.[49]

The doors of the temple were made of bronze and engraved with the labours of Heracles. They are described in detail by Silius Italicus.[50] Silius lists only ten, not twelve labours, and of these only six belong to the canonical list of the labours of Heracles. Given the fame of the temple, it would have been unwise for Silius to misrepresent what was to be found at Gades. It seems, therefore, that what was depicted were not the labours of Heracles as known to the classical world, but a different religious myth. The last of the scenes was the death of the hero on Mount Oeta, where Silius says: 'the great soul (of Hercules) is soaring up in flames to the stars'. This was not a popular topic in classical art, and is more likely to have been a depiction of the death and resurrection of Melqart. In Tyre, there was a local tradition of Heracles being burnt, a myth perhaps referred to by Nonnos.[51] The feast of Melqart's resurrection was kept in the town, with a major festival held every fifth year.[52] Perhaps Philostratus is

---

[40] Strabo, 3. 5. 7.   [41] Pliny, *NH* 2. 100.

[42] Silius Italicus, 3. 30–1; Philostratus, *Vit. Apol.* 5. 5, cf. 1 Kgs. 9: 25.

[43] Philostratus, *Vit. Apol.* 5. 5.   [44] Porphyry, *De Abstin.* 1. 25.   [45] Ibid.

[46] Lucian, *De Dea Syriaca* 15.   [47] Silius Italicus, 3. 22–3.

[48] Appian, *Ib.* 2.   [49] Arrian, 2. 16. 4.

[50] Silius Italicus, 3. 32 ff. with J. B. Tsirkin, 'The Labours, Death and Resurrection of Melqart as Depicted on the Gates of the Gades Herakleion', *RSF* 9 (1981), 21–7.

[51] See J. G. Frazer, *The Golden Bough*, pt. 4., *Adonis Attis Osiris* (3rd edn., 1927), i, ch. 5, 'The Burning of Melcarth'. One version of the death of the classical Hercules significantly places the site of his death not on Mount Oeta, but in Tyre, St Clemens Romanus, *Recognitiones* 10. 24 = Migne, *PG* 1. 1434. Nonnos (*Dionysiaca* 40. 369) describes Hercules as ἄναξ πυρός, which appears to be a reference to this myth.

[52] 2 Macc. 4. 18–20.

alluding to this feast when he states that the Gaditani are the only people to celebrate death in song.[53] The festival of Melqart was not uncommon in the Phoenician world, so it is difficult to see why Philostratus should single out the Gaditani in this way, but the allusion itself seems clear. The temple was said to contain the ashes of Heracles, strengthening the case for such a festival being held here.[54]

Pausanias mentions an incident which hints at a major religious festival held at Gades. He says that Cleon of Magnesia-on-the-Hermus saw a giant merman while returning to Gades after he and the rest of the crowd had sailed away from the island according to the instructions of Heracles, κατὰ τὸ Ἡρακλέους πρόσταγμα. This suggests that the festival involved the exclusion of foreigners from the island of the town. Such exclusion could be seen as a Semitic trait. It is not clear whether this festival was an annual one. It could have been a special festival, such as that at Tyre noted above, celebrated once every so many years.[55]

Little is known of the structure of the temple. It is said to have contained a large number of altars to abstract deities such as Old Age, Poverty, Death, and Art.[56] There was a statue of Alexander the Great, and possibly one of Themistocles in the precinct.[57] A tower is said to have been visible from the altar of the temple, presumably the main altar, and a tower is found on depictions of Eastern shrines on coins.[58] The temple appears on several coins of Hadrian, which show it as tetraprostyle with Corinthian columns, but this could be just a symbolic representation or the classical façade of the shrine.[59] One coin depicts a classical Heracles with his club standing in a *naiskos* of four pillars attended by two female figures. This should be symbolic since, as has been seen, there was no image of the god in the temple.

Apart from this major Punic temple which enjoyed empire-wide fame, the town also contained a temple to Cronos, the syncretized name of another major Punic god, Baʿal.[60] Clearly therefore the religious sympathies of the town's inhabitants had not been changed substantially by its contact with Rome.

Another, and very different, indication of Punic culture is Gades' reputation for dancing girls. All our sources which mention dancing girls from Spain link them firmly to the town. References to dancing girls

[53] Philostratus, *Vit. Apol.* 5. 4.   [54] Pomponius Mela, 3. 46.
[55] Pausanias, 10. 4. 6.   [56] Philostratus, *Vit. Apol.* 5. 4.
[57] Alexander: Suetonius, *Vit. Div. Iul.* 7; Themistocles: Philostratus, *Vit. Apol.* 5. 4.
[58] Porphyry, *De Abstin.* 1. 25. For towers on coins, see *BMCGC: Phoenicia* (1910), no. 38, pl. 12 no. 13; D. Harden, *The Phoenicians* (1980), pl. 102.
[59] *BMCRE* 3 (1936), pl. 48, nos. 17–20.   [60] Strabo, 3. 5. 3.

elsewhere invariably call them 'Syrian' or 'Phrygian', suggesting a cultural link between Gades and the East in this respect. A scholiast on Juvenal's eleventh satire makes this link clear. Glossing 'Gaditanae' he remarks: 'that is to say perhaps you are hoping that beautiful young Syrian girls are going to dance, since Gades was founded by Syrians and Africans.'[61] The evidence listed above shows that the town continued to have a strong Punic element in classical times. But we must remember that there was also another side to Gades' character. Philostratus says that the Gaditani were Hellenizers; Martial mentions a certain Canius of Gades as a literary figure; and Pliny notes that there were enthusiasts of Livy in Gades who travelled to Rome to meet him.[62] The town had a theatre, as is attested by archaeology (perhaps built by Balbus) and the grave of a Samnite gladiator has been found.[63] It is not surprising that the upper classes would imitate Roman ways and adopt Roman fashions, where these were seen to give advantage and prestige, and that the lower classes should adopt some forms of Roman entertainment, especially when they would have been paid for. Nevertheless this does not imply a full-scale adoption of Roman customs. A final indication of the town's Punic character and continuing links with North Africa is that King Juba II of Mauretania held an honorary duovirate in the town.[64] The kingdom of Mauretania was highly Punicized; the king also held this rank at Carthago Nova, another Punic foundation, making his office-holding in Gades highly suggestive of continuing Punic influence there.

Given the Punic element in the population along Baetica's southern coastline and the great prestige of the temple at Gades, dedications to Heracles in the province are as likely to be to Melqart in his syncretized form, as to the classical Heracles. At Osqua the temple dedicated to Heracles by L. Vibius Fetialis was probably a temple to Melqart, given the town's proximity to Gades;[65] and at Ostippo there is a dedication to Hercules Primigenius,[66] an epithet which only makes sense if applied to Melqart. An island off Onuba is recorded as being dedicated to Heracles.[67]

---

[61] 'Id est speras forsitan quod incipiant saltare delicatae ac pulchrae puellae Syriae: quoniam de Syriis et Afris Gadis condita est.' For general comments on this phenomenon, see A. García y Bellido, 'Las bailarinas gaditanas', *Veinticinco estampas de la España antigua* (1967), 102–5, and G. Wille, *Musica Romana* (1967), index s.v. Gaditanerinnen.

[62] Philostratus, *Vit. Apol.* 5. 8; Martial, 1. 61; Pliny, *Ep.* 2. 3.

[63] *AE* (1962), 58.   [64] Avienus, *Or. Mar.* 280–4.

[65] *AE* (1974), 381.   [66] *CIL* 2. 1436.

[67] Strabo, 3. 5. 5. This is quite possibly the island of Saltes at the mouth of the Ria de Huelva. The Muslim geographer al-Himyari records traces of ancient cult sites here, *Kitāb ar-Rawḍ*, 135 f. The island may perhaps be identified with Avienus' island of Cartare (*Ora Maritima* 255), whose name appears to have a Punic root.

This dedication of islands to the gods is a Punic practice, and similar islands of Heracles are attested at Carthago Nova and off Sardinia.[68]

Two similar dedications of islands to Juno, who is most likely to be, in these instances, the Punic goddess Tanit, are found in the province. These are near the Straits of Gibraltar,[69] and Gades.[70] The latter is specifically said to have been called the island of Juno 'ab indigenis' ('by the natives'). Two other shrines to Juno in this syncretic form are found at San Lucar de Barrameda at the mouth of the Baetis,[71] and at Cape Trafalgar, the *Promontorium Iunonis*.[72] In both cases a temple, as well as a sanctuary, is attested. At San Lucar de Barrameda, Strabo describes the sanctuary as that of the *Lux Dubia*, or Phosphorus, not of Hera/Juno.[73] This confirms the Punic nature of the shrine, as Tanit was a moon goddess: one of her most common symbols being the crescent moon.[74]

At Malaca, Avienus talks of an island dedicated to the moon and the *Dea Noctiluca*.[75] This is likely to have been another island dedicated to Tanit. Further inland, at Iliberris, a dedication to Luna dating to the third century AD has been found, which could be another syncretic dedication to the goddess.[76] Tanit could also have been syncretized with Venus in Baetica. Pliny, when discussing the *insula Iunonis* near Gades, mentions that it has also been known as Aphrodisias. Pliny's island may be the same as Avienus' island dedicated to Venus Marina, lying to the west of Gades, where the goddess had a temple and oracle.[77] The area near 'Tartessos' (identified in antiquity with either Carteia or Gades) was known as the *Campus Veneris*.[78] It may not be insignificant that Carteia itself was said to have once been called Heracleia,[79] and to have been settled, originally, by Phoenician settlers from Africa (perhaps some of the Blastophoenices).[80] The nearby town of Nebrissa had the epithet 'Veneria', suggesting a link with the goddess.

At San Lucar la Mayor a dedication to *Juno Regina* has been found, made by M. Calpurnius Seneca Fabius Turpio Sentinianus.[81] Sentinianus was the *primus pilus* of a legion and the *procurator* of the provinces of Tarraconensis and Vettoniensis. Again here we have an example of the

---

[68] Carthago Nova, Strabo, 3. 4. 6., 'Scombraria', the modern Escombreras near the harbour month; Sardinia, Pliny, *NH* 3. 7. 84.

[69] Strabo, 3. 5. 3.   [70] Pliny, *NH* 4. 120.   [71] Pomponius Mela, 3. 4.

[72] Pliny, *NH* 3. 7; Ptolemy, 2. 4. 5.   [73] Strabo, 3. 1. 9.

[74] See the enormous numbers of crescents which figure on dedicatory *stelae* at Sulci and Carthage, and Herodian, 5. 6. 4.

[75] Avienus, *Or. Mar.* 367–8, 428–31.   [76] *CIL* 2. 5509.

[77] Avienus, *Or. Mar.* 315.   [78] *CIL* 2. 844.

[79] Strabo, 3. 1. 7, perhaps hinting at an early link with Melqart.

[80] Pomponius Mela, 2. 96.   [81] *CIL* 2. 1267.

worship of a version of Tanit dating from the late imperial period. The root of the name of the modern Spanish town also suggests a reminiscence of the goddess concerned, given Strabo's identification of her as the *Lux Dubia*.

A more controversial instance of the goddess Tanit may be found at Tajo Montero, near the ancient town of Ostippo. A depiction of Artemis in a *naiskos* with a bird perched in the pediment has been found here. The goddess is depicted naked (although some commentators have seen traces of a cloak on the left shoulder) with a bow, quiver, and palm tree beside her. The stone is broken half-way down, so there is no way of telling what the figure is holding in its hands. García y Bellido dates the *stele* to the second century AD, from the lettering of an accompanying dedication by Annia Septuma, and believes that it shows a syncretized version of Tanit. There are, however, problems with this interpretation. First, Tanit was normally syncretized with Juno, not Artemis, and, although some inscriptions linking the two goddesses have been found, García y Bellido is forced to admit that the link is unusual.[82] Second, there is very little to substantiate the link between the two goddesses in this particular case. The palm tree in the background could be explained by a reference to Delos, renowned for its palm trees and for being the birthplace of Artemis.[83] Third, the sex of the figure is problematic. At least two commentators, Paris and Blech, have suggested that it is male, leading to a simple interpretation of the figure as Delian Apollo.[84] Iconography of an extremely similar sort (including the *naiskos*, palm, and bow and quiver) is associated with this god on the Apollo relief from the Villa Albani in Rome. Finally, although Punic dedications to Tanit often took the form of depicting the goddess in a *naiskos*, this is by no means solely a Punic form of dedication. A dedication to the goddess Brigantia, found at Birrens in Britain, shows the goddess concerned standing in a similar *naiskos*.[85] At Sulci an enormous collection of Tanit dedications has been found, none of which depicts Tanit in the same way as the stone from Tajo Montero. The goddess is invariably clothed, and normally holds her hands across her breast, or holds up a disc-shaped object in one hand. García y Bellido's best argument concerns the bird which is found in the *tympanum* of the *naiskos*. The dove, as has been seen, was regarded as holy in the Near East,

[82] A. García y Bellido, *Las esculturas romanas de España y Portugal* (1949), no. 392, lam. 277.

[83] See e.g. Homer, *Od.* 6. 163–4.

[84] P. Paris, *L'Espagne primitive* (1903), i. 332–43; M. Blech, 'Esculturas de Tajo Montero: una interpretación iconografica' in Arce (ed.), *La religión romana en Hispania*, 97–109.

[85] *RIB* 2091.

and here may show a Punic origin for the stone. Nevertheless there is no association of the dove with Tanit on the *stelae* from either Sulci or Carthage. The normal emblems found in the *tympanum* of these dedications are the disc and crescent sign of the goddess, a disc on its own, or a rosette.

It seems unlikely, therefore, that the Ostippo *stele* is a dedication to Tanit. Taken by itself, it is more likely to have been a dedication to Delian Apollo or Artemis. However, the stone was found in a group along with six others. One of these depicts the god Harpocrates giving his sign of silence,[86] another a bearded man holding a staff or sceptre, possibly the god Serapis. The Ostippo stones may therefore be a group dedicated by devotees of Isis, a goddess with an established cult on Delos, explaining her depiction here as Artemis. The bird in the *tympanum* could in this case be explained as the hawk of Horus. Its crude carving makes it unclear whether it is a dove or not.

Another possible case of Punic worship could be seen in the acts of the martyrs Justa and Rufina, dating to AD 287.[87] These two women were martyred for refusing to contribute a pot to the god Salabos and subsequently destroying his image. This god is probably some form of Adonis, and the pot would have been required to make a garden of Adonis. Although such forms of worship stem from the Near East, and so were possibly introduced into Spain by the Phoenicians, their immense popularity throughout the empire at this period makes it possible that the cult was merely a reflection of the times and shows no specific Punic influence in the province.

At Italica two dedications to Liber Pater, often syncretized with the Punic god Eshmun, have been found. The name of one dedicant is lost, while the other was called Saturninus.[88] The combination of a possibly Punic name and a possible Punic god is suggestive, but again perhaps an entirely non-Punic explanation would be equally valid. A further dedication to Liber Pater was made by the *duovir* L. Calpurnius Silvinus at Urgavo.[89] Urgavo's position in the north-west of the province might militate against a Punic link here, but it must be remembered that the town of Castulo, also found in this area, had once been under Punic influence and that Imilce, the name of Hannibal's bride, who came from this town, could have a Punic, rather than an Iberian, root.

---

[86] García y Bellido, *Las esculturas romanas de España y Portugal*, no. 395, lam. 280.

[87] Text in E. Florez, *España Sagrada* (1752), ix. 242 ff. See also F. Cumont, 'Les Syriens en Espagne et les Adonies à Séville', *Syria*, 7 (1927), 330 ff.

[88] *CIL* 2. 1108.   [89] *CIL* 2. 2105.

Toutain suggested that the cult of the *genius municipii* was a remnant of the Punic cult of individual gods of the city concerned.[90] Such gods would be known individually as Melqart, or lord of the city. In Toutain's day a total of seventy-two such inscriptions were known, and over half of these came from Roman Africa and Spain. The African examples were centred on old Punic towns, and the Spanish ones came mainly from Baetica. Of those that did not, many are from the Levant coast of the peninsula, another area where extensive Punic occupation had taken place, for example from Carthago Nova, Mentesa, and Laminium. The Baetican examples almost all fell into an area south of the Baetis. But Toutain's conjecture now seems less convincing as a purely Punic phenomenon: inscriptions honouring such deities have been found outside regions of Punic influence, for instance at Iponoba in Baetica and Conimbriga in Lusitania. However, given the parochial nature of Celtic and Iberian gods, this fact does not of itself disprove Toutain's hypothesis, but merely shows that a similar semi-syncretization of local gods to Roman forms took place in these areas as well as in the regions of Punic settlement.

Another Punic religious practice which survived in Spain is the method of disposing of the dead. The rock-cut tombs at Gades have already been mentioned, and further examples are to be found at Urso.[91] However, the best examples are found in the necropolis of Carmo. The standard form of tomb found here is that of a shaft with hand- and foot-holds (e.g. tomb 363), or a sloping shaft with stairs (e.g. tomb 50) leading down to a rock-cut chamber. This form of tomb is typically Punic in conception, having many parallels in Africa and the Phoenician homeland. The funerary chambers themselves, containing *loculi* for cinerary urns, are less Punic. The normal Punic rite of interment was inhumation, not cremation. The move to cremation may be a sign of increasing acculturation. However, cremations have been found in a purely Punic context, for example at Motya in Sicily. Many of the tombs at Carmo have classical-style wall-paintings in the funerary chamber. Birds are a common choice of subject, occurring, for example, in the Tomb of the Dove, the Tomb of the Three Doorways, the Tomb of the Plums, and the Tomb of the Cone Scales amongst others. This could indicate a Punic religious context, but is a common classical motif too. Of more interest is the fact that one cinerary urn from the cemetery carries the Punic name Urbanival.[92]

The tomb of Q. Postumius Hyginus and his wife, Postumia Cypare,

[90] Toutain, *Les Cultes paiens* (1907), i. 451–4.
[91] P. Paris, 'Antigua necrópolis y fortaleza de Osuna', *BRAH* 56 (1910), 201–19.
[92] *CIL* 2. 5427.

shows a mixing of funerary practices. The tomb is entered by a flight of steps on the Punic model, but then opens out into a courtyard which is more classical than Punic in conception. Off this courtyard opens a standard Punic funerary chamber which not only has *loculi* for cinerary urns, but also benches for inhumation burials. The lettering of Postumius' inscription suggests a date in the Antonine period, and the tomb shows an interesting new amalgam of cultures developing, with neither of the two old contributors managing entirely to supersede the other.

The richest tomb found in the cemetery, that of Servilia, the daughter of a local *duovir*, also shows this mixing of cultures. It is built in the form of a square colonnaded courtyard cut down into the rock, with a vaulted funerary chamber adjoining it on one side, and on another a small shrine to the deceased, where a high-quality marble statue of Servilia was found.[93] Although the tomb is, initially, much more classical in appearance than the others in the cemetery, its closest parallels are found in the Egyptianizing tombs of Hellenistic Alexandria in the necropolis of Mustafa Pasha, and similar rock-cut peristyle tombs found at Nea Paphos on Cyprus (the so-called Royal tombs).[94] Given the strong influence of Egyptian art on Punic culture, that Cyprus was an area of Phoenician settlement, and the context of our tomb, it appears that here we have an example of the persistence of Punic cultural values at the highest level of local society. Nevertheless the marble statue of Servilia, which is entirely classical, shows, like the tomb of Postumius, a mixing of cultures rather than the straightforward supersession of an old one by a new, or the survival of the latter unaffected by the former.

Bendála Galán believes that the Tomb of the Elephant in the necropolis was a shrine to Attis and Cybele, but provides no satisfactory arguments for this position. The sculpture carved into the wall of the courtyard of the tomb is more easily interpreted as a standard funerary motif than as a priest of the goddess, and his proposed sacrificial pit is too difficult of access for either *taurobolia or criobolia* to have been performed there. The presence of a well in the tomb need not indicate that it was used for ablutions other than those concerned with funerary rites, or in providing water for funeral feasts for which the two *triclinia* in the courtyard of the tomb seem to be areas. Both wells and *triclinia* are paralleled in other tombs found in the cemetery. Bendála's identification of a betyl in the

---

[93] M. Bendála Galán, *La necrópolis romana de Carmona* (1976), ch. 7.

[94] Alexandria: A. Adriani, *La Nécrople de Mustafa Pacha = Annuaire de Musée Greco-Romain* [of Alexandria] (1933–5). Nea Paphos: V. Karageorghis, *Cyprus* (1982), 176, pl. 126.

tomb is also problematic, the stone concerned being unshapen and too large for its proposed chamber. The presence of the carving of the elephant is mysterious. It is probably connected to the hope of eternal life, given the beast's reputation for longevity.

Another typically Punic style of tomb found in Baetica is the tower tomb, with parallels in Roman Africa and the Near East.[95] The most well-known Spanish example of a tomb built in this style is the Torre de los Escipiones near Tarraco. There are eight examples of tower tombs at Belo, the best example being the Hornillo de Sta Catalina. At Basilippo a further example appears in the Torre del Cincho.[96] This structure was built in three levels, divided by thin bands of tiles. The shape of the roof above the third level is unknown. It was made of *opus caementicum* and faced not with stone, but mortar. As there were quarries of good stone nearby in the Roman period this suggests economizing. Given the cost of a stone-faced structure, perhaps this is all the upper classes of a small town like Basilippo could afford. The highest level of the tomb had recesses for statuary, and at ground level, on the western side, a U-shaped niche communicates to an underground *bustum*. The latter feature is a common one on the tower tombs of Palmyra. A further tower tomb is to be found near Gerena. This, known as El Torril, again has an *opus caementicum* core with, on this occasion, a cladding of bricks. Other examples are to be found at Facialcazar, near Salpensa, Rio Tinto, and at Corduba. The last example has an underground *bustum*. At Iulippa a distyle funerary monument has been found built into the church of the present-day village, Zalamea de la Serena. It comprises two columns, probably surmounted by a statue in antiquity, mounted on a pilastered podium and it probably reached a height of 24 m. Again the monument is paralleled by others in the Near East.[97]

Another type of burial which is found in Baetica and has strong parallels in Roman Africa is the semicylindrical form of tomb known as a *cupa*. *Cupae* have been found at Gades, Belo, Rio Tinto, and Onuba in Baetica, at Mexilhoeir a Grande in the south of Portugal, and at several points in Tarraconensis. This form of burial is widespread in Africa, and the *cupae* at Belo show strong parallels with those found at Tipasa and Henchir Zaura. The tomb does not appear to be Punic, but rather African, in

---

[95] See C. Cid Priego, 'El sepulcro de Torre mediterráneo y sus relaciones con la tipología monumental', *Ampurias*, 11 (1949), 91–126.

[96] J. M. Rodríguez Hidalgo, 'Anotaciones en torno a Basilippo: La Torre del Cincho', *Habis* 10/11 (1979/80), 425–35.

[97] A García y Bellido and J. Menéndez Pidal, 'El distylo sepulcral romano de Iulipa (Zalamea)', *Anejos del Archivo español de arqueología*, 3 (1963).

origin. It is, however, found in many Punic towns and was probably introduced into Spain by Carthaginian colonists.

The link with Africa is likely to have helped sustain the persistence of Punic features in Baetica. The distance between the two provinces was negligible; Aulus Gellius pedantically argues that the passage from one to the other ought to be called a *transgressio* in order to emphasize this fact.[98] In the Claudian period we know that the governor of Baetica was charged with the responsibility of supplying Mauretania with corn.[99] The coins of Gades are commonly found on ancient sites in Africa,[100] and, according to Strabo, the fishing fleet of the town used to venture down the African coast as far as Lixus, another Punic foundation.[101] The *forum* complex of Belo, with its three separate temples and square shape, has close parallels with the old *forum* of the Punic town of Lepcis Magna. An example of the reinforcing effect which these links had in Baetica is seen at Italica, where the priestess Vibia Modesta, described as 'oriunda Mauretania', dedicated a silver statue on obtaining the priesthood for the second time to Isis, Ceres, and Juno Regina.[102] The last two of these goddesses are most likely to be Punic deities.

Vibia's high rank in Italica suggests that there was considerable inter-communication between the upper classes of Baetica and Africa. Further evidence of this, though in the reverse direction, is shown by the marriage of a *duovir* of Volubilis, L. Valerius Saturninus, to a wife from Conobaria in Baetica.[103] This continual communication would lead to considerably less pressure to acculturate than might have been the case if Baetica had not been adjacent to another area strongly influenced by Punic culture.

One aspect of the area's Punic religious past which seems to have survived at Belo, and which would have been strongly discouraged by Rome, is human sacrifice. At Belo fifteen adult skeletons have been found whose posture suggests that they had been victims of this practice. One appears to have had a sharp implement driven cleanly through his skull. The most surprising aspect of these remains is that they appear to date to the third century AD.[104] We know that ritual murder was part of Punic religion, but equally that Rome, with an abhorrence of the practice, endeavoured to stamp it out. Nevertheless according to Tertullian, human sacrifice had been practised with official connivance in Africa until at least

---

[98] Aulus Gellius, *NA* 10. 26. 6.   [99] Dio, 60. 24. 5.
[100] Monceaux, *Bull. de Corresp. Afric.* 2 (1884), 346, 350 ff.
[101] Strabo, 2. 3. 4.   [102] *AE* (1982), 521.   [103] *IAM* (2), 469.
[104] Paris, *Les Fouilles de Belo* (1923), ii. 91–4.

the reign of Tiberius, and continued in his own day in secret.[105] It is possible that the examples at Belo represent a sporadic outburst, as instances of thuggee still occur in India, or—perhaps given the third-century date—a reversion to ancestral practices at a time of great stress, for example in the Moorish invasions of Baetica which occurred in this century.[106]

Although some towns may have been of Punic appearance, very little in the way of Punic-inspired carving has been preserved in the province. Two exceptions to this, both dated by García y Bellido to the early imperial period, are a relief from Urso and a *stele* from Marchena.[107] The Urso relief depicts a deer feeding from a palm tree while suckling a fawn. It is carved from native stone, and non-classical techniques have been used for its execution. The theme is Punic in conception, and paralleled on some coins of Carthage. The *stele* from Marchena is worked in a similar way, depicting a leaping deer on one side and a palm tree on the other. Again the best parallels are to be found in Punic iconography.

The aspects of Punic culture discussed above have been in the non-political areas of civic life. It remains to ascertain whether Punic forms of organization also persisted in the political sphere. Here our evidence is much sparser. Certainly no Latin/Punic bilingual official inscriptions of the type found in Tripolitania have as yet been found in Spain, nor are there any known attestations of the title *suffete* by name. By the end of the republic Gades had *quattuorviri* elected on a Roman-style *comitia* system, perhaps hinting that other towns too had changed to a Roman system of administration.[108] On the other hand the political ambitions of the Balbi at

[105] Tertullian, *Apol.* 9. 2: 'Infantes penes Africam Saturno immolabantur palam usque ad proconsulatum Tiberii . . . teste militia patriae nostrae quae id ipsum munus illi proconsuli functa est. Sed nunc in occulto perseverat hoc sacrum facinus.' ('In Africa little children were sacrificed openly to Saturn down to the time of a proconsul of Tiberius . . . the soldiers of my homeland are witnesses as they served the proconsul in performing this task. Now this "holy" rite continues, but in secret.') 'Ad proconsulatum Tiberii' is normally interpreted as meaning 'down to the time of a proconsul of Tiberius'; however, it is possible that Tertullian is referring to a proconsul named Tiberius of the 2nd c. AD, in which case human sacrifice will have been practised openly within living memory of Tertullian. See the discussion in T. D. Barnes, *Tertullian* (2nd edn., 1985), 13 ff., and M. Leglay, *Saturne africain* (1966), 61 ff.

[106] The situation of Belo suggests that human sacrifice here is a Punic custom; however, at an earlier date, it was also a feature of Iberian religion: ritual graves have been found at both El Acebuchal (Sevilla) and La Joya (Huelva). See. R. J. Harrison, *Spain at the Dawn of History* (1988), 59.

[107] García y Bellido, *Las esculturas romanas de España y Portugal*, nos. 304 (Marchena) and 305 (Urso). Photographs on pl. 245.

[108] Cicero, *Ad Fam.* 10. 32.

Rome and their consequent need to appear as coming from a Roman background may have led to faster changes here than elsewhere. It is also important to recall that the greater part of our epigraphic evidence post-dates the Flavian Municipal Law and that the uniformity of the political structures found in Baetica may well be a product of this law imposing a blanket form of administrative structure on the Iberian peninsula. The scope of the grant rather than its nature could well be responsible for the uniformity that is found in the area. In this case we ought to see the phenomenon as an attempt to impose Roman forms not from ideological but from administrative imperatives.

Despite this uniformity after the enactment of the Flavian Municipal Law, some anomalies can be detected prior to this date which may suggest that administration was undertaken in a variety of ways in the province. At Ostippo[109] and Cartima[110] we find *decemviri* attested. At Ostippo, the *decemvir* concerned, Q. Larius Niger, has the title of *decemvir Maximus*. The relevant inscription from Ostippo dates to the Tiberian, that from Cartima to the Claudian, period. There are reasons to believe that Ostippo had a Punic element to its population. Ostippo is probably the Astapa of Livy, who described it at the time of the Punic Wars as a strong ally of Carthage, 'Carthaginiensium semper partis'.[111] The Marchena *stele* was found near the town, as were the reliefs from Tajo Montero, though, as has been seen, it is unlikely that the latter are a dedication to Tanit. Although we do not have a large number of inscriptions from the town, those we do have show a strong bias towards potentially Punic names such as Mummia Fortunata,[112] and Mettia Saturnina;[113] and others suggest African immigrants, such as Fulvia Maura,[114] and L. Mumminus Maurus.[115] The dedication to Heracles Primigenius, mentioned above, also suggests a Punic context. At Cartima, there is less evidence of a Punic background, but the town's name, possibly from the Punic root *qart*, or town, as it does not appear to be Iberian in origin, and its geographical position, both add support to such a hypothesis.

Given this background, it has been suggested that the decemvirate at these towns may have been a survival of a Punic system of government, whose chief magistrates would have been *suffetes*.[116] If this was the case, it

---

[109] *CIL* 2. 5048.   [110] *CIL* 2. 1953.

[111] Livy, 28. 22. The final holocaust of the town has been seen as showing Punic influence, but Pliny's account is too generic for such an argument to be convincing. See P. G. Walsh, *Livy: His Historical Aims and Methods* (1961), 194.

[112] *CIL* 2. 1449, although the name here may reflect her libertine status.

[113] *CIL* 2. 1461.   [114] *CIL* 2. 1453.   [115] *CIL* 2. 1462.

[116] T. R. S. Broughton, 'Municipal Institutions in Roman Spain', *CHM* 9/1 (1965), 126 ff.

is significant that although the post has remained Punic in inspiration, its title, for official purposes at least, has been baptized with a Latin name. Such a system may have persisted until Vespasian's grant of *ius Latii* and the town's consequent acquisition of municipal status.[117] Unfortunately, however, we know that at Carthage and other western Punic cities there were normally only two *suffetes*.[118] While *collegia* of ten and twenty magistrates are attested in some North African cities,[119] it would seem odd if towns which were Carthaginian colonies did not adopt Carthage's political system.

Nevertheless, even if we rule out a Punic derivation for the *decemviri*, their office does not seem to have been a standard Roman one.[120] A further inscription mentioning a *decemvir maxsimus* (*sic*) has recently been found attested on an inscription found at La Rambla (Cordoba).[121] The inscription dates from 49 BC, and records the building of a town gate by the *decemvir maxsumus* and an aedile. The precedence of the *decemvir* suggests that this was the higher of the two offices; the epithet *maxsumus* implies that perhaps the college of *decemviri* had a president. Unlike the aedile, who has a Roman name, M. Coranus Alpis, and enjoys a standard Roman title, the *decemvir* has an entirely native name, Binsnes Vercellonis f., which possibly betrays some Celtic influence.[122] There is no trace of Punic influence in this town, which in turn suggests that Thouvenot was right to see the *decemviri* of Baetica as a Turdetanian, rather than a Punic, cultural survival.[123]

Punic culture appears to have survived in Spain, therefore, mainly in non-administrative spheres of life such as religion, although here it re-

[117] See Broughton, 'Municipal Institutions in Roman Spain', 130 and n. 9.

[118] Cornelius Nepos, *Vita Hannibali* 7. 4: 'ut enim Romae consules, sic Karthagine quotannis annui bini reges creabantur' ('For as at Rome there are consuls, so at Carthage two kings who hold power for a year are created each year'). See A. Dupont-Sommer, 'Une nouvelle inscription punique de Carthage', *CRAI* (1968), 116 ff. for a *stele* from Carthage using a date based on two eponymous *suffetes*. A similar form of dating is found on a *stele* from Pauli Gerrei, *KAI* 66.

[119] M. G. Angeli Bertinelli, 'Roman-Punica Minima', *Atti del I Congresso internazionale di studi fenici e punici 1979* (1983), i. 253 ff. Aristotle, *Pol.* 2. 11, mentions boards of five, pentarchies, at Carthage.

[120] There are some Italian examples of *Xviri*: *ILS* 6649 (from Urbinum), 6586 (Falerii), 6269 (Ferentini), Cicero, *Ad Att.* 10. 13. 1 (Cumae). However, it seems unlikely that this anomaly would have been exported from Italy to the provinces; see P. J. Lacort Navarro *et al.*, 'Nuevas inscripciones latinas de Córdoba y su provincia', *Faventia*, 8/1 (1986), 69 ff., at p. 75 n. 23.

[121] Ibid. 70.   [122] Ibid. 73.

[123] Thouvenot, *Essai sur la province romaine de Bétique*, 220. See also the comments of J. A. Pérez, 'Un caso de pervivencia púnica durante el imperio romano: El municipio bético de Ostippo', *Memorias de historia antigua*, 5 (1981), 95 ff., at p. 96.

mained strong. At the beginning of the imperial period some of the towns on the Mediterranean coast had, according to contemporaries, a Punic rather than a classical appearance. These would definitely have included Gades and Malaca, and since Strabo only mentions Malaca as an aside, it is likely that other towns on this coast, such as Abdera and Sexi, also retained their Phoenician appearance. Abdera certainly, and perhaps other towns, still minted coins with Punic inscriptions and iconography in the Julio-Claudian period. Whether there was any attempt to rebuild these towns in a more classical manner as the imperial period went on is impossible to say, given our lack of archaeological evidence. Such development would depend primarily on whether the upper classes of the towns perceived any benefit in so doing. Some building developments which did occur, such as the *forum* complex at Belo, while being predominantly Roman, still retained some non-Roman features which might suggest a Punic aesthetic. It is possible, especially on the Mediterranean coast, that architects and builders to help with major works would have been hired from Roman Africa and so possessed some Punic aesthetic tastes themselves. Perhaps the most likely solution of the question of these towns' internal morphology is that while they would have been recognizable as towns to a traveller from Italy or Greece, they would always have had a slightly different 'feel' to them.

Despite the above evidence of cultural conservatism it is clear that conscious imitation of Roman customs also occurred in the Punic areas of Baetica. The best examples of this process are to be found in the careers of the Balbi of Gades, the younger Balbus going on to obtain a triumph,[124] and to write a learned work on Roman religious practices.[125] Others among the 500 *equites* of Gades would also have cultivated Roman manners. Philostratus describes the Gaditani as Hellenizers, ἐς τὰ Ἑλλήνων σπεύδουσιν.[126] The context of this remark, designed to point up the ignorance of the rest of the province as to the nature of the Olympic games, suggests that the affectation concerned was for the higher aspects of classical culture in general, rather than simply Greek customs. For the lower classes, however, there would seem little point in changing their way of life as there was nothing to gain by doing so; and it is probably amongst this element, unfortunately the least represented by our evidence, that Punic culture persisted most strongly.

Geographically the remains of Punic culture appear to fall into a distinct section of the province: the Mediterranean coast, the estuary of the

---

[124] Pliny, *NH* 5. 5. 36.   [125] Macrobius, *Sat.* 3. 6. 16.
[126] Philostratus, *Vit. Apol.* 5. 8.

Baetis up to, and around, Hispalis and Italica, and in the foothills and small valleys of Bastetania. A large proportion of this area corresponds, not surprisingly, with the judicial *conventus* of Gades, which may have been drawn up with these cultural regions in mind. Perhaps it is also significant that the *conventus* is outside Untermann's area of the highest density of epigraphic finds.[127] This may indicate a lack of investigation in this area, or alternatively show a reluctance to take up the 'epigraphic habit' by its inhabitants, many of whom may not have been habitual Latin speakers. The area is also, apart from a corridor running up from Malaca to Corduba, lacking in finds of classical sculpture. Again, this may possibly be because of lack of excavations, but it may also be part of an aversion to classical aesthetics. The lack is most noticeable at Gades itself.[128] In general it is easy to see why Agrippa came to his conclusions about the Punic origins of the towns of the southern and Mediterranean coasts of the province in his day, and it is likely that such origins would also have been readily apparent to a visitor some hundred years later.

From the above survey a variety of conclusions can be drawn. The first is that there appears to have been no strategy to enforce changes in cultural behaviour towards a standard norm by the governing power. A converse conclusion can also be drawn—namely that provincial groups perceived no reason to abandon wholesale their own cultural practices in favour of those of Rome. None the less some changes did occur. The political structures of the Punic towns of Baetica seem to conform closely to Roman norms. This may be in part because of the blanket grant of the *ius Latii* made by the Flavian Municipal Law; however, it may also have been thought advantageous to imitate this aspect of Roman life prior to this period, as seems to have been the case at Gades. It is impossible, of course, to ascertain whether such Roman titles were perceived by the local population as making a break with the past or whether they were simply seen as the continuation of older offices under new Latin titles.

Changes also occurred in non-political spheres. The cult activity at Gades and burial practices at Carmo show an intermingling of different traditions creating an end-product which, while owing much to all groups concerned, was distinct from all of them. In this context it is difficult to talk in a meaningful sense of either a process of 'Romanization' or native 'resistance' to Roman cultural patterns. A better term would be that

---

[127] Untermann, *Elementos de un atlas antroponímico de la Hispania antigua*, 18, map B.
[128] Niemeyer, 'Aspectos de la escultura romana de la península ibérica'.

devised by the Cuban sociologist Fernando Ortiz to describe his own society, namely 'transculturation'.[129]

Apart from its Punic population, Baetica also contained indigenous Iberian and Celtic communities. The most well-known piece of evidence for the survival, or otherwise, of the native Iberian culture is the statement of Strabo that the Iberians of Turdetania, especially those living by the Baetis, had become completely Romanized ($\tau\epsilon\lambda\acute{\epsilon}\omega\varsigma$ $\epsilon\grave{\iota}\varsigma$ $\tau\grave{o}\nu$ $P\omega\mu\alpha\acute{\iota}\omega\nu$ $\mu\epsilon\tau\alpha\beta\acute{\epsilon}\beta\lambda\eta\nu\tau\alpha\iota$ $\tau\varrho\acute{o}\pi o\nu$) and had forgotten their own language, and that a group of Iberians had become known as $\tau o\gamma\tilde{\alpha}\tau o\iota$ (toga-wearers) because of the completeness of this process. Most, he adds, had become $\varLambda\alpha\tau\tilde{\iota}\nu o\iota$ and received Roman settlers. $\varLambda\alpha\tau\tilde{\iota}\nu o\iota$ here suggests not a legal status, but a cultural state: that Turdetanians, without being Romans as such, were highly Romanized.[130] Strabo never visited Spain, and is drawing on earlier sources (although some of these, as has been seen above on his discussion of the population of Gades, appear to be contemporary, adding yet another problem to the equation). If he is correct, native culture should already have almost vanished by the beginning of the imperial period.

The passage contrasts oddly, however, with Strabo's comment of only two chapters previously, that the majority of towns in Turdetania were inhabited by Phoenicians.[131] There are a variety of possible solutions to this problem. The first is that Strabo is using more than one source for his account of Turdetania and confusing them. This, in turn, raises the question of why these sources differ. Perhaps distinct areas were covered by Strabo's various sources and so different conclusions were reached about the nature of the area. Alternatively there could be a chronological gap, Roman settlement occurring after the first source was written, but before the second. This does not, however, explain why the Phoenicians are left out of the picture in the later account.

Another answer could be that Strabo is making slightly different statements in each case. In the first of the two passages he says that it is the majority of *poleis* in Turdetania which are inhabited by Phoenicians, whereas nothing is said about the nature of the Turdetanian settlements. Nevertheless he does seem to imply that the Turdetanians lived in towns, noting that one of the reasons that the neighbouring Celts are not as prosperous as the Turdetanians is that they live in villages, $\varkappa\omega\mu\eta\delta\grave{o}\nu$ $\zeta\tilde{\omega}\sigma\iota\nu$, implying that the Turdetanians did not. Nevertheless it could still be argued that Strabo's emphasis on the adoption of Roman manners and the reception of Roman settlers as the main force in civilizing the Iberians,

---

[129] See F. Ortiz, *Contrapunteo cubano entre tabaco y el azucar* (1963).
[130] Strabo, 3. 2. 15.   [131] Ibid. 3. 2. 13.

along with his mention of the three jointly settled *coloniae* as focal points for civilization, implies that it was only after the Romans arrived that the native population became urbanized.

This would leave a picture of Phoenician towns and non-town-dwelling Iberians in the Baetis valley, the latter urbanizing only under Roman pressure. This is unsatisfactory. There is little concrete evidence for Roman mass migration to the province in the republican period (see Chapter 2). Settlement seems to have consisted of a wealthier class of Romans who formed *conventus* in already existing towns, rather than creating new ones on virgin sites. Moreover, our limited archaeological information about the Iberians in this area, supplemented by more extensive information from the Levant and Catalonia, suggests that the Iberians did live in small towns.

A more likely solution is that the areas covered by Strabo's two sources are different, and that this explains their divergence. If the author of one source knew chiefly Gades and the Mediterranean coast, and had travelled only a little up the Baetis valley, he would form the conclusion that the area was mainly inhabited by Phoenicians, and knowing that the area was once ruled by Carthage, draw a general conclusion about the whole of Turdetania from this. There is a hint that this form of deduction has taken place, as the relevant passage states that the people of the area became so utterly subjected to the Phoenicians that the majority of the towns here are inhabited by Phoenicians. A traveller who penetrated further up the Baetis valley might well have formed a different impression of the province, leading to the view of Romanization which we find two chapters further on.

Again, however, it is necessary to see if this second picture is correct. Whoever wrote Strabo's initial source was probably entertained by Roman settlers, and it is likely that he would have come into contact only with Latin-speaking Iberians, probably of the upper classes, or estate workers who knew Latin. The statement that the adoption of Roman customs was particularly marked along the Baetis valley suggests that this was the case, this being where the majority of Roman estates would have been situated. The statement is likely to be a generalization from limited experience of the Baetis valley, and cannot be regarded as a reliable source for the large areas of Baetica, such as Baeturia, which lay outside this area, and perhaps not for the Baetis valley as a whole.

In stark contrast to Strabo, who wishes to give a civilized picture of the province, Philostratus, writing in the third century AD, gives almost the reverse impression, saying that when Nero announced his triple victory at the Olympic games, although his message was understood in Gades, the rest of the province, never having seen a tragedy or a lyre contest, imagined that the emperor had won a victory over a people called the Olympians.[132] Philostratus also notes that the inhabitants of the city of Ipola in Baetica reacted with panic the first time they saw a tragic actor, thinking that he was some form of demon.[133] Ipola cannot be traced apart from Philostratus' account, but the name does not sound unreasonable for the province.

Obviously Philostratus is exaggerating the depth of ignorance shown in Baetica concerning classical customs. It is inconceivable that the *coloniae* of the province would not have understood Nero's decree. This reaction of other smaller cities to it is, however, entirely credible. It could be argued that Philostratus is merely exploiting Baetica as a 'far-away place' to tell exotic stories of, but by the third century AD, the date at which he wrote, this would not have been the case. It is best to see Philostratus' account as a salutary corrective to the enthusiastic accounts of Strabo about the nature of life in Baetica.

One area of the province where Philostratus' account might hold good is the area to the north of Corduba stretching across to the *colonia* of Acci. Extensive work has been carried out on the pre-Roman sites of this area, which shows that the vast majority of them continued in use into the Roman period.[134] These sites, known as 'recintos', have two basic forms. The first is that of a small tower built of Cyclopean masonry, normally measuring approximately 10 × 10 m. Examples of this kind of *recinto* can be found at Las Piedras de Gilicia, La Tejuela, San Nicolas, La Oreja de la Mula, and many other sites. All those listed above, and many more, have traces of occupation well into the imperial period. Unfortunately no systematic excavation has taken place at any of these sites. They may have been used seasonally, but the lack of other settlements in the area concerned, and their highly strategic positions, normally commanding the surrounding countryside, make this unlikely. Their small size suggests that they may have been used as central refuges in times of danger, like the peel towers of northern England. In this case they would probably have had other houses built around them. Unfortunately this will not be known until systematic excavation takes place.

---

[132] Philostratus, *Vit. Apol.* 5. 8.

[133] Ibid. 5. 9.

[134] See F. Valverde y Perales, *Historia de la villa de Baena* (repr. 1982); J. Bernier Luque et al., *Nuevas yacimientos arqueológicos en Córdoba y Jaén* (1981); J. Serrano Carrillo and J. A. Morena López, *Arqueología inédita de Córdoba y Jaén* (1984); J. Fortea Pérez and J. Bernier Lugue, *Recintos y fortificaciones ibéricas de la Bética* (1970).

The second kind of *recinto* is much larger, enclosing an entire hilltop with walling. These walls are not built in the Cyclopean style, but rather are of smaller stones and are reminiscent of the Iberian wall excavated by Engel and Paris at Urso, suggesting that they postdate the earlier structures. Again many show signs of habitation well into the principate.

Cerro del Minguilar provides an interesting example of this second type of *recinto*. Its walls cover an area of *c*.40,000 square metres. Excavations here at the beginning of the twentieth century uncovered four marble statues, comprising three togate males, including a youth wearing a *bulla*, and a seated female; there were also houses with rooms whose walls had been decorated with yellow and black plaster, and whose floors had been hardened with a form of red plaster. Other finds included an 'enormous' building, regarded as a temple by the excavator, traces of lead and ceramic piping, a stone water-channel running for 10 m., three column bases, a large number of pottery fragments, and two large cisterns.

Three of the statues were found on a paved area extending for 18 m. and of unknown depth on which there appeared to be three pedestals for statue bases. This was interpreted by the excavator as a *forum*, which appears a reasonable conjecture.[135] It is clear from the small number of inscriptions found at the site that Cerro del Minguilar was the Roman site of Iponoba, probably the Hippo Nova of Pliny.[136] The ceramic stamps of a P. Rocius Cleantus have been found on the site,[137] a name, which, if not a misspelling of Roscius, suggests a Celtic element in the population. There were some Roman magistracies in the town as the discovery of a dedication by C. Cornelius Fidelis Saturninus, an *Augustalis*, shows.[138] A recently discovered inscription dedicated to the *Genius M.M. Flavi(i) Iponobensis* shows that the site was included in Vespasian's grant of the *ius Latii*.[139]

The site provides us with a fine example of Ortiz's concept of transculturation—the end-product is neither Roman nor Iberian but a result of the intermingling of Roman and non-Roman customs. As can be seen, while there are a substantial number of Roman features present in Iponoba, the site also differs in many respects from the town in the standard classical sense of the word. Its inclusion in Pliny's list of towns of the province serves as a warning that we ought not to assume that all

[135] F. Valverde y Perales, 'Antigüedades de Baena', *BRAH* 40 (1902), 253 ff., *BRAH* 43 (1903), 521 ff., *BRAH* 46 (1905), 167–8.
[136] *CIL* 2. 1638.   [137] *AE* (1983), 535.   [138] *AE* (1904) 81.
[139] A. M. Muñoz Amilibia, 'Excavaciones de Iponoba, novedades arqueológicas', *Segovia: Symposium de arqueologia romana* (1977), 280.

these towns were settlements on the classical model. Moreover its inclusion in the grant of the *ius Latii* shows that the complete adoption of Roman cultural norms was not a necessary qualification for this status.

Other *recintos* also appear to have been recognized 'urban' centres in the imperial period. Cerro de los Infantes, near Pinos Puente, should be identified as the site of the town of Ilurco. The centre of this site was dominated by a large oval cistern whose axes measured 8.5 × 7.9 m. An inscription, sadly undatable, gives the name of one of the town's inhabitants as Urcestar Tascaseceris f.,[140] a native name. Another stone, dating to the second century AD, records that the town's *ordo* (this title again suggests that some Roman features were to be found in the town, although it could be a Latin translation of a native term) gave a burial place to Fabia Broccilla.[141] This name has a Celtic root, suggesting that part of the town's population was Celtic. It is interesting that Fabia's father was called L. Fabius Avitus, a far more Roman-style name. Roman nomenclature may have been perceived to be of more advantage to males than females and the sexes could have received names accordingly. If so, the adoption of Roman names in this area cannot be seen as a wholehearted embrace of Roman customs, but rather as cultural imitation limited to those circumstances where it was perceived as advantageous.

Despite its somewhat non-Roman appearance, Ilurco appears to have had magistrates with Roman titles, as well as an *ordo*. A *duovir* called P. Cornelius Callicus, and described as an *Ilurconensis*, is attested at a site near Granada.[142] This combination of a predominantly native site with Roman legal terminology is an example of the accommodation of Roman forms to native circumstances dubbed *interpretatio peregrina* by Galsterer and discussed at length in Chapter 6.

Another *recinto* occupied in the imperial period was Torreparedones, dominating the Guadajoz valley, an important route to the south. Its walls enclosed an area of 108,000 square metres, enough to hold some 800 houses. They are of the same type as at Urso and have traces of similar semicircular bastions. Inside the circuit is a *recinto* of the older style, perhaps used as a strong point and showing the expansion of the community concerned. Fragments of Roman pottery, part of a marble cornice, and traces of water piping have also been found within the walls along with a sanctuary which yielded twenty-five undated crude stone figures. The most interesting aspect of the site is the presence of the mausoleum of the Pompeii family, found within the walls at El Cortijo de los Vir-

---

[140] *CIL* 2. 2067.   [141] *CIL* 2. 2064.   [142] *NAH* 10–12 (1966–8), 275.

genes. This contained twelve inscriptions, of which only three do not show signs of native nomenclature.[143] The style of lettering dates the inscriptions to the Augustan period. Among those interred were M. Pompeius Q. fil. Gal. Ictsnis, the first of the family to become a *duovir*,[144] Cn. Pompeius Cn. fil. Gal. Afer, aedile and *duovir*,[145] Q. Pompeius Q.f. Velaunis,[146] Ildrons Velaunis f.,[147] and Igalchis Idrons f.[148]

These inscriptions are notable for several reasons. First, the names of the two office-holders include a tribal affiliation, showing them to have been Roman citizens, on their epitaphs. This hints that Torreparedones was one of the towns which Pliny records as having old Latin rights. In support of this is the strategic position commanded by the site. It would have been well worth while for the central authorities to placate the leaders of this community. If this is the case, the nature of the site shows that the adoption of Roman customs was not a criterion for such a grant. The second point of interest is that although Afer has a completely Roman name, there does not seem to be any attempt in general to adopt Roman nomenclature. Ildrons is probably the son of Q. Pompeius Velaunis, and Igalchis his son. Here we see a move away from a semi-Romanized name to fully native ones. It is possible that Roman-style names were adopted only if they became necessary and that otherwise native nomenclature was retained. If Ildrons and Igalchis died young there would have been no need for them to adopt Latin names. In contrast to these completely native male names, the three female names, Pompeia Q.f. Nanna,[149] Iunia L.f. Insghana,[150] and Fabia M.f. Aninna,[151] are all semi-Roman while retaining native elements. It has often been asserted that the Punic name Hanno is attested here by breaking the inscription Seseanbahan Nonis f.[152] at the 'h' in the preceding name. However, 'Nonis f.' is carved on a separate line and there is no good reason for this amendment.

Whilst the most well known, these three *recintos* are by no means the only examples in the area. At Torre Alta an area of *c.*10,000 square metres is enclosed. A cistern is again a major feature of the site. In the centre of the enclosed area huts measuring 2 × 1.6 m. had been cut down into the living rock to the depth of 0.6 m. Pottery attests occupation in the imperial period, as do finds of coins struck at Emerita in the reign of Tiberius. At El Salobrar the area enclosed is 8 hectares, and the centre is occupied by

---

[143] *CIL* 2. 1585–96. The location of the mausoleum seems in breach of the general Roman practice of forbidding burial within a city and raises the question of the status of the walled enclosure in the Roman period.

[144] *CIL* 2. 1585. [145] *CIL* 2. 1596. [146] *CIL* 2. 1589. [147] *CIL* 2. 1590.
[148] *CIL* 2. 1591. [149] *CIL* 2. 1588. [150] *CIL* 2. 1593. [151] *CIL* 2. 1586.
[152] *CIL* 2. 1594.

a cistern of *opus caementicum* measuring 11.5 × 5 × 3 m., closely resembling those found by the Baetis at Carchena, which date from the early principate. A *sestertius* from the Julio-Claudian period has been found, along with pottery dating from the Iberian to the Arabic period. Other similar sites include Cerro de Sta María (30 hectares), La Camora (10 hectares), Cerro Boyero (16 hectares), and Plaza de Armas (10 hectares). It is important to realize that settlements of these sizes were comparable to those of the more southerly parts of Baetica. Carmo was 47 hectares in size, but more typical are Ostippo at *c*.13.5 hectares and Ilipa at 12.6 hectares.

It appears, therefore, that life in this northern area of the province was very different from that in the Baetis valley. Settlements remained on dominant hilltop positions and retained many native features. Although the town magistrates were referred to in Roman terms, native nomenclature also persisted. There seems to have been no pressure by Rome to change this style of life, and following the grant of *Latinitas* such settlements received a status equal to that of the more conventional lowland towns, as the case of Iponoba shows.

This form of settlement continued to exist throughout the imperial Roman period and beyond. The Arabic geographer, al-Idrisi, when describing the region in his own day, notes that there were many fortified places, which resembled towns and were well provisioned.[153] This is a perfect description of the type of *recinto* described above, several of which have yielded Arabic pottery sherds.

The *recinto*-type culture may also have persisted in other parts of the province. The town of Lacipo, in the hills of Bastetania, was surrounded by Cyclopean walls and commanded the entrance to the Guadiaro valley. Q. Fabius Varus, the *quinquevir* and *pontifex* of the town, dedicated a *hypaetrum* to Augustus here.[154] The dedication is probably Tiberian in date. The date of the inscription suggests that the office of *quinquevir*, if it is not merely a stonecutter's error for *quattuorvir*,[155] may be an anomalous native magistracy, like the *decemviri* of Cartima, Ostippo, and La Rambla discussed above. The work of López Palomo has shown that *recintos* were

---

[153] Al-Idrisi, *Description de l'Afrique et de l'Espagne*, trans. R. P. A. Dozy and M. J. De Goeje (2nd edn., 1969), ch. 203.

[154] R. Puertas Tricas, 'Nuevo epigrafe monumental de Lacipo', *Mainake*, 1 (1979), 99 ff.

[155] The view of R. Étienne, 'Culte impérial et architecture à propos d'une inscription de Lacipo (Bétique)', *ZPE* 43 (1981), 135 ff. However, see J. González, 'Un *Vvir* de Lacipo/Casares (Málaga)', *Actas del 1 Congreso andaluz de estudios clásicos* (1982), 223 ff., for a defence of Puertas Tricas's reading.

also occupied on the higher slopes of the Singilis valley in the imperial period.[156]

Towns in the areas of the province away from the Baetis valley which were not hilltop sites also show the persistence of native culture. At Epora a Flavian inscription records a Calpurnia L.l. Uprenna and a Fulcinia L.f. Attunna.[157] The inscription is of especial interest, as not only is the name of Lucius' freedwoman Iberian, but so is that of his daughter, showing that cultural survival was not just a phenomenon in the lowest classes of society, but also occurred among those wealthy enough to own slaves. It is possible that the male name here can be restored as Lucius Calpurnius Fulcinius. If so, his daughter's name shows a 'regression' to native nomenclature, or that Roman names were embraced only for reasons of social advantage. In the latter case it would not be necessary for Lucius' daughter to have a fully Roman name and its absence here perhaps shows that such names were adopted only reluctantly. A *flamen Augustalis* from the same town, dated by his tomb to the late first or early second century, also has a semi-Iberian name, P. Attenius Afer.[158] At Urgavo, a *duovir* of the town was called M. Horatius Bodonilu and his wife Lucretia Sergeton, again an indication of the persistence of native culture among the upper classes.[159]

At Igabrum, an inscription records a dedication to the Domina Daeva, a goddess of Celtic origin, by Valeria Comse.[160] At Ipagrum an inscription has been found reading, 'Ceturgi mater p(osuit) anorum L PIS STTL DMS'.[161] Ceturgis is a Celtic name, and the misspelling of 'annorum' and the placing of the formula DMS at the end rather than at the beginning of the inscription, suggest that the stonecutter concerned was not at home in the classical milieu, and may merely have been copying out by rote, not understanding what he was carving.

At Iliturgi, there is a large cistern in the town, which appears to be a typical Iberian feature.[162] In addition two triangular blocks have been found, dating to the mid- or late second century AD, carved with a gorgon's head, the treatment of which is Celtic in style.[163] Another set

[156] L. A. López Palomo, 'Testimonios de la iberización al sur de Córdoba y Sevilla', *16 CNA* (1983), 795–800.

[157] *CIL* 2. 2160.   [158] *CIL* 2. 2159.   [159] *CIL* 2. 2114 = *AE* (1965), 90.

[160] *AE* (1983), 541.   [161] *ILER* 4261.

[162] See the examples discussed above and the cistern found at Ullastret, M. Aurora Martin Ortega, *Ullastret, Poblat Iberic* (1985), 20–1.

[163] L. Baena del Alcázar, 'Esculturas de Mengibar', *BSAA* 48 (1982), 111–20.

of reliefs from the town has a funerary context, with two *erotes* flanking a garland of acanthus leaves containing various fruits. The treatment of the *erotes*, especially their facial features, is more reminiscent of Iberian than of classical sculpture.[164] These date to the late second or early third century AD. The area in general has yielded a series of reliefs, the most famous being the 'mining' relief from Linares, which, while dealing with classical subjects, or subjects which would be regarded as suitable for sculpture, are worked to native aesthetic standards. These include the 'Oxherd' of Castulo, the 'Athlete' of Bobadilla de Alcaudete and the 'Heracles' of Alcala la Real.[165] At Torredonjimeno, a Bacchant's head has been found where the facial treatment is Iberian in inspiration along with a 'Nemesis' in marble which is Celtic in style.[166]

The presence of these sculptures shows that classical tastes did not entirely oust native aesthetics in this part of the province. Although the subjects treated are classical, there is still either a desire to render them in a native way, or perhaps an inability to do otherwise. The region is lacking in finds of classical sculpture and lies outside Untermann's area of the densest inscription finds.

At the mining town of Sisapo there is a sharp break in the styles of living found on the two hills of the 10-hectare site. On one hill ashlar masonry and traces of Roman pottery have been found, whereas on the other round huts were still being occupied. The most likely explanation for this divide is that one hill was occupied by the Roman overseers of the mine and the other by the native workforce.[167] Native nomenclature persisted here, as is shown by an inscription of the *socii Sisaponenses* found at Capua, where the *vilicus* of the *societas* has the Iberian name Epapra.[168] At the mines of Rio Tinto and the associated village of Nerva, a similar lack of Roman cultural life is found. Inscriptions from the site are cut extremely poorly, while the miners attested have native names, such as Boutimandus,[169] which use Celtic forms of filiation. In one case a child, L. Helvius Lupus, takes his name from his mother, Helvia Secundilla, rather than from his father, Probus. This may indicate the persistence of a Celtic

---

[164] L. Baena del Alcázar, 'Esculturas de Mengibar', *BSAA* 48 (1982), 111–18.

[165] L. Baena del Alcázar, 'Consderaciones sobre la escultura romana de la provincia de Jaén', *Actas del I Congreso andaluz de estudios clásicos* (1982), 137 ff.

[166] E. Romero da Torres, 'Inscripciones inéditas de Alcaudete y Torredonjimeno en la provincia de Jaén', *BRAH* 65 (1914), 624–8.

[167] Sillières, 'Sisapo: Prospections et découvertes'.

[168] *Socii Sisaponenses*: Pliny, *NH* 33. 7. 118; Epapra: *CIL* 10. 3964.

[169] Almagro Basch, *Huelva: Prehistoria y antigüedad*, no. 5, p. 284.

form of filiation.[170] This practice also appears at Andevalo, where an individual named Avelliun (a native ending, or an engraver's error for -*ium*) Acallae is recorded.[171] Two Celtic heads of a horned deity, carved in a Celtic style, have also been found at the site, but it is impossible to date them securely.[172]

Evidence for the continuation of the Celtic cult of the head is also found at Arucci, where two Celtic-style heads have been found carved into architectural elements, one of which appears to date from the second century AD.[173] A further sign of Celtic religion can be found at Pozoblanco (Cordoba) where a dedication to the Celtic deities, the Louci Iuteri, was recovered.[174] The presence of these heads and other vestiges of Celtic religion noted above lead us to a general consideration of religious practice in the province. It has been frequently asserted that the native religion of Baetica, unlike that of the Punic community, quickly died out in the Roman period. It is true that the region has not yielded anything like the same number of inscriptions to native gods as has, for example, the north-west of Spain. The situation may not, however, be as clear cut as this suggests. Two problems immediately present themselves. One is that this assumption avoids the problems raised by syncretism. It is not certain that if a provincial made a dedication to a classical god in Latin he was necessarily thinking of the god in his classical form. Other pressures may have been at work; it could, for example, have been regarded as socially advantageous to address the god in Latin, and consequently with his Latin title.

The other, more serious, problem concerns the nature of Iberian religious practices in this part of Spain. These are described by Strabo when he discusses the ceremonies that were performed at the 'Sacred Cape'. There was no temple at the Sacred Cape, but only stones in groups of three or four which were turned in some way ($\sigma\tau\rho\acute{\epsilon}\varphi\epsilon\sigma\theta\alpha\iota$); a libation was poured, and the stones were moved back ($\mu\epsilon\tau\alpha\varphi\acute{\epsilon}\rho\epsilon\sigma\theta\alpha\iota$).[175] Presumably the sense here is that a stone was moved, a libation was poured beneath it, and the stone was returned to its original position. If this is a description

---

[170] *AE* (1965), 298: 'L. Helvius Lupus Emeritensis mens. VIII HSE STTL. Fac. c(uraverunt) Helvia Secundilla m(ater) et Probus pat(e)r'.

[171] Almagro Basch, *Huelva: Prehistoria y antigüedad*, no. 4, p. 284.

[172] A. Blanco Freijeiro, 'Antigüedades de Rio Tinto', *Zephyrus*, 13 (1962), 31–45. Blanco associates the heads with the god Vestius Aloniecus, found in Galicia. However, horned gods are found all over the Celtic world, so this connection is not secure; see A. Ross, *Pagan Celtic Britain* (1967), ch. 3, 'The Horned God in Britain', for a general survey.

[173] Almagro Basch, *Huelva: Prehistoria y antigüedad*, 305–6.

[174] *CIL* 2. 2849.   [175] Strabo, 3. 1. 4.

of the form Iberian rites normally took, it would be impossible to detect them even if they continued into the imperial period.[176]

The native god Neto is attested as being worshipped in the late imperial period at Acci, a *colonia* which originally lay in the far west of the province but was later transferred to the province of Tarraconensis, by the colonists there.[177] The form of the god's image was said to be like that of Mars with a radiate crown. Neto is also attested at Conimbriga in Lusitania.[178] A bust of the god has been found at Iptucci in Baetica,[179] and another bust with a radiate crown found by Engel and Paris at Urso may be a second depiction of this god.

A more important native deity in Baetica was the goddess Ataecina, who is often given the epithet Turobrigensis.[180] Turobriga is listed by Pliny as a town in Celtic Baeturia in the north of Baetica.[181] Apart from this notice in Pliny, the only other reference to Turobriga is from Arucci, where Baebia Crinita is described as a *sacerdos Turobrigensis*.[182] It has been suggested that this means 'priestess of [the goddess Ataecina] Turobrigensis', attesting worship outside the cult's centre, but a more natural reading is 'priestess of Turobriga', indicating a normal civic office. Over a dozen dedications to the goddess are known, mainly from the area between the Baetis and the Tagus. Many of these are from Lusitania, which suggests that the northern areas of Baetica looked towards this province as much as towards the Baetis valley. The present inscriptions need not mean that the goddess was of no importance in Baetica, as Turobriga has not yet been located. It is likely that a large number of inscriptions to the goddess would be found if her shrine was located (this is certainly the case with another Iberian deity Endovellicus, the majority of dedications to whom come from his sanctuary at San Miguel da Mota). The goddess received a civic dedication from Ulia at Cabeza del Griego. The relevant inscription reads 'Dominae S(acrum) Tur(ibrigensi) A(taecinae) Ul(i)enses ara posuerunt ex v(oto)' ('Sacred to our Mistress of Turobriga Ataecina. The people of Ulia set up this altar in accordance with their vow').[183] This implies that the goddess was regarded as of sufficient importance to be honoured by a city away from its own territory.

---

[176] It is significant in this respect that the most completely excavated Iberian sites show no sign of temple buildings. See J. Pou, J. Sanmartí, and J. Santacana, *The Iberian Citadel of Calafell* (1993).

[177] Macrobius, *Sat.* 1. 19. 5.   [178] *CIL* 2. 365.   [179] *BRAH* 30, p. 285.

[180] e.g. *CIL* 2. 462, *ILER* 732. For a full discussion of Ataecina, see R. López Melero, 'Nueva evidencia sobre el culto de Ategina: El epigrafe de Bienvenida', C. Chaparro Gómez (ed.), *Manifestaciones religiosas en la Lusitania* (1986), 98 ff.

[181] Pliny, *NH* 3. 14.   [182] *CIL* 2. 964 = *ILER* 1760.   [183] *CIL* 2. 5877.

The inscription suggests that there was a shrine to the goddess at Cabeza del Griego, but no trace of such a sanctuary has been found, perhaps because of the lack of substantial buildings at these sites, as mentioned above. At both Cerro de los Santos and San Miguel da Mota the actual temple buildings of the sanctuary are remarkably small, given the number of votive offerings found. A possible representation of the goddess has been found on a pottery sherd from Castulo; if the identification is correct, it again shows that Ataecina commanded devotion well away from her home area.[184] The nature of the goddess is not known. It has been suggested that the root 'AT-' is linked with 'ater', and that Ataecina should therefore be a chthonic deity. In support of this is the fact that one of the inscriptions is a *defixio* for theft.[185] If this assumption is correct, another shrine of the goddess may have been recorded by Avienus, who states: 'iugum inde rursus et sacrum infernae deae divesque fanum, penetral abstrusi cavi adytumque caecum' ('thence we reach the holy hill of the goddess of the underworld and her wealthy shrine, it lies in the innermost place of a hidden cave, a sanctuary devoid of light'). Schulten believes that Avienus is referring to Ataecina here, and locates the site of the sanctuary at La Rábida by Onuba on the Atlantic coast of the province.[186] An inscription from Sardinia has been interpreted as reading 'D(eae) S(acrum) A(taecinae) T(urobrigensi)' ('dedicated to the goddess Ataecina of Turobriga').[187] This, if true, implies that Ataecina was worshipped beyond Baeturia, the dedication probably being made by Spanish sailors *en route* to Italy or Africa.

Another native god whose cult seems to have persisted into the imperial period is 'Andebalo'. Ceán Bermúdez reports that on a hill called the Cerro Andebalo he found a temple dedicated to this god. The hill is close to the modern village of Cabezas Rubrias, normally linked with the Ad Rubrias of the *Antonine Itinerary*. The site is again in Baeturia. The god concerned could be a version of Endovellicus, but the distance from that god's main shrine may rule this out. In general, interpretation is difficult as there has been no attempt to follow up Ceán Bermúdez's claims.[188]

[184] A. Blanco Freijeiro, 'Un interesante fragmento ceramico en el museo arqueologico de Linares', *Oretania*, 8–9 (1961), 93–5.

[185] H. Balmori, 'Ataecina, Adaegina', *Emerita*, 3 (1935), 214–24, *CIL* 2. 462.

[186] Avienus, *Ora Maritima* 241 ff., with A. Schulten, *FHA* 1 (1922), 91 f. See also G. Bonsor, 'Tartessos', *BRAH* 79 (1921), 57 ff.

[187] A. Balil, 'En torno a las relaciones de Cerdaña e Hispania en la época romana', *Studi Sardi*, 14/15 (2) (1955/7), 130–3; *CIL* 10. 2. 7557.

[188] J. A. Ceán Bermúdez, *Sumario de las antigüedades romanas que hay en España* (1832), 260.

At Nescania, there is a dedication to the god Sciyvita.[189] No parallels to this god have been found, and it is best to assume that he was a local Iberian deity. It is noteworthy that Nescania was situated in the mountains of Bastetania, away from the Baetis valley. The occurrence of the *Domina Daeva* in the north-west of the province has already been mentioned.

Another form of Iberian cult which continued into the Roman period was that connected with worship at caves.[190] At Cueva del Valle, 6 km. to the east of Zalamea de la Serena, are traces of a cave where, judging by deposits of pottery, cult activity continued well into the imperial period.[191] This form of worship can be paralleled by the cult of Fortuna practised until the late empire in the Cueva Negra in Murcia (Tarraconensis).[192]

It can be seen, therefore, that there are fewer dedications to native gods in Baetica than elsewhere in Spain. These dedications increase considerably outside the Baetis valley, suggesting that the pull of the old gods was considerably stronger in these areas, although it must be remembered that Iberian worship appears to have been so ephemeral in its rites that continuing practices elsewhere could easily have been overlooked or have left no trace in the archaeological record.

In Baeturia, an area comprising over a third of the province's total land area, the cult of the local goddess Ataecina appears to have remained strong, judging by the spread of dedications already known. The discovery of the site of her centre of worship, Turobriga, would probably confirm this view even more substantially. As has been seen, several sites in this area have also yielded evidence of a persistence of Celtic religious practices. Apart from this evidence of continuing native cults, Baeturia in general seems to have adopted considerably fewer Roman customs than the lowland areas of the Baetis valley to its south. It is lacking in Roman buildings, has yielded little classical sculpture, and is away from Untermann's area of densest finds of inscriptions.

In this it is paralleled by Bastetania, the mountainous area to the south of the Baetis valley. Here we also find a lack of Roman buildings, statuary, and inscriptions. These hints that the area was not strongly affected by Roman culture are supported by the strange god of Nescania discussed above. Strabo, too, confirms this view in his account of the region in which

[189] *CIL* 2. 5491.

[190] J. M. Blázquez, *Primitivas religiones Ibéricas* (1983), ii. 204–6.

[191] A. García y Bellido and J. Menéndez Pidal, *El distylo sepulcral romano de Iulipa (Zalamea)*, in *Anejos del Archivo español de arqueologia*, 3 (1963).

[192] A. González Blanco *et al.*, *La cueva negra de Fortuna (Murcia) y sus tituli picti* (1987).

the Bastetanians are regarded as being similar to the other hill-dwellers of Spain.[193] The walls of Acinippo, the major town of the region, which does show signs of extensive adoption of Roman practices, appear to have been built in the same style as the Iberian wall at Urso, suggesting that the town was a native site at the beginning of the imperial period and gradually developed its Roman features when the aristocracy of the town saw the advantages of doing so. The town of Sabora, in the same region, remained a hilltop site until the reign of Vespasian,[194] and so did Lacipo and Iliberris throughout the Roman period.

In contrast to these two areas, the Baetis valley would have presented a picture of an area much more at home with the Roman way of life. It is here that epigraphic finds are densest, and that the greater part of the province's classical statuary has been found. The reason for this contrast lies in the fact that the valley was the most fertile part of the province, and the area from which its wealth was derived. Accordingly it attracted the majority of Roman settlers, not only in the form of town life, but also in the establishment of *villae*. This area of the province consequently contained the highest number of Romans and enjoyed the greatest amount of contact with Roman culture. This contact would have been increased by the fact that it was this area which exported olive oil to Rome, and so would have had the strongest links with the empire at large. These links were thus not to an area of a predominantly similar culture, as were the links of the Mediterranean coast to Roman Africa. The pressure for the local aristocracy in this area to modify their way of life, and so seem to be part of the ruling élite of society—hence worthy of respect to the lower classes of Iberians, and at the same time 'civilized' and acceptable in the Roman society which they endeavoured to join—would consequently have been far stronger than in the other regions of the province. In these regions there was much less settlement, and no equivalent to the olive-oil trade. Consequently there was less contact with Roman culture, and its imitation did not offer the same social advantages, with the result that the incentive to abandon ancestral customs was far weaker.

The process of change was, nevertheless, a gradual one even in the Baetis valley. At Munigua, Iberian-style settlement persisted until the building of the major sanctuary in the Flavian period. An Iberian god may have continued to have been worshipped in some form after this, if the

---

[193] Strabo, 3. 3. 7. One possible problem here is Strabo's tendency to use geography as a measure of civilization. See P. Thollard, *Barbarie et civilisation chez Strabon* (1987). It could be argued that as Strabo never visited the region he is merely theorizing here.

[194] *CIL* 2. 1423 = *ILS* 6092.

small shrine to *Dis Pater* found in the *forum* here is, as its excavator thinks, that of a syncretized Iberian deity.[195] At Corduba a carved ship's prow, while classically conceived, has its *proembolium* carved in the form of an Iberian lion. Given the nature of the rest of the carving, this seems to have been from deliberate choice, rather than lack of ability.[196] At Belo, half of the column capitals in the Claudian *basilica* are carved in a native interpretation of the Corinthian order. This may have been due to lack of ability, but it is difficult to explain, if so, why the other seven capitals of the *basilica* are standard Corinthian capitals. At Carteia, a major building, dating, probably, to the early imperial period, incorporates kneeling bulls into its capitals. The bull was a common animal on Iberian monuments, and its incorporation here should be seen as a continuation of this tradition.

A study of nomenclature also shows that initially at least some Iberians were reluctant to abandon their traditional names. At Ilipa an inscription, dated by Étienne to the Augustan period, records an Urchail Attita f. Chilasurgun, who built, or restored, the town gates.[197] The expenditure involved indicates that Urchail would have been a member of the town's aristocracy. At Nebrissa a dedication firmly dated to the Claudian period was made by Terpulia Sauni f. in accordance with the will of her husband, Albans Sunna.[198] Above the inscription is a carving of Atlas holding up a globe. This carving is classical in conception, and the ability to commission such a work shows that those concerned were reasonably wealthy. The whole piece indicates a middle stage in cultural adaptation where the advantages of change were not yet firm enough to ensure a total adoption of classical customs. Such nomenclature does die out, however, with the passage of time, and most aristocrats have entirely Roman names. Others such as L. Attius Vetto, *duovir* and *flamen* of Canama, have Romanized their names (in this case the stem Att-) to such a degree that they are perfectly acceptable Latin.[199]

It is, however, unwise to concentrate too strongly on the upper classes of the area. Terracottas found at Corduba, and around the Hispalis region, show that popular art was less affected by Rome, and that native art-forms continued to persist. In nomenclature, too, native forms continue. At Carmo, an Ugao (cf. the town name, Ugia) occurs,[200] and the native name

---

[195] W. Grünhagen, 'El monumento a Dis Pater de Munigua', 201–8. Perhaps the deity concerned was the same as that worshipped at the Iberian shrine of Cigarralejo (Mula, Murcia), where 175 votive statuettes of horses have been found (see Harrison, *Spain at the Dawn of History*, 130 and figs. 82–3).

[196] Blanco Freijeiro, 'Vestigios de Córdoba romana', 109–23.

[197] *CIL* 2. 1087.   [198] *CIL* 2. 1302.   [199] *CIL* 2. 1074.   [200] *CIL* 2. 1383.

Attita is found on pottery stamps;[201] at Italica the Iberian name Acci Odon f. is attested,[202] along with Celtic names such as Brita.[203] This name is also found at Jimenez de la Frontera.[204] At Corduba an L. Cornelius Caranto is attested,[205] along with Celtic names such as Sentia Mapalia.[206] At nearby Carbula a further Celtic name, L. Alius Cloutius, is found.[207] A Susinna is known at Astigi.[208] There are two attestations of the female Iberian name Attenia at Ilipa.[209] At Hispalis, the Iberian names Agria Matuna[210] and Viria (cf. Viriatus) Severa[211] are recorded. At Morón (ancient name un-known) the related name Avircia is attested,[212] along with a further Celtic name, Abascantus.[213] At Marchena the name Spalia, which should be connected with the root forming the names of the towns Spalis and Hispalis, appears.[214]

The stones on which these names are recorded tend to be modest, indicating that their owners were not in the higher echelons of society. From them we can conjecture that the use of native nomenclature also persisted amongst the poorest elements of society who were unable to pay for memorials of stone. Such nomenclature appears to have carried on in use throughout the Roman period, as occasional Iberian names appear on early Christian inscriptions of the late imperial/Visigothic period. Among these are Ikillio (cf. Icieus[215] also attested here),[216] and Acantia (cf. Aecantus) of Corduba,[217] Istorna from Salpensa, [218] and Trebtes (cf. Trepte at Tarraco[219] and Trette from Emerita[220]) from Morón.[221]

Some forms of native burial customs also seem to have survived. At the necropolis at Carmo, as well as Punic rock-cut tombs, there are cremation burials in an inner trench cut into the centre of a larger trench, the inner trench being covered with flagstones or tiles. This form of burial predates the Roman period and is found at many Iron Age sites in the region such as that at Acebuchal. Such burials also appear to have continued in the imperial period at the necropolis of Setefilla. In addition, five large circular tumuli, dating from the imperial period, have been found in the necropolis; this form of burial also predates the Roman period, as graves from Tutugi show.

On a smaller scale, native forms of funeral *stelae* also persisted into the imperial period. At Jerez de los Caballeros the grave of a legionary soldier,

[201] *EE* 8. 95; the name is also found at Ilipa, *CIL* 2. 1087.   [202] *EE* 9. 202.
[203] *BRAH* 72 (1918), 178.   [204] *CIL* 2. 1335.   [205] *CIL* 2. 2286.
[206] *CIL* 2. 5537.   [207] *CIL* 2. 2323.   [208] *BRAH* 21 (1892), 352.
[209] *CIL* 2. 1092, *CIL* 2. 1100.   [210] *CIL* 2. 1209.   [211] *CIL* 2. 1250.
[212] *ILER* 6016.   [213] *CIL* 2. 2248b.   [214] *CIL* 2. 1402.   [215] *CIL* 2. 2317.
[216] *BRAH* 65 (1914), 557.   [217] *ICERV* 165.   [218] Ibid. 130.
[219] Ibid. 333b.   [220] *ILER* 6205.   [221] *ICERV* 148.

M. Aurelius Abbicus, has been found. Not only had Abbicus preserved a Celtic name despite serving in the legions, but his long, thin tombstone owes more to native tradition than Roman custom, showing that the Roman army was not as powerful an agent of Romanization as is sometimes thought.[222]

Another form of native *stele* which survived was rounded at the top, often displaying a rosette in the *tympanum* so formed. Large numbers are to be found in central and north-west Spain. Four examples have been found at Astigi,[223] two at Ostippo, both of freedwomen,[224] one at Urso, also of a freedwoman,[225] one at Hasta Regia, with the native name Cultronia,[226] and seven in Sabora.[227]

At Belo many of the tombs in the necropolis have small, crude busts, know locally as *munecos*, in front of them. The only parallel for this practice is at the Iberian village of Taratrado, destroyed in the fourth century BC. Some, but not all, of the *munecos* have painted noses, eyes, and mouths. The majority are turned to face the sea. Some appear before tombs whose occupants' names suggest that they were of Punic or Iberian stock, for example tomb 814, that of L. Siscinius Honoratus and his wife, Siscinia Novata, and tomb 351, belonging to M. Sempronius Saturninus. Others, however, appear before tombs whose occupants had completely Roman names, for example, tomb 523, that of L. Annius Plautus. This practice continued well into the imperial period. Saturninus' tomb can be dated to the reign of Marcus Aurelius and that of Plautinus to the reign of Hadrian. Given the generally Roman appearance of Belo at this time, the survival of this practice is a good example of the partial and selective nature of cultural change and intermixture in the province.

Other forms of native organization may also have survived to a degree greater than our epigraphic record might suggest. At Arva we find an inscription, dating from the reign of Trajan, which records a dedication by the *centuriae* Ores, Manens, Halos, Erques, Beres, Arvaberes, Isines, and Isurgut to their *patronus* and *pontifex*, Q. Fulvius Carisianus.[228] This is the only attestation of organization by *centuriae* in Baetica, and so there

---

[222] *AE* (1980), 562, picture in M. L. Albertos Firmat, 'Un soldado de la legión décima', *BSAA* 46 (1980), 201–5; pre-Roman examples are displayed in Caceres and Badajoz archaeological museums.

[223] e.g. *AE* (1978), 406 and the remarks of P. Rodríguez Oliva and R. Atencia Páez, 'Estelas Saborenses', *BSAA* 49 (1983), 152 n. 2.

[224] *CIL* 2. 1449, 1458.　　　[225] *AE* (1978), 417.　　　[226] *IRPC* 34.

[227] Rodríguez Oliva and Atencia Páez, 'Estelas Saborenses', 151 ff.

[228] *CIL* 2. 1064.

must be a question as to what is meant by this term. Nevertheless the *centuria* was a common form of social organization in the north-west Spain,[229] which suggests that here we have evidence of the persistence of native forms of organization. Such a hypothesis is supported by the fact that the names of the *centuriae* here are entirely Iberian, suggesting that the social groupings which they represented were also native. That Caris-ianus was styled the priest as well as the patron of the *centuriae* suggests that these groups still had some social validity, and were not merely an administrative convenience. Arva was situated on the banks of the Baetis in the centre of the olive-oil producing region, and the persistence of such groups here at such a relatively late date suggests that Iberian structures were still important to many in the province. The upper classes' relation-ship with the lower orders of society may have remained defined in terms of Iberian and not Roman status-groups. This phenomenon has existed in many modern colonial societies where the upper classes, while adopting the customs of the colonial power to try to gain access to the ruling group, are still linked by traditional ties to the rest of their society. This hypoth-esis of a Iberian 'countryside' in Baetica is strengthened by the fact that Iberian-style grain silos were used throughout the Roman period, and various measurements of land were known by Iberian terms. Varro records that land-measurement in the area was recorded by the *iugum*, rather than the Roman *iugerum*, in his day,[230] and writing at the end of antiquity Isidore tells us that the non-Roman terms 'arapennis' and 'porca' were given to areas 120 × 120 feet and 830 × 830 feet respective-ly.[231] The fact that Isidore is familiar with such vocabulary suggests that it was in use throughout the Roman period.

In conclusion therefore we can see that separate areas in Baetica dif-fered radically in the degree of Roman culture that they adopted. There would have a sharp contrast between the towns of the upland areas of the north and north-west of the province and Bastetania, and those of the Baetis valley. In the former areas towns would have been fewer in number and more widely dispersed, and many of those that did exist here would not have conformed in many ways to the criteria normally accepted as defining a classical town. All would have lacked the decoration commonly found in such towns, or have rendered it in a native way. It is possible that in these areas Celtic, and Iberian, continued as living tongues. Tacitus notes that the Termestinienses of central Spain still used their native

---

[229] Tranoy, *La Galice romaine*, 371 ff., although see contra M. L. Albertos Firmat, *Organ-izaciones suprafamiliares en la Hispania antigua* (1975), 63 ff.
[230] Varro, *RR* 1. 10.   [231] Isidore, *Etym.* 15. 15. 4, 15. 15. 6.

tongue in the reign of Tiberius,[232] and Eutropius, a sixth-century priest of Valencia, suggests that native languages were continuing in use in his area.[233]

On the Mediterranean coast of the province another set of distinctive towns was to be found. These would have been more familiar in appearance to a visitor from Rome, but might well have still retained a 'feel' of otherness in the way they were laid out. Some religious practices found in them would not have been those of Rome, although it must be added that this would not have caused any great surprise or concern. Perhaps more surprising would have been the general lack of classical works of art. It is conceivable that Punic would be spoken as well as Latin in towns such as Gades. This must have been the case in Abdera in the Julio-Claudian period. The Baetis valley would have seemed the most familiar area of the province, with many towns having Roman-style public buildings and some being laid out on grid patterns. The aristocracy would have had Roman names and spoken Latin. Nevertheless the towns of the area would still have had some noticeable anomalies. Their size was generally small and many, when they were not by the river itself, would have still been hilltop sites. It is likely that the impression of a high degree of absorption of Roman culture would have disappeared in the countryside and may well have been weaker in the lower-class areas of the towns themselves.

The survey above also suggests that the adoption of Roman customs was a 'bottom-up' rather than a 'top-down' phenomenon where the ruled rather than the ruling power were the driving force in conscious cultural change. 'Romanization' therefore is best seen not as a policy of the Roman authorities, but rather as the product of disparate acts of imitation pursued for self-advantage by the provincial communities themselves. The level of such imitation varied with the amount of gain perceived. Hence Roman nomenclature was embraced by the upper classes and Roman-style public works were built where those concerned saw a chance of being assimilated into a higher social group, with the possible advantages to be gained from this. Other areas upon which Rome did not place great emphasis, such as religion, frequently continued as before or exhibited a mixture of Roman and non-Roman practice. At this point we have no method of determining which cultural tradition is uppermost in the practitioner's mind. It would be naïve to regard urbanization *per se* as part of

---

[232] Tacitus, *Ann.* 4. 45.

[233] *Liber de Simultudine Carnis Peccati* (Migne, *PL* suppl. 1, 55 ff.) Text edited by G. Morin, *Études, textes, découvertes Marsedsous* (1913), 107–50 = *Anecdota Maredsolana* (2nd ser., 1931), 81 ff.

this imitative process, given the pre-existing urban traditions of both the Punic and Iberian communities in Baetica.

Nevertheless, while the view that there was a conscious attempt to change native cultural practices by Rome appears to be incorrect, it seems equally wrong to posit a model where all adoption of Roman models is merely imitative—a façade grudgingly erected by native communities.[234] To examine the question of the impact of Rome on the native cultures of Baetica in terms of a dichotomy of 'Romanization' versus 'native resistance' seems in itself a dangerous methodological error as it creates a tendency to view societies as static rather than evolving organisms. The end-product of Roman involvement in Baetica was neither a society which moved entirely to a Roman way of life nor a community that rejected such practices in their entirety nor yet a society that contained two mutually exclusive parallel groups of cultural ideas. Rather the province presents the viewer with a new society where different cultural patterns fused together to form not a collage of old customs, but new practices born out of this cultural mixture—a mixture whose ingredients themselves would differ in both content and proportions in different areas and among the different social classes of the province. A synthesis so produced is best described neither as the end-product of a process of 'Romanization' nor in terms of native resistance to such a process, but rather in terms of the transculturation of two cultures into a third, new culture.

[234] For a notable exposition of this point of view, see Collingwood's views on Romano-British art in ch. 15 of R. G. Collingwood and J. N. L. Myres, *Roman Britain and the English Settlements* (1937).

9

Conclusions

As will have become clear, no one simple model adequately explains urban development in Baetica in the early imperial period. This should not be surprising, given the geographical and cultural diversity of the province, and the fact that Rome does not appear to have attempted actively to impose a standard pattern on the region. The province was much less influenced by Roman cultural patterns at the beginning of our period than is commonly assumed, and this too must be borne in mind when assessing its overall development.

Change in the urban environment in Baetica in the early imperial period was piecemeal; initiatives came from the ruled rather than the rulers, and as a consequence were highly selective, and often a response to specific events rather than exemplifying a general trend. Examples of this are the development of Gades by the Balbi, with an eye on their political careers at Rome, the growth of Belo, stimulated by Claudius' campaigns in Mauretania, and most notably the general upsurge in building which took place after Vespasian's grant of *Latinitas* to the province, shown, for example, by the building programme at Munigua. As opposed to this 'bottom-up' activity, there is no positive evidence that there was frequent action taken either by governors of the province, or the *patroni* of individual towns, to speed up the process of urbanization as part of a long-term plan for the area.

The different areas of the province show different levels of urbanization. The area where Roman influence was at its height was the 'core' of the province: the valleys of the Baetis and of its major tributary, the Singilis. This region constituted the wealthiest part of the province, attracting the most settlers and enjoying the most contact with Rome, all of which led to a relatively high degree of acculturation to Roman patterns of life. The vast majority of the Roman buildings of the province are to be found here, reflecting a high degree of cultural assimilation among the upper class of the region who would have the wealth to erect these structures.

The élite of this 'core' area were the section of the native community which most enthusiastically adopted foreign patterns of life, as is demonstrated by the names of the wealthy oil-traders of the area and the amount of Roman architecture found here. This phenomenon can be attributed not only to the high degree of contact with Rome which the area enjoyed, but also to the fact that compared to the Punic population of the Mediterranean coast, or the Celtic tribes in the province's highlands, both of whom lived in close proximity to populations of similar cultural outlook, the Iberian population of the 'core' area was culturally isolated, giving the intrusive Roman culture greater influence.

These differences must affect our interpretation of the most important development in the legal life of the province: Vespasian's grant of *Latinitas* to Spain and the subsequent promulgation of the Flavian Municipal Law under Domitian. Vespasian's actions do not appear to have been motivated by a desire to reward previous adaptations among the native communities towards a Roman norm which had already taken place (this cannot be the case if the grant was given, as our evidence suggests, to the entire peninsula, not just to Baetica); nor consciously to stimulate this process (if this was the intention, the consequent inability of the Spanish towns to reach any higher status than that of the *ius Latii* which they had been awarded, shows that it failed to achieve its objective in a spectacular manner); but it seems rather that the emperor was forced to make the grant for reasons of state which extended well beyond Spain.

The highly Roman Flavian Municipal Law which was the legacy of this process leaves us with many difficulties. The largest of these is the presumption by the law of a total transformation of the inhabitants of the province from *peregrini to cives Latini*, who enjoyed rights very similar to those of Roman citizens themselves. How realistic is such an assumption? Given the varied development of the province in other fields, it is likely that here too there would have been a wide spectrum of responses to the law. We should probably see the law not as a definite description of what town life was actually like in the province, but as a document, drafted centrally at Rome, providing an ideal of what town life ought to have been like. It thus provided a blueprint towards which communities could evolve, rather than something to be instantly implemented in all its aspects. The degree of comprehension would vary with the position of the towns within the province. At the 'core' of the province where contact with Rome was high, much, if not all, of the law would have been implemented as envisaged by its Roman creators. However, in the more inaccessible parts of the province the law was probably subject to a looser interpretation, named by Galsterer an *interpretatio peregrina*. This would have involved both its assimilation, to some degree, to prior local practice, and procedures based on what was believed to be, rather than what was, meant by the law. These anomalies seem to have been rectified in a random way, probably by individual initiative in seeking out the correct interpretation, or perhaps by positive action in this respect by some governors of the province. The geographical arrangement of the judicial *conventus* of the province, which reflects the predominant interest of Rome in its lowland zone, bears out such an interpretation. As the provincial governor would travel around the *conventus* capitals to give judgement, their locations can tell us something about the internal infrastructure of the province and the areas regarded as of importance. Baetica was divided into four *conventus*; one was sited at Gades, the obvious choice for an area comprising the Mediterranean coastal strip; while the other three were located at Corduba, the head of the navigable Baetis, Hispalis, the limit for sea-going vessels on the Baetis, and Astigi, the navigable limit of the Baetis' main tributary, the Singilis. The *Antonine Itinerary* also shows this lowland bias. Only three routes cross the Sierra Morena into Lusitania, and there are no recorded routes across the Andalusian Corderilla to the Mediterranean strip.[1] Such routes did exist of course, but their lack of interest to Rome shows its relative indifference to these regions, which constitute half the total area of the province.

Although the local aristocracy in the Baetis valley adopted Roman customs with some enthusiasm, outstanding individuals are few in number. The Senecan family based around Corduba, and their associates such as the orators Statorius Victor,[2] and Porcius Latro,[3] are representatives of the 'Hispanienses'—that is, Roman settlers—not of a totally changed indigenous upper class. This is also the case with the 'Spanish' emperors, Trajan and Hadrian, and the family of Marcus Aurelius, which hailed from Ucubi; and it may well also be true of other provincial notables such as Sextus Marius, the Corduban mine-owner, who gave his name to the Sierra Morena and was reputably the richest man in Spain at the time of his execution by Tiberius,[4] and of Aemilius Regulus, who was involved in the assassination of Caligula.[5] The senators attested as hailing from the province cluster around the *coloniae* and many of these would have again been members of the settler class—that is, *Hispanienses*, rather

[1] J. M. Roldán Hervás, *Itineraria Hispanica* (1965), esp. lam. VI.
[2] Seneca, *Suas.* 2. 18. [3] Seneca, *Controv.* 1 pr. 16; 9 pr. 3.
[4] Tacitus, *Ann.* 6. 19. [5] Josephus, *Ant. J.* 19. 1. 3.

than *Hispani* proper.[6] A recent survey of the senators of the province was therefore correct to describe this group as a relatively closed circle.[7] The same pattern is repeated with the equestrian order. There would have been a larger number of Baetican *equites* than senators. Strabo states that there were 500 resident at Gades in his day; however, this will have been an abnormally high number reflecting Gades' trading role. Nevertheless very few *equites* are known by name; of a sample of eight of these studied by Pflaum, two are simply known to have been from Baetica; of the other six, all but one are from colonial sites or Gades.[8] The exception is Quintius Hispan(us?) of Obulco, whose name suggests that he was a native Iberian and who had a reasonably distinguished career abroad as well as rising to the top of the municipal *cursus*.[9] It appears therefore that like their senatorial counterparts the *equites* of the province were concentrated almost exclusively in its major urban centres. Again a majority of them would have been *Hispanienses*, not *Hispani*. The Praetorian Prefect of AD 118/19, P. Acilius Attianus,[10] known to be an *Italicensis*, may have been a *Hispanus*, as his *cognomen* has a possibly Iberian root; but this cannot be established with certainty.

Below this upper class the degree of cultural change remains unclear, though it would be reasonable to assume that it was stronger in lowland areas and that in general it grew over time. Nevertheless we see a persistence in the use of Iberian names, and the continuance of dual communities in some towns may also hint at a continuing settler–native divide; although here it is uncertain which side, or whether both, was responsible for this. The continued existence of *centuriae*, even in the Baetis valley, suggests that at a lower level society remained more native in outlook, and that members of the aristocracy had to some degree a 'dual life', leading a Roman-style existence at one level, but not abandoning the old native structures which bound them to their followers.

On Horvath's bipolar schemata therefore the lowland part of the prov-

[6] A. Caballos Rufino, 'Los miembros del senado de epoca de Vespasiano originarios de la provincia Hispania Ulterior Baetica', in *Actas del 1 Coloquio de historia antigua de Andalucia*, ii (1993). In this survey 45% of those listed were inhabitants of Italica or the provicial capital Corduba. Further colonial sites comprise another 30% of the total.

[7] C. Castillo García, 'Los senadores de la Bética', *Gerión*, 2 (1984), 239–50, at p. 248: 'un núcleo relativamente cerrado'.

[8] H. G. Pflaum, 'La Part prise par les chevaliers romains originaires d'Espagne à l'administration impériale', in A. Piganiol and M. Terrasse (eds.), *Les Empereurs romains d'Espagne* (1965), 87–121.

[9] *CIL* 2. 2129 = *ILS* 1404.

[10] *ILS* 8999.

ince appears to exhibit the 'colonial' version of 'assimilation'. Nevertheless his construct fits awkwardly into the Baetican reality, as the large numbers of settlers he envisages for such a model are not to be found in the province. It appears that the prestige of Rome alone was a sufficient incentive to imitate Roman practice. This might lead us to ask whether the premisses of such a model (premisses strongly fortified by use of terminology such as 'Romanization') are in fact of any use when looking at the life of a Roman province. Any consideration of cultural change will need to take into account the phenomenon dubbed *interpretatio peregrina* by Galsterer and dealt with more fully by Ortiz under the name of 'transculturation', meaning the blending of Roman forms and institutions into their native equivalents. The end-product of this process is something intelligible to both Roman and native in terms of their own culture, yet does not fit into either entirely. A good example of this duality is the continuing existence of the *hospitium* agreement between towns. *Hospitia*, as has been seen, were a standard Roman form of agreement and are found in other *provinciae*. Nevertheless in Spain they are a Roman form of prior native practice, as can be seen from extant pre-Roman versions. The end result is a form of document which is neither entirely Hispanic nor Roman, but forms an overlap between the two cultures, something which, while highly visible in this case, would probably have been a common aspect of the province's life in many fields. Another example, prior to Vespasian's grant of *Latium*, are the *decemviri* found at some towns: here a native magistracy receives a Roman title, but it is not clear how much the new title changed the functions of the old office.

Away from the central, lowland area, the penetration of Roman customs into everyday life seems much weaker. The Punic civilization kept many of its old features, notably its religious practices, most obviously exemplified by the temple of Heracles/Melqart at Gades. More surprisingly, some of its administrative features may also have been retained, for example the *veteres ordines* found at some towns. No doubt this cultural resilience was fortified by the region's proximity to, and close links with, Punic Africa. The highlands of the province also retained many native features in the face of Roman indifference. This can be seen in the retention of *recinto* settlements, which Rome was prepared to treat on equal terms with the more classically urban settlements of the Baetis valley, and the only partial adoption of Roman nomenclature. As can be seen from the case of Iponoba, Roman administrative titles were used by the magistrates of such communities, but it is unclear if these would have been understood in the same way as a Roman would understand them.

The sheer inaccessibility of much of this area in antiquity would have aided its native conservatism, as would the proximity of Celtic Lusitania. Pliny says of the inhabitants of Celtic Baeturia that: 'ex Lusitania advenisse manifestum est sacris, lingua, oppidorum vocabulis' ('they have clearly come from Lusitania as can be seen from their religious practices, language, and the titles of their towns'),[11] implying an almost total lack of Roman customs here either in his own day, or that of his (probably Augustan) sources. This view is supported by the predominance of native finds, and evidence for high rates of immigration from neighbouring Lusitania, in the mining sites from the Huelva region.

Once again a bipolar approach describes the social reality of these areas in an inadequate fashion. Here the nearest point in Horvath's model would be that of 'Imperialist Equilibrium'—that is, the retention of native culture. But this again is not the whole truth, for some aspects of Roman culture were adopted, and at some sites in an impressive manner, for example at Regina in the middle of Baeturia. Throughout the province therefore it is noticeable that the notion of dividing up aspects of its life into 'Roman' and 'non-Roman' proves insufficient at best and futile or even misleading at worst. What we are offered is instead a complex interaction between several cultures—an interaction which produced a new set of social arrangements which themselves varied widely both from area to area and from social class to social class. An urge to change from a traditional way of life would have depended on many disparate factors: the amount of contact with Rome, often limited by geographical considerations; the desire, or lack of it, to integrate with the Roman system; and the financial ability to carry out these wishes.

The province's development therefore exhibits a mosaic of different choices and patterns of development. As important, however, is the fact that no one of these brought about a purely 'Roman' or retained a purely 'native' society. Cultural borrowing inevitably changes the practice borrowed, and resistance to change also changes the structure of the resisting society as it adapts to meet a new 'threat'. The cultural diversity of Baetica, normally referred to as 'highly Romanized' in broad surveys of the Roman empire, is a salutary warning to those who would see the 'Romanization' of the Roman empire as a natural and uniform phenomenon initiated purely on the part of Rome towards her grateful or unwilling subject nation. Indeed the reality of life in the province is as good a plea as any for this misleading term to be dropped from the examination

[11] Pliny, *NH* 3. 1. 13.

of Roman provincial life and reason enough to agree with López Castro's statement that: 'it would be best to reject the use of the concept of "Romanization"; at least in the form in which it has come to be used up to the present day . . . The unthinking and mechanical use of this concept stops "Romanized" peoples being the subject of their own history'.[12]

[12] 'Conviene rechazar el uso del concepto de 'romanizacion; al menos tal como se ha venido hasta ahora. El uso irreflexivo y mécanico del concepto de romanizacion hurta a los pueblos "romanizados" la posibilidad de ser subjetos de su propria historia.' J. L. López Castro, 'El concepto de romanizacion y los Fenicios en la Hispania republicana: Problemas historiograficos', in J. L. López Castro and M. Carrilero Millán (eds.), *La colonizacion fenicia en el sur de la peninsula iberica* (1992), 161.

BIBLIOGRAPHY

GENERAL WORKS

ABBOT, F., and JOHNSON, A. C., *Municipal Administration in the Roman Empire* (Princeton, 1926).

ABRAMS, P., and WRIGLEY, E. A. (eds.), *Towns in Societies* (Cambridge, 1978).

ALCOCK, S. E., 'Archaeology and Imperialism: Roman Expansion and the Greek City', *Journal of Mediterranean Archaeology*, 2/1 (1989), 87 ff.

ALFÖLDY, G., 'Notes sur la relation entre le droit de cité et la nomenclature dans l'empire romain', *Latomus*, 25 (1966), 37 ff.

ARNOLD, W. T., *The Roman System of Provincial Administration to the Accession of Constantine the Great* (Oxford, 1906).

ASTON, M., and BOND, J., *The Landscape of Towns* (London, 1976).

BARTEL, B., 'Colonialism and Cultural Responses', *World Archaeology*, 12 (1980–1), 11 ff.

BLAGG, T., and MILLETT, M. (eds.), *The Early Roman Empire in the West* (Oxford, 1990).

BOSWORTH, A., 'Vespasian and the Provinces: Some Problems of the Early 70s AD', *Athenaeum*, 51 (1973), 49 ff.

BRADFORD, J., *Ancient Landscapes* (London, 1957).

BRAUND, D. (ed.), *The Administration of the Roman Empire 241 BC–AD 193* (Exeter, 1988).

BRUNT, P., *Italian Manpower* (Oxford, 1971).

—— 'The Romanization of Local Ruling Classes', in D. Pippidi (ed.), *Assimilation et résistance à la culture gréco-romaine dans le monde ancien* (Bucharest, 1976).

—— *Select Texts of the Digest* (Oxford, 1979).

BURNETT, A. M., and CRAWFORD, M., *The Coinage of the Roman World in the Late Republic* (Oxford, 1987).

CLAVEL, M., and LÉVÈQUE, P., *Villes et structures urbaines dans l'occident romain* (Paris, 1971).

CRAWFORD, M., *Coinage and Money under the Roman Republic* (London, 1985).

—— 'The Laws of the Romans: Knowledge and Diffusion', in J. González and J. Arce (eds.), *Estudios sobre la Tabula Siarensis* (Madrid, 1988).

CROOK, J. A., *Law and Life of Rome* (London, 1967).

CUNLIFFE, B., and ROWLEY, T. (eds.), *Oppida*, BAR suppl. series II (Oxford, 1976).

DILKE, O. A. W., *The Roman Land Surveyors* (Newton Abbot, 1971).

FISHWICK, D., *The Imperial Cult in the Latin West* (Leiden, 1987).

FREDRIKSEN, M. W., 'The Republican Municipal Laws: Errors and Drafts', *JRS* 55 (1965), 183 ff.

GALSTERER, H., 'Roman Laws in the Provinces: Some Problems of Transmission', in M. Crawford (ed.), *L'impero romano e le strutture economiche e sociali delle province* (Como, 1986), 13 ff.

GASCOU, J., 'Municipia Civium Romanorum', *Latomus*, 30 (1971), 133 ff.

GRANT, M., *From Imperium to Auctoritas* (Cambridge, 1946).

HARDEN, D., *The Phoenicians* (London, 1980).

HARMAND, L., *L'Occident romain* (Paris, 1960).

HORVATH, R. J., 'A Definition of Colonialism', *Current Anthropology*, 13 (1972), 45 ff.

HUMBERT, M., 'Le Droit latin imperial', *Ktema*, 6 (1981), 207 ff.

HUMPHREY, J. H., *Roman Circuses* (London, 1986).

JOHNSON, A. C., *et al.*, *Ancient Roman Statutes* (Austin, Tex., 1961).

MACDONALD, W. L., *The Architecture of the Roman Empire*, ii (New Haven and London, 1986).

MILLAR, F. G. B., *The Emperor in the Roman World* (London, 1977).

MILLETT, M., *The Romanization of Britain* (Cambridge, 1990).

—— 'Romanization: Historical Issues and Archaeological Interpretation', in Blagg and Millett (eds.), *The Early Roman Empire in the West* (Oxford, 1990).

MOSCATI, S., *The World of the Phoenicians* (London, 1973).

OWENS, E. J., 'Roman Town Planning', in I. M. Barton (ed.), *Roman Public Buildings* (Exeter, 1989), 7 ff.

—— *The City in the Greek and Roman World* (London, 1991).

PIPPIDI, D. (ed.), *Assimilation et résistance à la culture gréco-romaine dans le monde ancien* (Bucharest, 1976).

REID, J. S., *The Municipalities of the Roman Empire* (Cambridge, 1913).

RODRIGUEZ NEILA, J. F., 'Municipia', *Memorias de historia antigua*, 6 (1976), 147 ff.

—— 'La situación socio-political de los incolae', *Memorias de historia antigua*, 11 (1978), 147 ff.

SALMON, E. T., *Roman Colonization under the Republic* (London, 1969).

SAUMAGNE, C., *Le Droit latin et les cités romaines sous l'empire* (Paris, 1965).

SHERWIN-WHITE, A., *The Roman Citizenship* (2nd edn., Oxford, 1973).

SIRKS, A. J. B., 'The Lex Iunia and the Effects of Informal Manumission and Iteration', *RIDA*, 30 (1983), 211 ff.

SJÖBERG, G., *The Preindustrial City* (New York and London, 1960).

SYME, R., *Colonial Elites* (London, 1958).

THOMAS, J. A. C., *Textbook of Roman Law* (New York, 1976).

WILSON, A. J. N., *Emigration from Italy in the Republican Age of Rome* (Manchester, 1966).

WORKS ON THE IBERIAN PENINSULA

ABAD CASAL, A., *El Guadalquivir, via fluvial romana* (Seville, 1975).

ABASCAL, J. M., and ESPINOSA, U., *La ciudad hispano-romana: Privilegio y poder* (Logroño, 1989).

Actas del simposio 'El teatro en la Hispania romana' (Badajoz, 1982).

ALBERTINI, E., *Les Divisions administratives de l'Espagne romaine* (Paris, 1923).

ALBERTOS FIRMAT, M. L., *La onomastica personal primitiva de Hispania Tarraconensis y Betica* (Salamanca, 1966).

——'Nuevos antroponimos hispanicos', *Emerita*, 40 (1972), 1 and 287 ff.

ALMAGRO BASCH, M., *Huelva: Prehistoria y antigüedad* (Madrid, 1974).

ALVAREZ MARTINEZ, J. M., 'Las termas romanas de Alange', *Habis*, 3 (1972), 267 ff.

——'Alange y sus termas romanas', *Revista de estudios extremeños*, 29 (1973), 445 ff.

——'El teatro romano de Regina', in *Actas del simposio 'El teatro en la Hispania romana'* (Badajoz, 1982) 267 ff.

AMO Y DE LA HERA, M. DEL, 'El teatro de Acinipo', in *Actas del simposio 'El teatro en la Hispania romana'* (Badajoz, 1982).

ARCE, J. (ed.), *La religión romana en Hispania* (Madrid, 1981).

ARRIBAS, A., *The Iberians* (London, 1964).

ATENCIA PÁEZ, R., *La ciudad romana de Singilia Barba (Antequera-Málaga)* (Malaga, 1988).

BAENA DEL ALCAZAR, L., 'Esculturas romanas de Mengibar', *BSAA* 48 (1982), 111 ff.

——'Relieves romanas de Mengibar (Jaen)', *Italica*, 17 (1984), 127 ff.

BALIL, A., 'En torno a las relaciones de Cerdeña e Hispania en la epoca romana', *Studi Sardi*, 14/15 (1955/7), 130 ff.

——*Casa y urbanismo en la España antigua* (Santiago de Compostela, 1972–4).

BELEN DEAMOS, M., *et al.*, 'Excavaciones en Niebla', *16th CNA* (1983), 971 ff.

BELTRÁN, A., 'Sobre los Balbi de Cádiz', *A.e.A.* 25 (1952), 142 ff.

BENDÁLA GALÁN, M., *La necropolis romana de Carmona* (Seville, 1976).

——'La perduración púnica en los tiempos romanos: El caso de Carmona', *Huelva archaeologica*, 6 (1982), 193 ff.

——(ed.), *La ciudad hispanorromana* (Barcelona, 1993).

BERNIER LUQUE, J., *Corduba, tierra nuestra* (Cordoba, 1978).

—— *et al.*, *Nuevos yacimientos arqueológicos en Córdoba y Jaén* (Cordoba, 1981).

BLANCO FREIJEIRO, A., 'De situ Iliturgis', *A.e.A.* 33 (1960), 193 ff.

——'Antigüedades de Rio Tinto', *Zephyrus*, 13 (1962), 31 ff.

——'Vestigios de Corduba romana', *Habis*, 1 (1970), 109 ff.

——*Historia de Sevilla*, i. *La ciudad antigua* (3rd edn., Seville, 1989).

——and CORZO SÁNCHEZ, R., 'El urbanismo romano de la Bética', in *Symposion de ciudades augusteas* (Zaragoza, 1976), i. 137 ff.

BLÁZQUEZ, J. M., *Historia economica de la Hispania romana* (Bilbao, 1978).

——and GARCIA-GELABERT, M. P., *Ca'stulo, ciudad ibero-romana* (Madrid, 1994).

BLECH, M., 'Esculturas de Tajo Montero: Una interpretación iconografica', in J. Arce (ed.), *La religión romana en Hispania* (Madrid, 1981).

BONSOR, G., 'Les Colonies preromaines de la valle du Betis', *RA* 35 (1899), 126 ff., 232 ff., 376 ff.

——*The Archaeological Expedition along the Guadalquivir* (New York, 1931).

——*An Archaeological Sketchbook of the Roman Necropolis at Carmona* (New York, 1931).

BOUCHIER, E., *Spain under the Roman Empire* (Oxford, 1914).

BROUGHTON, T. R. S., 'Municipal Institutions in Roman Spain', *CHM* 9/1 (1965), 126 ff.

CABALLOS RUFINO, A., 'Colonia Claritas Iulia Ucubi', *Habis*, 9 (1978), 273 ff.

——'Iptuci, civitas stipendaria del conventus Gaditanus', *Gades*, 7 (1981), 37 ff.

CABO, A., *Historia de España Alfaguara*, i (Madrid, 1973).

CAMPOS, J., and GONZALEZ, J., 'Los foros de Hispalis, colonia romula', *A.e.A.* 60 (1987), 123 ff.

CANTO, A. M., 'Un nuevo documento de Paulo Emilio en la Hispania Ulterior', *Reunion sobre epigrafia Hispanica de época Romano-Republicana* (Zaragoza, 1986), 227 ff.

——'A propos de la loi municipale de Corticata, Cortegana, Huelva, Espagne', *ZPE* 63 (1986), 217 ff.

CARO BAROJA, J., *Los pueblos de España*, i (Madrid, 1990).

CASAS MORALES, A., 'Baza', *NAH* 2 (1953), 207–8.

CASTILLO, C., *Prosopographia Baetica* (Pamplona, 1965).

——'Hispanos y Romanos en Corduba', *Historia antigua*, 4 (1974), 191 f.

CASTRO, A. DE, *Historia de Cádiz* (Cádiz, 1858).

CHAVES TRISTAN, F., *Las monedas de Italica* (2nd edn., Seville, 1979).

CHIC GARCIA, G., 'Consideraciones sobre la navigabilidad del Guadalquivir en época romana', *Gades*, 1 (1974), 7 ff.

——'El tráfico en el Guadalquivir y el transporte de las anforas', *Anales de la Universidad de Cádiz*, 1 (1984).

COLLANTES TERAN, F., 'Cantillana', *NAH* 2 (1953), 134.

CORZO SÁNCHEZ, R., *Osuna de Pompeyo a César: Excavaciones en la muralla republicana* (Seville, 1977).

——and JIMÉNEZ, A., 'La organización territorial de la "Baetica"', *A.e.A.* 53 (1980), 21 ff.

CURCHIN, L. A., *Roman Spain: Conquest and Assimilation* (London, 1991).

——'The Romanization of Spain: An Overview', *Classical Views*, 30/3 (1986), 271 ff.

DIAZ TEJERA, A., *Sevilla en los textos clásicos greco-latinos* (Seville, 1982).

DILKE, O. A. W., 'Roman Colonization in Spain: A Comparison with Other

Areas', in *Actes du IIe Congrès de l'Études des Cultures de la Mediterranée Occidentale* (1978), 59 ff.

DIOS DE LA RADA Y DELGADO, J. DE, 'Nertobriga Beturica', *BRAH* 24 (1894), 164 ff.

DIXON, P., *The Iberians of Spain* (Oxford, 1940).

DOMERGUE, C., *Belo*, i. *La stratigraphie* (Paris, 1973).

—— *Les Mines de la péninsule ibérique dans l'antiquité romaine* (Rome, 1990).

EDMONDSON, J. C., *Two Industries in Roman Lusitania: Mining and Garum Production*, BAR, IS 362 (Oxford, 1987).

—— 'Romanization and Urban Development in Lusitania', in Blagg and Millett (eds.), *The Early Roman Empire in the West* (Oxford, 1990), 151 ff.

ENGEL, A., and PARIS, P., 'Une fortresse ibérique à Osuna', *NAMSC* 13 (1906), 357 ff.

ESTUVE GUERRO, M., 'Las excavaciones de Asta Regia', *A.e.A.* 15 (1942), 245 ff.

—— *Excavaciones de Asta Regia 1942–3* (Madrid, 1945).

ÉTIENNE, R., *Le Culte impérial dans les provinces ibériques* (Paris, 1958).

—— *Les Fouilles de Conimbriga* (Paris, 1977–9).

FERNÁNDEZ, R. R., *La ciudad romana de Ilici* (Alicante, 1975).

FERNÁNDEZ CHICARRO, C., 'Informe arqueológico de los hallazgos en Andalucía', *7 CNA* (Barcelona, 1960), 65 ff.

—— 'Informe sobre las excavaciones del anfiteatro romano de Carmona', *13 CNA* (Zaragoza, 1975), 855 ff.

—— and OLIVELLA, A., 'Informe sobre las excavaciones del anfiteatro romano de Carmona', *NAH* 5 (1972), 119 ff.

FERNÁNDEZ GÓMEZ, F., 'Nuevos fragmentos de leyes municipales y otros bronces epigráficos de la Bética en el museo arqueologico de Sevilla', *ZPE* 86 (1991), 121 ff.

FERNÁNDEZ LÓPEZ, M., *Necropolis romana de Carmona, tumba del elefante* (Seville, 1899).

—— *La historia de Carmona* (repr. Seville, 1969).

FERREIRO LÓPEZ, M., 'Asta Regia segun los geografos antiguos', *Gades*, 9 (1983).

FITA, F., 'Los callenses Aeneanici del Arahal y de Montellano', *BRAH* 31 (1894), 381 ff.

FORTEA PEREZ, J., and BERNIER LUGUE, J., *Recintos y fortificaciones ibéricas de la Bética* (Salamanca, 1970).

GALSTERER, H., *Untersuchungen zum römischen Städtewesen auf der iberischen Halbinsel suppl. Madrider Mitteilungen* (Berlin, 1971).

—— 'Municipium Flavium Irnitanum: A Latin Town in Spain', *JRS* 78 (1988), 78 ff.

—— 'The Tabula Siarensis and Augustan Municipalization in Baetica', in J. González and J. Arce (eds.), *Estudios sobre la Tabula Siarensis* (Madrid, 1988), 61 ff.

GARCÍA Y BELLIDO, A., *España y los españoles hace dos mil años* (Madrid, 1945).
——*La España del siglo primero de nuestra era* (Madrid, 1947).
——*Las esculturas romanas de España y Portugal* (Madrid, 1949).
——'Iocosae Gades', *BRAH* 129 (1951), 73 ff.
——*Las colonias romanas de Hispania* (Madrid, 1959).
——'Lapidas funerarias de gladiatores de Hispania', *A.e.A.* 33 (1960), 123 ff.
——'Disperción y concentración de itinerantes de la España romana', *Archivium*, 12 (1963).
——'Hercules Gaditanus', *A.e.A.* 36 (1963) 68 ff.
——'Deidades semitas en la España antiqua', *Sefarad*, 24 (1964).
——'El templo romano de Corduba', *Oretania*, 16–17–18 (1964), 156 ff.
——'La latinazación de Hispania', *A.e.A.* 40 (1967), 3 ff.
——*Les Religions orientales dans l'Espagne romaine* (Leiden, 1967).
——*Italica* (Madrid, 1985 edn.).
——and MENÉNDEZ PIDAL, J., 'El distylo sepulcral romano de Iulipa (Zalamea)', in *Anejos del Archivo español de arqueologia*, 3 (1963).
GARCÍA-BELLIDO, Ma. P., '¿Colonia Augusta Gaditana?', *A.e.A.* 61 (1988), 324 ff.
GASCOU, J., 'La Tabula Siarensis et le problème des municipes romains hors d'Italie', *Latomus*, 45 (1986), 541 ff.
GIMÉNEZ REYNA, S., 'Antequera', *NAH* 2 (1953), 207.
GONZÁLEZ, J., 'Ilorci', *Habis*, 7 (1976), 391 ff.
——*Inscripciones romanas de la provincia de Cádiz* (Cádiz, 1982).
——'La Tabula Siarensis, Fortunales Siarenses et Municipia civium Romanorum', *ZPE* 55 (1984), 55 ff.
——'Italica, municipium iuris Latini', *MCV* 20 (1984), 17 ff.
——'The *Lex Irnitana*: A New Copy of the Flavian Municipal Law', *JRS* 76 (1986), 147 ff.
——'Los municipia civium Romanorum y la lex Irnitana', *Habis*, 17 (1986), 221 ff.
——'El ius Latii y la lex Irnitana', *Athenaeum*, 75 (1987), 317 ff.
——'More on the Italica Fragment of Lex Municipalis', *ZPE* 70 (1987), 217 ff.
——'Epigrafia del yacimiento de La Cañada', in Gonzalez and Arce (eds.), *Estudios sobre la Tabula Siarensis* (Madrid, 1988), 91 ff.
——*Inscripciones romanas y visigodas de Utrera* (Seville, 1988).
——(ed.), *Estudios sobre Urso* (1989).
——*Bronces juridicos romanos de Andalucía* (Seville, 1990).
——and ARCE, J. (eds.), *Estudios sobre la Tabula Siarensis* (Madrid, 1988).
GONZÁLEZ HURTADO DE MENDOZA, M. F., and MARTIN DE LA TORRE, M., *Historia y reconstrucción del teatro romano de Málaga* (Malaga, 1982).
GONZÁLEZ ROMAN, C. (ed.), *La Bética en su problemática historia* (Granada, 1991).
GRIFFIN, M., 'The Elder Seneca and Spain', *JRS* 62 (1972), 1 ff.
GRÜNHAGEN, W., 'Excavaciones del Sanctuario de Tarrazos de Munigua', *5th CNA* (Zaragoza, 1957), 275 ff.

——'El monumento a Dis Pater de Munigua', in *Segovia: Symposium de arqueologia romana* (Barcelona, 1977), 201 ff.

——and HAUSCHILD, T., 'Sucinto informe sobre las excavaciones arqueológicas en Munigua en 1973', *NAH* 5 (1977), 105 ff.

——and —— 'Sucinto informe...en 1974', *NAH* 6 (1979), 283 ff.

——and —— 'Sucinto informe...en 1976', *NAH* 6 (1979), 301 ff.

GUTIERREZ BEHEMERID, M. A., 'Sobre la sistematización del capitel Corintio en la peninsula Ibérica', *BSAA* 48 (1982), 25 ff.

——'El capital corintizante: Su difusión en la peninsula Ibérica', *BSAA* 48 (1983), 73 ff.

HANARD, G., 'Note propos des leges Salpensana et Irnitana', *RIDA* 34 (1987), 173 ff.

HARDY, E., *Three Spanish Charters and Other Documents* (Oxford, 1912).

HARRISON, R. J., *Spain at the Dawn of History* (London, 1988).

HENDERSON, M. I., 'Julius Caesar and Latium in Spain', *JRS* 32 (1942), 1 ff.

HIMYARI, AL-, *Kitāb ar-Rawḍ al-Miṭār fī Habar al-Akṭār*, trans. E. Levi-Provençal (Leiden, 1938).

HOYOS, B., 'The Romanization of Spain: A Study of Settlement and Administration to 14 AD', unpubl. D.Phil thesis (Oxford University, 1971).

——'In Defence of C.I.L. 2.760', *Athenaeum*, 56 (1978), 390 ff.

——'The Elder Pliny's Titled Baetican Towns', *Historia*, 28 (1979), 439 ff.

IBAÑEZ CASTRO, A., *Córdoba Hispano-Romana* (Cordoba, 1983).

ISSERLIN, B. S. J., 'Report on the Archaeological Trial Excavations Undertaken at Malaga in 1974', *Actes du IIᵉ Congrès de l'Études des Cultures de la Mediterranée Occidentale* (1978), 65 ff.

JIMÉNEZ, A., 'Arquitectura romana', in *Segovia: Symposium de arqueologia romana* (Barcelona, 1977), 223 ff.

KEAY, S., *Roman Spain* (London, 1988).

—— 'The Romanisation of Turdetania', Oxford Journal of Archaeology, 11/3 (1992).

KNAPP, R. C., *Aspects of the Roman Experience in Iberia 206–100 BC* (Valladolid and Alava, 1977).

——*Roman Córdoba* (Berkeley and London, 1983).

——'Spain', in A. M. Burnett and M. Crawford (eds.), *The Coinage of the Roman World in the Late Republic* (Oxford, 1987).

KOCH, K. M., 'Observaciones sobre la permanancia del substrato púnico en la peninsula ibérica', in F. Jordan (ed.), *Actas del I Coloquio sobre lenguas y culturas prerromanas de la peninsula ibérica* (Salamanca, 1976).

LA CHICA CASSINELLO, G., 'Inscripción dedicada a Tiberio Sempronio Graccho', *NAH* 6 (1956/61), 178 ff.

LACORT NAVARRO, P. J., *et al.*, 'Nuevas inscripciones latinas de Cordoba y su provincia', *Faventia*, 8/1 (1986), 69 ff.

LEÓN ALONSO, P. (ed.), *Italica = EAE 121* (1982).

——*Traianeum de Italica* (Seville, 1988).

LEROUX, P., *L'Armée romaine et l'organization des provinces ibériques d'Auguste à l'invasion de 409* (Paris, 1982).

——'Municipe et droit Latin en Hispania sous l'empire', *RHDFE* (1986), 325 ff.

LÓPEZ CASTRO, J., *Hispania Poena: los Fenicios en la Hispania romana* (Barcelona, 1995).

——and CARRILERO MILLÁN, M. (eds.), *La colonización fenicia en el sur de la peninsula iberica: 100 años de investigación* (Almeria, 1992).

LÓPEZ GÓMEZ, A., *Estudios sobre centuriaciones romanas en España* (Madrid, 1974).

LUZÓN NOGUÉ, J. M., 'El teatro romano de Italica', *Actas del simposio 'El teatro en la Hispania romana'* (Badajoz, 1982), 183 ff.

MCEIDERRY, J., 'Vespasian's Reconstruction of Spain', *JRS* 8 (1918), 53 ff. and *JRS* 9 (1919), 86 ff.

MCKENNA, S. J., *Paganism and Pagan Survivals in Spain up to the Fall of the Visigothic Kingdom* (1938).

MACKIE, N., 'Augustan Colonies in Mauretania', *Historia*, 32 (1983), 332 ff.

——*Local Administration in Roman Spain* (Oxford, 1983).

MANGAS, J., 'Servidumbre comunitaria en la Bética prerromana', *Memorias de historia antigua*, 1 (1977), 151 ff.

MARCOS POUS, A., 'La ley municipal de Ostippo', *Corduba*, 12 (1982–3), 43 ff.

MELIDA, J., *Monumentos Romanos en España* (Madrid, 1925).

MILLAN LEÓN, J., *Ilipa Magna* (Cordoba, 1989).

MOLINA GONZÁLEZ, F., and ROLDÁN HERVÁS, J. M., *Historia de Granada*, i (Granada, 1983).

MONTENEGRO, A., 'Problemas y nuevas perspectivas en el estudio de la Hispania de Vespasiano', *Historia antigua*, 5 (1975), 1 ff.

MORA, G., 'Las termas romanas en Hispania', *A.e.A.* 54 (1981), 32 ff.

MOUTINHO ALARCO, A., *et al.*, *Ruinas de Conimbriga* (1986).

MUÑIZ COELLO, J., 'Aspectos sociales y economicos de Malaca romana', *Habis*, 6 (1975), 241 ff.

——'Notas sobre Cartima romana', in *Actas del 1 Congreso de la historia de Andalucía* (Cordoba, 1983).

NIEMEYER, H. G., 'Aspectos de la escultura romana de la peninsula ibérica', *14th CNA* (Zaragoza, 1977), 915 ff.

OLID, F., 'Osuna', *NAH* 3/4 (1954/5), 310.

ORDOÑEZ AGULLA, S., *Colonia Augusta Firma Astigi* (Seville, 1988).

D'ORS, A., 'Una nueva table emeritense de hospitium publicum', *Emerita*, 16 (1948), 46 ff.

——*Epigrafía jurídica de la España romana* (Madrid, 1953).

——'El bronce de Belo', *Emerita*, 27 (1959), 367 ff.

——'La ley municipal de Basilipo', *Emerita*, 73 (1985), 31 ff.

PADILLA MONGE, A., 'Asido Caesarina: Consideraciones acerca de su "status"', *Habis*, 16 (1985), 307 ff.

PARIS, P., *L'Espagne primitive* (Paris, 1903).

—— *Promenades archéologiques en l'Espagne* (Paris, 1910).

—— *Les Fouilles de Belo* (Bordeaux and Paris, 1923).

PASTOR MUÑOZ, M., 'La economia en el municipio romano de Iliberris', *Historia antigua*, 9–10 (1979–80), 197 ff.

—— *Inscripciones latinas de la provincia de Granada* (Granada, 1987).

PEREZ, J. A., 'Un caso de pervivencia púnica durante el imperio romano: El municipio bético de Ostippo', *Memorias de historia antigua*, 5 (1981), 95 ff.

PIERNAVIEJA, P., 'Dos notas sobre los antiguos "ludi" españoles', *12 CNA* (Zaragoza, 1973), 579 ff.

—— 'Los circos de Hispania', in *Segovia: Symposium de arqueologia romana* (1977), 309 ff.

PONISCH, M., *Implantation rurale sur la bas Guadalquivir* (Madrid, 1974).

—— 'El teatro de Belo', *NAH* 10 (1980), 307 ff.

—— and DE SANCHA, S., 'Le teatre à Belo', *MCV* (1979), 559 ff.

—— and —— 'Le teatre à Belo', *MCV* (1980), 357 ff.

PRESADO VELO, F. J., *et al.*, *Carteia*, i = *EAE 120* (1982).

PRIETO ARCINIEGA, A., 'La pervivencia del elemento indigena en la Bética', *Faventia*, 2/1 (1980), 37 ff.

PUERTAS TRICAS, R., *Estudios sobre la ciudad romana de Lacipo* (Cordoba, 1980).

—— 'El teatro romano de Malaga', *Actas del simposio 'El teatro romano en la Hispania romana'* (Badajoz, 1982), 203 ff.

RAMIREZ DELGADO, J. R., *Los primitivos nucleos de asentamiento en la ciudad de Cádiz* (Cádiz, 1982).

REMESAL RODRÍGUEZ, J., 'La economia oleicola Bética, nuevas formas de analis', *A.e.A.* 50–1 (1977/8), 87 ff.

RICHMOND, I. A., 'The First Years of Emerita Augusta', *Archaeological Journal*, 87 (1930), 98 ff.

RODRÍGUEZ HIDALGO, J. M., 'Anotaciones en torno a Basilippo: La Torre del Cincho', *Habis*, 10/11 (1979/80), 425 ff.

RODRÍGUEZ NEILA, J. F., *Los Balbos de Cádiz* (Seville, 1973).

—— *Sociedad y administración local en la Bética romana* (Cordoba, 1981).

RODRÍGUEZ OLIVA, P., 'La arqueologia romana de Algeciras', *Segovia: Symposium de arqueologia romana* (Barcelona, 1977).

—— 'Municipium Barbesulanum', *Baetica*, 1 (1978), 207 ff.

—— 'Sobre el culto de Dea Luna en Málaga', *Jabega*, 21 (1985), 49 ff.

—— Notas sobre Anticaria Sulpicia', *Jabega*, 24 (1988), 19 ff.

—— and ALENCIA PÁEZ, R., 'Estelas Saborenses', *BSAA* 49 (1983), 151 ff.

RODRÍGUEZ TEMIÑO, I., 'Algunas cuestiones sobre el urbanismo de *Hispalis* en época republicana', *Habis*, 22 (1991), 157 ff.

ROLDÁN HERVAS, J., 'El elemento indigena en las guerras civiles en Hispania', *Hispania antigua*, 2 (1972), 102 ff.

—— *Hispania y el ejercito romano* (Granada, 1974).

——*La España romana* (Madrid, 1989).

——*et al.*, *La Andalucía romana* (1989).

SANTERO, J. M., 'Colonia Iulia Gemella Acci', *Habis*, 3 (1972), 203 ff.

SANTOS GENER, S., 'Rute (Zambra)', *NAH 1* (1952).

——'Zuheros', *NAH 2* (1953).

SANTOS YANGUAS, N., 'Las invasiones de Moros en la Bética del siglo II D.N.E.', *Gades*, 5 (1981), 51 ff.

SCHULTEN, A., *Fontes Hispaniae Antiquae*, vols. i–ix (Barcelona, 1922–47).

SEGURA ARISTA, M. L., *La ciudad ibero-romana de Igabrum* (Cordoba, 1988).

SERRANO CARRILLO, J., and MORENA LÓPEZ, J., *Arqueologia inédita de Córdoba y Jaén* (Cordoba, 1984).

SERRANO DELGADO, J. M., *La colonia romana de 'Tucci'* (Cordoba, 1987).

SILLIÈRES, P., 'Sisapo: Prospections et découvertes', *A.e.A.* 53 (1980), 49 ff.

STYLOW, A., 'Inscripciones latinas de sur de la provincia de Córdoba', *Gerion*, 1 (1983), 267 ff.

SUTHERLAND, C. H. V., 'Aspects of Imperialism in Roman Spain', *JRS* 24 (1934), 31 ff.

——*The Romans in Spain* (London, 1939).

SYME, R., 'Hadrian and Italica', *JRS* 54 (1964), 142 ff.

TERRASSE, M. H., and PIGANIOL, A. (eds.), *Les Empereurs romains de l'Espagne* (Paris, 1965).

THOUVENOT, R., *Essai sur la province romaine de Bétique* (2nd edn., Paris, 1973).

TOVAR, A., *Iberische Landeskunde*, i. *Baetica* (Baden-Baden, 1974).

TRANOY, A., *La Galice romaine* (Paris, 1981).

TRIGUEROS, M., 'La Torre (Corduba)', *NAH 2* (1953), 231.

TRILLMICH, W., and ZANKER, P. (eds.), *Stadtbild und Ideologie: Die Monumentalisierung hispanischer Städte zwischen Republik und Kaiserzeit* (Munich, 1990).

TSIRKIN, J. B., 'The Labours, Death, and Resurrection of Melqart as Depicted on the Gates of the Gades Herakleion', *RSF* 9 (1981).

——'The South of Spain in the Civil War of 40–45 [*sic*] BC', *A.e.A.* 54 (1981), 91 ff.

——'The Phoenician Civilization of Roman Spain', *Gerion*, 3 (1985), 245 ff.

UNTERMANN, J., *Elementos de un atlas antroponímico de la Hispania antigua* (Madrid, 1965).

VALVERDE Y PERALES, F., 'Antigüedades romanos y visigothicos de Baena', *BRAH* 40 (1902), 513 ff.

——'Antigüedades romanas de Andalucía: Excavaciones en el cerro del Minguillar cerca de Baena', *BRAH* 46 (1905), 167 f.

——*Historia de la villa, de Baena* (Cordoba, repr. 1982).

VIVES, J., *Inscripciones latinas de España romana* (Barcelona, 1971).

VIVES Y ESCUDERO, A., *La moneda hispanica* (Madrid, 1926).

WIEGELS, R., *Die Tribusinschriften des römischen Hispanien* (Berlin, 1985).

WISEMAN, F. J., *Roman Spain* (London, 1956).

WOODS, D., 'Carteia and Tartessos', *5 Symposio de prehistoria peninsular* (Barcelona, 1968), 251 ff.

YOSHIMURA, T., 'The Legio Vernacula of Pompey', *JCS* 8 (1960), 74 ff.

INDEX